THE UNBOUNDED LEVEL OF THE MIND

The Unbounded Level of the Mind

Rod Macdonald's Legal Imagination

Edited by

RICHARD JANDA, ROSALIE JUKIER, AND DANIEL JUTRAS

Published for the Faculty of Law, McGill University
by
McGill-Queen's University Press
Montreal & Kingston • London • Ithaca

ISBN 978-0-7735-4523-6 (cloth)
ISBN 978-0-7735-4524-3 (paper)
ISBN 978-0-7735-8341-2 (ePDF)
ISBN 978-0-7735-8342-9 (ePUB)

Legal deposit second quarter 2015
Bibliothèque nationale du Québec

McGill-Queen's University Press acknowledges the support of the Canada Council for the Arts for our publishing program. We also acknowledge the financial support of the Government of Canada through the Canada Book Fund for our publishing activities.

Library and Archives Canada Cataloguing in Publication

The unbounded level of the mind: Rod Macdonald's legal imagination/ edited by Richard Janda, Rosalie Jukier, and Daniel Jutras.

Proceedings of a symposium held in honour of McGill Dean of Law Rod Macdonald, 'The Unbounded Level of the Mind: Rod Macdonald's Legal Imagination' held at the Faculty of Law, McGill University from February 7-8, 2014.
Issued in print and electronic formats.
ISBN 978-0-7735-4523-6 (bound). – ISBN 978-0-7735-4524-3 (pbk.). – ISBN 978-0-7735-8341-2 (pdf). – ISBN 978-0-7735-8342-9 (epub)

1. Macdonald, Roderick A., 1948–2014. 2. Law – Canada. I. Janda, Richard, editor II. Jukier, Rosalie, editor III. Jutras, Daniel, editor IV. McGill University. Faculty of Law, issuing body

KE448.U53 2015 349.71 C2015-902237-1
C2015-902238-X

This book was typeset by Interscript in 10.5/13 Sabon.

MIX
Paper | Supporting responsible forestry
FSC® C013604
FSC www.fsc.org

Contents

PART TWO: LESSONS FROM ROD MACDONALD'S EVERYDAY LIFE

Acknowledgments

The publication of this book is the product of an irrepressible desire to honour Roderick A. Macdonald through a careful and creative exploration of his scholarly voice. This desire was shared by dozens of people, each of whom made it possible for this wonderful volume to come to light. The efforts of this group began with an enormously successful symposium, held at the Faculty of Law at McGill University on 7 and 8 February, 2014, with Rod, his wife, Shelley Freeman, and their children, Madeleine and Aidan, in attendance. Close to 300 legal academics, scholars from other disciplines, students, lawyers, judges, and friends of Rod Macdonald made the trip to McGill on these two days to create the primary material for the book that you now hold in your hands. There are many people to thank for making the symposium the success it was, including many student and faculty volunteers ably led by McGill law student Olivier Jarda.

Turning the content of the symposium into an archive of the remarkable scholarship that took place on those two days involved the work of many people to whom we owe our thanks. In particular, we would like to thank Dia Dabby, DCL candidate at McGill's Faculty of Law, for her attentive and insightful assistance, as well as Julie Fontaine and Libby Parker, administrative coordinators in the Faculty of Law, who provided invaluable administrative support in putting together the manuscript. Ms Dabby, Ms Fontaine, and Ms Parker should find here the expression of our enormous gratitude. Finally, we wish to thank McGill-Queen's University Press, and in particular Dorothy Turnbull and Jessica Howarth.

Richard Janda, Rosalie Jukier, and Daniel Jutras

Preface

How does one write a preface to a postscript, a prologue to an epilogue? Perhaps by reminding oneself that Rod Macdonald's life and work remain so vivid and such a constant touchstone for those who knew and engaged with him that it seems natural to reflect on him prospectively rather than retrospectively. The three of us joined McGill's Faculty of Law as young scholars in the 1980s, at the outset of Rod's deanship. We have spent our entire academic careers in this environment. We have been accustomed to thinking of his past as his prologue, to waiting in anticipation for the next transformation of his thinking. Indeed, to the very end of his life, Rod himself wondered what could and would be next.

It was in the spirit of preface and prologue that more than 300 people gathered to discuss the influence of Rod's scholarship and its prospects for future research. On 7–8 February 2014, four months before he passed away on 13 June 2014, jurists and academics gathered in the Moot Court of McGill University's Faculty of Law to ponder his life's work. There, friends, colleagues, students, mentors, mentees, and admirers spent two intense and memorable days in Rod's company and that of his wife, Shelley Freeman, and their children, Madeleine and Aidan, often overwhelmed by the scope and scale of his scholarship and accomplishments.

When it was decided to convene around Rod's work, it had been difficult, as the interview with Paul Kennedy in this volume testifies, to convince him of the need to have such a symposium while he was still alive. But the way into Rod's heart was to explain, as persuasively as possible, that we wanted to do this because we needed it for ourselves, not because we wanted to celebrate him. On the strict condition that the gathering was not to be either maudlin or adulatory, Rod agreed to the venture. The symposium was not to be an encampment for old guards.

Nor was it to be a self-congratulatory McGill affair. He wanted it to focus on how his work had been received, especially critically, across the country and indeed around the world.

It was fascinating unto itself to watch Rod turn his mind to the themes that had cut across his work and continued to preoccupy his inquiry. When presented with a list that included access to justice, legal pluralism, constitutional law, secured transactions, administrative process, and legal education, Rod was disappointed at the lack of understanding of his method of analysis. The sense of the verb was missing from that list. He did not engage with a series of nouns. He had never organized his questions around the characteristics of subject matter. All subject matter was fundamentally intertwined. For Rod, it was deeply misleading to seek to delimit, say, the zone of secured transactions from the zone of access to justice. Rod focused on our modes of agency: how and why we engage with the world, not what kinds of things we observe in it. Thus, he settled the themes of our symposium upon "Producing Fairness," "Pluralizing the Subject," "Kaleidoscopic Federalism," "The Priority of Distributive Justice," "Contextualizing Governance," and "Pursuing Virtue." By that stroke alone, everything to be discussed spoke to everything else. The thematically interwoven character of his endeavour became apparent. The choice to focus on these themes meant that some aspects of Rod's phenomenal scholarly output were not specifically addressed at the symposium. By way of example, inquiry into his remarkable and meticulous work as a historian of McGill's Faculty of Law, and his uniquely insightful publications on the voice, culture, and epistemology of Quebec civil law, reluctantly had to be postponed to another day.

Rod's curriculum vitae is notoriously epic, and his publication list seems interminable. How then to produce serious and sustained engagement over the course of two days with a body of work of that proportion? The answer, of course, was to pick a subset of his writing suggestive of the whole. Rod himself selected five works to reflect each theme, and our speakers were asked to consider, first, the impact that those works had had on them and second, the effect they would have on future scholarship. The list of works in question is appended to this volume.

There was also something to be learned from the way Rod, when consulted, put his mind to who should be invited to speak. Rod had a horror of being in the presence of a band of acolytes. Thus, it was of great significance that the tone of discussion be set by someone whose own body of thought, in Rod's judgment, was of greater significance than his own and who, though a careful and sympathetic reader of Rod's work, would nevertheless produce a critical assessment. Harry Arthurs was therefore selected to be the keynote speaker, and once Harry agreed – instantly, as was true of everyone else – the rest could fall into place. Harry Arthurs's presence, as well as that of Angela Swan, John Whyte, Guy Rocher, and David Mullan, among others, was also important as a way of acknowledging the debt Rod felt to scholars who had anticipated his own preoccupations.

At the other end of the spectrum lay young and emerging scholars whose work Rod felt would eclipse his own. A final word, he believed, should come from someone Rod felt embodied the student who had taught the teacher. Thus, Desmond Manderson became the bookend to Harry Arthurs.

The attempt to put the symposium together while we could still be with Rod placed us under an impossible time constraint. Rod himself imagined a rather intimate affair assembling those few people who would be available. Yet the impossibility and audacity of the event attracted people to it, proving Rod's dictum that "if it's not impossible, it's not worth doing." Thus, Justice Rosalie Abella of the Supreme Court of Canada turned her agenda upside down. Stephen Toope, then president of the University of British Columbia, put everything else on hold. Partners from law firms in Chicago and Los Angeles took temporary leave of their clients. Law deans from across Canada either came or provided subsidies for colleagues and students to attend. The intimate affair became the largest symposium ever staged at the faculty. Students at McGill who had never had Rod as a professor not only swarmed to the event but also poured themselves into organizing and facilitating it. It was also especially meaningful and moving that Rod's long-time friend and co-researcher, Andrée Lajoie, launched the publication of her biography, *La vie intellectuelle de Roderick Macdonald: un engagement*, at the symposium.

This collection of essays is formed around papers that emerged from the presentations made at the symposium. They are grouped around three themes: Lessons of Rod Macdonald's Scholarship, Lessons of Rod Macdonald's Life, and Lessons of Rod Macdonald in His Own Words. The titles of these three parts were inspired by Rod's ground-breaking work, *Lessons of Everyday Law*.

In part 1, Lessons of Rod Macdonald's Scholarship, twenty-five scholars explore the six symposium themes, from a critical perspective, in light of the selected texts. Inevitably, as indeed we had hoped, the themes interweave, and these scholarly papers provide a three-dimensional unity to Rod's body of thought. In part 2, Lessons of Rod Macdonald's Life, fourteen scholars reflect on particular experiences, encounters, and contributions that have marked them and the wider community. Although Rod listened during the symposium and did not speak, his voice all but taken away by disease, we nevertheless have been most fortunate to include him in his own words. As the symposium was coming together, the thought arose to approach Alison Cook of the CBC Radio program "Ideas" and offer access to the symposium recordings. Alison wondered whether Rod might be up to an interview, and Rod agreed, relying on a prosthesis to make himself intelligible. This led to an *Ideas* program about Rod, and the CBC has generously agreed to allow the publication of the full transcript of the interview with host Paul Kennedy. In addition, we have been given permission to publish a remarkable interview with Rod conducted by Professor Andrea Brighenti of the University of Trento in 2004 that served as background to the interview conducted by Paul Kennedy. These two interviews, separated by a decade, form part 3: Lessons of Rod Macdonald in His Own Words.

The title of this collection, and indeed of the symposium, is *The Unbounded Level of the Mind: Rod Macdonald's Legal Imagination.* Alexander Pope's *Essay on Criticism* of 1711 remains an enduring source of reflection on critique and virtue. Rod certainly took to heart Pope's injunction that "a little learning is a dangerous thing," constantly seeking to reposition and reorient his standpoint on what he knew. These were the lines from Pope's poem that inspired the title:

> While from the bounded level of our mind
> Short views we take, nor see the lengths behind,
> But, more advanced, behold with strange surprise
> New distant scenes of endless science rise!

Rod's tireless effort to resist the short view, to escape the tyranny of the tried and true, and to venture into unexplored territory, characterized the unbounded level of his mind. Shelley Freeman's wonderful painting, *Pothole*, which graces the cover of this book and became the symbol of the symposium, conveys aesthetically the trappings of mind Rod resisted and the perimeters of thought where he was happiest and most comfortable. To know, through Rod's work, that there is indeed an unbounded level of the mind is the best possible prologue to future inquiry.

Richard Janda, Rosalie Jukier, Daniel Jutras

THE UNBOUNDED LEVEL OF THE MIND

Biography of Rod Macdonald

A teacher first and foremost, Roderick A. Macdonald will be remembered as one of the most important scholars and thinkers in McGill University's history. He was a mentor and inspiration to generations of students and law professors and a transformative force at the Faculty of Law, at the university, in Canadian society, and in the broader world.

Professor Macdonald came to McGill University in 1979. His term as dean of the Faculty of Law, from 1984 to 1989, was a leap forward for McGill. His bold vision of legal education, his extraordinary energy as a scholar, his ability to redefine and reimagine the boundaries of law, his deep commitment to justice, his unfailing integrity, and his unique dedication to his students and colleagues – all of these continue to this day to define the mission and aspirations of McGill's Faculty of Law.

Born in Ontario in 1948, Rod Macdonald spent his formative years working at a summer camp in central Ontario and developing a taste for folk music and protest songs that never left him. He completed his legal education in Ontario (BA York, 1969; LLB Osgoode Hall, 1972; LLL Ottawa, 1974; LLM Toronto, 1975). Macdonald then took his first position as a legal academic at Windsor University's Law Faculty, one of a group of scholars committed to access to justice and law reform initiatives. He came to Montreal a few years later, joining a faculty that was already defined by mixity and *métissage*, in civil law and common law, in French and in English.

McGill's path as a bijural, bilingual, cosmopolitan institution was in the works, and Macdonald gave it a rich and principled grounding in a pluralistic conception of law. Professor Macdonald's steadfast commitment to bilingualism, legal pluralism, interdisciplinarity, and dialogue formed the intellectual spine of, and was integral to, the genesis of McGill's pioneering program. The program's linguistic, transnational, and dialogic nature is rooted directly in the values that Professor Macdonald espoused and encouraged at the faculty. Roderick Macdonald's inventiveness as a teacher, his use of music, visual arts, and theatrical performance in the classroom, gave his students the confidence to explore their own representations of law and their moral, ethical, political, and social role as jurists. For Professor Macdonald, every moment was a teaching and learning moment; every professor was a learner as well as a teacher; every student was worthy of deep respect and consideration. He always knew how to appeal to each person's better self.

As one of the most influential legal scholars of his generation, Professor Macdonald authored three books and was the editor of six edited collections. He published more than one hundred major journal articles, as well as dozens of chapters in edited collections, Law Reform Commission reports, and commissioned research studies and reports, both nationally and internationally. His work on the civil law tradition, on legal theory and legal history, on administrative and constitutional law, on secured transactions, on the theory and practice of legal education, on legal pluralism and diversity, and on access to justice literally redefined each of these fields. His capacity to bring unique and original insight to the broadest range of issues in public law and private law will remain unparalleled.

Professor Macdonald was also convinced of his duty to serve the community at large and remained throughout his life an engaged academic and public actor. Soon after his term as dean of the Faculty of Law, Roderick Macdonald chaired the Task Force on Access to Justice of the Quebec Ministry of Justice, producing a report that formed the basis of revisions to the legal aid plan, the small claims court, class actions, and civil procedure generally. Over the years, Professor Macdonald prepared studies and reports for several royal commissions, including the Royal Commission on Canada's Economic Prospects and the Royal Commission on Aboriginal Peoples. He was frequently consulted by law reform commissions in Canada and abroad. He prepared the major background study on alternatives to civil litigation for the Ontario Civil Justice Review. He worked as a leading consultant to the federal Department of Justice in connection with the Project to Harmonize Federal Legislation with the Civil Code of Quebec and produced three major studies for that project. He was the author of influential reports to the Canadian Department of Justice on *Constitutional Implications of the Civil Code of Quebec* (1996), to the Senate Committee on Illegal Drugs (2002), and to the Law Society of Upper Canada on *Access to Justice* (2003). More recently, Professor Macdonald produced a report for the Quebec Justice Minister on measures to prevent Strategic Lawsuits Against Public Participation (SLAPPS) and made representations to the Bouchard–Taylor Commission. At the time of his death in June 2014, Professor Macdonald was serving as one of the three commissioners on the Charbonneau Commission on public contracts in the construction industry.

One of his most prominent contributions came from his tenure as the founding president of the Law Commission of Canada (1997–2000). During this period, Professor Macdonald essentially reimagined what such an institution could do and how. Far from becoming a "service organization" for lawyers and politicians, Macdonald's Law Commission seized instead an opportunity to support and stimulate debate on the broadest questions of the role of law in society, on the one hand, and to engage the whole community from primary schools to civil society in such a project, on the other. This creative vision can be seen in the discussion papers and reports the commission authored under his supervision, including *Recognizing and Supporting Close Personal Relationships between Adults* and *Restoring Dignity: Responding to Child Abuse in Canadian Institutions*. The same unfailing sense of creative and compassionate imagination can be seen to animate every one of the Law Commission's innovative projects during the term of his presidency. In three years Macdonald turned a new institution – now disbanded by the federal government – into a celebrated model for such institutions around the world.

Rod Macdonald also gained prominence through his work in the international community. In 2003, he was engaged as an external consultant by the World Bank to assist in crafting Ukraine's laws on secured transactions. Moreover, from 2002 to 2011, he served as a member of the Canadian delegation on secured transactions of the United Nations Commission on International Trade Law (UNCITRAL). In the latter capacity, he made invaluable contributions to the preparation of UNCITRAL's Legislative Guide on Secured Transactions.

Roderick Macdonald was universally regarded as one of Canada's most distinguished intellectuals. In November 2008, he was elected the 111th president of the Royal Society of Canada (RSC). He was and remains the only law professor ever to have been elected president of the RSC and served from November 2009 to November 2011. In November 2012, Governor General David Johnston announced that the new reading room in Walter House, the Royal Society of Canada's headquarters in Ottawa, would be named the Macdonald Reading Room in Professor Macdonald's honour in recognition of his years of service.

Over the course of his career, Roderick Macdonald received many prestigious awards underlining his extraordinary contributions. He was appointed a Fellow of the Pierre Elliott Trudeau Foundation in 2004. In 2007, he received the Killam Prize for the Social Sciences awarded by the Canada Council, as well as the Sir William Dawson Medal for the Social Sciences of the Royal Society of Canada. In 2010, Professor Macdonald was honoured by the Canadian Bar Association with the Ramon Hnatyshyn Medal. His contributions were underlined again by the Canadian Bar Association (Quebec division) in 2012, which gave him the Médaille Paul-André Crépeau. Professor Macdonald received an honorary doctorate from Université de Montréal in 2010 and from Osgoode Hall Law School in 2011, as well as the Ordre du mérite from the Section de droit civil of the Faculty of Law, University of Ottawa, in 2007. In 2012, Roderick Macdonald was made an Officer of the Order of Canada, and a year later he was awarded the Queen Elizabeth II Diamond Jubilee Medal. Finally, in 2014, he was named to the Cercle Yves Caron by Paul-André Crépeau Centre for Private and Comparative Law.

At McGill, Professor Macdonald was the recipient of the 2012 John W. Durnford Teaching Excellence Award. To this day, he is the only McGill professor to have received both of the university's highest awards: the Lifetime Achievement Award for Leadership in Learning in 2011 and the McGill University Medal for Exceptional Academic Achievement in 2014.

PART ONE

Lessons from Rod Macdonald's Scholarship

1

Opening Remarks: My "Very Idea" of Rod – and Yours

HARRY ARTHURS

The very idea of law must be autobiographical.[1]

Introducing a collection of essays on the legal imagination of Rod Macdonald would be a daunting task under any circumstances. It is made even more so by the constraints under which I labour. I can't hope to match the comprehensive overview that Andrée Lajoie provides in her book about Rod.[2] Nor can I compete with the focused exploration of specific aspects of Rod's work found in the papers that emerged from the symposium. Nor, because he has forbidden us to be maudlin, can I do what I would like most to do – devote this text to the expression of my admiration and affection for Rod. I have therefore taken my cue from something Rod said frequently and in various formulations: "The very idea of law must be autobiographical."[3] If that's true, then the "very idea" of Rod himself must be "autobiographical." I'm therefore going to begin our collection by sharing my autobiographical – and consequently idiosyncratic – idea of Rod and his work. This idea has been shaped by our many encounters over some four decades. It may not accord with your idea of Rod's scholarship or, for that matter, with his. However, because Rod himself strongly advocates "pluralizing the legal subject," it will be interesting to see what happens when we put his theory into practice.

For convenience's sake, I'm going to engage with four aspects of Rod Macdonald's work that have variously impressed, persuaded, puzzled, and exasperated me – sometimes all at once. Specifically, I will address

Rod Macdonald's antipathy to borders and boundaries, his relentless search for virtue, his style of argumentation, and finally, his inclination to magic realism.

Savant sans frontières

We live in a world where in many respects borders seem to be hardening – borders between nations, classes, religions, cultures, ethnicities, epistemologies, ideologies, professional specialisms, academic disciplines, and legal regimes, to name a few. They are hardening despite the Enlightenment, technology, globalization, and, alas, despite the best efforts of Roderick A. Macdonald, who rejected borders. "Personal" or "political" or "professional": for him, these were just labels that obscure more than they reveal. Teacher or student: for him, both were equal partners in the search for understanding. Mathematics or music, genetics or jurisprudence, it was all the same to Rod: just another useful way of looking at life. High law or low law, common law or civil law: all way-stations along his transsystemic, transdisciplinary road to better understanding. Building docks in Ontario's cottage country or creating a legal framework for secured transactions in Ukraine: for Rod, these were just occasions for shaping appropriate responses to people's particular circumstances and varied needs.

In short, Rod was the quintessential *savant sans frontières*. He constantly demonstrated how and why we must deconstruct concepts and break down categories that impede the search for understanding, justice, and virtue. He did this by insisting not only on the possibility of integrating all forms of knowledge but on the inevitability of people's interconnectedness, on the inescapable *mixité* of communities, on the hybridity of institutions and the contingency of rules, and, above all, on the role of the individual as the ultimate source and destination of legal and moral knowledge, agency, and responsibility.

Rod's open-borders policy made huge intellectual demands on him and, frankly, on his readers. For instance, in a recent article, he discusses musicology, biology, and virology as metaphors for norm migration.[4] However, after ensuring that readers have mastered these difficult subjects, he rejects them all and takes refuge on the moral high ground of Aristotelian philosophy. Why, I am tempted to ask, did he not start where he was ultimately going to end up? The answer surely is that for Rod, the journey – the border-crossing – is at least as important as the destination.

In Search of Virtue

And yet, the destination is important as well. Rod was always searching for virtue, for the moral high ground. In that article on norm migration, he relies on the concept of *phronesis*, which was central to his own thinking, namely: "[T]he capacity to be sensitive to the particularities of a given situation is a necessary condition for moral agency. Even if universal moral principles were to exist, they would not be self-applying. The moral agent … is never relieved of the responsibility for making decisions. As moral agents we must therefore constantly reassess what it is we think we know. This, in turn, means cultivating openness to and reciprocity with others."[5]

So far so good. However, the article deals with attempts to standardize certain rules of international trade law. As far as I have been able to observe, "cultivating openness to and reciprocity with others" has not been a prominent feature of the so-called Washington Consensus, nor of regimes of trade law, nor of actual/existing international business relationships. "Openness" and "reciprocity," I contend, are likely to become more widespread (if at all) only with a change in power relations, which is to say only after the current model of US-led neo-liberal globalization enters its declining stages.

In his work, if only occasionally, Rod acknowledges the existence of power: "Human beings are social animals who find meaning in the relationships they build with others [he says somewhere] but … [s]adly, these relationships are not always bilateral or equitable, for human beings in the Western cultural tradition also appear to have an insatiable appetite to project their views about life, community, social organization, spirituality and justice onto others … through … episodic violence … through psychological manipulation … through religious crusades … and sometimes by economic coercion."[6]

If our appetite for power and domination is indeed insatiable, if the means we are prepared to use are so despicable, how does this square with our innate responsibility and capacity as moral agents? In Rod's view, this contradiction is attributable in part to our reliance on the state. He characterizes the state as "the primary vehicle for self-assertion and domination of the other," and he insists that "whether exercised for malignant or benign purposes, political power … tends toward authoritarian subjugation."[7]

How, then, did he propose to reverse the tendency toward subjugation? Rod genuinely favoured giving priority to distributive rather than restorative justice, which made him a "small-s," "small-d" social democrat. However, because he was uneasy about the state, Rod could also be called a diffident social democrat. He mustered much more enthusiasm for ideas and initiatives that empower individuals: acknowledgment that they constitute the state rather than vice versa, for example; affirmation of their status as legal agents rather than legal subjects; the provision to citizens of opportunities and resources that will translate these concepts into practical reality; the "unbundling" of state functions to make them more responsive to the needs and desires of citizens. Don't misunderstand me. Rod was no egoist, let alone a closet libertarian; he never was a market fundamentalist. It is just that he laid out his own unique route to the moral high ground of social democracy, of distributive justice, by way of individual capacity and responsibility.

Methodology

My "very idea" of Rod – perhaps mistaken – is that he chose that route partly because of his preferred methodologies, partly because of his temperament. I'll explore those two notions in that order – methodology first. Though he dazzled in almost any intellectual vernacular, Rod's preferred methodologies seem to be philosophy and poetry. Aristotle's concept of *phronesis*, already mentioned, captures a central aspect of his approach to life and therefore to law. This constitutes just one of many instances when he used philosophical methods to work toward his conclusions and philosophical concepts to encapsulate those conclusions in his memorable prose. Indeed, *Lessons from Everyday Law*[8] is arguably lodged in the philosophic tradition of inductive argument from the observed experience of everyday life. Yet Rod was not just a philosopher. He was also a poet, a skilled practitioner of metaphor, allusion, allegory. "Allegory," he explained, "… is a vehicle for *phronesis*, a form of expression that does not allow for a final propositional message that is separate from the story itself, easily transmissible, formulaic and universalized"[9] – a form of expression, in other words, that ensures that each reader, each listener, will have to pursue virtue by trying to understand themselves and others.

A philosopher and a poet, then, but apparently not an empirical social scientist. For example, in a 2006 piece, Rod and David Sandomierski wrote: "[w]hile we locate ourselves as legal pluralists, we nonetheless take our distance from empirical, social scientific conceptions of legal pluralism."[10] Indeed, Rod took his distance from empirical social science in many similar statements. However, such disclaimers must be taken with a grain of salt. Rod – the *savant sans frontières* – was constitutionally incapable of taking his distance from any form of knowledge, any mode of analysis, that provides enlightenment. For example, his wonderful essay, "Office Politics,"[11] reveals him to be an anthropologist, an ethnomethodologist of the first order, as does *Lessons of Everyday Law*.[12] Moreover, his understanding of institutions like federalism, relationships like families, and processes like lawmaking is thoroughly grounded in empirical evidence including – as his footnotes often reveal – evidence amassed by the very social scientists from whom he distanced himself. I concede that the social sciences do not appear to be his preferred mode of analysis. This, as he himself acknowledged,[13] constitutes something of a "paradox" for someone as deeply involved in society and social relations. This paradox can be resolved, I think, by considering his relationship with reality.

Magic Realism

Here is how the Macdonald–Sandomierski article I've just mentioned describes legal reality: "Legal norms, in whatever site of law, are imagined by human beings, given expression by human beings, lived by human beings, followed by human beings, modified by human beings, rejected by human beings – in a word, constituted by human beings not primarily as passive legal subjects, but above all as active legal agents."[14]

I have no problem with this formulation, as far as it goes, but there does seem to be something missing. That missing element is power[15] – power that permeates many sites of law, that warps human imaginations, that stunts freedom of expression, that prevents people from adhering to certain legal norms or forces them to do so against their will. All too often, indeed, power trumps *phronesis* and determines whether human beings become passive legal subjects or active legal agents or neither – but simply disenfranchised, debilitated, or even dead. I've made this point to Rod over the years: "I have the sense [I wrote to him once] that you continue to overestimate the power of the individual, to underestimate the power of the state, class, culture, and corporation … I sense that a more tragic view of life, a recognition of its large and little brutalities has to be introduced into your picture of identity-negotiating citizens."[16] Rod responded by calling me a "tragic realist." I retaliated by calling him a "magic realist." On reflection, I think my flippant rejoinder was not far off the mark.

Rod – in his work as in his life – engaged with reality as a thoroughgoing optimist or, as I call him, a magic realist. By contrast, I'm at best a Gramscian optimist – an optimist of the will but a pessimist of the intellect. I believe – like Gramsci and unlike Rod – that "man is ... a product of history, not of nature." Seeing Rod as a magic realist helps to explain a lot – especially his always-imaginative and well-conceived projects to levitate justice: to mobilize ordinary Canadians in a bottom-up process of law reform; to unbundle government programs to allow citizens to shape their own identity; to introduce a new "Swiss Army knife of governance" that will ensure social justice while preventing the growth of an overbearing state; to invent a transsystemic legal education that will not only be able to resist the intense parochialism of the bar but ultimately transform our understanding of law.

Truly, truly I admire the noble ambitions and imaginative design of each of these projects. But they do represent a magical view of reality, a determined optimism that isn't quite quixotic but nonetheless fails to factor power into the equation. Rod, I conclude, took his distance from empirical social science because it was foreign to his nature and – as he perceived it – at odds with the concept of *phronesis* that informs so much of his thinking.

This point can be illustrated through "Office Politics": recall that that article concerns the allocation of newly vacated offices in a law faculty. It is epistolary in form: it reproduces an imagined exchange of memos between the dean and faculty members asserting their claims to the office they think they deserve, as well as challenging the claims of others and in some cases impugning the dean's fairness and good faith. The narrative demonstrates, according to him, "the value of constitutive practice for reaffirming the subtle and informal normative orders that make associational life possible."[17] It's his article, and he was entitled to draw his own conclusions. However, stated as it is, Rod's conclusion confirms to me that he was indeed a magic realist. Everyone in the story – save "the dean," save Rod himself – seems utterly unconcerned about "associational life." On the contrary, each faculty member seems to be driven not to improve the quality of collegial relations or to secure justice or virtue but rather to expend precious intellectual and moral capital in an effort to enhance personal comfort, convenience, or prestige.

A final example illustrates Rod's magical realism. In the mid-1990s, Rod and I were members of the law program of the Canadian Institute for Advanced Research. Fraser Mustard, the founder and then director of the institute, was incapable of conducting a conversation that did not include mention of "the gradient." The gradient in question was the product of a sophisticated epidemiological study, known as the Whitehall Study, that closely linked health outcomes to socio-economic status. Very crudely put, the gradient showed that the higher your status, the better your prospects of living a long, healthy, productive, and satisfying life.[18] As a tragic realist, I thought this was what Bora Laskin used to call "a penetrating glimpse into the obvious." Indeed, the same gradient seemed to me to determine a whole host of outcomes, from people's political influence, to their access to social and cultural goods, to their enjoyment of legal rights. However, mere mention of "the gradient" drove Rod to distraction. There were other reasons, no doubt, but at some level, I think, Rod's optimism, his magic realism, would not allow him to accept the determinism implicit in the very notion of a "gradient."[19] He just could not acknowledge that socio-economic status is what makes some people into active legal agents and others into passive legal subjects.

A New Research Agenda

We've all been challenged to identify the implications of Rod's work for future research. I think I've now identified a key item on that agenda. On the one hand, we are all attracted by Rod's commitment to *phronesis*, his vision of individuals as moral and legal agents: it is a vision that not only promises a better society for all of us but a better life for each of us – a life exemplified by the one Rod made for himself. But on the other hand, I'm surely not the only tragic realist present. Many of us – as was Rod – are deeply concerned about the powerful and destructive forces at loose in the world. Many of us are convinced that power can seldom be challenged effectively by individuals – even exceptional individuals – and even steadfast practitioners of *phronesis*. And many of us are convinced that new and better forms of political, economic, and social relations are essentially projects that require collective action and, in many cases, state action. Here is my nomination for a future, Rod-inflected research question: how can we push back the forces of injustice and selfishness, how can we mobilize for positive collective action, how can we create effective institutions and governments, how can we build a just society – without, at the same time, impairing our individual capacity, and denying our individual responsibility, for moral and legal action?

Conclusion

I said at the outset that my "very idea" of Rod is necessarily autobiographical and therefore likely different from yours. Now I want to shift my ground. At any academic gathering, the only person wearing a bow tie he has tied with his own two hands was likely to be Rod. In that sense, the "very idea" of Rod begins for all of us with the man himself, with his unique human qualities, with the breadth of his interests and the depths of his understanding, with his unrelenting search for meaning and for justice. All of these function as a bow tie. They give his work remarkable intellectual coherence and imprint it with a unique moral DNA. If there were such a thing as a blind tasting of legal scholarship, Rod's work would be instantly recognizable. That's why I think I can conclude in a very matter-of-fact, non-maudlin way by saying that Rod was *sui generis*. He was one of Canada's most conscientious and constructive citizens, one of its most imaginative and influential scholars, and one of its most decent human beings. That is my "very idea" of Rod, and I'm sure it's yours as well.

NOTES

1 Martha-Marie Kleinhans and Roderick Macdonald, "What Is a *Critical* Legal Pluralism?" *Canadian Journal of Law and Society* 12 (1997): 46.
2 Andrée Lajoie, *La vie intellectuelle de Roderick Macdonald: un engagement* (Montreal: Thémis, 2014).
3 Keinhans and Macdonald, 46.
4 Macdonald, "Three Metaphors of Norm Migration in International Context," *Brooklyn Journal of International Law* 34 (2009): 603.
5 Ibid., 652.
6 Macdonald, "The Political Economy of the Federal Spending Power," *Queen's Law Journal* 34: (2008): 251.
7 Ibid., 252.
8 Macdonald, *Lessons of Everyday Law* (Montreal: McGill-Queen's University Press for the School of Policy Studies, Queen's University, and the Law Commission of Canada, 2002).
9 Lajoie, 7.
10 Roderick Macdonald and David Sandomierski, "Against Nomopolies," *Northern Ireland Legal Quarterly* 57 (2006): 616.
11 Macdonald, "Office Politics," *University of Toronto Law Journal* 40 (1990): 419.
12 Supra note 8.

13 Personal email correspondence from Rod Macdonald to Harry Arthurs, 29 November 2013.
14 Supra note 10 at 614–15.
15 In that same piece, Macdonald and Sandomierski maintain that "whether law is a closed normative system, or whether its rules, practices and institutions are permeated by other social, economic and political norms is, for present purposes, immaterial" (612).
16 Personal email correspondence from Harry Arthurs to Rod Macdonald, 28 January 2004.
17 Supra note 11 at 419.
18 For a very brief summary of the argument, see Fraser Mustard, "Free Market Capitalism, Social Accountability and Equity in Early Human (Child) Development," *Pediatrics and Child Health* 13 (2008): 839, http://www.ncbi.nlm.nih.gov/pmc/articles/PMC2603502.
19 He provides his own account of this experience in "Transdisciplinarity and Trust," in *Transdisciplinarity: Recreating Integrated Knowledge*, edited by M. Somerville and D. Rapport (Oxford: EOLSS Publishers, 2000), 74–5.

2

L'équité à la portée de toutes et tous

NATHALIE DES ROSIERS

Herménégilde Chiasson, le poète acadien, décrit les textes, les mots, les œuvres comme des bouteilles qu'on lance à la mer et qui aboutissent au bout du monde, qui sont ouvertes et découvertes par des personnes autres que soi. C'était tout un plaisir que de rouvrir des bouteilles enfouies afin de relire les textes de Rod Macdonald regroupés sous le thème « La production de l'équité ».

In one of the texts to be reviewed in this session, Rod Macdonald questions whether there is such thing as "objectivity."[1] This was reassuring to me as I embarked on the task at hand, because the texts that I am to present have been so close to my life, so imbedded in my thinking, that I am not sure that I can sufficiently detach myself from them to read them properly, let alone summarize them. Nous lisons tous Rod Macdonald avec nos propres perspectives. C'est le but de notre symposium d'explorer nos propres et diverses compréhensions de sa pensée. C'est dans cet esprit et bien modestement que je vous offre les remarques suivantes.

Chaque être humain a la capacité et la responsabilité de produire l'équité. Ce n'est pas tant dans la reproduction des règles que se vit et se pratique l'équité, mais dans l'exercice de rapports interpersonnels plus ou moins proches et exempts d'exploitation. La question du pouvoir n'est pas esquivée dans ce contexte. La distribution inégale du pouvoir est une réalité. L'équité se mesure par la capacité de reconnaître cette inégalité de pouvoir et par la responsabilité et l'imputabilité des gens qui détiennent le pouvoir de l'exercer vertueusement dans un contexte en constante évaluation.

Le droit ne produit pas nécessairement l'équité, mais il doit et peut libérer la capacité des individus de le faire et d'agir justement. Les institutions que les humains créent pour produire l'équité ou pour vivre de façon plus équitable peuvent être manipulées et produire l'injustice. Une attention constante doit donc être portée à leur design pour qu'elles puissent rappeler aux êtres humains leurs responsabilités et créer la possibilité pour eux d'être justes. De « bonnes » institutions doivent exiger des êtres humains qu'ils remplissent leurs responsabilités et qu'ils soient vertueux (ce sujet sera abordé plus tard). Elles leur imposent une imputabilité lorsqu'ils ne le font pas. Ce n'est pas que le droit formel ne soit pas pertinent à la production de l'équité, mais simplement qu'il n'est pas en soi porteur d'équité et qu'il peut facilement produire et légitimer l'iniquité tout autant que l'équité. L'équité ne se produit pas dans l'abstrait, mais dans le concret des rapports humains, elle est fragile et dynamique et se vit et se reproduit dans le quotidien par la voie d'une myriade d'interactions entre les personnes et entre les communautés. C'est le droit « vivant » que Rod Macdonald a enseigné.

In the texts that are the subject of this part, the production of fairness by all is sought. I will first review the five texts, then offer brief concluding remarks.

Embracing Responsibility

Restoring Dignity[2] was the breathtaking and ground-breaking report that the Law Commission of Canada produced in 2000. The subject, the responsibility of present Canadian society for the racist policies of the past – namely, the residential schools – demanded a contextualized approach to the production of fairness. Yet how can you be fair in responding to such widespread, profound, lasting wounds in the relationship between Aboriginal people and the government of Canada? And how can you be fair in trying to give voice to the hurt and profoundly wounded children of the past?

"By embracing responsibility," Rod Macdonald would answer. The report is well known for its thoughtful and comprehensive approach. It suggests that everyone in Canada bears a responsibility to help in the healing and that many institutions can produce fairness and must do so. Fairness is not only governmental but produced by a wide array of actors, including the judiciary, the law societies, the universities, and the Canadian public. C'est cette dimension de l'éclatement des responsabilités pour la production de l'équité qui retient notre attention. Taking responsibility is about change and future action and prevention. It is about listening to the people who have been hurt and designing responses with them in mind.

The process of law reform undertaken for the report was in itself designed to produce fairness. Law reform must take into account and begin with the voice of the survivors. It must start from a perspective of responding to the complexity of their needs. The report also recognizes that the harm was not only individual but collectively experienced and reproduced.

Moving beyond government as the target of law reform, demanding more of all institutions, was a key aspect of the report. It was transformative for the law reform world. It pushed law reform beyond legislative suggestions and beyond a narrow governmental focus.

To produce fairness for survivors of childhood sexual abuse demanded more than a few legal pronouncements but rather a radical transformation of the approach that Canada had toward the issue. The government certainly had a role to play – to set up compensation schemes, to facilitate access to healing funds, to support community healing and to apologize – but others did as well, irrespective of their level of "guilt" or participation. A society that cares about fairness seeks to respond meaningfully to the legacies of racism and violence. I think that it is the attention to the survivors, to the roles of a multiplicity of actors, to the demands of action and prevention, that make this report so important for the development of law reform.

Confronting Neutrality

Ten years after *Restoring Dignity*, Rod Macdonald produced another law reform agenda, this time for the Bastarache Commission on Judicial Appointments,[3] which directly confronted the idea of neutrality, the subjectivity/objectivity dilemma, and the role of "politics" (positive and negative) in choosing powerful actors. The report is about institutional design to produce fairness and instill virtue in powerful actors – namely, the judges. In the passage on whether it is "possible to discipline subjective judgement about judicial appointment,"[4] Roderick Macdonald invites us to reflect on the following: there is no perfect system; no system, however good, always functions perfectly. Nevertheless, we can minimize the "manipulation" or gaming of the process and invest in transparency and accountability. Making our subjectivity clearer, identifying it, speaking about it, not hiding it or masking it will enhance fairness. Recognizing the dangers of manipulation will also enhance fairness.

The report recognizes the subtle ways in which judges can be influenced and "politicized" in the wrong ways. For me, it is again this broad approach that recognizes the dynamic nature of interaction, the wisdom about human nature, and the frailties of our attempts to secure fairness that constitutes the hallmark of the report. The recommendations of are far-ranging, confronting the silences of current processes as well as their perverse effects. All aspects of the reward, nomination, and promotion of judges must be looked at if we want to produce fairness. We should aim to appoint and promote judges who will be virtuous, directly confront their own biases and failings, and self-reflect as a way to ensure the production of fairness.

Lessons of Everyday Law

The nobility of the everyday law is celebrated in *Lessons of Everyday Law*.[5] Dans ce livre extraordinaire, Rod Macdonald reprend les chroniques mensuelles qu'il faisait à la commission pour expliquer avec anecdotes et petites histoires certains aspects fondamentaux du droit : pourquoi a-t-on un processus législatif ? Qu'est-ce qui est juste ? Pour qui ?
Ce sont les nouvelles fables de La Fontaine, ces leçons qui nous restent après que nous avons tout oublié. Il s'agit de la démonstration d'une approche pédagogique qui engage les lecteurs dans l'histoire pour les faire réfléchir.

Because fairness is within everybody's reach, because it can be achieved and must be experienced at the day-to-day level, the book speaks directly to the tensions about the hierarchy of modes of speech in speaking about law, in owning legal knowledge and distributing it. There is something radical in explaining Lon Fuller with short histories of one's family holidays.

Personal Relationships

"Perspectives on Personal Relationships"[6] presents a radical approach to questioning legal language and categories with a view to assessing whether they liberate people and allow them to be fair or, on the contrary, force them into unhealthy choices. It questions whether the law and the state should highlight and reinforce certain relationships and not others. The context of this paper can be understood in terms of the following background: in 1999, the Law Commission was engaged in a study of law and relationships – personal, social, economic, and governance relationships – as a way of avoiding the definitional limitations of doing family law, criminal law, commercial law, and public law. This approach was designed to force the commission to question the way in which family law evokes a certain grouping of persons and ignores others. The "relationships" approach meant embracing legal pluralism and avoiding the language of rights. This approach served as a constant reminder of the need to question our legal reflexes and our often narrow legal imagination.

At that time, there was no legal recognition of same-sex marriage, which was still being debated. The idea of engaging in a conversation that would posit that marriage may have been overused by the legislator as a proxy to capture psychological or economic interdependence was controversial. For some proponents of same-sex marriage, the debate should not engage with big questions that detracted from a narrower frame of the question of equality as to whether gays and lesbians could marry. As someone at the conference said: "Before reorganizing the furniture in the house of marriage, let us in." "Perspectives on Personal Relationships" aimed to invite people to think outside the box about the nature of personal relationships and the role of the state in structuring and supporting relationships or being neutral toward personal choices of citizens. Did the law help people achieve fairness and be non-exploitative in all their personal relationships, whether with their helpers/caretakers or housemates, irrespective of sexual intimacy?

A paragraph in "Perspectives on Personal Relationships" summarizes Rod Macdonald's thinking on the law reform enterprise:

> Let us suppose for a moment that Parliament were to acknowledge that its social policy goal should be that of supporting stable, nurturing, adult relationship … the technical issue is whether there are better or worse ways of drafting legislation in order to accomplish these goals. Two complementary inquiries are engaged: what new concepts of law can be imagined? More important, what are the new ways to imagine concepts of law? Let me be clear about the difference. The first is instrumental: how to better line up policy and legal definition. The second is profoundly symbolic: how to do law reform in a manner that captures the loyalty and fidelity of citizens to the implicit values being advanced.[7]

Again, the project is about the clarification of what is at stake, of what is really going on, of who is winning and who is losing as a result of the present legitimized and legalized arrangements. It is not only about whether the legislative objectives are well served by legal language but about whether the objectives are the right ones. The inquiry is also about the "perverse effects" of the concepts used: it is not sufficient to support marriage in a limited way if it undermines the ability of human beings to be free to explore fairness and responsibility in other valuable and important relationships.

A Theory of Procedural Fairness

Rod Macdonald développe sa théorie de la justice procédurale, une précurseure des idées exposées ici, dans un article datant de 1981: [8] "It is not enough just to follow rules to be fair. A narrowly defined and decontextualized approach to decision-making and process participation leads to masking unfairness and legitimizing unjust results."

Rod Macdonald explique que les principes de la justice procédurale doivent viser la qualité de la participation des personnes affectées et le processus de raisonnement, soit l'explication donnée pour expliquer les résultats d'un processus décisionnel.

Ces deux éléments expliquent bien la production de l'équité. Il s'agit de permettre aux individus de bien se comprendre, d'avoir la chance d'être équitables, d'agir « moralement », et d'être transparentes. Il s'agit également de les empêcher de se cacher derrière le droit pour justifier un manque de courage, une discrimination, un jugement mesquin ou un exercice abusif du pouvoir.

Giving attention to the issue of "quality" of participation does not mean eschewing the possibility of disenfranchisement or of power imbalance. Indeed, recognition of the contextual approach to determine "quality" participation leads to imagining many ways in which one can facilitate participation. For example, the presence of an interpreter, accommodating time or spatial needs, providing legal representation, meeting demands for information exchange or disclosure are all measures aimed at responding proactively to a demand for participation. A contextualized approach to quality participation requires attention to the broadly understood needs of the participants. The second point of the theory of procedural fairness is a constant in Rod's work: he is searching for transparent decision-making, more transparent than is often the case. His insistence on rationality does not lead to an abstract rationality disconnected from the needs of the participants: rationality is about the explanation and communication of a moral decision reached honestly and virtuously.

The Influence of Rod Macdonald's Work

How has Rod Macdonald's work influenced mine? For me, he was a liberation theorist (or a liberation terrorist). Although it is impossible to emulate his imagination, energy, and brilliance, it is stimulating to push ourselves into more theoretically challenging places and put "law in action" as one of the focuses of our inquiries.

To insist on honesty in inquiry throughout by identifying all factors – the religious, the moral, the physical, the power dynamics, the sociological, and the psychological – to get a truer picture of what is going on is always implicit in Rod Macdonald's work. This was the liberation for me: I integrated the need to look more rigorously at legal categorizations and accepted concepts, to engage more purposefully with legal pluralism, and to recognize the fluidity and erratic nature of our expectations about legal outcomes.

Rod Macdonald's work also allowed me to attempt to maximize the power of humans – at times, at the margins, in the right circumstances – to do the right thing and to be engaged in the production of fairness. It also forced me to continue to insist that institutions – legal, educational, public, private, charitable, small or large – offer transparency, honesty, self-reflection, and self-learning and to demand that institutions be concerned about their capacity to produce both fairness and unfairness and aim to construct and reconstruct themselves with this question constantly in mind.

The Future of Rod Macdonald's Work

Rod Macdonald's work suggests that there are many questions left unanswered. Among them, how do we reinvent old hierarchies, limitative and oppressive, and ensure that they remain dismantled and do not re-emerge in new clothes?

In administrative and policy design, how do we ensure that organizations are self-reflective, beyond self-indulgent lip service? Can we use and design mechanisms of evaluation that speak to the issues of power dynamics essential to a clear understanding of the production of fairness?

How do we study the silences of the law, the silences that oppress and fundamentally undermine the production of fairness?

Si la production de l'équité est plus que le simple respect des règles de droit, comment refléter cette conception si riche de nos aspirations dans toute notre compréhension du droit, de son enseignement, et de sa production ?

NOTES

1 Roderick Macdonald, "Parametres of Politics in Judicial Appointments" (prepared for the Bastarache Commission on Judicial Appointments, 2010).
2 Law Commission of Canada, *Restoring Dignity: Responding to Child Abuse in Canadian Institutions, Executive Summary* (Ottawa: Law Commission of Canada, 2000), http://publications.gc.ca/collections/collection_2008/lcc-cdc/JL2-7-2000-1E.pdf (with S. Zimmerman et al.).
3 Macdonald, "Parametres of Politics," 20.
4 Ibid., 20–9.
5 Macdonald, *Lessons of Everyday Law* (Montreal: McGill-Queen's University Press for the School of Policy Studies, Queen's University, and the Law Commission of Canada, 2002).
6 Macdonald, "Perspectives on Personal Relationships" (Opening address to the Conference on Domestic Partnerships, Queen's University, Kingston, 22 October 1999).
7 Ibid., 8.
8 Macdonald, "A Theory of Procedural Fairness," *Windsor Year Book of Access to Justice* 1 (1981): 3–34.

3

Law – Eight Days a Week

SHAUNA VAN PRAAGH

There is never enough time. It is always tempting to think about what we could or would do if we had more. I begin my contribution by reflecting about what I could have done had I had more time. Based on the wide array of Rod Macdonald's work related to "Producing Fairness," I could have written an essay on his vision of dignity and its centrality in assessing the responsiveness of state and non-state law to shared commitments and multiple identities.[1] I could have focused on Rod Macdonald's insistence on listening, sharing, and finding words and actions that foster collaboration. I could have traced the human interactions that ground so many of his projects, including rethinking close personal relationships, processes of selecting judges, supporting responsible choices, or identifying the enterprise of law across sites of institution-building. But it was a busy week, and I just didn't have time. Instead, I am left to contemplate my agenda, to remind myself of how I have filled the hours and days of one week in the life of a law teacher, and to rediscover the insights into the practices and meanings of law that come from all of the things that require so much time.

On *Saturday*, I picked up a printed booklet of photo-essays prepared by Canadian and Israeli law students in my intensive seminar, Socio-economic Justice: Children at Play, one component of a 2013 Hebrew University–McGill University summer program. Course participants explored ways in which children's experiences enrich understanding and practice related to socio-economic fairness and, conversely, ways in which socio-economic context shapes the needs, claims, and responsibilities of young people. We examined the potential and perils of the language of individual rights, on one hand, and of the language of protection, on the other. While both capture something important about human dignity and social values, both can be misleading. Children themselves – just like the boy scouts in Rod Macdonald's essay on social ordering in *Lessons of Everyday Law* or the kids he quotes who protest, "It's not fair, he hit me first"[2] – teach us important lessons as jurists. The photo-essays show children as the future for Bedouin families and villages, as wielders of toy guns in a market, or as vendors for their family businesses, as observers, negotiators, critics, and artists. They are never simple victims, sole claimants, or self-assured actors. As *Restoring Dignity*, the Law Commission's report on responses to institutional child abuse, reminds us, the way "we treat our children and how we allow them to be treated reveals much about ourselves and about our values as a society."[3] By following children, law students can explore the paths they will take as jurists – as dreamers and drafters, translators and teachers, storytellers, advocates, consultants, and companions.

On *Sunday*, I worked on a report on Integration Week, the first full week of formal legal education for McGill's entering law students in September of 2013. For five days, all first-year law students and first-year law professors engaged in a sustained conversation about law's interaction with past, present, and future; about the doors that beckon before the law; about the projects that call upon jurists to connect human needs, human voices, human actions, and human institutions. One of the days of that Integration Week centred on residential schools as an introduction to studying law in Canada, to understanding roles and responsibilities and responses, to thinking about sites and structures for restoring dignity to individuals, families, communities, and entire societies. To start the day, students heard excerpts from accounts given by survivors of residential school – read aloud by upper-year students situated all around McGill's Moot Court – and were thus invited to pay attention to the intersection of empathy and analysis, narrative and argument. They also began that day, and indeed their legal education, with Rod Macdonald's voice in their heads: the voice behind the Law Commission recommendations that labelled the perspective of survivors of institutional child abuse as central to the effectiveness of response, that reminded us that government does not have a monopoly on meaningful redress, that combined acknowledgment, accountability, memory, and public awareness.[4]

On *Monday*, I taught a class of Extra-Contractual Obligations/Torts, a mandatory integrated private law course in the first year of McGill's program of legal education. This week we focused on relational loss – the damage suffered by victims "par ricochet," understood as secondary because their loss stems from the injury or death of someone else.[5] As we see, that someone else is usually a loved one, and the private law has a range of specific mechanisms for recognizing and underscoring particular relationships. More than a decade ago, I wrote a report for the Law Commission of Canada on the picture of relationships that count in the private law of civil wrongs.[6] Understandably reluctant to turn grief into a fully compensable harm, private law quietly plays its part in supporting only some horizontal and vertical human relationships. It thus becomes one of the many places to pay attention to the questions posed by Rod Macdonald: "Are there things that happen in relationships that we see as socially beneficial, such that we should actually orient our legal-regulatory regimes to promote relationships, rather than just targeting individuals?"[7] What are the dominant socio-cultural-religious structures that articulate and organize the conceptual frame for a whole series of social and legal policies? These may sound like particularly difficult questions for first-year law students, but they are crucial to making connections between private law principles and the human activities and encounters that they attempt to reflect and regulate.

On *Tuesday*, I taught a session of a seminar in Legal Education – a course I am teaching for the first time, in the syllabus of which I have noted my debt to Rod Macdonald, its long-time professor, and the materials of which open with Rod Macdonald's "Academic Questions" and close with Harry Arthurs's "The Future of Legal Education: Three Visions and a Prediction."[8] Participants in the course discuss the contours of legal education; the law faculty's place in the university; the connection between learning law and preparing for a life as a jurist; the roles of law teachers, scholars, and deans. Recently, I used the example of teaching the well-known tort law case of *Palsgraf*[9] to provoke a discussion among seminar participants of what first-year law students learn and how. One of the doctoral candidates asked, "Do you teach tort law to your students or instead how to think like lawyers?" As Rod Macdonald might say, it was a good teaching and learning moment. "Both, all of the time" is the obvious answer: "each through the other." The question invites a discussion of how students learn not just how to think like lawyers but to listen, and do, and create, and team-build, and express appropriate humility like lawyers. How we help them do that as their teachers is crucial. How do we ensure that students, as Rod asked of judges, "retain the precious idealism of youth – those moments of wide-eyed wonderment that impel the constant discovery and rediscovery of self?"[10] Constant questioning of the forms and functions of legal education helps to ensure that learning in a classroom, like decision-making in a courtroom, can be characterized by exploration and wonder.

On *Wednesday*, I helped sort through proposals for the 2014 annual meeting of the Canadian Association of Law Teachers. The theme of the conference, designed by those entrusted with guidance of the association, is "Open Doors: Teaching and Learning Law for Justice." Law teachers are invited to reflect on faculties of law as important sites for thinking about justice and fairness, regulation and governance, and nourishing of life projects. Law, as Rod Macdonald says in "A Theory of Procedural Fairness," is a "natural and creative phenomenon arising from human conduct."[11] On the agenda is a discussion of the future of the Canadian Association of Law Teachers itself. Rod Macdonald's "Parametres of Politics," focused on the process of choosing judges, holds important lessons; so does "Sometimes It's Better Just to Fix the Dock" and "Who Do You Think You Are Anyway?"[12] Who do we think we are as teachers of law? Among our many identities that count, do we include members of a countrywide collective with shared objectives and priorities? In what ways can we revise structures upon which the nurturing of identities depends? Rod Macdonald reminds us that judges have lived engaged lives in the community where they have experienced the joys, frustrations, aspirations, and disappointments of life. So too have law professors. Those life experiences enrich the contributions and human dimensions we bring to the task. They inform the ways that legal educators can design and then open wide the doors of legal education for justice.

On *Thursday*, I took myself to a Montreal neighbourhood café for the morning to treat myself to some thinking time devoted to a project in progress. The project is focused on the ways in which judging can be importantly linked to teaching and university leadership, to public policy engagement and institutional reform, to the content and method of lawmaking. Centred on the trajectory of one person engaged in all of these forms of the practice of law, the character of the project might be characterized as biographical. Biography often suggests the narrating of life story and the listing of achievements and accolades. But the biography of a jurist, as Rod Macdonald might insist as a corollary to his essay "What You See Depends on Where You Stand,"[13] must pay attention instead to all of the stuff in between the events and the awards and the marked moments. The project is particularly challenging not because of its subject but because of the way in which it forces its author to examine the importance of perspective. Writing as a law professor, especially about the paths leading from a legal education to overlapping roles and responsibilities, requires recognition of reliance on colleagues and friends and students and life partners or, in other words, of relationships as what Rod Macdonald labels the bedrock of law.[14] This project serves as reminder that our research and writing always force reflection on our ongoing engagement with law – whether found in judgments or charters, constitutions or local by-laws, committee guidelines, or even children's stories.

This brings me to the *everyday* – the children. Each and every day in every one of my weeks includes parenting and the reasons, rules, resistance, and renewal that are all part of the unrecorded reality of family life. In "But Everyone Else Is Allowed," Rod Macdonald distinguishes arbitrary from responsible parents by focusing on the need to listen to children's arguments about the very meaning, scope, and malleability of the rules. As he says, "Wise parents know that their rules alone do not provide specific solutions to specific problems."[15] That kind of wisdom is hard to develop and maintain. This is teaching and learning around the clock, about fairness, limits, transparency, explicit expectations, implicit norms, natural consequences, empowerment. Concrete children's gifts chosen and presented by Rod Macdonald include a Swiss Army knife and a subscription to *The New York Review of Books*. Of course, those gifts deliver thinly disguised lessons to parents: to encourage the children to find their own tools and words, create their own projects, and ask their own questions. None of this makes dinner table conversations any easier – but those conversations are the shapers of everyday, Rod Macdonald's primary sources for reflecting on law's structures and potential.

And so I arrive at *Friday – today*, the day to join with others to consider the implication of Rod Macdonald's work for future directions in research, writing, and teaching. With my agenda in hand, I am already looking ahead to tomorrow and the next day. I may not have had enough time. But throughout the week I was immersed in doing law in the ways Rod Macdonald envisages, describes, and prescribes, even if I didn't name them. Sometimes our sources are so integrated into our work that the footnotes fade. As Rod Macdonald might say, sometimes the most important things have to remain unstated, just as he insists that sometimes we don't need specific rules but rather general expressions of shared commitment.[16] The diary of a law professor can feel full of nothing but blocks of under-inspired teaching, partial learning, best-in-the-circumstances decision-making, adequate reason-providing, less-than-perfect attempts to show respect for another's dignity, messy combinations of self-doubt and stepping up. Perhaps all of that is the content and method of a life of teaching and writing, creating and connecting, listening and reaching out.

The published words of Rod Macdonald can provide both compass and content for ongoing projects. They can explain, justify, and give meaning to so much of what fills the agendas of the weeks, years, and careers of law teachers and scholars, practitioners and policy-makers. But quiet conversations can also set directions. Two decades ago, Rod Macdonald invited a young would-be McGill law professor for a first walk and talk – in a snowstorm while we both ate Laura Secord ice cream cones. I don't remember the exact words. But for Rod, even an ice cream moment in a blizzard could be an invitation to consider the intersections of law and everyday life. It was a lesson on what was important, a realization that a few snowflakes couldn't get in the way of sharing ideas and stories. It was a meeting and moment not inscribed in any agenda but instead a sign of boundless time and space and ideas to follow.

NOTES

1 Law Commission of Canada, *Restoring Dignity: Responding to Child Abuse in Canadian Institutions, Executive Summary* (Ottawa: Law Commission of Canada, 2000), http://publications.gc.ca/collections/collection_2008/lcc-cdc/JL2-7-2000-1E.pdf (with S. Zimmerman et al.).
2 Roderick Macdonald, "It's Not Fair, He Hit Me First!" in *Lessons of Everyday Law* (Montreal: McGill-Queen's University Press for the School of Policy Studies, Queen's University, and the Law Commission of Canada, 2002), 95–8.
3 Law Commission of Canada, *Restoring Dignity*, 1.
4 Ibid., 2, 9.
5 We read, for example, *Régent Taxi c Congrégation des petits frères de Marie*, [1929] SCR 650; *Augustus v. Gosset*, [1996] 3 SCR 269; Shauna Van Praagh, "Who Lost What? Relationship and Relational Loss," *Supreme Court Law Review* 17 (2) (2002): 269–87.
6 Law Commission of Canada, *Compensation for Relational Harm*, by Shauna Van Praagh (Ottawa: Law Commission of Canada, 2001).
7 Macdonald, "Perspectives on Personal Relationships" (Opening address to the Conference on Domestic Partnerships, Queen's University, Kingston, 22 October 1999), 4.
8 Macdonald, "Academic Questions," *Legal Education Review* 3 (1992): 61–74; Harry W. Arthurs, "The Future of Legal Education: Three Visions and a Prediction," *Alberta Law Review* 51 (4) (2014): 705–16.

9 Van Praagh, "*Palsgraf* as 'Transsystemic' Tort Law," *Journal of Comparative Law* 6 (2) (2011): 243–61.
10 Macdonald, "Parametres of Politics in Judicial Appointments" (Prepared for the Bastarache Commission on Judicial Appointments, 2010), 16–17.
11 Macdonald, "A Theory of Procedural Fairness," *Windsor Year Book of Access to Justice* 1 (1981): 7.
12 Macdonald, "Sometimes It's Better Just to Fix the Dock," in *Lessons of Everyday Law*, 55–8; Macdonald, "Who Do You Think You Are Anyway?" in *Lessons of Everyday Law*, 120–4.
13 Macdonald, "What You See Depends on Where You Stand," in *Lessons of Everyday Law*, 115–19.
14 Macdonald, "Everyday Life and Everyday Law," in *Lessons of Everyday Law*, 3.
15 Macdonald, "... But Everyone Else Is Allowed To," in *Lessons of Everyday Law*, 86.
16 Macdonald, "If It Goes without Saying, Does It Go Better When You Say It?" in *Lessons of Everyday Law*, 36.

4

Roderick Macdonald's Andragogy: Producing Fairness through Education

SUZANNE BOUCLIN

The texts that the "Producing Fairness" panel was asked to discuss may be explicitly about fairness; implicitly and inferentially, however, I believe, they are all about teaching and learning. In these texts, which explore how each human being bears a responsibility for producing fairness, Rod also asks us to consider how legal education – in whatever form or mode or on whatever site – can generate more just conditions of interaction.

In this contribution, I borrow a passage from one of his articles to suggest that there is an underlying invitation in almost all of his writings, regardless of their subject matter or form, to endeavour toward an "ethics of education." Rod's hypothesis is that all relationships – including those between students and professors – are best informed by virtue ethics and consequently "by recourse to conceptions of human and intellectual flourishing."[1] Students and professors, like all moral actors, are better situated to judge and guide their behaviour, he believes, "with reference to the internal morality of the relationship" rather than to "externally imposed and ostensibly objective and universalizable rules" used to determine when a conflict of interest has arisen and how best to address it.[2]

In what follows, I draw on one passage from Rod's early work on procedural fairness[3] as a means of discussing how his theory of andragogy (the education of *adults* rather than children)[4] manifests concretely in the classroom. I then move on to relate his scholarly writing to the teaching materials from his Legal Education Seminar (LES)[5] as a means of illuminating a broader vision of teaching that highlights some of his concerns about the instrumentalization of legal education while foregrounding his profound belief in and optimism about people's desire and potential to achieve a more just world. I do so by relating his scholarly writing to the teaching materials from his LES.

The LES is an upper-year seminar, developed by Rod and still offered at the Faculty of Law at McGill University.[6] Intended primarily for students contemplating a teaching career, the course was designed to help students gain awareness of, and critically engage with, their tacit assumptions about law and legal education.[7] The course has three overarching objectives. Procedurally, LES aims to "review the aims, goals, methods, and techniques" of legal education in North American universities.[8] Substantively, the seminar asks epistemological questions such as: What is law? What is legal knowledge? How is legal knowledge acquired? How is it circulated?[9] Instrumentally, the seminar aspires to enrich the teaching and learning experiences of students and professors.[10] The LES is the performance of his theory of andragogy,[11] which flows from several assumptions: students have *self-concept* and consequently have resolved identity formation issues; students' *experiences* are a resource in their learning; students have a *readiness to learn*; students have an *orientation to learning* toward problem-solving; *motivation to learn* is internal, and consequently students ought to be treated as self-directed in their learning.[12]

The assumptions that undergird Rod's andragogy stem, I suggest, at least in part from his earlier scholarship on procedural fairness. In "A Theory of Procedural Fairness," he explains that fairness in decision-making can be evaluated according to two criteria: the meaningfulness of the participation afforded to those affected by the decision-making and whether the character of the reasons for the decision have been properly conveyed.[13] This article is rich on a number of levels, but I found his description of the minimum rights that should be afforded to all participants in non-adjudicative decision-making to be its most compelling feature. These rights include:[14]

1 The right to know in advance the subject matter to be decided and the authority under which the decision is to be taken.
2 The right to an adjournment in order to prepare submissions fully.
3 The right to engage counsel to assist in the presentation of fact and opinions, access other submissions, and file supplementary comment.
4 The right to know the general policy of the decision-maker in advance.

5 The right to move for re-argument, reception of additional evidence, and reconsideration.
6 The right to appeal any decision upon its merits.[15]

These principles of procedural fairness form what I understand to be Rod's pedagogical injunctions as developed in his Legal Education Seminar. Below, I recast each of the rights afforded to participants in political decision-making as rights afforded by Rod to his law students.

Participants have the right to know in advance the subject matter of the point to be decided.

It is unfair to have students guess what is expected of them during evaluations. When designing law courses, professors should be explicit about their pedagogical choices, including course materials and evaluations. Rod explains:

> There is a sense of distrust in the accuracy of evaluating a student's performance. Some of this suspicion stems from the inherent weaknesses of such a system: professorial subjectivity, artificial curving of grades and arbitrariness are among the most common complaints. Some of the scepticism, however, originates from the unreliability of assessments themselves. The distinction between a B+ and A– for example is rarely made clear. The lack of feedback and transparency in the marking scheme fuels the argument that there is no justification for the assigned grades. Improved assessment strategies can not only help restore the integrity of a grading system, but can provide a more rewarding experience for the student.[16]

The ethics of teaching, according to Rod, includes a responsibility to clearly explain to students, in advance of their assessments, the criteria against which their work will be measured.

Participants have the right to an adjournment and to prepare submissions fully.

Students should come to class prepared and should be active participants in class, but participation also includes self-reflection after "official," explicit classroom time. Education extends beyond explicit aspects of such law education and well beyond the classroom experience. Rod makes this plain in the LES syllabus: "Legal education [embraces] not just the activities of a law faculty, but also legal education in other departments of the University, in secondary schools, in NGOs and trade unions, and public legal education generally; legal education not just in its North American context, but also legal education in European universities, polytechnic institutions, through apprenticeship training and through bar admission courses; legal education not just in formal settings, but also informal legal education on the street, in prisons, and in other normative communities."[17]

Rod asked professors and students to consider the implicit education of law students through those teaching and learning moments that are peripheral to professors' institutional roles, whether through guest lectures, judging competitive moots, participating in and attending conferences, and, especially, email and everyday conversation. Students should be afforded an appropriate amount of time to prepare for these interactions and to reflect on them as part of their legal education.

> *Participants have the right to engage counsel to assist in the presentation of fact and opinions, access other submissions, and file supplementary comment.*

Students lead complex lives and have diverse perspectives that can serve as resources in their learning as well as buttress those of their peers and professors. While Rod firmly believed that "students must take charge of their own education," such individual responsibilization is not the same as individualism. In fact, three-hour-long, individual final exams that look backward to assess the degree to which students have absorbed data may not, at least on their own, be the most effective means of assessing skills or knowledge. Instead, he favoured collegial approaches to learning that draw on "the collective strength of [the learning community's] members."[18] Consequently, a strong component of Rod's evaluations in the LES was to provide students with multiple modes of feedback (including the presence of peer evaluators who were, along with him, "co-responsible for providing feedback"). Legal education should invite collaborative assignments between first-year and upper-year students and among students of different disciplines and should encourage peer-to-peer feedback within cohorts. Such assessments can be an iterative, future-oriented, ongoing, and interactive tool that enables students to test their understanding of the material presented. In his LES, Rod included six such forms of evaluation, each with the following features: "First, the process will be *continual*, beginning on the first day and continuing throughout the semester. Second, the process will comprise both *informal* and *formal* components. Third, the process will be *interactive* and involve continual feedback from me to you. Fourth, you will have a chance to *tailor-make* the evaluation process to your own needs and work with me in its specific design."[19]

Participants have the right to know the general policy of the decision-maker in advance.

Teaching requires a level of transparency and of awareness of the beliefs, backgrounds, and self-concepts that shape the way we teach. Rod expresses this belief as an overarching principle of the LES. Consider this passage from a class entitled "Who Am I and Why Am I Here?": "The overall theme [of today's seminar] is to test whether any body of knowledge exists independently of the intellectual commitments of the teacher who teaches and the students who learn. In particular we will explore the extent to which the way one teaches and learns is not influenced by personal learning styles and personal beliefs about who one is and what one is seeking to get out of a legal education."[20] In order for students to know the assumptions that underlie professors' decisions, professors must first be able to articulate and stand for what they believe.

Participants have the right to move for re-argument and reconsideration.

Students should be able to learn through their mistakes. Self-assessments feature prominently in LES because they encourage additional reflection after class and permit students to discover or confirm their own learning styles and strengths. When asked about his teaching methods, Rod explained: "People sometimes ask me what my ambition is as a law professor. I say that I hope my students know more about themselves at the end of the course than they did at the beginning."[21]

Self-assessments and assignments that promote self-reflection can enable teachers to assess different learning styles in a fair and equitable manner and can help them to probe students' progress over time as well as encourage self-improvement. Rod's view that self-reflection can promote deep learning stemmed from his belief that it is actually through mistakes and the reconsideration of those mistakes that learning truly happens. In a class that explores the meaning of education, he reminded his students that "to be alive is to risk, and to risk is to make mistakes. Teaching that human failings are inescapable and that the recognition of failing is a first step towards redemption is the lesson that is taught at the coffee house as much as it is taught in the corridor, on the bus, or in the classroom."[22]

Participants have a right to appeal a decision on the merits.

There should be appropriate channels for formative assessments of professors in ways that invite them also to learn and improve over time. Professors are human beings who, however diligent, will make mistakes. As mentioned above, all mistakes are teaching moments, yet in the university context, some mistakes made by professors have consequences for students.

These six injunctions gleaned from his work on procedure demonstrate how – in whatever context Rod is writing – he is often also talking about how we might reinvigorate legal education to provide more a rewarding experience for students and professors. By way of demonstration, let me point to a few passages from the other texts assigned to this panel. Legal education, he explains in *Everyday Law*, is a series of interactions and inquiries that aim at human and intellectual flourishing.[23] Every encounter may be an opportunity for self-discovery and joint discovery, and "if one does not respond [to such opportunities to build relationships], one misses the chance to educate"[24] and, I add, to be educated. In "Parametres of Politics in Judicial Appointments," Rod reminds us that "education must aim to embolden [us] to resist the siren songs of conventional adulthood – most notably reputation and popular acclaim – and to retain the precious idealism of youth – those moments of wide-eyed wonderment that impel the constant discovery and rediscovery of self."[25]

In all of this work, Rod enjoins us to make education – our own education and that of our students – part of a worthwhile life project. He iterates that the instrumental purpose of legal education is acquiring valuable skills, tools, habits, and knowledge that will help to make good jurists and judges but that that aim should not displace the true character of education: fostering the opportunities, inquiries, interactions, and discoveries that nurture the kind of virtues that will help to produce a more just society.

NOTES

1 Roderick Macdonald, "Relationships and Ethics," Reading Guide Memo 20, Legal Education Seminar (LAWG-525), McGill University, Faculty of Law, 10 November 2008 (on file with author).

2 Ibid.

3 Macdonald, "A Theory of Procedural Fairness," *Windsor Year Book of Access to Justice* 1 (1981): 3–34.
4 Macdonald, "'Alternative' Pedagogies/Andragogies," Lesson Plan 15, Legal Education Seminar, 21 October 2008 (on file with author). He distinguishes his theory from a *peda*gogical approach, which implies that law students are children. See also "Knowles Andragogy," http://www.learningandteachinginfo/learning/knowlesa.htm; Mark K. Smith, Infed, "Andragogy: What Is It and Does It Help Thinking about Adult Learning?" 28 January 2005, http://www.infed.org/lifelonglearning/b-andra.htm.
5 I had the great pleasure of co-teaching LES with Rod in 2008 and took over the course for him in 2010 while he underwent one of several treatments for cancer.
6 Macdonald, "Legal Education Seminar," Syllabus, McGill University, Faculty of Law, fall 2008; Macdonald, "LAWG-525 Legal Education Seminar," Courses Overview, McGill University, 2008, http://www.mcgill.ca/study/2012-2013/courses/lawg-525.
7 Macdonald, "Legal Education Seminar," Syllabus, McGill University, Faculty of Law, fall 2008, 1.
8 Ibid., 2.
9 Ibid.
10 Ibid.
11 Macdonald, "'Alternative' Pedagogies/Andragogies."
12 Macdonald, "'Alternative' Pedagogies/Andragogies," Reading Guide Memo 15, Legal Education Seminar (LAWG-525), McGill University, Faculty of Law, 21 October 2008) on file with author).
13 Macdonald, "Theory of Procedural Fairness," 5.
14 Ibid., 19.
15 Ibid.
16 Macdonald, "Assessment and Evaluation," Reading Guide Memo 18, Legal Education Seminar (LAWG-525), McGill University, Faculty of Law, 5 November 2008 (on file with author).
17 Macdonald, "Legal Education Seminar," 1.
18 Macdonald, "Liberal Theories of Education," Recap Memo 9, Legal Education Seminar (LAWG-525), McGill University, Faculty of Law, 1 October 2008, 1 (on file with author).
19 The six modes of evaluation are: Classroom Participation (Pass-Fail); Field Trips (Pass-Fail); Web-Platform Participation (Pass-Fail); Teaching (33%); Peer Evaluation (Pass-Fail); Designing a Law Course (67%).
20 Macdonald, "Who Am I and Why Am I Here?" Reading Guide Memo 2, Legal Education Seminar (LAWG-525), McGill University, Faculty of Law, 8 September 2008 (on file with author).

21 Neale McDevitt, "Rod Macdonald," *McGill Reporter* 16 October 2014, http://publications.mcgill.ca/reporter/2011/12/rod-macdonald-a-lifetime-educating-not-indoctrinating.
22 Macdonald, "Professing to Education or Educating to Profess: What Do I Believe …?" Handout 7, Legal Education Seminar (LAWG-525), McGill University, Faculty of Law, 24 September 2008, 9 (on file with author).
23 Macdonald, *Lessons of Everyday Law* (Montreal: McGill-Queen's University Press for the School of Policy Studies, Queen's University, and the Law Commission of Canada, 2002).
24 Macdonald, "Professing to Education," 14.
25 Macdonald, "Parametres of Politics in Judicial Appointments" (Prepared for the Bastarache Commission on Judicial Appointments, 2010), 17.

5

Mixed Method, Controversy, and Abiding Influence

ROBERT LECKEY

In this brief text, I address the impact of Roderick Macdonald's scholarship on my work. I focus on the Law Commission of Canada's report *Beyond Conjugality*[1] and on "Parametres of Politics in Judicial Appointments," the expert study prepared for the Inquiry Commission into the appointment process for judges to the Court of Quebec, municipal courts, and the Tribunal administratif du Québec (the Bastarache Commission).[2] These texts appeared with others on the short list for the "Producing Fairness" panel. Much of Rod's scholarship continues to influence me, and I might easily have focused on other texts of his. If I could have selected other texts, however, the matters I highlight here would apply to most of them. To identify the impact of Rod's scholarship, I separate his methodology from his political sensibility or posture. I also identify some implications of Rod's scholarship for future research. For that issue, I focus on *Beyond Conjugality*.

Methodology

Beyond Conjugality and "Parametres of Politics in Judicial Appointments" both set out questions to direct our thinking of appropriate legal approaches to a complex issue. One addresses recognizing and regulating adult interdependent relationships, the other, selecting judges. The methodological point I want to draw out is Rod's way of transposing registers or lines of inquiry from one area of legal inquiry to another. In this way, he deploys a distinctive kind of mixed methodology.

When examining close personal relationships, he displays great sensitivity to affective dynamics. He also shows, however, a clear-eyed, dispassionate willingness to broach the matter as if it were any other regulatory challenge. Some of his writing on intimate relationships, then, is emotionally cool. Rod asks: What are our legislative objectives here? What are the instrument choices? What are the costs and benefits of each instrument choice? How much space is there for self-regulation (e.g., for individuals to designate the relationships that matter most to them)? Can we recognize relationships for some purposes and not others?

In effect, Rod's analysis around the use of the conjugal relationship as the vehicle for delivering social programs pushes aside romantic assumptions about the couple that might cloud our appreciation of the regulatory stakes. I think of that work as borrowing the technical, analytical Rod so well known to his colleagues in the field of secured lending and transplanting him in the field of family law and social policy – in which graze the sacred cows of marriage and the exclusive romantic couple.[3] I hasten to add that on these matters, his questioning rests on a vast knowledge of how law and the state function – of the intricacies of the private law of marriage and family relationships, of general private law, and of the public programs of taxation, social welfare, and other benefits. Rod's grasp of how such regimes interact has influenced and improved my own work.[4]

The dispassionate analysis that the Law Commission undertook using this methodology led to recommendations that many statutes cease making the conjugal couple central. It led, indeed, to the idea that it might be good for the state to get out of the marriage business, although doing so might be politically unfeasible.

Then, in the judicial appointments piece, we see a similar methodological move but reversed in affective terms. Many people speak of the judicial appointment issue as if we can do it neutrally, apolitically – as if we can speak in objective terms of the best-qualified judge and imagine that an appointments process would arrive at only him or her. Counterintuitively, Rod's paper for the Bastarache Commission takes the human elements as its point of departure. It foregrounds the necessity, for the rule of law, of having a human judiciary, underscoring that subjective human judgment necessarily inheres in the application of legal rules. The paper also emphasizes the ineluctability of human judgment and human considerations in a selection process. Tackling assumptions about objective decision-making, he imagines a situation in which a committee has an agreed list of fifty criteria, agreed weighting of the criteria, a requirement to rank each candidate on each criterion, and a requirement to tally their total results. He writes that "it would be tendentious to claim that a candidate with the highest total score, say 2,753 points, is 'objectively best' or even that such a candidate is 'objectively better' than a candidate with 2,748 points ... The most that one could deduce from such a process is that candidates above a certain threshold would be acceptable, and candidates above some other threshold would likely be excellent candidates."[5] His overall argument is that disciplining subjective judgment about judicial appointments is possible, but eradicating it is not.

The methodological idea, then, is that Rod's texts bring together different modes of inquiry and different kinds of concerns in unexpected but analytically rich and productive ways. These texts, written in different settings, model the integration and methodological and intellectual pluralism that have deeply affected my scholarly work.

Political Posture

Each of these texts – not to mention others during Rod Macdonald's career – was potentially politically controversial. The personal relationships piece incurred the ire of a prominent lawyer fighting for gay and lesbian equality rights. That activist felt that the time wasn't ripe for questioning the state's global approach to regulating intimate relationships when fighting gay men's and lesbians' exclusion from such regulation topped the agenda.

The judicial appointment paper dared to distinguish illegitimate from legitimate political considerations. In other words, it accepted that judicial appointments properly involve some political considerations.[6] Doing that was risky and controversial at a moment when public discourse attacked the idea of legitimate political decisions and leading opinion-makers regarded as suspect any involvement in the political process by someone eventually named a judge. The climate of a witch-hunt surrounded the Bastarache Commission's work, with the idea that organizing work or a donation of $100 to a political party by someone whom that party later named a judge had tainted the whole thing. (Nobody, it seemed, paused to ask how many former political organizers and donors to each political party, once in office, had been passed over for judgeships.)

Rod Macdonald was fearless, or at least he appeared fearless, in voicing hypotheses, critiques, and conclusions that might irritate or anger people, even people who would expect to be his allies. As someone who tries to merge academically rigorous critique with activism around sexual justice issues, I bear his example in mind. He showed us that the scholar's job isn't always to make friends.[7]

Implications for Future Research

What implications does Rod Macdonald's work on personal relationships, including *Beyond Conjugality*, have for future research? This question is important, especially since the federal government has shut down the Law Commission, although it has never repealed its enabling legislation.[8] Its website no longer exists – a reminder that even in the Internet era, it's sensible to put paper copies of publications in libraries.

Scholars continue to read *Beyond Conjugality*, to cite it, and to find inspiration in it. I attended an international conference at which American scholars discussed it extensively in a presentation. I also edited an interdisciplinary, international collection, chapters of which refer to *Beyond Conjugality*, using its methodology to raise concerns about the taxation regime's focus on the conjugal couple.[9]

In my view, an aggressively fairness-based analysis of relationships is especially crucial now. Legislative and judicial measures to make same-sex marriage possible and to address the economic fallout of unmarried cohabitation appear to lead people to assume that we have dealt appropriately with all relevant relationships. That assumption is false. It may be that Rod's thinking on adult relationships came before its time. In any event, it dovetails with work published more than a decade afterwards on questions such as those who are living-apart-together.[10] His sensitivity to the pluralism of adult relationships would also make space for recent conversations on being single.[11]

These remarks, and the conference from which they derived, bear on Rod's scholarship. It is obvious to turn to his published writing, which has significantly influenced scholars around the world and will continue to do so. Before closing, I would add that Rod invested countless hours in scholarship of another kind, namely, commenting on the draft work of colleagues and students. At moments, you might have suspected that Rod wanted every paper of yours, too, to be about legal pluralism. Rod Macdonald's methodology and intellectual fearlessness, and the force of his ideas, will be with me and with many others for the rest of our scholarly lives.

NOTES

For comments on earlier versions, the author is grateful to Fraser Harland, Thomas Touchie, and Shauna Van Praagh.

1 Law Commission of Canada, *Beyond Conjugality: Recognizing and Supporting Close Personal Adult Relationships* (Ottawa: Law Commission of Canada, 2001); see also Roderick Macdonald and Nathalie Des Rosiers, "Recognizing and Supporting Close Personal Relationships between Adults" (Ottawa: Law Commission of Canada, 2000); Roderick Macdonald and Thomas McMorrow, "Wedding a Critical Legal Pluralism to the Laws of Close Personal Adult Relationships," *European Journal of Legal Studies* 1 (2007): 1.

2 Macdonald, "Parametres of Politics in Judicial Appointments" (Prepared for the Bastarache Commission on Judicial Appointments, 2010). I should disclose that I served as director of research for the commission and in that capacity I commissioned Rod's study and edited it.

3 See, for example, my distinction between the streams of functionalist and autonomy-based discourse regarding cohabitation, which reflected the influence of Rod's work on secured transactions: Robert Leckey, "Cohabitation and Comparative Method," *Modern Law Review* 72 (1) (2009).

4 Leckey, "Families in the Eyes of the Law: Contemporary Challenges and the Grip of the Past," in *IRPP Choices* (Montreal: Institute for Research on Public Policy, 2009); Leckey, "Bankruptcy, Provincial Law, and the Family Farm," *Canadian Bar Review* 91 (2) (2012); Leckey, "Strange Bedfellows," *University of Toronto Law Journal* 64 (5) (2014).

5 Macdonald, "Parametres of Politics," 207.

6 Ibid., 213.

7 For papers that press against the gay-rights orthodoxy, see Leckey, "Thick Instrumentalism and Comparative Constitutionalism: The Case of Gay Rights," *Columbia Human Rights Law Review* 40 (2) (2009); Leckey, "Must Equal Mean Identical? Same-Sex Couples and Marriage," *International Journal of Law in Context* 10 (1) (2014).

8 Law Commission of Canada Act, S.C. 1996, c. 9.

9 Kim Brooks, "Cameos from the Margins of Conjugality," in *After Legal Equality: Family, Sex, Kinship*, edited by Robert Leckey (Abingdon: Routledge, 2015), 99–100; Claire Young, "Taxing Times for Lesbians and Gay Men: Twenty Years Later," in *After Legal Equality: Family, Sex, Kinship*, edited by Robert Leckey (Abingdon: Routledge, 2015), 143–4.

10 See, e.g., Vicky Lyssens-Danneboom, Sven Eggermont, and Dimitri Mortelmans, "Living Apart Together (LAT) and Law: Exploring Legal

Expectations among LAT Individuals in Belgium," *Social and Legal Studies* 22 (3) (2013); Simon Duncan et al., "Legal Rights for People Who 'Live Apart Together'?" *Journal of Social Welfare and Family Law* 34 (4) (2012).

11 Michael Cobb, *Single: Arguments for the Uncoupled* (New York: New York Uuniversity Press, 2012).

6

From the Perspective of Personhood: Thoughts on Rod Macdonald's Conception of Procedural Fairness

KRISTEN RUNDLE

A conversation in early 1998 with Jeremy Webber, then recently appointed as dean of Sydney Law School, led somehow to the prescription that I ought to be put in a box and sent to work with Rod Macdonald. This I did as an LLM student at McGill in 2000–01, where I wrote a thesis under his supervision that I now see as having laid the groundwork for everything I have done since.

The road to that thesis involved many hours in Rod's office talking about ideas. I learned a lot about a lot of things during those conversations, but I especially learned some crucial things about perspective. By "perspective," I mean to indicate two things. First, I have in mind Rod's own perspective – specifically, how he always kept the abstract and the real, the normative and the practice, not only both in view but in contact with each other. In the Macdonald cast of mind, therefore, we find none of the siloed silliness of insulated concepts untainted by the vagaries of the real world, or any sense of a real world that somehow gets on without honouring the significance of ideas. But I also mean to signal how in following that cast of mind, irrespective of the problem at hand, we are led to consider the perspective of the person on the bottom, the person in the middle, the person to the side, the person at the top, those who have come before, and those who are yet to come, not to mention the rest.

In my contribution to the panel "Producing Fairness," I will take both these senses of perspective, but especially the latter, as the foundation for some remarks on Rod's 1981 article, "A Theory of Procedural Fairness."[1] Procedural fairness, he argues, is a much more rich and demanding affair than we might otherwise have assumed. Any "general concept" of procedural fairness, must therefore reflect this complexity at the same time that it offers a coherent perspective on a distinctive ideal.[2] Though the ambitions of the essay are large, their pursuit comes wrapped in Rod's characteristic way of seeking rupture at the same time that he delivers rigour, committed at every turn to embracing variation rather than simplifying it. Accordingly, the central argument of the piece is that we miss something essential as theory and risk courting failure in practice if we align our thinking about procedural fairness to the specificities of the modality – adjudication – that has historically been the natural home for its demands. Rather, a theory of procedural fairness appropriate to *all* kinds of legal activity must direct itself to "two complementary features of any decision-making process": (i) the quality of the participation that should be afforded to persons affected by a decision and (ii) the kinds of reasons that properly may be offered in support of the decision that results.[3]

Much of the essay is occupied with an extended analysis of the implications of these two features for different modalities of ordering. How might the demands of procedural fairness translate to property? Or mediation? Or politics? But it is by asking *why* these two features should be so central to a theory of procedural fairness that the underlying impulse of each is revealed. The demand that participation afforded to affected persons must be of a certain quality, Rod explains, speaks to the relation between "enfranchisement and justice." The demand that certain kinds of reasons should be offered in support of a decision in turn invites us to consider the connection between "justification and justice."[4] Enfranchisement and justification, therefore, lie at the heart of the rationale for procedural fairness and so must also occupy a central place within any theory that seeks to capture the distinctive character of its normative demands.

This is the core argument, and it is helpful to pause and note that much is made throughout the analysis of its indebtedness to the work of Lon Fuller. Certainly, this debt is readily apparent in how the first limb of Rod's prescription for a theory of procedural fairness is clearly inspired by Fuller's idea that the very distinctiveness of adjudication consists in the mode of participation that it affords to its parties.[5] Marks of Fuller's analytical methods also abound, perhaps most obviously in Rod's way of refining his arguments about what procedural fairness demands by reference to hypothetical instances of its apparent failure.[6] Still, Rod's analysis goes, and continued in later work to go, into territory that was far less explored by Fuller. Specifically, what we get from Rod's analysis is a deep concern for what each kind of process that might be brought to the resolution of a given problem *will mean* for those who are affected by it.

This, for me, is where the nub of Rod's thinking on procedural fairness lies: in its concern for conditions of personhood within decision-making processes. The claim, therefore, is that that there should be no theorization of the normative demands of procedural fairness that does not start and end in the figure of the person, attending closely to conditions that might generate intelligibility, to her, about what is happening to her in the present, as well as, when relevant, what has happened to her in the past. To speak of procedural fairness in Rod's lexicon is to ponder how the possibility of the enfranchisement of persons can be generated through a process design appropriate not just to some intended end but also to its capacity to make sense to the expectations and experiences of those who participate within it.

To this end, it is important to note the emphasis Rod gives to the matter of choice of process paradigm.[7] This point, though surely not something we would typically subsume within the demands of procedural fairness, signals Rod's enduring awareness of how what is at stake in such a choice is not merely the efficacy of a given process (though it is, of course, also that) but the much more fundamental matter of its intelligibility to its participants. Accordingly, the insight offered is that if personhood is to be constituted and sustained within such processes, respect for it must, wherever possible, begin at the beginning by allowing those affected to play a role in choosing the process itself. Because without this attention to how conditions of personhood might be generated by processes, as well as potentially negated by them, the game might well be over before it even begins.

The foregoing is, of course, just one reading of Rod's theory of procedural fairness. But it is, I want to suggest, entirely compatible not only with what was to come in Rod's work but with what we might now develop out of the frame he laid down. On what was to come, anyone familiar with his contribution to both the theorization and practice of the design of administrative processes will recognize his efforts to develop and apply the insights contained in the 1981 essay. One especially striking example is his authorship of the Law Commission of Canada's *Restoring Dignity* reference in response to child institutionalization. Here the question of choice of process, placed front and centre, is driven by a deep recognition of just how crucial appropriate modes of participation will be to a process designed to both confront an agonizing history and establish conditions for a more enfranchised future.[8]

The question of what might be further developed out of Rod's thinking on procedural fairness is, of course, in our hands now. With an eye to this, therefore, I offer the following suggestion. The wide variety of modalities that comprise the landscape of contemporary administrative governance, and the kinds of threats to personhood that they might pose, could not have been fully in view when he penned his theory of procedural fairness. But if we understand the essence of his prescriptions for procedural fairness as concerned with how conditions of personhood and intelligibility can be both generated and undermined within settings of administrative governance, their continuing salience is obvious. Indeed, it is precisely because Rod's approach is simultaneously focused (in its commitment to enfranchisement and justification) and flexible (in its demand to rethink the requirements of procedural fairness in novel contexts) that its counsel remains so fundamentally important.

The most striking feature of this contemporary landscape is, of course, its commitment to neo-liberal ideology and the orientation to things private that this necessarily entails. Though incorporating a range of institutional designs, this commitment is particularly evident in the allocation of government functions between public and private agents in accordance with market-based principles through a turn to contract. The argument that such arrangements promote economic efficiency is perhaps better advertised than it is proven. Either way, the point for present purposes is that its implications for other conditions and values have, so far, been much less thought through. Among these neglected sites of analysis is precisely what I have suggested lies at the heart of Rod's theory of procedural fairness: namely, a concern for the relationship between institutional design and conditions of personhood.

This question, I fear, has become something of an "externality" to the feverishness with which the counsel of neo-liberal thought has been brought to bear on the redesign of the administrative state. The reasons for this neglect are, however, not hard to find: questions of personhood, beyond the conditions and capacities required to be a rational economic actor, are not easily grasped within the conceptual frame of neo-liberalism. Nor, I would speculate, are they readily translatable to the contractual mode through which that frame is so regularly implemented. Instead, as powers and functions are assigned to private parties through contract, we must expect that ideas of responsibility and accountability will necessarily be reconfigured.

The human dimensions of this scene are then further obscured by the way that the embrace of contract as a modality of government has retained, at its core, an essentially unreformed idea of contract itself as an arrangement that binds only its parties and, in the ordinary case, to which only its parties might be privy. This understanding, however, misses the key point, which is that when applied in the context of public governance, the private form of contract also becomes a modality of public ordering and thus affects persons beyond the contracting parties in significant ways. The traditional contractual language of "third party beneficiaries" does little to grasp the complex position in which such persons are situated. For them, the worry goes, the oft-asserted enfranchising promise of contract might be anything but. It might instead, in certain conditions, lead much more directly than its bureaucratic predecessors to the frightening spectre of the objectified "administered man."

To propose that the idea of procedural fairness casts an important light on the concerns about personhood to which these arrangements may give rise might seem an unusual move. After all, the domain of contract is not one we typically associate with talk of "processes." Indeed, even Rod – at least at the time of writing the 1981 essay – did not envisage the modality of contract as generating any complex demands of procedural fairness, concerned, as it is by design, with the participatory needs of its parties alone.[9] To leave the story there, however, would be short-sighted. Rod's thinking on procedural fairness is, or could be, fundamentally important to gaining perspective on the dynamics of this picture, as well as to shaping a normative response to the concerns that it raises.

To see why and how, we might begin by recalling that the neo-liberal project, being fundamentally an administrative project, goes directly to the space where people actually experience their relations with the state as well as with fellow citizens. A multitude of complex and varied human experiences thus fills the space that leads to the end-game of measurable efficiencies. It is here, I want to suggest, that the demands of procedural fairness as elaborated by Rod signal their importance. The first step, therefore, must be one of diagnosis. How, especially in "human services" contexts that implicate a high degree of human vulnerability on the part of affected persons, might we transpose the imperatives of procedural fairness to a neo-liberal register? If one is the "beneficiary" of an outsourced prison, or immigration removal service, or elder-care home, or children's home, one is not, as mentioned above, ordinarily party to the contracts that institute that service arrangement or able to access the account of intentions and responsibilities recorded in those contracts. How, therefore, to frame and assert necessary conditions for personhood in such contexts?

This is clearly not a question that can be effectively answered by applying a checklist of so-called required steps, themselves generated out of an entirely different context, to a novel institutional arrangement. The necessary next step, therefore, must be reconceptualization, something Rod himself undertook when he sought to liberate the idea of procedural fairness from received, adjudication-based prescriptions. But however that reconceptualization might be rendered into actual institutional design, it must be guided by the fundamental commitment to enfranchised personhood that lies at the nub of Rod's position. As expressed succinctly in "A Theory of Procedural Fairness," the concept arises because administrative officials "are authorized to make decisions which may have a direct and substantial impact upon individual citizens, and the manner of their action may be either fair or unfair."[10] This has not changed, in any way, simply because we have reconfigured the formal and conceptual architecture within which the "direct and substantial impact" of those decisions and experiences now occurs. The demands of procedural fairness transcend such specificities, and at the heart of Rod's account is the argument that the latter must be beholden to the former, rather than the other way around.

We can also see the pressing relevance of Rod's thinking on procedural fairness to the enduring feature of the administrative realm.[11] Historically, we have understood this responsibility as bound up, in fundamental ways, with what it means to participate within a public as opposed to a private realm. We expect something different, something more, of those who discharge the demands of a public space than we do of private actors acting privately. The neo-liberal turn, however, complicates this idea considerably. There is a real risk that the generative conditions for the development of a public ethos on the part of administrative actors will be vulnerable to neglect within frames that take their animating modus operandi from private principles.

How, then, might the idea of procedural fairness help us to reclaim and reassert a demand for a distinctly "public" ethos on the part of administrative actors? Though surely more is needed, the concept is nonetheless a powerful one precisely for how it speaks to a relational consciousness and to a demand for equal treatment within that consciousness, which cannot be fully grasped within privately motivated interactions. To even speak in the vocabulary of procedural fairness in response to neo-liberal institutional design, therefore, is to (re)assert a particular view of politics, committed to public relationships, that insists on the realization of the distinctive value of such relationships in the exercise of public power. The fact that this power might, in some instances, be channelled through a private legal form is and must be beside the point. The very demands of procedural fairness are demands of a distinctly "public" perspective.

These reflections might seem some distance from the concerns elaborated in "A Theory of Procedural Fairness." But it is not just because I knew Rod and have a sense of his cast of mind that I want to insist that he would not think so. The way he chose to end the 1981 essay provides support for this view. Having been immersed in the intricacies of process paradigms and the construction of taxonomies intended to capture their organizing items of "participation, principle, correlation and locus of decision,"[12] he concludes, as we might expect, by aiming high. A theory of procedural fairness, he claims, "is a powerful means of access to major problems of legal and political philosophy: in other words, an understanding of the relationship between enfranchisement and justice, between justification and justice (both fundamental to a theory of procedural fairness) supposes an understanding of concepts such as society, state, law, and community."[13]

This statement rings as true today as it did when Rod wrote it. Still, there is modesty to its claim that I, for one, am happy to dispense with. Indeed, his theory of procedural fairness "supposes an understanding" of these fundamentals of legal and political life. But it is also capable, in what today might be urgently important ways, of shaping them. The foregoing remarks on the interface between the demands of procedural fairness and the contemporary landscape of neo-liberal institutional design have pointed to just one prism through which that normative potential might be explored. There will surely be others, and their investigation will, I hope, be inspired by the spirit of creativity and wisdom, rigour and rupture, of the original author. Because whether we are equipped for its demands or not, this is simply what comes with the territory of following a cast of mind that, at every turn, attempted to reconcile what is constant with what is new.

To conclude, then, the following truths might be noted. There will always be persons, they will always have to live with and among each other, they will always be different from one another, and they will always have needs. Equally, there will always be institutions, in one guise or another, and these will always shape our individual and shared lives in fundamental ways. And, finally, there will always be ideas, whether reclaimed from the past or invented anew, and we will always, most definitely, need them. These things don't change. But what Rod Macdonald would remind us is that from time to time, situation to situation, our perspective on them must.

NOTES

1 Roderick Macdonald, "A Theory of Procedural Fairness," *Windsor Year Book of Access to Justice* 1 (1981): 3–34.
2 Ibid., 4.
3 Ibid., 5.
4 Ibid.
5 Namely, the opportunity to offer proofs and reasoned arguments to an independent adjudicator: see "The Forms and Limits of Adjudication," an essay that remained in draft form at the time of Fuller's death but was published posthumously in *Harvard Law Review* 92 (1978): 353 and referred to in Macdonald, "A Theory of Procedural Fairness," 13–14.
6 This approach, which runs throughout the article, commences with the "preliminary" suggestion that "a decision is tainted by procedural unfairness if either the quality of participation afforded to affected parties is inappropriate to the decision-making process undertaken or the kinds of reasons offered in support of the decision are inappropriate to the process followed" (Macdonald, "A Theory of Procedural Fairness," 5).
7 Ibid., 32.
8 Law Commission of Canada, *Restoring Dignity: Responding to Child Abuse in Canadian Institutions, Executive Summary* (Ottawa: Law Commission of Canada, 2000), especially 12–13, http://publications.gc.ca/collections/collection_2008/lcc-cdc/JL2-7-2000-1E.pdf (with S. Zimmerman et al.).
9 Macdonald, "A Theory of Procedural Fairness," 11, 15.
10 Ibid., 8.
11 Ibid., 29.
12 Ibid., 15.
13 Ibid., 33–4.

7

Radi- Criti- Pluri-

JACQUES VANDERLINDEN

In the summer of 1992, when we decided, my wife and I, to settle down at Shediac Cape, New Brunswick, my main task, academically speaking, was to attempt a contribution to the established international reputation of the University of Moncton and, owing to the generosity of the latter, to complete three books that were at various stages in their publication process when I left Europe.[1] Legal pluralism was totally absent from my mind, especially since I had just published two short papers[2] on the subject in which I completely reversed the content of a twenty-year-old predecessor paper of mine.[3] All three papers on pluralism were accidents in my academic career, and their production was entirely the result of outside intervention.[4] Legal pluralism was absolutely not my cup of tea, since I did not have a great affinity for legal theory. To be frank, if I had followed my own inclinations, I would have been a historian, a linguist, or a social anthropologist – certainly not a lawyer.

My relationship to legal pluralism changed after an invitation from Andrée Lajoie[5] to attend, listen, and deliver some concluding remarks at a conference at the Université de Montréal of which the masterminds were, apart from Andrée Lajoie, Rod Macdonald, Richard Janda, and Guy Rocher. I knew none of the four, although Rod and Guy were familiar with some of my writings; furthermore, I had absolutely no idea of what the words *surdétermination* and *effectivité*, which appeared in the title of the conference side by side with legal pluralism, meant. My embarrassment grew when I saw that the dictionaries lying on my table did not include these two words; yet I accepted the challenge because this seemed a good occasion to discover and study something new, beyond my own rudiments of legal pluralism.

These rudiments were that:

1 Legal pluralism had to be looked at *outside* of any legal system; any different, distinct treatment of the subject of law was a differentiation within the system but not pluralism.
2 The subject of lawS – mind the heavy type and capital of the last letter – operated at the heart of legal pluralism – the only place where it could sit – with a constant choice for the legal subject among the many laws that factual evidence showed he was willy-nilly connected to.

This was my "new conception," and it was immediately applied in 1993 when I discovered the history of law in Acadia[6] and maintained[7] when I was invited by Andrée Lajoie to close the symposium in Montreal. It opened on Friday, 20 October 1995. On that day to remember, at lunchtime, I knew for certain that I would never again walk alone on the path of radical legal pluralism. This was the immediate conviction of one of my-still-to-come inner selves, and it would rapidly become known in Canadian academic circles. Some years later, in the early 2000s, in an application for funding to the Social Sciences and Humanities Research Council of Canada, a colleague proposed a program based on legal pluralism but was careful to underscore emphatically that this was not a legal pluralism of the kind Macdonald and Vanderlinden were conceiving. There we were: forever united.

I simply knew that, accompanied by such a Mentor, I would from then on study another kind of legal pluralism. I don't know whether we were the very models of a modern major-general, but the paradox was there, neither critical nor radical: Mentor was some fifteen years younger than Telemachus! So what?

The first question asked by the organizers of this symposium about Rod Macdonald's work was: "What was the impact of the set of texts[8] chosen for the panel 'Pluralizing the Subject' on my own work?" The general impact was quite simple: *the discovery of a new world.*

Globally, I was passing from law as a "fact" to "imagining" law. This was something *completely* foreign to me, a person who detested theorizing and concentrated on facts in the everyday legal life of common people, as Rod so magnificently does in his *Lessons of Everyday Law.*[9] I'll follow the order of Rod's papers that were submitted to us, picking in each of them the major ideas that progressively enlarged my horizons, even if intuitively I had occasionally imagined them. No need to say that by then I fully subscribed to them, even if one of my inner selves sometimes hesitated to immediately follow what Mentor suggested. It is also true that I still led quite a busy life between Belgium, France, and Canada and occasionally neither possessed the theoretical background nor found the relaxation necessary to following the complexities of critical legal pluralism. But I had the feeling that I was enlarging my recently discovered inner selves without limit.

Furthermore, Rod played a decisive role in the qualification of my pluralism as "radical." For a long time, I hesitated to call it that. During that time, colleagues were engaged in debating the distinction between hard as opposed to soft or strong as opposed to weak pluralisms. In a decisive email – I do not remember the date – he told me that the adjective "radical" derived from the Latin, *radix* – which I knew – but went further and said that we both looked for the deepest root of legal pluralism and that, in that respect, "radical" was entirely suitable, at least for my pluralism, since he had already coined the expression "critical legal pluralism" for his. My doubts were gone.

And this is the place and opportunity for me to definitively clarify a capital point. I read recently under an authoritative pen that Rod at one time abandoned his critical legal pluralism for my radical one; this was justified on the basis of document 3 (referred to in note 8 above). To the best of my reading of that text and my exchanges with Rod in the following ten years, there is no evidence whatsoever for such a change of mind on his part.

When I looked at the five texts I was assigned to read, my feeling was that my challenge was well nigh insuperable. Rather than paraphrasing these 130 or so pages (theoretically in five minutes), I decided to jump from text to text in a chronological[10] sequence, trying to indicate which words or phrases appeared to me as new in the progression of the expression of Rod's ideas successively influencing my mind over the course of time.[11] This I would do with practically no comment unless such comment appeared unavoidable. This is not to say, of course, that this approach leads to what Jean-Guy Belley once called "a path analysis" of Rod's thinking. I would rather say that each of his contributions represents for me a new stone for the building, thus opening new perspectives over the course of time and leading to a reassessment of the fundamental principles[12] enunciated in his first text of 1997 with Martha-Marie Kleinhans.

Here is how I look at it in a "kaleidoscopic" way (another of Rod's most stimulating images), my Mentor inviting me in each case to slightly rotate the cardboard tube and discover another rearrangement resulting from his boundless imagination.

More plainly, for me, it means moving:

1 *From* a law- and forum-shopping subject of lawS (JV 1992)
To a *creative* subject *inventing narrations* (RM 1997). Until then I had never contemplated the subject as "creating" anything but only as "choosing" between existing laws to which he was subject. As to narrations, in their esoteric quality I confined them in Brussels to the restricted company of legal philosophers interested in and familiar with Ronald Dworkin or Peter Brooks.
2 *From* a law- and forum-shopping subject of lawS (JV 1992)
To a *non-definitional* way of framing my inquiry about law in an attempt to *symbolize* human conduct and interaction as governed by rules (RM 2005). In contrast to Rod's novel approach, the problem of the definition of law pervades writings by European scholars, particularly those of anthropologists and sociologists who are interested in legal pluralism. The latter include one of the most famous, whom Rod quotes as having had a "powerful influence" on his thinking,[13] Jean Carbonnier. As for symbolization, it embarrassed me the most, since it was my life that was its object, something I would never have imagined.
3 *From* a law- and forum-shopping subject of lawS (JV 1992)
To the agency of people to create, narrate, iterate, mediate and *negotiate* plural identities *both* vis-à-vis the law of the state and in the diverse non-state legal regimes they build with others (RM 2006). In my legal education, the law is in principle simply non-negotiable, exactly as there is no non-state legal regime. This is monism, for which Rod's perspective enunciated here is blasphemy and would have led him to the stake some centuries ago!
4 *From* a law- and forum-shopping subject of lawS (JV 1992)
To a pluralistic law *re-substance, which is* the antithesis of unitary law re-form (RM 2007), as formulated in the last conference in which I participated with Rod in Louisiana. It "illuminated legal change" as I had practised it many times when participating in the preparation of a code of investments in Kinshasa or doing the same sort of job in Edinburgh with the Scottish Law Commission, preparing alongside the English commission a code on contracts for the two countries.
5 *From* a law- and forum-shopping subject of lawS (JV 1992)
To a legal pluralism, which is *neither* in itself an analytical model *nor* an invitation to chaos but a way of *portraying non-chirographic*

> *legal phenomena in relation to one another and in their full richness of detail* (RM 2011). For someone who had begun and spent his academic life studying, teaching, and debating "custom" in mediaeval Europe and Africa, the reference to non-chirographic *legal* phenomena opened endless new avenues.

There is no need to elaborate on the impact these successive texts have had on the work of a resolute non-theorist! The question to be answered is: Is it still the same head that rests on my shoulders?

The second question asked by the symposium organizers was: "What implications does Rod's contribution have for my future research?" The answer is: innumerable ones, among which, *for inner-self reasons*, are implications for my work on the cases of pre-legal western European societies and pre-colonial African societies. These are among my topics of long-standing predilection, since I began teaching legal history in 1958 and did fieldwork in the Zande country (Belgian Congo) in 1959. In both cases, I was confronted with "custom." Radical legal pluralism leads me today to an unfinished reassessment in the theorization of that formal "source of law." Theorization? Did you read theorization? Here enters *L'Apprenti sorcier* at last unmasked!

The societies I have just mentioned were (and in some cases still are) *living* their laws predominantly *with* a minimal amount of writing. Hence, for "lawyers" from the *outside* world looking into them, a reference to what they know as "custom" is "*ius non scriptum*" or, in Rod's words, "non-chirographic law," i.e., a law not necessarily "expressed in the written words of a natural language," while for people acting in their daily lives *inside* these societies, each of them imagines in his multiple selves ad hoc *solutions*, which he confronts in palavers with the other members of his society in order to restore peace within the latter, be it in the Inuit or the Zande country.

And when Northern American or European (or even – alas! – some of the Americanized or Europeanized local) lawyers are confronted with that way of dealing with social tensions, they (1) find the mediation process between the local inner selves incomprehensible, time-consuming, and going nowhere (hence the pejorative sense attributed in their language to the word "palaver") and (2) press the local people with a question which for them has no sense: "Why do you reach that solution?" The only quite natural answer – which does not satisfy the lawyers' longing for a pre-existing norm from which the solution is deduced – is: "Because we do so" or, to cut short the insistence: "Because we have always done so," which, in fact, refers to the history of the process much more than to the solution but puts the lawyers on a more familiar ground, that of "custom" in their system of thought.

If one accepts this factual description and rejects this example of what I have elsewhere termed by a neologism, "analocalism,"[14] we are left with the question: How do we qualify what happens in pre-colonial and pre-legal societies before self-proclaimed "lawyers" appear in them?

Why not call it genuine critical or radical legal pluralism at its best, given that no state law intervenes in the process of mediation between the people's inner selves?[15] It will of course be a totally open and popular non-chirographic critical or radical legal pluralism symbolized by the "it depends" – the answer of Chief Ukwatutu, when, in 1959, I tried to elicit from him a definite answer to a question about the outcome of a particular legal conflict. His answer clearly opened the road to a collective mediation of inner selves in order to restore peace in the social unit concerned. As another of my mentors, Amadou Hampate Ba, once suggested to me in a language more adequate for the global person I was then carrying with me before Rod came along: "There are many persons in the person of man."

Today, "seas between us braid hae roard sin auld lang syne," and what precedes are only simple imaginings of a now slightly less artless aging companion nearly twenty years after meeting his Mentor.

All the rest is silence
On the other side of the wall,
And the silence ripeness,
And the ripeness all.[16]

For everything just depicted, "the great and good debt that cannot be paid,"[17] including our many other shared adventures, I could only find four miserable words, which I borrow from Franz Schubert addressing himself in the same mood "An die Muzik":

Rod, accomplice and Mentor, "*Ich danke dir dafür.*"

NOTES

The author wholeheartedly thanks the editors of this volume and the staff at MQUP for their kind translation of his original text from "Vanderglish" into Queen's English.

1 *Pierre Ryckmans (1891–1959) – Coloniser dans l'honneur* (Brussels: De Boeck-Wesmael, 1994); *L'uranium, la Belgique et les Puissances* (Brussels: De Boeck-Wesmael, 1994) (with P. Buch); *Comparer les droits* (Brussels: Kluwer, 1995).

2 Jacques Vanderlinden, "Return to Legal Pluralism – Twenty Years Later," *Journal of Legal Pluralism* 28 (1991): 149–57; Vanderlinden, "Vers une conception nouvelle du pluralisme juridique," *Revue de la recherche juridique – Droit prospectif* (1993): 573–83.

3 Vanderlinden, "Le pluralisme juridique, Essai de synthèse," in *Études sur le pluralisme juridique* (Brussels: Éditions de l'Institut de Sociologie, 1972), 19–56.

4 These accidents are recorded in Vanderlinden, *Les pluralismes juridiques* (Brussels: Bruylant, 2013) in which sixteen articles or excerpts of articles devoted to the subject have been republished with short comments.

5 Andrée Lajoie only knew me through the concluding remarks to a conference, which I had delivered at Mont-Orford in 1994. It became the introductory chapter of *Interpréter le droit: le sens, l'interprète, la machine*, edited by C. Thomasset and D. Bourcier (Brussels: Bruylant, 1997), under the title "Regards candides sur les sciences du texte juridique," 1–30.

6 Vanderlinden, "La double colonisation juridique de l'Acadie aux XVIIe et XVIIIe siècles," Académie royale des Sciences d'Outre-Mer, *Bulletin des séances*, 39 (1993): 361–84, reprinted in *Regards d'un historien du droit sur l'Acadie aux XVIIe et XVIIIe siècles*, 1–34 (Moncton, Université de Moncton, Institut d'études acadiennes, 2008).

7 Vanderlinden, "Les Amérindiens du Nord à l'heure du pluralisme juridique?" Académie royale des sciences d'outre-mer, *Bulletin des séances*, 41 (1995): 299–317, reprinted in part in Vanderlinden, *Les pluralismes juridiques*, 97–104.

8 This refers to five texts by Rod: "What Is a *Critical* Legal Pluralism?" *Canadian Journal of Law and Society* 12 (1997): 25–46 (with Martha-Marie Kleinhans); "Legal Republicanism and Legal Pluralism," in *Human Diversity and the Law*, edited by M. Bussani and M. Graziadei (Brussels: Bruylant, 2005), 43–70; "Here, There ... and Everywhere," in *Étudier et enseigner le droit: hier, aujourd'hui et demain – Études offertes à Jacques Vanderlinden*, edited by N. Kasirer (Montreal: Éditions Yvon Blais, 2006), 381–413; "Unitary Law Re-form, Pluralistic Law Re-substance: Illuminating Legal Change," *Louisiana Law Review* 67 (2007): 1,114–60; "Custom Made – For a Non-chirographic Critical Legal Pluralism," *Canadian Journal of Law and Society* 26 (2011): 301–27.

9 Macdonald, *Lessons of Everyday Law*. (Montreal: McGill-Queen's University Press for the School of Policy Studies, Queen's University, andthe Law Commission of Canada, 2002).

10 This could only be done on the basis of the dates of publication, because in some cases it was impossible for me to say exactly when its content became public. A good example of that is the first one, published in 1997 and referring to a text as "forthcoming" in 1998, while I knew of it in 1995 as a participant at the conference where it was first read and communicated to me for the final synthesis of the meeting.

11 In the chronological order of publication of Rod's five papers mentioned in note 8 to which I refer by "RM" below, followed by their year of publication, the starting point being always my conception of 1992.

12 This is needed, as I experienced myself, because in most cases, one is addressing a new public that is not necessarily familiar with the fundamentals. Thus repetitions are unavoidable from one text to the other.

13 Macdonald, *Lessons of Everyday Law*, 14.

14 Vanderlinden, *Les pluralismes juridiques*, 363, where it designates the unjustified transfer of a notion applicable in one place into another where it is not, on the model of anachronism for such a transfer in time.

15 This would more aptly be called "Rendre la production du droit au peuple," which I envisaged in *Politique africaine* 62 (1996): 83–94.

16 I discovered Wystan H. Auden's poetry through a summer course in Cambridge in 1953 and re-explored it by the grace of Rod through our correspondence.

17 G.K. Chesterton, *St. Francis of Assisi* (London: Hodder and Stoughton, 1951), 189.

8

Daddy, Is the Sky Higher Than the Ceiling? Roderick Alexander Macdonald's Federal Epistemology and Ontology

JEAN LECLAIR

Il ne coupait pas son blé de peur d'abimer les marguerites.

Jules Renard[1]

In an entry in his journal, the French writer Jules Renard records the following question asked by his daughter: "Daddy, is the sky higher than the ceiling?"[2] Since the beginning of his career, Rod has asked analogous questions. Brilliant, gigantic questions forcing us to investigate how we know what we know and, consequently, to acknowledge the kind of facts we perceive as constituent elements of reality.

Asking Fundamental Questions

What is Rod's epistemology and ontology? What did he see out there? And why did he see such things? What part does this play in his understanding of the legal phenomenon and of federalism? Answering these questions is fundamental if we wish to follow the kaleidoscopic brick road that he finds federalism to be.

The best summary of Rod's perspective on society and law is encapsulated in the following passage taken from one of Lon L. Fuller's articles[3]: "Some of the most important and complex systems of order we know have come into existence, not by a single act of creation, but through the cumulative effect of countless purposive directions of human effort. Examples of such systems are language, economic markets, scientific theory, the common law, and on a homelier plane, a footpath through a woodland." Some elements of the architectonic structure of Rod's understanding of society and law may be distilled from this quote.[4]

First, society, communities, as well as countries and states, are not "facts of nature"; rather, they are human creations.[5] They are the product of human interaction, i.e., interactions between generally rational individuals embedded in historically and socially contingent contexts.

Second, although these individuals are certainly enmeshed in a great many human associations, they are not passive subjects of these corporate bodies. They not only forge these multifarious communities, but they transform them over time. Collective identities are dialogic as they are formed in interaction with others. But so are individual identities as they are formed in "interaction with one's understanding of how one conceives oneself."[6] All individual identities are also plural, since human beings are always the locus of multiple allegiances. From the individual's point of view, therefore, the communities enjoying pride of place in the formal constitution (provincial political communities and the federal or national political community) do not exhaust the meaningful places of affect making up his or her life.

Third, if we admit that groups are only the product of human interaction and that individuals can affiliate with others for a plethora of reasons, the perfect homogeneity of majorities and minorities is but an illusion. Such homogeneity exists only at the price of what Amartya Sen calls a miniaturization of human beings.[7] If both the members of the majorities and those of the minorities are reduced to one arbitrarily chosen identity referent (say, language in the first case and religion in the other), then, yes, homogeneity exists, but at the price of deep diversity. In a word, our social world is not confined to the human associations – provinces, nations, and states – into which political parties and ideologues of all creeds wish to embalm us. And the more we tend to essentialize our own selves, the more we tend to envisage others in the same reified fashion.

Fourth, if we wish to respect the inevitable diversity of our modern communities and to avoid the appeal of homogenization, then we must seek ways of fostering the loyalty of all. Allowing all to participate is the only path toward such an objective. All other courses (assimilation, forced emigration) are denials of our ingrained individual plurality. Again, in the words of Lon Fuller, participation compels us all to "open up, maintain, and preserve the integrity of the channels of communication by which men convey to one another what they perceive, feel and desire."[8] Although it imposes a heavier burden on the majority – however the latter may be composed – the members of the minority also share the responsibility of making such participation possible.

For this participation to be meaningful, citizens must be allowed to debate society's most fundamental questions in the freest possible manner. Their voices, therefore, must not be stifled by having to be translated into the stultifying language of rights and other legal categories. They must be free to appeal to a morality of aspiration, one that tolerates, but also encourages, "poetical discourses of open justification," rather than to a morality of duty, typically embodied in "the constraining language of legal rights or constitutional jurisdiction."[9] Those participating in the realm of politics, i.e., the public arena where allocative and distributional decisions are taken, must not be shackled by a disembodied vocabulary.

Fifth, it goes without saying that what is true of the advent of systems of order in general particularly applies to legal orders. Rod understood law as the product of human interaction, not as a commodity solely manufactured by the state's legislative, executive, and judicial branches. Legalism disqualifies law understood as a social phenomenon and dispossesses citizens of the power and responsibility to solve their own problems. In fact, mesmerized as it is by state laws and structures, legalism constitutes an epistemological obstacle to any non-state legal perspective. If one can only envisage law as state-produced, then one's (lack of) legal imagination will confine the realm of legal reforms to state-implemented solutions, confirming Abraham Maslow's quip: "if all you have is a hammer, every problem looks like a nail."[10] In conflating justice with state law, legalism also elevates confrontational adjudicative procedures to the status of the most appropriate modes of delivering justice. By equating justice with the resolution of disputes, legalism naturally focuses on cures rather than on prevention. It builds upon a negative conception of freedom – freedom from external restraint – to the detriment of a more empowering definition according to which freedom is conceived as the "freedom to participate effectively in the processes and institutions by which policy (public or private) is debated."[11]

For Rod, the state is certainly not the only locus of justice, and he rightfully questioned why all our interactions should be mediated through the language of rights. According to him, individual agents not only constantly negotiate their identities with others and themselves, they also continually negotiate among the several legal orders that attract their loyalty and their commitment.

The Impact of Asking Fundamental Questions

How do these considerations impinge on Rod's constitutional and federal perspectives? First, in his pluralistic perspective, federalism is not confined to state governance; rather, it mirrors what is and what has always been "the normal condition of human interaction."[12] The family is, for instance, the quintessential example of a federal union. It involves allocation of power, multiple and competing sources of authority, and close relationships in which the complex and overlapping identities of the reflexive members interact. The same goes for bridge clubs, universities, business organizations, religious institutions, and so on. At the state level, once you "abandon the fixation on the territorial nation-state … new vistas of federal experience and practice appear."[13]

Second, and tying in with his understanding of federalism, Rod's pluralistic constitutionalism commands that all state structures (constitutional, political, legal, and administrative) at once "symbolize" diversity and promote the "flourishing of diversity in practice,"[14] thus allowing for the blossoming of a veritable culture of civic tolerance. More specifically, this approach argues "for institutions and principles of governance that cannot be captured by single constituencies, and cannot be dominated by conjunctions of majorities that identify themselves by language, culture or ethnicity."[15]

Third, Rod rejected logocentrism, i.e., the belief that a constitution can be reified to its written incarnation. Our federal legal order is made up of explicit texts but also of implicit constitutional norms and of political practices and constitutional conventions. The meaning of explicit texts must be nourished by an understanding of the entirety of our constitutional inheritance (our prior explicit constitutions of 1774, 1791, etc.). However, still more is needed because "a living constitutional order constantly mediates the claims of history [the lessons of which should not be overstated[16]] and the claims of necessity," thus the need for resorting to political practices and constitutional conventions.[17] For citizens to commit to such practices, however, the practices must be in tune with the lived experiences and expectations of the citizens of the state.[18]

Fourth, in Rod's pluralistic perspective, the political tradition of a state has less to do with what can be deciphered from the written scriptures of formal constitutions than with the central questions that recurrently animate the "constitutional (or constitutive) conversation" of the polity.[19] "In Canada, [according to him,] we debate foundational questions about the kind of society we wish to build and maintain – questions about equality, poverty, liberty and personal security – by reference to the organization of constitutional authority."[20] This conversation, he claims, revolves around three fundamental themes, all closely linked to the issue of federalism:

1 The issue of membership. (For instance, in view of its demographic heterogeneity, who are Canada's constituent actors? Do Quebec and the Aboriginal peoples of Canada deserve a special status in our polity?)
2 The issue of constitutional continuity and adaptability. (For instance, should we subject all of our political transformations to a volitional model of constitutional amendment and forswear the more organic means of change that typified our constitutional regime prior to 1982? In other words, should we completely jettison an evolutionary constitutionalism in favour of a revolutionary one?) This issue of constitutional continuity and adaptability also raises the issue of the locus of sovereignty (does it reside in the Queen, in Parliament, in the courts, in the Constitution, in the people, or in the peoples?)
3 The issue of framework and institutions of governance. (How is the shifting balance of authority between central and more local governments to be maintained both formally and in practice?).

Rod's rejection of logocentrism triumphs in his claim that formal constitutional texts are in fact epiphenomenal. Canada's constitutive conversation, he argues, is more intimately linked to the successive and various national policies that Canadians have chosen over the course of their history than with the text of any of our constitution acts adopted since 1867. The form taken by some of these national policies goes a long way, he says, toward explaining the estrangement of Quebec.

And as for Quebec, Rod not only believed that it "is truly a province unlike all the others" but claimed that Canada will not survive unless Quebec's specificity is eventually recognized "both symbolically through the distinct society clause and institutionally through a constitutional veto."[21] According to him, Quebec's special status rests on many foundations. First, Quebec's perennial concern about the need to protect its socio-cultural specificity has played a key role "in creating the heterogeneous polity called Canada that is now celebrated around the world."[22]

Second, Quebec has played a key role in revealing that one of Canada's recurring constitutional issues has had to do more with assessing the limits of asymmetry than with imposing uniformity. Third, Quebec has also been one of the prime movers of Canada's evolutionary rather than revolutionary constitutionalism since 1763, thus helping to create "a governance structure that has been justly celebrated around the world for its continuity and adaptability."[23] Finally, he says, the whole idea of choosing a federal system was based on the acknowledgment of "the special role that the government of Quebec [had and still] has in fostering the French language in Canada."[24] Explicit recognition is thus a "*sine qua non*"[25] if the purpose of constitutional reform is to convince French-Canadian Québécois that they are being offered a meaningful participation. The claim of Aboriginal peoples for explicit recognition of their inherent right to self-government is of the same type.

Commentaires

Je m'en tiendrai à trois commentaires au sujet de cette pensée foisonnante. Je tiens à souligner que Rod Macdonald n'ignore pas les questions que je soulève ici. Toutefois, dans les textes que j'ai pu lire, il ne les explore pas en profondeur.

Premier commentaire : s'il chérit le fédéralisme en tant qu'incarnation du pluralisme social et juridique, pour moi, qui n'ai pas son optimisme, ce régime trouve sa vertu en tant qu'incarnation du constitutionnalisme. Je m'inscris ainsi dans une longue tradition libérale, celle qui veut que le pouvoir arrête le pouvoir. Ainsi, comme l'a si bien démontré Rod, en reconnaissant le caractère pluriel de nos identités individuelles, le fédéralisme confère une légitimité à une posture politique souvent décriée par les nationalistes de tout acabit, celle du citoyen qui, satisfait d'appartenir *simultanément* à deux communautés politiques (la québécoise *et* la canadienne), renvoie dos à dos deux formes de monismes nationalistes qui l'obligent constamment à choisir l'une ou l'autre cocarde parce qu'elles sont toutes deux mortellement allergiques à la double appartenance. [26]

La logique fédérale confère également une légitimité à la posture de la citoyenne québécoise musulmane qui, satisfaite d'appartenir *simultanément* à la communauté politique québécoise *et* à sa communauté de foi, renvoie dos à dos la crispation identitaire des Québécois canadiens-français et le monisme religieux des mollahs radicaux. Pour moi aussi, donc, le fédéralisme ne s'épuise pas dans les articles 91 et 92 de la Loi constitutionnelle de 1867.

Deuxième commentaire : bien que l'idée ne soit pas mauvaise, loin de là, je ne pense pas que la reconnaissance explicite du caractère distinct du Québec mette jamais un terme aux réclamations de celui-ci. La solution au problème québécois se trouve peut-être ailleurs. Je n'ai pas le temps d'élaborer, mais, selon moi, le problème du fédéralisme au Canada est avant tout un problème de démocratie. [27] La concentration du pouvoir dans les mains des exécutifs provinciaux et de l'executif fédéral contribue à une représentation outrancièrement réifiée de nos identités, de nos préoccupations et de nos intérêts respectifs de citoyens. Le gouvernement fédéral parle-t-il vraiment pour tous les Canadiens ? Le gouvernement du Québec parle-t-il vraiment pour tous les Québécois ? Le parlementarisme qui érige les exécutifs fédéral et provinciaux en titulaires uniques du droit de parler au nom de tous vient renforcer l'idée véhiculée par les tribunaux selon laquelle le fédéralisme se résume à une lutte sans merci entre des gouvernements qui sont présumés représenter parfaitement l'ensemble de leurs commettants. Le discours politique et le discours judiciaire se soutiennent donc mutuellement lorsque vient le temps d'affirmer que le fédéralisme n'est pas une affaire de citoyens, mais de gouvernements.

Troisième commentaire : quand je réfléchis à ma posture intellectuelle qui s'apparente à celle de Rod, je me demande parfois si elle ne constitue pas une morale trop exigeante. Est-ce que l'idéal de l'être humain investi du pouvoir de définir lui-même ses valeurs et ses priorités, capable de multiplier les allégeances sans avoir l'impression de se perdre, de l'être humain « master of his/her fate, captain of his/her soul » est un idéal qu'un grand nombre de personnes ne veulent pas ou ne peuvent pas poursuivre ? Est-ce que la solitude, les angoisses et les responsabilités associées à l'exercice de la liberté individuelle ne sont pas une charge si lourde que la tentation de se fondre dans un grand tout, de succomber au monisme, n'est pas irrésistible lorsque l'appel est lancé ? En effet, comme le souligne Amartya Sen, « on peut se demander pourquoi cette idéologie de la singularité [le monisme identitaire] rencontre un tel succès malgré son extraordinaire naïveté dans un monde à l'évidence pluriel. N'envisager un individu qu'en fonction de l'une de ses nombreuses identités est on ne peut plus simpliste… pourtant, à en juger par son efficacité, cette illusion savamment cultivée est assez facile à soutenir et à promouvoir. »[28]

Quoi qu'il en soit de ces questions, il est maintenant temps de conclure. As I mentioned, in his inquiries about constitutional law and federalism, Rod never sought answers in the written frieze of constitutional temples. Rather, he looked about him, appraising how his fellow citizens worked out their problems, mobilizing as best they could their always-imperfect knowledge about our imperfect world, aiming at the coalescence of their multifarious aspirations, hoping for the best. To the child's question as to whether the sky is higher than the ceiling, Rod might have given one of his usual disconcerting answers: no, the sky is in fact lower than the ceiling, and so are the stars. If you peer down instead of up, and if you look closely, you might see their reflection in the rain puddles. Rod always sought *grandeur* where no one expected to find it.

NOTES

1 *Journal 1887–1910*, 107 (25 July 1892) (Paris: coll. Bouquins, Robert Laffont 1990).

2 *Journal 1887–1910*, 278 (9 September 1896): "Baïe demande: 'est-ce que le ciel est plus haut que le plafond?'"

3 Lon L. Fuller, "Freedom: A Suggested Analysis," *Harvard Law Review* 68 (1955): 1,322.

4 All ideas expressed in the first part of this paper were articulated by Rod in some fashion or another in the following pieces: "Access to Justice and Law Reform," *Windsor Year Book of Access to Justice* 10 (1990): 287–337; "The New Zealand Bill of Rights Act: How Far Should It Stretch?" *New Zealand Law Conference* (1993): 94–193; "Three Centuries of Constitutional Making in Canada: Will There Be a Fourth?" *University of British Columbia Law Review* 30 (1996): 211–34; "The Design of Constitutions to Accommodate Linguistic, Cultural and Ethnic Diversity: The Canadian Experiment," in *Dual Images: Multiculturalism on Two Sides of the Atlantic*, edited by K. Kulcsar and D. Szabo (Budapest: Royal Society of Canada and Hungarian Academy of the Sciences, 1996), 52–84; "Kaleidoscopic Federalism," in *The States and Moods of Federalism: Governance, Identity and Methodology*, edited by J.-F. Gaudreault-DesBiens and F. Gélinas (Montreal: Blais, 2005), 261–83; "The Political Economy of the Federal Spending Power," *Queen's Law Journal* 34 (2008): 249–304; "Canada's Third National Policy: The Epiphenomenal or the Real Constitution?" *University of Toronto Law Journal* 59 (2009): 469–523 (with Robert Wolfe). To avoid burdening the text with a profusion of footnotes, only direct quotes will be referenced.

5 Macdonald, "Canada's Third National Policy," 482.

6 Macdonald, "Kaleidoscopic Federalism," 276.

7 Amartya Sen, *Identité et violence* (Paris: Odile Jacob, 2007), 17.

8 Fuller, *The Morality of Law*, 2nd edn (New Haven: Yale University Press, 1969), 185–6.

9 Macdonald, "Design of Constitutions," 83.

10 Macdonald, "Access to Justice and Law Reform," 303.
11 Macdonald, "The New Zealand Bill of Rights Act," 157.
12 Macdonald, "Kaleidoscopic Federalism," 263.
13 Ibid., 263.
14 Macdonald, "Design of Constitutions," 75.
15 Ibid., 83.
16 Macdonald, "Three Centuries," 221, 227.
17 Macdonald, "Political Economy," 254.
18 Macdonald, "Design of Constitutions," 59.
19 Macdonald, "Canada's Third National Policy," 471.
20 Macdonald, "Three Centuries," 216.
21 Ibid., 231.
22 Ibid., 224.
23 Ibid., 226.
24 Ibid., 231.
25 Ibid., 231.
26 J'ai abordé ces questions dans plusieurs articles, notamment : « "Vive le Québec libre !" Liberté(s) et fédéralisme », *Revue québécoise de droit constitutionnel* 3 (2010) 11 p.; « Le fédéralisme comme refus des monismes nationalistes », dans Dimitrios Karmis et François Rocher (dir.), *La dynamique confiance-méfiance dans les démocraties multinationales. Le Canada sous l'angle comparatif* (Québec : Presses de l'Université Laval, 2012), 209–43 ; « Le fédéralisme : un terreau fertile pour gérer un monde incertain », dans Ghislain Otis et Martin Papillon (dir.), *Fédéralisme et gouvernance autochtone/Federalism and Aboriginal Governance* (Québec : Les Presses de l'Université Laval, 2013), 21–50; «Socrates, Odysseus and Federalism», *The Review of Constitutional Studies/Revue d'études constitutionnelles* 18 (2013), 1–18 ; «Military Historiography, Warriors and Soldiers: The Normative Impact of Epistemological Choices», à paraître dans Patrick Macklem et Douglas Sanderson (dir.), *Essays on the Constitutional Entrenchment of Aboriginal and Treaty Rights*.
27 Voir Jean Leclair, « The Securities Reference: The Ghost of Political Representation Comes Knocking at Federalism's Door» , texte présenté à l'occasion du 42nd Annual Workshop on Consumer and Commercial Law qui s'est tenu à la Schulich School of Law de la Dalhousie University à Halifax, en octobre 2012; accessible en ligne : ssrn.com/abstract=2189661.
28 Sen, *Identité et violence*, 239. Le rapport *Fonder l'avenir. Le temps de la conciliation* de la Commission de consultation sur les pratiques d'accommodement reliées aux différences culturelles (2008), rédigé par Gérard Bouchard et Charles Taylor, souligne le danger de se replier sur des identités réifiées : « Le principal danger qui nous guette, c'est que les groupes qui

composent notre société en viennent à conjuguer leur méfiance et leurs peurs réciproques (en bonne partie non fondées) et mettent ainsi en péril les processus de rapprochement en cours. En d'autres termes : que nos peurs imaginaires engendrent un danger réel. Nous pensons notamment à cette identité québécoise encore fragile qui a pris forme au cours des dernières décennies et qui continue de grandir au-delà de nos différences (ou plus exactement, à même nos différences). Par ailleurs, et comme il se doit, elle se nourrit abondamment, mais librement, de l'héritage canadien-français, un héritage très riche qui accède ainsi à une nouvelle vie, non pas en se refermant, mais en s'ouvrant à l'apport créatif et fécond de l'Autre; c'est précisément ce qu'il a fait à maintes reprises dans le passé. En somme, c'est l'avenir de la nation québécoise qui se joue ici» (242).

9

The Unbounded Public Law Imagination of Roderick A. Macdonald

HOI L. KONG

The organizers of the symposium from which this collection of papers originated presented the "Kaleidoscopic Federalism" panelists with two questions: what impact has Rod Macdonald's scholarship had on the field of public law, and what was its influence on our own scholarship? In what I think of as a quintessential Rod manoeuvre, I will not quite answer those questions. Often, when I asked him a question, he would point out that there were issues that needed to be addressed before it could be broached. And often, he would, instead of answering the question precisely as posed, offer a response to what he thought was the deeper inquiry that lay beneath the surface of my query. I will undertake these two manoeuvres in this essay. First, because it would be difficult to speak to the entirety of Rod's public law scholarship, I will in Part I trace out two main themes in his writing in this field: (1) the influence of Lon Fuller's theory of legal forms on his federalism scholarship and (2) the relevance of legal pluralism to that body of scholarship. Second, I will address what I see as the deeper issues that lie beneath the question about influence. When we speak of influence in academia, we might be tempted to imagine that earlier generations of scholars bestow their ideas upon later generations who develop them for a new time and a new set of circumstances. But the relationship between past and present ideas, between teachers and students, can be more complex than this. Sometimes a later generation can, by drawing upon the sources of its predecessors, respond to questions that the earlier generation could not formulate clearly for itself. In this essay, I will track the flow of ideas across two generations of scholars, from Lon Fuller to Rod and from

Rod to one of his students, Kristen Rundle; in Part II, I will examine how Rundle has interpreted Fuller in ways that clarify Rod's own thought and vindicate his hopes for legal pluralism.

Part I: The Morality of Legal Forms and Law Beyond the State

Selecting a set of themes on which to focus, in a body of scholarship as wide-ranging and eclectic as Rod Macdonald's, would seem to present a serious if not insurmountable challenge. As the table of contents of this collection makes clear, he wrote in an almost unimaginably diverse set of fields. Moreover, a glance at the footnotes in his works reveals a mind that found inspiration in a dazzling array of cultural artefacts. For example, in his article "Custom Made – For a Non-chirographic Critical Legal Pluralism,"[1] he begins with a disquisition on the Protestant Reformation in which he cites authors including Thomas Hobbes and Jimmy Carter and makes reference to several works on the history of the Bible. Toward the middle of the paper, he illustrates a point about interpretation by discussing in some detail (1) the rules of cricket, (2) a canonical text on cricket, and (3) a five-part documentary about cricket. The range of references in that article is by no means unrepresentative. Yet within the flurry of cultural references and across the spectrum of fields in which he wrote, one can trace leitmotifs. Indeed, the text of "Custom Made" is, like many of his articles, filled with references to Fuller's work, and the title refers to critical legal pluralism, a concept that Rod coined in an article co-written with Martha-Marie Kleinhans[2] and that he developed over almost two decades of writing. I think, therefore, that I am on solid ground when I select Fuller's legal theory and legal pluralism as lenses through which to view Rod's public law scholarship.

Fuller and the Form(s) of Federalism

Lon Fuller's influence on Rod's work was deep and far-reaching. He was aware of his intellectual debt to Fuller and in the preface to *Lessons of Everyday Law* acknowledges the ways in which Fuller shaped his thought: "Throughout this collection, readers will discern the powerful influence of Lon Fuller and, to a somewhat lesser degree, Jean Carbonnier. I never met either. Yet much of what I think I know about the law I have learned from their writings and from the writings of others about them. I would be honoured if knowledgeable readers were to judge me to have been a good student."[3]

Rod was a very good student of Fuller. Indeed, I vividly recall him, in the last year of his life, engaged in passionate debate with colleagues in the faculty common room, citing Fuller and referring to a specific page and edition of *The Morality of Law*. The deep imprint of Fuller is evident in his federalism scholarship and is revealed in the citations to Fuller that are scattered throughout his oeuvre. Perhaps the most telling reference is in the form of a paraphrase of Fuller at the end of his book chapter "The Design of Constitutions to Accommodate Linguistic, Cultural and Ethnic Diversity: The Canadian Experiment."[4] It is worth quoting, because it reveals much about his understanding of the significance of law and legal forms: "The one indisputable element of substantive natural law, I believe, has no theological content. It is, rather, a way of being: open up, maintain and channel the channels of communication through which people may communicate with each other about their hopes, their fears and their aspirations."[5]

Legal forms mattered for Rod, because he understood that they serve well-defined and valuable purposes. They enable those affected by law to identify and clarify the ends they seek and to communicate to one another and to others the reasons for valuing and pursuing those ends. Fuller saw these functions in the formality requirements of contract law. For Fuller, formalities serve communicative objectives (he labelled them the channelling and evidentiary functions), and they encourage contracting parties to reflect on their actions.[6] Following Fuller, Rod argues that in order to assess whether any particular legal form serves this purpose of facilitating the identification and communication of specific ends, we would need to examine carefully its internal architecture and the contexts in which it operates.

He describes the internal architecture of federalism's legal form in "Kaleidoscopic Federalism": "Federalism is centrally about the deduction, division, and allocation of power, about multiple and competing sources of authority, and about the complex and overlapping identities of agents."[7] According to Rod, those who fall within the regulatory ambit of a successful federation find in its formal architecture means of articulating, communicating, and pursuing their aspirations. And although the form of federalism has the primary attributes just described, there are infinite variations possible, and they manifest themselves in the vast diversity of federations that exist today and across time. Understood in this light, there is nothing inevitable or necessary about the success of a given federation, and when federalism's forms fail to respond to the felt exigencies of those who inhabit a federation, it can falter, before re-establishing its balance, or it can fail. This is the lesson that we can draw from his magisterial article,

"Three Centuries of Constitutional Making in Canada: Will There Be a Fourth?"[8] In each cycle of constitutional reform that he analyzes, we can see shifts in the forms of Canadian federalism in response to changes in the identity, aspirations, and claims of stakeholders in the federation.

Legal Pluralism and Federalism beyond the State

This emphasis in Rod's writing on those who are affected by legal forms is tied closely to his embrace of legal pluralism. He wrote extensively on legal pluralism, and I will not attempt to capture the full breadth of his thought here. Instead, I will focus on the central insight that is relevant for his understanding of federalism. According to Rod's version of legal pluralism, law is not exclusively an output of the state. In "Kaleidoscope Federalism," he makes the daring claims that federalism, as a legal structure, can be found in families and even in the individual self. The latter claim is vintage Rod Macdonald: original, counterintuitive, and presented in Delphic terms. Here is how it is phrased: "The truest federalism is a psychological federalism that decomposes not political and anthropological affiliations but individual subjects themselves."[9] It is important to be clear about the nature of this claim and the one about families. He is not saying that families and individuals should be understood *by analogy* to the constitutional structure of federations. Instead, he is saying that families and individuals are *themselves* federations.

How might we interpret this Delphic utterance? We have seen that for Rod, the distinctive *formal features* of federalism lie in how it structures relationships by splicing and allocating authority and creating cross-cutting affiliations. Given this conception of federalism, one can see how every family, with its distinct and overlapping allocations of authority and loyalty, can be seen as a federation. An individual can also be a federation, in this view, if we understand every individual to be comprised of multiple roles that are structured in ways that disperse and order decision-making power among the various facets of the self. For example, as a law professor, I am a colleague to the administrative and professorial corps of the Faculty of Law at McGill, but I count among that same group of people some very close friends. An additional layer of complexity is added by the fact that I am an associate dean. My various roles generate a diverse set of loyalties and commitments that overlap and, at times, enter into tension with one another. At various moments in my daily life, I need to prioritize some roles and loyalties, and at other times, I order my priorities differently. Finally, and to return to Rod's paraphrase of Fuller cited above, it is often in the very act of ordering my priorities and identifying claims on my loyalties that I can make clear to myself my understanding of the various dimensions of my identity and communicate that always-contingent understanding to others. It is through the federal forms within my psyche that, according to Rod, I engage in the conceptual, communicative, and moral activities that he associated with law.

At this point in the argument, the sympathetic reader might accept Rod's general view of federalism, including the extensions of the argument into the novel territory of the family and the self. Yet even the sympathetic reader might resist the claim that the "federation" of the family or of the self should be understood as a *legal* regime. Law, the sympathetic yet sceptical reader might continue, lies within the exclusive province of the state, and we distort the concept of law when we remove it from that context. In particular, we lose sight of what makes law distinctive as a mode of social ordering when we ignore the role of officials in formulating, interpreting, applying, and enforcing the law. This view of law as inextricably tied to the state and its officials, our sympathetic but sceptical reader might say, is commonly shared, and to use the word "law" in Rod's unfamiliar way is confusing and unproductive.

Rod was aware of these arguments against his theory of legal pluralism. Yet his responses to them are often elusive. Here, from "Kaleidoscope Federalism," is the contrast that he draws between legal pluralism and the commonly accepted view of law that I have just articulated: "By imagining law as a mode of giving particular sense to particular ideas in particular places, legal pluralism shifts inquiry towards thinking of law as meaning, not machinery (as aspiration, not structure; as narrative, not norm)."[10]

I suspect that our sympathetic yet sceptical reader would not be convinced by this formulation and would see in it an evasion rather than a response. She might register two specific objections. First, she might say that there are many modes of "giving particular meaning to particular ideas in particular places," including novels, movies, and poems, but there is no obvious basis for calling all or indeed any of them law. Second, she might say that even if we accept that legal pluralism shifts the focus of analysis in the ways that Rod identifies, it is by no means clear that it does so in ways that are faithful to the phenomenon it purports to represent. Put slightly differently, our sympathetic but sceptical reader might say that even if shifting the focus of analysis in the ways that Rod suggests would allow us to emphasize qualities that we would want to see in law, he has provided us with no argument to convince us that these qualities are in fact essential to the law.

But to frame the challenges in these terms is perhaps to misunderstand Rod's purposes in writing. In his contribution to this volume, Jeremy Webber argues that Rod often wrote in a prophetic voice, a voice that exhorts us to see the world as it should be and to strive to remake the world in that image. If Webber is right, and we are willing to accept these prophetic terms in which the case for legal pluralism is put, then the terrain of argument changes. Instead of asking whether law is as Rod presented it, one might ask whether it is plausible to believe that understanding the law in the way that he urged us to would lead us to make the world into the kind of place he thought it should be.

The prophetic intent in his writing expresses itself in specific ways. For instance, Rod juxtaposes his position against positivism, which he defines as "the belief that a hard *ex ante* criterion may be propounded for distinguishing that which is, and that which is not, law."[11] Although this juxtaposition contains qualifiers that weaken the contrast, we can detect in it at least a partial abandonment of the goal of analytic clarity in favour of something like the exhortative voice. In what follows, I hope to show that legal pluralism can be defended analytically and in ways that vindicate Rod's ideas about the purposes of legal regulation. I began this part with a quotation in which he expressed the hope that he would be considered a good student of Fuller's. In the next part, I will examine the work of one of his students, and I hope to show that, as good students often do, she is able to address challenges that were incompletely met in her teacher's work.

Part II: The Public Law Imagination of Rod Macdonald's Students

In the preface to *Forms Liberate: Reclaiming the Jurisprudence of Lon L. Fuller*, Kristen Rundle writes: "tracing the genesis of the ideas contained in these pages to conversations in 2001, I wish to convey my deep thanks to Rod Macdonald for his inspiration and generosity, then and since."[12] In the summer of 2013, Rod and a group of McGill colleagues read Rundle's book together, and I can say with confidence that he reciprocated her thanks. In the paragraphs that follow, I will show why Rod was justified in feeling grateful.

Unlike Rod, Rundle has interpreted Fuller in order to derive the essential elements of law and to clearly distinguish law from non-law. Rundle argues that for Fuller, laws that are in compliance with the rule of law create obligations (1) on the part of rulers to govern with respect for the agency of citizens and (2) on the part of citizens to respect laws evincing this kind of respect. In other words, laws that are worthy of the appellation properly address themselves to citizens in ways that create a relationship of reciprocity between lawgiver and citizen. It is this relationship of reciprocity that constitutes the basis of legitimacy of a legal order, and if a lawgiver undermines this relationship through, for instance, acting like a tyrant, the resulting governance order is no longer one of law, and the citizen has no obligations of fidelity toward it.[13] Rundle further argues that according to Fuller, laws, properly understood, have embedded within them the assumption that citizens have the *capacity* to engage with the law as responsible agents.[14] One implication of this conception of the rule of law has been drawn out by Rundle. She argues that the principles of the rule of law (non-retroactivity, non-contradiction, congruence, publicity, etc.) are indicative but not exhaustive of a concern for the underlying ideal of respect for citizen's moral agency.[15] It is important to note that, according to Fuller, we can question whether a set of rules amounts to a system of laws when there is a "total failure" to respect one or more principles of the rule of law.[16] A body of regulation that fails in this systematic way is not worthy of the appellation of law, because it fails to evince respect for the form of moral agency that Rundle has revealed to be essential to the Fullerian conception of the rule of law.

Rundle's interpretation of Fuller has implications for Rod's theory of legal pluralism. Recall that, according to Rod, law can exist even in the absence of the state and its officials. Rundle's arguments about the Fullerian conception of the rule of law provide the analytical structure that supports what might otherwise appear to be a prophetic, if not gnomic, claim. Interpreting Fuller through the eyes of Rundle and Rod, one might say that law is defined not by the imprimatur of the state but by those formal qualities that evidence a respect for human agency. According to this view of law, legislation is not law because it is the handiwork of state legislators but because it has formal qualities that create a relationship of reciprocal influence between law-maker and law-receiver. Similarly, a contract is not law because it is recognized or enforced by judges in the courts of the state. Rather, a contract is law in the Fullerian universe because it enables contracting parties to conceive, communicate, and pursue their ends. Rundle's reading of Fuller, therefore, provides criteria for distinguishing law from non-law and reveals that one need not abandon the pursuit of analytical clarity, as Rod at times seems to do, in order to arrive at his conclusions about legal pluralism.

I close this paper with some thoughts about what this view of legal pluralism might mean for Rod's prophetic goals. First, it might encourage us to evaluate state law with an increased sensitivity to the ways in which its forms can be structured to achieve the moral ends that Rod and Fuller understood to be intrinsic to law. In administrative law, this might mean concentrating attention on designing institutional processes that ensure that officials are answerable to citizens, rather than focusing exclusively on whether particular administrative actions were authorized by statute. The focus, in other words, would be on questions of agency rather than pedigree. Similarly, the constitutional professor influenced by legal pluralism might turn from questions of constitutional validity and pour her energies into designing constitutional structures that create opportunities for citizens to participate effectively in lawmaking. Finally, if we were to see the world through legal pluralist eyes, we would become more aware of countless quotidian opportunities to structure human relationships and interactions so that they evince a deep regard for, and facilitate the exercise of, human agency. And if we were to cultivate this awareness, it might lead us to strive to construct the rules and procedures governing our playgrounds, faculty committees, and households in ways that facilitate the arising of just, decent, and respectful relationships. That, I believe, was the ultimate goal of Rod's restlessly seeking, and unbounded, public law imagination.

NOTES

This text derives from my symposium presentation, and, consistent with the practice at that gathering, I have decided to refer to Professor Macdonald throughout this text as "Rod." I owe a debt of deep gratitude to him, and this essay is but a small gesture of thanks. I am also grateful to the symposium organizers and McGill's Faculty of Law for hosting the event and arranging for the publication of the presentations. I especially thank Richard Janda, who in leading the organization of the event made real for Rod the hope expressed by Saint John of the Cross that "in the evening of life, you will be examined with love."

1 I thank Sarah Chênevert-Beaudoin for her help with the formatting of these citations. Roderick Macdonald, "Custom Made – For a Non-chirographic Critical Legal Pluralism," *Canadian Journal of Law and Society* 26 (2011): 301–27.

2 Martha-Marie Kleinhans and Roderick Macdonald, "What Is a *Critical* Legal Pluralism?" *Canadian Journal of Law and Society* 12 (1997): 25–46.
3 Macdonald, *Lessons of Everyday Law* (Montreal: McGill-Queen's University Press for the School of Policy Studies, Queen's University, and the Law Commission of Canada, 2002), xv.
4 Macdonald, "The Design of Constitutions to Accommodate Linguistic, Cultural and Ethnic Diversity: The Canadian Experiment," in *Dual Images: Multiculturalism on Two Sides of the Atlantic*, edited by K. Kulcsar and D. Szabo (Budapest: Royal Society of Canada and Hungarian Academy for the Sciences, 1996), 52–84.
5 Ibid., 84.
6 Lon L. Fuller, "Consideration and Form," *Columbia Law Review* 41 (1941): 799–824.
7 Macdonald, "Kaleidoscopic Federalism," in *The States and Moods of Federalism: Governance, Identity and Methodology*, edited by J.-F. Gaudreault-DesBiens and F. Gélinas (Montreal: Blais, 2005), 263.
8 Macdonald, "Three Centuries of Constitutional Making in Canada: Will There Be a Fourth?" *University of British Columbia Law Review* 30 (1996): 211–34.
9 Macdonald, "Kaleidoscopic Federalism," 275.
10 Ibid., 279.
11 Roderick Macdonald and David Sandomierski, "Against Nomopolies," *Northern Ireland Legal Quarterly* 57 (2006): 615.
12 Kristen Rundle, *Forms Liberate: Reclaiming the Jurisprudence of Lon L. Fuller* (Portland: Hart, 2012), vii.
13 Ibid., ch. 1. Rod Macdonald has similarly argued that laws offer hypotheses of interaction that citizens can construct and interpret. See, e.g., Macdonald, "The Fridge-Door Statute," *McGill Law Journal* 47 (2002): 33. Jeremy Waldron calls this aspect of Fuller's conception of the rule of law "self-application": Jeremy Waldron, *Dignity, Rank, and Rights* (New York: Oxford University Press, 2012), 53.
14 Rundle argues, "To be a legal subject, Fuller insists, is not merely to be a member of a 'subservient populace ready to do what they are told to do,' but rather to be a participant in a distinctly constituted social condition in which one is respected as an agent" (Rundle, "Form and Agency in Raz's Legal Positivism," *Law and Philosophy* 32 (6) (2012): 771. Similarly, according to Colleen Murphy, "[r]eciprocity plays a key role in Fuller's account of duty; according to him, the existence of duties depends partly on the behavior of others ... In the legal context, citizens have a duty to

follow legal rules provided those rules outline a standard that citizens are knowledgeable of, capable of following, and that is actually used to judge their conduct" (Colleen Murphy, "Lon Fuller and the Moral Value of the Rule of Law," *Law and Philosophy* 24 (3) (2005): 242).

15 Rundle writes: "the message that Fuller sought to convey through his model of the internal morality of law is distorted if we regard it as a checklist of criteria that require exhaustive and inflexible application. Instead ... the eight principles must be understood as larger than the sum of their parts, a representation of how governance through general rules works and is made possible and which includes respect for the legal subject as an agent as part of law's form" (Rundle, *Forms Liberate*, 141).

16 Ibid., 39.

10

Kaleidoscopic Multilateralism: Lon Fuller, Rod Macdonald, and the WTO

ROBERT WOLFE

When Rod Macdonald was president of the Law Commission of Canada, a picture of his family fixing the dock at their summer cottage appeared on the commission website illustrating one of his president's messages. I have been using that story in my policy analysis course ever since.[1] Students who have taken my course in different years have been known to identify each other when they meet by asking "what's a dock?" At the symposium, Justice Rosalie Abella of the Supreme Court of Canada recalled him asking a similar question about a table in the introduction to a course on jurisprudence. The answer to this classic Macdonald question about a dock and whether it needs fixing depends on your purposes, not simply the thing itself. The cottage dock can be a place to tie up a sailboat or for a teenager to get a tan; it can be broken because the family's purposes have changed or because the ice shattered it, again. We cannot decide what to do, in other words, if we do not know what the problem is. And the problem with the same dock can differ for the children and the grandparents, or the family and their neighbours, or cottagers and the municipality. Life is kaleidoscopic, whether we are thinking of the family or the multilateral trading system.

Rod's metaphors for law reform apply to most of life. I am a political scientist, not a lawyer. I cannot speak to his influence on legal scholarship; instead, I will talk about how his legal imagination has influenced my own scholarship. In trying to show that influence, I will begin with the first of two papers we wrote together. My contribution to the paper on Canada's national policies was more political economy than legal theory; what I took from that exercise in humility (every draft came back quickly and more sophisticated than what he received) was the idea of the epiphenomenal constitution.[2] He inverts the usual story – social interaction, not the text, is constitutive. The paper took years to emerge – even after we decided that our extended conversations needed to be written down.

So what came first? The last spike in the Canadian Pacific Railway? Or something else? One of the key claims in our national policy paper is that constitutions are policy tools. That is, the Canadian nineteenth-century policy objective required a transcontinental railway and a transcontinental constitutional framework. The British North America Act[3] of 1867 in this conception is a tool of the first national policy, not the other way around, although building the railway became a key plank in the great 1879 general election. The 1982 Charter of Rights and Freedoms[4] might be a harbinger of what we called the third national policy in an era when citizen agency matters more than railways. And before the objective, before the scholarship, there is the old guard.

Rod's "old guard" paper uses a summer camp as an example.[5] The essence of the story is his observation that without informal associations and groups, which he calls the "old guard," most complex institutions could not function.[6] Reading about the overlapping sets of informal, implicit, and inchoate associations that shape the camp's collective enterprise was a M. Jourdain moment for me. Who knew I had been part of such a sophisticated institution? We both worked at Camp Kandalore throughout our time in university. I followed him into the senior staff of the camp in 1970, but I think I was already part of the camp's old guard, not that anybody would have identified themselves in that way. In the only picture of the group that I have, Rod is leading from behind in the back row, and the camp owner is off to the far side of the photo. The point of the national policy papers is that the written constitution is epiphenomenal. The point of old guards is that a formal job title is also epiphenomenal.

In 1970, Rod was the camp's chief operating officer; I was the program director who had to co-ordinate a group of senior staff, including section directors responsible for 200 campers of different age groups and other directors responsible for groups of activity instructors and canoe trip guides. We had almost no hierarchy governing the 100 staff. We all wanted the campers to have a good time, but we had a problem because each section's needs shifted almost on a daily basis depending on which groups were in camp or out on a canoe trip. He suggested that I chair a weekly meeting called "This Hour Has Seven Days"[7] where everyone involved could bargain over the allocation of available resources. At our kaleidoscopic summer camp, he imagined a program that could vary week by week depending on circumstances. He was already thinking about institutional design when he was still an undergrad.

The old guard observation applies to the governance of summer camps, international organizations, and law schools. The first few times I read "Office Politics," which came out while I was preparing for PHD comprehensives, I was mesmerized by the play of different theoretical rationales for decision.[8] It took me a while to note the two things that the article leaves to the reader to figure out: who got the office, and who made the decision? The tension in the answer is inherent in Rod's work. Institutions have formally designated decision-makers. But the institution is better governed when she has consulted the old guard.

My first career was as a foreign service officer. In 1980, at my request, Rod helped the Professional Association of Foreign Service Officers prepare a brief for the McDougall Commission[9] on how to reform the rules that applied to our lives abroad. The brief I now know was classic Rod Macdonald: he argues for giving officers greater autonomy in how we managed such matters as getting ourselves from Ottawa to a new posting abroad; he argues from the start for guidelines over rules.[10]

Most of the work in my second career as an academic is about trade and global governance in some way or another, and especially the World Trade Organization (WTO). When we talk about the WTO, fundamentally a contract among its members, we talk about reciprocity and obligation. Naturally, Rod kept suggesting things I should read that offered a richer way of thinking about such institutions. The ideas that proved especially helpful were implicit and interactional law in the legal process theory of Lon Fuller[11] and legal pluralism in Rod's own work.[12] The way in which they address the nature of social order, good institutional design, and law as a social construction resonated with my understanding of the role of institutions in the establishment of a stable and prosperous global order.

One of the things I try to understand is how a complex international organization, with vast differences in capacity and interests among its members, can make decisions. Thinking about a kaleidoscopic institution with more than one old guard helps. Every member of the WTO naturally insists on *participation* in making decisions that affect their country directly while having *influence* on decisions that affect the evolving structure of rules. But plenary meetings of 160+ members in any WTO body are held only for transparency: the real work is done in

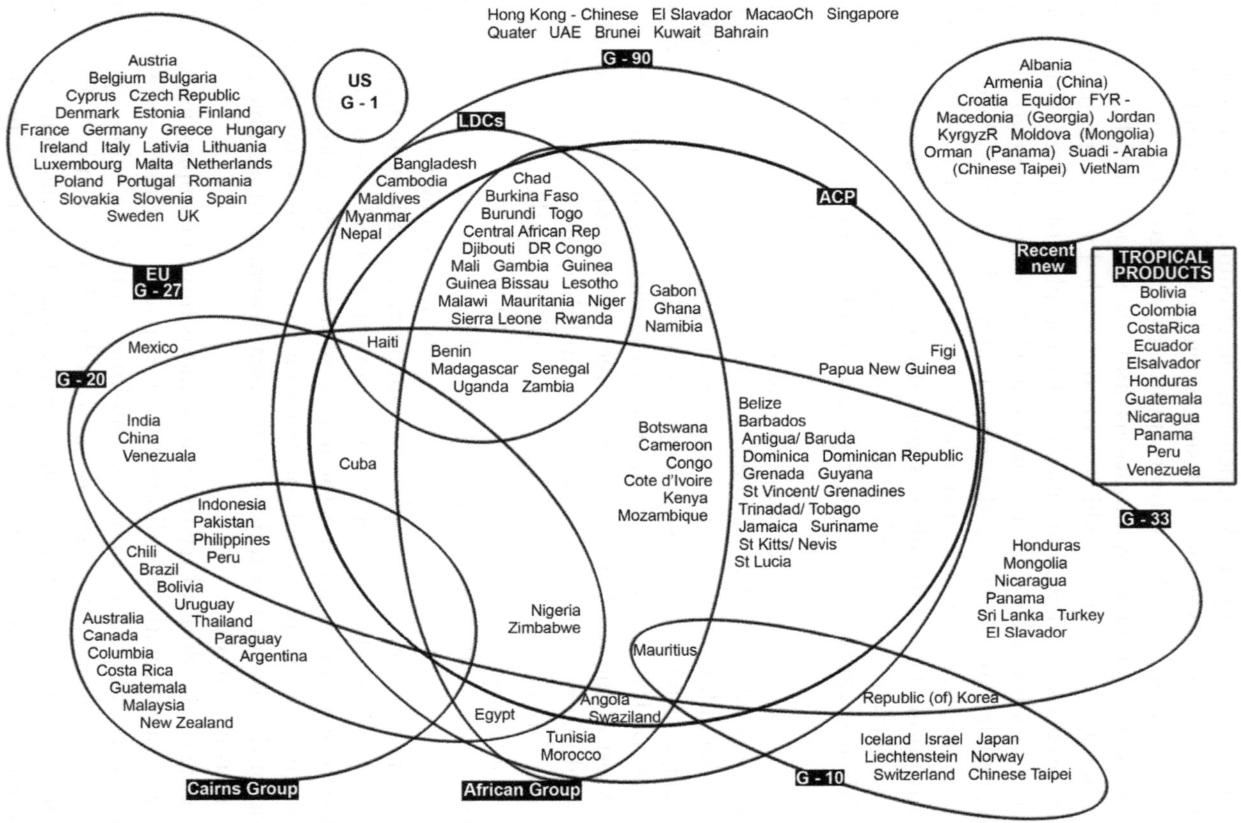

Figure 1 Clubs in the WTO agriculture negotiations

informal meetings. The largest players are present at virtually all such meetings, however constructed, but most members are represented by the co-ordinator of their club.[13] The chart in figure 1 was prepared by the WTO Secretariat to help people understand the clubs active in the Doha Round agriculture negotiations.

The pattern is different for other negotiating groups. Anybody who studies only formal WTO bodies, or even the visible clubs, will not understand how decisions emerge and therefore might not understand what the decisions mean. That is, understanding ultimate codification requires understanding what was at stake and the forces in play.

I have looked closely at how the WTO interacts with participants in the regulation of food safety in an amateur application of legal pluralism ideas.[14] Every country has a food safety regulator. They mostly get on with it, but within a multilateral normative framework. There have been literally thousands of formal notifications of new or changed regulations to the WTO. A few hundred have been raised in the Sanitary and Phyto-Sanitary Measures Committee. A couple of dozen have become formal disputes, and a handful have been appealed all the way through the dispute settlement system. Legal normativity in this domain matters for all of us who like to eat safe food, but it does not come from WTO adjudication. The observations about the food safety domain seem to hold across all of the WTO agreements, even subsidies. We observe that a great deal of collective life in the trading system is never notified to the WTO. We also observe that many disputes are avoided, and conflicts resolved, without formal adjudication.

Contra centralism, I have found in my empirical work, neither states nor any of the other actors in global collective life stand in a hierarchical relation to each other: social order is possible, even if it is not a single unified social order.[15] Contra legal positivism, therefore, it is never easy to know what the law is a priori in a given context, but the fact of a written treaty is not determinative; contra monism, no international organization or state has a monopoly of law in its domain. It is not helpful, therefore, to define WTO law in terms of its texts, and its evolution in terms of disputes, for that is to define the thing by breaches, not by adherence to its normative order. In this view of law as plural, implicit, and pervasive, the famous WTO dispute settlement system plays only a small, if important, part in the maintenance of a rule of law.

Much of my work on the WTO explores its sophisticated transparency and accountability mechanisms.[16] Accountability regimes commend themselves neither on their technical merits nor their democratic virtue but because of the purposes they serve both for those seeking accountability and for those called to account: people engaging in the process on both sides have to see the benefit for themselves; otherwise, accountability cannot work. That means the process starts with *ex ante* accountability to oneself, and then to one's peers, before considering the possibility of *ex post* accountability to others.[17]

How then do we understand the reciprocal obligation of the trading system? It begins with accepting that reciprocity means that law is not a "one-way street"; it depends on collaboration among actors to build shared understandings[18] and confidence in the (diffuse) reciprocity of the system. Following Fuller's conception of law's "inner morality,"[19] fidelity to law depends on others also having fidelity to law.[20] Accountability mechanisms are best understood, therefore, as interactional opportunities for the constant development and affirmation of shared understanding of what fidelity to WTO obligations entails. If a committee makes a series of decisions in a certain way, actors (or, at least, active participants, admittedly a subset of the membership) know what the WTO law is without codification in the treaty or an appellate body decision. Members hold each other to account for meeting their mutual obligations under the WTO contract, and only members can decide whether the explanations and justifications offered are sufficient.[21] No external entity can subject the WTO to judicial review. In this sense, reciprocity and non-discrimination are both the ends and the means of WTO; they are its purpose as well as its process.

In a different application of Rod's pluralism, I have argued that it is misleading to dream of an overarching constitution in which the relations of Canadians and Americans can be subsumed in a strong state-to-state framework with a single set of coherent policy tools.[22] Instead of the concrete metaphor of an overarching bridge, or one comprehensive treaty, I borrowed the pluralist metaphor of the legal framework as a *kaleidoscope*, with its constantly shifting shapes and colours, just like our many shared institutions.[23] The kaleidoscopic North American constitution has been evolving at least since the Jay Treaty of 1794. The NAFTA texts work well, but they do not work alone in guiding the interactions of millions of traders. Hundreds of treaties, arrangements, and joint organizations govern aspects of the Canada–US relationship. Canadians meet with their American counterparts in academic societies and professional associations. Many provinces are members of US state associations. Thousands of firms have integrated operations across borders, and myriad standard-setting bodies affect industrial and commercial practices.

Borrowing another metaphor from Rod, I contrasted the image of the president and the prime minister signing a single written constitution meant to solve all the residual problems of NAFTA with the image of a Swiss Army knife: not a single tool, or even the same tool for every person, but a collection of tools infinitely adaptable to the purposes of millions of users.[24] In Swiss Army knife diplomacy, Canada–US relations are everyone's responsibility, not just that of leaders, and everyone creates their own knife, their own set of tools. Managing Canada–US relations requires the continuous engagement of Canadian officials, legislators, politicians, businessmen, lobbyists, and others from all levels of Canadian life. Critics in the business community have misunderstood this observation, thinking it means accepting the status quo or dealing with irritants exclusively on a case-by-case basis, but I advocate no such lassitude with respect to Canada's most important foreign relationship. Rather, I argue that an activist approach to North American security and prosperity can be managed within institutions that are constantly being reshaped by the daily interaction of millions of North Americans.

I want to conclude by returning to the national policy and why I was placed on the symposium panel on federalism. In the second paper we wrote together, Rod and I again use his metaphor of a Swiss Army knife.[25] Every citizen soldier needs one, but citizens no more want the same things from government than they want identical gadgets on their Swiss knife. This analogy allows us to see how almost everything in the Internet era is being unbundled and re-aggregated in novel ways. The phenomenon we call the "third national policy" in Canada can be observed in other places too. The focus of the changes is on citizens, not jurisdiction. Finding the fit between the pluralism of citizen desire and the structures of federalism, or multilateralism, is central to twenty-first-century governance.

The national policy story is ultimately about citizen agency, which for me is the point of the legal pluralism hypothesis. That is, it is against all binary choices. Pluralists think individuals can have many identities, and the menu usually has more than two options. So Rod and I argue that the objective of Canada's emerging third national policy is that people need not be forced to pick only one identity, which does not mean that anything goes. Our governance structures must enable citizens to lead self-directed lives of their own choosing. My kaleidoscopic understanding of the trading system is similar. The WTO does not force every country to have the same policy. It only requires non-discrimination. The constitutive basis of any governance structure lies in the ability of people to talk to each other, to discuss problems in collective life. The notion that texts are epiphenomena is, I think, an idea that Rod derived first from Fuller. Texts matter, but the source of normativity is social interaction. That idea has influenced how I think about the trading system. It holds for families, summer camps, law schools, and international regimes. And it will continue to influence my teaching and research.

NOTES

1 Roderick Macdonald, "Sometimes It's Better Just to Fix the Dock," in *Lessons of Everyday Law* (Montreal: McGill-Queen's University Press for the School of Policy Studies, Queen's University, and the Law Commission of Canada, 2002), 55–8.
2 Roderick Macdonald and Robert Wolfe, "Canada's Third National Policy: The Epiphenomenal or the Real Constitution?" *University of Toronto Law Journal* 59 (2009): 469–523.
3 Constitution Act, 1867 (UK), 30 & 31 Vict, c 3.
4 Canadian Charter of Rights and Freedoms, Part I of the Constitution Act, 1982, being Schedule B to the Canada Act 1982 (UK), 1982, c 11.
5 Macdonald, "Les vieilles gardes: hypothèses sur l'émergence des normes, l'internormativité et le désordre à travers une typologie des institutions normatives," in *Le droit soluble [:] contributions québécoises à l'étude l'internormativité*, edited by Jean-Guy Belley (Paris: Librairie générale de droit et de jurisprudence, 1996), 233–72.
6 Macdonald, "Old Guards," in *Lessons of Everyday Law*, 130–4.
7 "This Hour Has Seven Days" was a controversial CBC-TV newsmagazine that ran in the mid-1960s.
8 Macdonald, "Office Politics," *University of Toronto Law Journal* 40 (1990): 419–76.
9 Canada, *Report of the Royal Commission on Conditions of Foreign Service* (Ottawa: Minister of Supply and Services, 1981).
10 Macdonald, "Is Law about Issuing Orders or Making Rules?" in *Lessons of Everyday Law*, 28–32.
11 Lon L. Fuller, *The Law in Quest of Itself* (Chicago: The Foundation Press, 1940); Fuller, *The Morality of Law*, rev. edn (New Haven and London: Yale University Press, 1969).
12 Macdonald, "Metaphors of Multiplicity: Civil Society, Regimes, and Legal Pluralism," *Arizona Journal of Comparative and International Law* 15 (1998): 69–91; Macdonald, "The Legal Mediation of Social Diversity," in *The Conditions of Diversity in Multinational Democracies*, edited by Alain-G. Gagnon, Montserrat Guibernau, and François Rocher (Montreal: Institute for Research on Public Policy, 2003), xi, 351.

13 Robert Wolfe, "Canada's Adventures in Clubland: Trade Clubs and Political Influence," in *Canada among Nations 2007: Room for Manoeuvre*, edited by Jean Daudelin and Daniel Schwanen (Montreal and Kingston: McGill-Queen's University Press, 2008), 181–97. Note that figure 1 appears in that text as figure 9.1 (source: International Centre for Trade and Sustainable Development and WTO Secretariat).
14 Wolfe, "See You in Geneva? Legal (Mis)Representations of the Trading System," *European Journal of International Relations* 11 (3) (2005): 339–65.
15 Macdonald, "The Fridge-Door Statute," *McGill Law Journal* 47 (2001): 13–38.
16 Wolfe, "Letting the Sun Shine in at the WTO: How Transparency Brings the Trading System to Life" (World Trade Organization: Staff Working Paper ERSD-2013-03, March 2013); Wolfe, "An Anatomy of Accountability at the WTO," *Global Policy* (2015)
17 Macdonald, "The Acoustics of Accountability: Towards Well-Tempered Tribunals," in *Judicial Integrity*, edited by A. Sajo (Leiden: Martinus Nijhoff, 2004), 141–81.
18 Jutta Brunnée and Stephen J. Toope, *Legitimacy and Legality in International Law: An Interactional Account* (Cambridge and New York: Cambridge University Press, 2010).
19 Fuller, *The Morality of Law*.
20 Brunnée and Toope.
21 Friedrich Kratochwil and John Gerard Ruggie, "International Organization: A State of the Art on the Art of the State," *International Organization* 40 (4) (1986): 753–75.
22 Wolfe, "See You in Washington? A Pluralist Perspective on North American Institutions," *Choices* 9 (4) (2003): 1–24.
23 Macdonald, "Kaleidoscopic Federalism," in *The States and Moods of Federalism: Governance, Identity, and Methodology*, edited by J.-F. Gaudreault-DesBiens and F. Gélinas (Montreal: Blais, 2005), 261–83.
24 Macdonald, "The Swiss Army Knife of Governance" (Paper delivered to the Instrument of Choice in Global Democracies Conference, Faculty of Law, McGill University, Montreal, 26–8 September 2002).
25 Macdonald and Wolfe, "Is Citizen Federalism Canada's Third National Policy?" in *State of the Federation, 2010: Shifting Power, the New Ontario and What It Means for Canada*, edited by Matthew Mendelsohn, Joshua Hjartarson, and James Pearce (Montreal and Kingston: McGill-Queen's University Press, 2013), 165–84.

11

Constitutional Experience

JOHN D. WHYTE

Perhaps the most significant leitmotif in Rod Macdonald's scholarship, and especially in his writings on the Constitution, is the behavioural or social foundation for what is constituted as our basic political order. He adopted a socio-generative conception of constitutional order; it is the quotidian practices of a nation's people in response to their changing needs and purposes that are the true influences in constitutional development.[1] His view of constitutionalism is an appealing version of the "we the people" idea that legitimates constitutional formation, and this, in turn, creates popular commitment to constitutionalism. Shifts in constitutional order should not be seen as coming from stirring declarations and revolutionary concepts as much as emerging from peaceable transformations of social practice and beliefs that reflect new sensibilities, changing ethics, and emerging ideas about what the nation should be. In the words of Michel Foucault, "thus we are always in the position of beginning again."[2]

Macdonald's constitutionalism is not closely bound by theories of the state, received structures of governance and accountability, or the historic concerns that shaped the nation's formation. More significant have been the shifts in state structure brought about through practices and values.[3] There is no socially detached template that determines, once and for all, the structure of government. The polity operates in ways that reflect how we relate to each other, how we lead our lives, and what we yearn for and conceive our purposes to be. Patterns of attachment and reliance between citizens provide the most genuine way to understand the course of constitutional development.

For Macdonald, the precise constitutional form of federalism is only a metaphor for the deeper truth of *métissage* – the process of generating new identities and new entities through the constant mixing of the different ways and values of different communities.[4] The structure of the federal state permits the marrying of diverse and established communities into a single entity – into a nation. Just as individuals live through encounters between their own diverse and multi-sourced selves so, too, the communities brought into a common political structure negotiate and renegotiate the terms of relationship and the preservation of identity. As individuals flourish when the elements of their identity are received in a spirit of acceptance – and pride – our *métissagiste* political community develops best under practices – and regimes – of reconciliation and mutual acceptance.

This view of the deep human meaning behind choices of constitutional formation serves two valuable purposes. First, it allows us to grasp the deep purposes served by political structures, and this helps us to recognize both what is truly valuable and what are non-essential refinements. From this we understand how to preserve the integrity of the structures that we have agreed to be bound by. The second purpose is the mirror image of this; understanding the deeper purposes behind political structures reveals the necessity of reforms to the constitutional order. The virtues that we seek to have reflected in political structures will not always be achieved as practices change, and new structures or constraints will become necessary in order to preserve underlying purposes. The organic nature of institutions and human society produce correspondingly organic constitutional development. The needed changes in the constitutional order arise from social changes. In this way, constitutional development is pluralist, populist, and democratic.

Federalism is an expression of the human aspiration to meld freedom with order, independence with membership, diversity with a common cause, and dynamism with predictability. The process of federal relationship is of greater longevity, greater durability, greater breadth, and greater vibrancy than any specific structure of political authority can capture. Federalism captures both the aspiration for a statecraft that creates an effective relationship between centres of state authority and the inevitability of change that flows from such a relationship. In "Kaleidoscopic Federalism," Macdonald writes: "in case there remains any doubt about the matter, I do advance in my paper a normative theory of federalism – it is a theory that is grounded in philosophical premises about human beings and human capacities, about relationships and social interaction and about the instantiation of human agency in diverse sites of normative commitment."[5] And then, in order to demonstrate how universal, how much above, and how much below, the precise constructions of a state's polity the idea of federalism truly is, he goes on to say how much of the same ideas of authority and established terms of relationship, and how much of the same dynamism, contextualization, and adaptability, that are found in the ordinary experiences of kinship can also be found in state federalism. He writes, "Already my children know and understand the federal complexities of divided sovereignty and overlapping attributions."[6]

However, there are more structured and more constrained understandings of statecraft than the understanding based on constant social reconstruction or that follows the changing dictates of social needs and values. In the formation of the national constitution, federalism is chosen as a specific constitutional construct based on specific protections, commitments, and promises and with fixed assurances to the citizens who live under it. It is dangerous not to see the bargain in such arrangements or to treat them as perennially negotiable. Federalism conveys more restraint than is provided by the large and general ideas of polyarchy and accommodation.

Constitutional dynamism takes place through more or less formal processes. One of these processes is controlled by the strictures of democracy. It is based on the double aspect of democratic self-determination.[7] One aspect of political self-determination is found in moments of high politics in which there is formal identification of the changes to be made to the political order and a more thorough regard paid by political leaders to the preferences – or the consent – of the general population. The measure of popular consent is taken through one deliberative process or another, each age, it seems, seeking a more hearty form of consent than previously adopted. The shifting process of high politics is distinct from the everyday processes of ordinary politics, which do not engage the wishes of the population except through the periodic political calculations of citizens based on evaluating the record of governance in light of past promises, or calculating which political leadership will meet the emerging challenges to the state, or attaching political preference to general ideas such as liberty, or the socialization of needs, or the moral imperative to protect people. Nevertheless, it can be convincingly claimed that the force behind formal constitutional reform is not found in the acts of political authority and formal consent as much as it is in social evolution and changing beliefs about what citizens are due or what is the right range of the state's concern and action.

Second, the constitutional order is also open to revision through judicial decisions on the meaning and application of the constitutional text (including the text found in prior judicial determinations of the constitution's meaning). At first glance, this process may not seem to be one based on shifts in social practice and moral vision. Yet it well may be. In Canada, constitutional adjudication has gone through notable swings – swings from decentralization to centralization, from indifference to citizen entitlement and a lack of concern over loss of liberty, integrity, or well-being to a high degree of attention to protecting them, and from constitutional formalism to regard for workable state functioning. It would be an exercise of refined analysis to identify in each of these examples the exact sources of the changes in constitutional interpretation. It is, however, more likely that they reflect changes in social values and needs and changes that track a popular consensus than that they are driven by doctrines of established constitutional jurisprudence. For instance, the marked difference between the Supreme Court's majority opinion in the *Patriation Reference*[8] on the legal requirements for requesting the British Parliament to make a change to the Canadian Constitution and that Court's majority opinion in *Reference re Secession of Quebec*[9] on the constitutional rules for effecting the secession of a province from Canada demonstrates a shift away from preserving the Constitution's formal legal character to developing an essentialist understanding of the nation and a structural understanding of national consent – a shift that reflects a commitment to basing the exercise of higher law on the idea of national will. Although the Macdonald view of constitution as being made in the streets, and for the present time, must meet the claim of formalism and constraint that attaches to judicial review, it is hardly disproven by this claim.

But the Macdonald view of the nature of constitutional change does face a challenge. This challenge arises from the appropriation by those in privileged positions of the constitution's effects – and its development. While constitutional dynamism flows from social values and needs, the values and needs that are reflected are those that belong to the privileged. State organization is not a passive taker of changing human aspirations but a mighty and ongoing force that sets our relationships and community purposes but does so in ways that frequently favour existing advantage. The social tendencies that impel constitutional change are formed through the state as handmaiden of established powers and through placing citizens in fixed relationships and with fixed purposes and functions long before they can form and pursue their deepest dreams – the dreams of freedom, self-fulfillment, mutual support, and caring.

Consider two examples of constitutional unresponsiveness to changing social values. One relates to the obdurate effects of a historical constitutional arrangement of inter-societal dominance notwithstanding an evolved political social context, and the other relates to trends in constitutional interpretation.

The first instance engages the constitutional relationship of government with indigenous communities. This relationship is an instance of an older constitutional mechanism – the power to place political communities under trusteeship. This tradition shows its face explicitly in the Constitution Act, 1867[10] in the provisions relating to inter-jurisdictional supervision (in powers relating to sectarian education and in the power to suspend the enactment of legislation) or in the overriding legislative powers (the disallowance of legislation). These powers have now largely fallen into disuse. But with respect to Aboriginal peoples, the federal government's supervisory powers have not been fundamentally affected by either the organic development toward constitutionally recognized parties negotiating as equals or by the historical trend of moving away from national trusteeship over indigenous peoples. The attempts to find the trope that would signal and induce national resolve to move past trusteeship are legion – there have been repeated attempts through constitutional, political, and judicial proposals to establish a language of reconciliation based on a greater parity between political communities – expressions and ideas such as Aboriginal rights, Aboriginal title, the treaty relationship, the inherent right of self-government, federal fiduciary responsibility, honour of the Crown, duty to consult, the Declaration of the Rights Indigenous Peoples, negotiated self-government agreements, and so on.

These utterances reflect a conception of the political space for indigenous peoples that has been developed in recognition of the intra-nation incommensurability of the experiences, conditions, and needs of settler and indigenous populations. But they have not amounted to a new constitutional order. For a constitutional dynamic that we celebrate for its capacity to absorb changing moral sensibilities and evolving conceptions of justice, there is a marked woodenness in the governmental failure to recognize this relationship's organic development. This failure to acknowledge the political (and material) needs of indigenous peoples continues unabated with ongoing destruction of indigenous integrity. Federal and provincial interests in exercising control over, and gaining economic rents from, ever greater territory make the relationship with indigenous peoples based on the idea of reconciling competing jurisdictions less likely – or more conflicted. The normal constitutional aspiration to be an effective instrument of recognition and preservation of all manner of multiplicities – regional, ethnic, religious, and original – continues to fail when it comes to the recognition and accommodation of indigenous difference.

The second instance of constitutionalism's fixed interests is seen in the structural relationship between the instruments of liberal democracy and the privileged treatment of commerce. This relationship has its roots in the European intellectual culture that, since the Middle Ages, became focused on the centralization of knowledge. This process depended on finding a common ground for knowledge and, hence, it was a process for creating a general standard for knowing truth. But the tendency of this intellectual process (or, as some might suggest, the *incentive* for this process) of ordering knowledge and regulating the demonstration of truth was not, directly, enlightenment but rather creating conditions for economic dynamism that would lead to an increase in personal and community wealth. Knowledge mobility adds to economic mobility, which increases wealth through the creation of the common knowledge base essential to a common market. Knowledge mobility also enhances the economic factors of scale and efficiency, and these factors lead to growth and greater wealth.[11] Since the mid–twelfth century, the culture of refining knowledge has served to support wealth-seeking. Apart from anything else, this has been a powerful imperialist venture; the value of common knowledge has served to justify the extirpation of its enemies – superstition, some elements of faith and religious practice, and the uncritical acceptance of dogma and local belief. Wealth-seeking has marshalled the ideas of science and moral philosophy, as well as social endeavour and politics, to create a world of common understanding.

Ideas about common knowledge and wealth generation have been matched by ideas about the appropriate political structure. These are, first, that centralizing knowledge disturbs received knowledge, undermines the embedded privilege of "knowing," and replaces them with challenges to any authority that is not based on the new intellectual currency. Second, commercial dynamism depends on the political stability that makes economic endeavour rewarding and investment a sensible gamble. Activism in markets depends on an absence of revolution.

Ultimately, and over a millennium of state development, two large political constructions have emerged to correspond to the needs of wealth production and stable markets. The quest for political stability was achieved – very slowly – through early versions of democracy, which, again slowly, embodied the idea that political changes require broad subscription – at least broader than the will of a victorious strongman or a usurper who seizes power and then turns state power to his advantage. This evolution has controlled the lurching between generals and tribal upstarts, between kings and bourgeoisie, and between sectarian competitors. The second construction is constitutionalism, which is typically designed to suppress the resentments that cause rebellion through checking the outlandish or oppressive exercise of political office and to remove the tendency to revolution on the part of minorities and groups by making provision to ensure they are not left out of the state's operation and concern.

This historical narrative told in broad strokes connects the development of democracy and constitutionalism to the needs of markets – or to commercial flourishing. While this marriage may have sustained a balance that has been of greater world benefit than leaving tyranny unchecked, it is, nevertheless, imperialism – the imperialism of commerce.[12] And Canadian federalism has been a part of it. There is no shaking away the wealth-seeking purposes of our dominant constitutional ideas. Neither Canadian federalism itself nor the dynamism that has driven its development has been shaped as much by our souls' wishes, our spirits' insights, or our ample needs for sustaining human relationships as by constitutionalism and federalism being an instrumental part of the millennial evolution of political structures that engender positive conditions for markets.

The inertial tendency of political structures toward commerce has not necessarily been hostile to humans' needs and aspirations. The rule of law and democracy, principles that enable economic mobility, social dynamism, and political stability, have not been terrible guides for living together. The processes by which wealth is increased have likely provided more human care and comfort than maintaining a rigid politico-economic situation that perpetuated mean and desperate want. And when the two – commercial wealth through liberalism and desperate want – have occurred together, which certainly happened often enough, perhaps it has been resting political legitimacy on the principle of democracy that has allowed social movements, over time, to defeat exclusion and exploitation.

Not only is Canada's founding based on principles that favour commerce, its constitutional development carries forward this program.

Recent developments in Canadian federalism jurisprudence reflect the influence of commercial interests. First, the two general descriptions of federal jurisdiction – general regulation of trade and the national dimension conception of the peace, order, and good government power – had been interpreted mainly to provide purposive explanations of the trade power and the general power. But in recent decades they have been reinterpreted as substantive – and potentially substantial – categories of federal jurisdiction.[13] A way has opened for a newly activist national state to pursue national commercial interests to the displacement of local regulatory priorities.

Second, the Supreme Court has shown enthusiasm for suppressing the constitutional concepts of exclusive legislative powers and interjurisdictional immunity in favour of broad jurisdictional concurrency and, therefore, much enlarged federal regulatory authority.[14] This potential for enlarged federal authority has created a tendency to remove protections for citizens and local interests and has conferred expanded national capacity to produce common market conditions that will facilitate the increase of commercial strength.

Third, there has been, under the banner of respecting traditional federalism, abandonment of intergovernmental negotiations and discussions between Canada's governments – a process that has been effective in securing both constitutional reform and Canada's development as a socially activist state. This has led to a wholesale retreat from considering policies that need to be developed through political engagement between the many Canadian political communities. These policies would bear on citizens outside commercial interests and would not directly relate to developing economic capacity; they include such things as disease control and prevention, wildlife preservation, health care, global warming, urban transportation, municipal infrastructure, crime prevention, research, and scientific discovery.

These simultaneous tendencies toward greater federal regulatory control and away from the mechanisms for developing needed national social policy conduce to low state engagement with social conditions in favour of national economic activity. Political power is exercised away from the diverse and particular interests of people – and peoples – and toward the common link of commerce.

Such developments in the functioning of the Canadian constitutional order do, of course, reflect the connection between changes in that order and a change in social values and interests, but these changes predominantly favour commercial interests. They structurally give markets more weight than the life experiences, social needs, and aspirations of citizens. But this tendency, while structural, should not be seen as constant. There have been moments of transformation that have produced efforts to realize social justice or citizen entitlement. There has also been a theology of Canadian federalism that claims that federalism's deepest purpose is the creation of governing structures that respect social relationships and honour aspirations of personal fulfillment. Historical grand arcs do not capture all of the turns of history.[15]

Macdonald was not wrong in seeing federalism as being made in the streets of our communities. But it seems at least partially a mistake not to recognize that Canadian constitutionalism tends not to stray far from the millennially established ideal of cosmopolitan governance that finds its common and enduring interest tied to serving commercial interests rather than to liberating citizens so that they can meet their particular needs and shape their personal identities. The citizens of this democratic, constitutionally grounded nation may be situated as agents of change, reform, and self-determination, but equally they are situated as captives of the structures that generate economic growth and serve commerce.

NOTES

1 The conception of citizen agency in constitutional development is described under the heading of "Plural Modes: Territorial, Personal and Psychological Federalism," in Roderick Macdonald, "Kaleidoscopic Federalism," in *The States and Moods of Federalism: Governance, Identity and Methodology*, edited by J.-F. Gaudreault-DesBiens and F. Gélinas (Montreal: Blais, 2005), 273.

2 Michel Foucault, "What Is Enlightenment?" in *The Foucault Reader*, edited by Paul Rabinow (New York: Pantheon Books, 1984), 47.

3 Macdonald does not, however, exclude the significance of constitutional mechanisms, texts, and institutions or formal interpretive decisions. He opposes these sources of constitutionalism being "fetishized." See "The Political Economy of the Federal Spending Power," *Queen's Law Journal* 34 (2008): 252–3.

4 Macdonald, "Kaleidoscopic Federalism," 270.

5 Macdonald, "Kaleidoscopic Federalism" (Paper delivered to the International Conference on Federalism, sponsored by the Forum of Federations, Montreal, 8 November 2002), 1.

6 Ibid., 4.

7 See Bruce Ackerman, "The Storrs Lectures: Discovering the Constitution," *Yale Law Journal* 93 (1984): 1,093.

8 [1981] 1 S.C.R. 753.
9 [1998] 2 S.C.R. 217.
10 Constitution Act, 1867 (UK), 30 & 31 Vict, c 3.
11 Some of this history is set out in Albert O. Hirschman, *The Passions and the Interests: Political Arguments for Capitalism before Its Triumph* (Princeton: Princeton Classics, 2013).
12 For a description on the processes by which constitutionalism is held in place and serves the world hegemony of free markets through the persistent structures of post-colonial imperialism, see James Tully, *Public Philosophy in a New Key, Vol. II: Imperialism and Civic Freedom*, ch. 5, "On Law, Democracy and Imperialism" (Cambridge: Cambridge University Press, 2008), 127–65.
13 Respectively, *General Motors of Canada v. City National Leasing*, [1989] 1 S.C.R. 641, and *R. v. Crown Zellerbach Ltd.*, [1988] 1 S.C.R. 401.
14 *Canadian Western Bank v. Alberta*, [2007] 2 S.C.R. 3.
15 Perhaps nowhere is this so well demonstrated in the Canadian constitutional context as in Roderick Macdonald and Robert Wolfe, "Canada's Third National Policy: The Epiphenomenal or the Real Constitution," *University of Toronto Law Journal* 59 (2009): 469–523.

12

The Priority of Distributive Justice: Roderick Macdonald and the Reform of Secured Transactions Law

CATHERINE WALSH

Introduction

Although Rod Macdonald's scholarship spanned the full spectrum of private law, the five texts selected for the symposium panel on "The Priority of Distributive Justice" are all drawn from his work in relation to the law of security on property. This is not a surprising choice – among private law subjects, the law of security on property most directly engages distributive justice issues. To understand why, consider that debtor–creditor and insolvency laws in Western legal traditions generally treat a defaulting debtor's assets as subject to seizure and sale by its creditors, with the proceeds then distributed among them proportionately to their claims. Secured creditors seek to escape the principle of creditor equality by bargaining for the right to have property of their debtors appropriated to the payment of their debts in preference to the claims of other creditors. Thus, security is essentially a private bargain "between A and B that C take nothing,"[1] with C representing the collectivity of A's unsecured creditors that would otherwise get to share in the value of B's assets in the event that there is insufficient value to pay everybody.

The distributional consequences of prioritizing secured creditors did not radically disrupt the principle of creditor equality as long as the law of security was limited in its objects to specific parcels of land and possessory pledges of tangible movables and reified intangibles. These limitations meant that there usually were sufficient debtor assets left over for creditor equality to remain the baseline principle. Since the nineteenth century, however, with the ever-increasing demand for credit brought about by industrialization, creditors have sought ways to take security over the full range of a debtor's movable property, present and future, tangible and intangible, without the need to dispossess the debtor. The broader the range of assets capable of being made the object of security, the greater the potential wealth transfer from unsecured creditors to secured creditors. Expanding the scope of potential collateral also increases the likelihood that multiple creditors may bargain for security on the same asset, raising distributive justice issues among secured creditors. Should the secured creditor who is first on the scene inevitably prevail, or do countervailing considerations militate in favour of carving out super-priority exceptions for particular classes of secured creditors?

Before turning to Rod Macdonald's approach to these distributive justice issues, I think it is useful to offer some more general observations about the five texts assigned to this panel, their common elements, and what they reveal of his ideas about the reform and modernization of secured transactions law.

Pluralism and the Pursuit of Secured Transactions Law Reform

The past half-century or so has seen enormous resources devoted to the reform and modernization of secured transactions law, first at the national level and – at least since the emphasis on the importance of "legal security for property rights" in the 1989 Washington Consensus – at the transnational and global level. As the title to Rod Macdonald's "Article 9 Norm Entrepreneurship"[2] paper reflects, Article 9 of the Uniform Commercial Code in the United States has often been promoted as the optimal reform model in these initiatives.

Throughout his career, Rod Macdonald was actively involved in secured transactions law reform. Three experiences in particular informed his thinking and scholarship.[3] Between 1984 and 1989, he participated in a working group of the Quebec Ministry of Justice that examined the proposals of the Civil Code Revision Office for security on property and that produced the first draft of what became the new regime of security in the 1994 Civil Code of Quebec. In 2003, he was engaged as an external consultant by the World Bank to assist in crafting

Ukraine's new Charge Law, proclaimed in force in 2004. From 2002 to 2009, he served as a member of the Canadian delegation to Working Group VI on secured transactions of the United Nations Commission on International Trade Law (UNCITRAL). In the latter capacity, he made invaluable contributions to the preparation of UNCITRAL's Legislative Guide on Secured Transactions (2007),[4] a comparative exposition of the multiple issues that must be attended to in designing and executing a regime in this field.

The five texts selected for this panel are all very much rooted in Rod Macdonald's lived commitment in the pursuit of secured transactions reform to the Aristotelian concept of *phronesis*, or practical wisdom, meaning "moral sensitivity, perception, imagination, and judgment informed by experience."[5] In line with that orientation, all five texts seek to inculcate an informed scepticism of single-model approaches – particularly models like Article 9 that focus only on the interests of consensual secured creditors – to the diversity of interests and perspectives that must be identified and balanced in crafting an effective reform of secured transactions law. Methodologically, Rod Macdonald accomplishes his goal by exposing the panoply of legal, extra-legal, and institutional considerations that must be attended to in undertaking secured transactions reforms and why differences in the legal traditions and economic, political, and social contexts of different states across time and space make perfect harmonization or transplantation of law unattainable and undesirable.

Stylistically, these texts reflect Rod Macdonald's signature use of metaphor, allegory, and wordplay to communicate his ideas. Perhaps the most extensively elaborated example is found in his article entitled "Three Metaphors of Norm Migration in International Context."[6] His aim here is to challenge the simplistic assumptions underlying rhetorical appeals to the metaphors of harmonization, transplantation, and viral propagation to promote global norms along the lines of Article 9. He advances his thesis by exposing the lessons to be derived from the disciplinary origins of these three metaphors in music, botany, and epidemiology.

So from music we learn that perfect legal harmonization is impossible; tuning compromises are necessary to achieve something approximating harmony, and the choice of instrument, key, and tonal range affects the relative degree of harmony obtained. Rod Macdonald then applies these insights to explain the imperfect level of harmonization achieved between the real security regime adopted in the 1994 Civil Code of Quebec and the Article 9–derived Personal Property Security Acts (PPSAs) in the Canadian common law provinces. Like Article 9, the PPSAs are organized around a functional concept of "security interest" in which all transactions that deploy a property right to secure an obligation are brought within a single legislative framework regardless of their form. In line with functionalist logic, the code drafters initially proposed adoption of a single nominate form of security called the hypothec, with all transactions intended as security brought within the hypothecary regime through a mechanism called the "presumption of hypothec." In the end, the presumption of hypothec was rejected. While the Civil Code folds all prior forms of nominate security into the single concept of a hypothec, it continues to recognize the possibility of obtaining security through the transfer or retention of title. Functionalism in outcome is instead (somewhat imperfectly) achieved by subjecting these title-based security devices to rules that are analogous (but not identical) to those applicable to hypothecs. While unsympathetic to the ideological and atavistic impulses that he believes informed the rejection of the presumption of hypothec, Rod Macdonald nonetheless sees the Quebec experience as evidencing the inevitability of tuning compromises in the harmonization process.

Botany teaches us similar lessons in relation to the metaphor of legal transplants: there cannot be a perfect transplant; the specificities of the local ecosystem may require *ex ante* adaptive compromises, leaving further *ex post* adjustments to develop over time once the transplant takes root. Rod Macdonald applies these insights in explaining the reform of Ukraine's secured transactions law. Rather than transplanting the complexity of finely tuned rules reflected in the most recent iteration of Article 9, the Ukraine Charge Law instead adopted a bare-bones regime targeted at the most basic types of business and consumer collateral – equipment, inventory, accounts receivable, and consumer durables. As he observes, this reform strategy was aimed at ensuring that the basic concepts and institutions of a modern security regime would take firm root in Ukraine's unfamiliar soil and that *ex post* demands for further adaptations to facilitate security in more rarified forms of intangible collateral would emerge over time, as indeed they had through the various iterations of Article 9 in the United States.

Epidemiology teaches us that viral propagation depends on a complexity of factors, including the strength of the vectors of transmission and the relative susceptibility of the host. Rod Macdonald applies this insight to the process that led to the adoption of the UNCITRAL

Legislative Guide on Secured Transactions (ULGST). As he observes, the key objective underlying the ULGST was said to be the promotion of greater access to credit at lower cost, and, perhaps predictably in light of that goal, it ended up largely recommending the basic features of the Article 9 model. Nonetheless, certain aspects of the Article 9 model encountered strong resistance among some member states in the deliberation process, as reflected in the detailed commentary set out in the ULGST. Some of these points of resistance were rooted in policy differences regarding the extent of protection to be extended to secured creditors or particular classes of secured creditors; others were rooted in differences in legal tradition – for example, the desire of some states to preserve recognition of the distinct character of reservations of title by vendors and lessors as alternative modes of financing the acquisition of assets. For Rod Macdonald, these points of resistance imply three conclusions. First, the global propagation of the Article 9 "virus" through the ULGST may be less extensive than anticipated. Second, closer attention to the need to balance diverse interests and to take account of diverse legal, social, political, and economic contexts in different states in the articulation of the key objectives of the ULGST might have enhanced the chances of widespread "infection." Finally, just as viruses can mutate in a new host and re-infect the initial host, states with legal regimes derived from the Article 9 model may need to adapt their own regimes to take account of these points of resistance if their secured creditors are to succeed in the transnational credit sphere.

Rod Macdonald's resistance to single-model law reform approaches is, of course, consistent with the pluralistic theoretical instincts that inform his scholarship across all legal fields. But his pluralism here, as everywhere, is tempered. He finds much to admire in the Article 9 organizational framework and functionalist orientation and regards its core principles and general objectives as ones that should be pursued in any reform of secured transactions law. His concern is that successful secured transactions reform can only be achieved if reformers attend to the local social and political context in the implementation process, if laws are articulated in a manner that respects the legal traditions, private law conceptual structures, and drafting conventions of the enacting state, and, of paramount importance, if the reform process ensures that the interests of all potential creditors, not just secured creditors, are represented in the reform process. This last point takes us to Rod Macdonald's views on the distributional effects of security, as reflected throughout the five texts assigned to this panel, to which we now turn.

Distributive Justice between Secured and Unsecured Creditors

The priority accorded to secured creditors over the claims of unsecured creditors has traditionally been justified according to the inherent logic of party autonomy and freedom of alienability of private property. But the broader the range of potential collateral, the greater the potential diminishment of the asset pool available to unsecured creditors. Consequently, the expansion of the range of permissible collateral to encompass virtually the entirety of a debtor's potential insolvency estate has generated considerable controversy in the academic literature, especially in the United States. The distributive goals underpinning principles of freedom of contract and private property plausibly justify vesting secured creditors with an indefeasible priority only to the extent that unsecured creditors can somehow be seen as having consented to their subordinate position by failing to bargain for a first-priority security right or by adjusting their contract terms to take account of the risk that the debtor's assets may be encumbered and therefore unavailable to them as a source of repayment should the debtor default. But not all creditors are able to adjust to the priority risk posed by security – the debtor's employees and small trade suppliers, for example, typically lack the bargaining power to do so. And some creditors do not choose to enter into a credit relationship with their debtor – tort victims and environmental damage claimants, for example, are involuntary creditors. Governments likewise may be seen as involuntary creditors in respect of claims for tax and other revenue arrears in the sense that they did not choose to lend this money to their citizens.

Some argue that the social costs and unfairness of subordinating involuntary and non-adjusting creditors to the claims of consensual secured creditors should be addressed by awarding them a preferential charge on the proceeds realized from the debtor's encumbered assets or by setting aside a certain proportion of those proceeds to feed their claims. Others take the position that the overall economic benefit to society of giving an indefeasible priority to consensual secured creditors – increased access to credit at lower cost – justifies any unfair distributive effects this may have on some unsecured claimants.[7]

Rod Macdonald rejects this latter theorem as unproven and indeed incapable of proof. More generally, he rejects the assumption that the paramount objective of a secured transactions law is to promote access to private credit at lower cost. The promotion of lower-cost access to credit (and debt) is not the only public good or necessarily a self-evident good. Overall economic efficiency must be balanced against other legislative and policy goals that a state might wish to achieve in its secured transactions law and about which states might reasonably differ. As he observes, a state with well-developed and well-funded social welfare and social insurance programs may well be prepared to adopt a regime of insolvency preferences that heavily favours consensual secured lenders over the revenue claims of the state or the wage or pension claims of the debtor's employees. But in many other states, super-priority entitlement may be needed in order to preserve the financial solvency of these same programs.

Consistent with his pluralistic instincts, Rod Macdonald does not advocate any particular formula or template for determining when non-consensual security rights or preferences should trump the claims of consensual secured lenders. His primary concern is in ensuring that the interests of all creditors are fully taken into account in the secured transactions reform process so that each state may make a conscious and informed policy choice. To that end, he is critical of reform models like Article 9 that focus exclusively on consensual secured transactions, relegating considerations of the distributive consequences for unsecured creditors to other law. In his view, secured transactions reform projects should be comprehensive in scope, covering both consensual security and non-consensual preferences and security rights both within and outside the context of formal insolvency proceedings. This approach obligates a state to determine at the outset of the reform process the balance it wishes to draw between facilitating consensual secured lending and protecting non-adjusting and involuntary creditors and avoids the risk of inadvertently giving implicit precedence to the interests of consensual security-holders.

As an example of how a security regime that focuses exclusively on advancing the interests of consensual secured creditors may end up over-protecting their interests at the expense of unsecured creditors, Rod Macdonald points to Article 9's treatment of the proceeds of encumbered assets, an approach carried over in the ULGST. Subject to contrary agreement, an Article 9 security interest automatically extends to any new assets received "on account" of the encumbered assets, regardless of whether these proceeds replace the original collateral or constitute additional revenues and regardless of whether their value exceeds that of the collateral. This approach is based on the contestable assumption that secured creditors reasonably expect that their security will cover every conceivable asset that can be said to be derived from their collateral and should not have to set out that expectation expressly in their security agreement. But default contractual rules that expand the range of assets caught by a security right further diminish the scope of assets available to unsecured creditors. In view of this distributional impact, Rod Macdonald argues that the burden should be on the secured creditor to explicitly describe in its security agreement the types of non-replacement proceeds to which its security right is intended to extend.

Distributive Justice among Secured Creditors

Expanding the collateral base available to secured creditors enables them to take an effective security right not just in the specific assets of a debtor but also in generic categories of assets and indeed in the entirety of a debtor's movable assets, present and future. This increases the likelihood that secured creditors will come into competition with each other. Traditionally, competitions are resolved according to the simple justice of temporal priority: the first-in-time creditor wins, provided it takes the necessary steps to make its security right effective against third parties. Typically, this requires dispossession of the grantor (possible only for tangible assets currently owned by the grantor) or public registration for non-possessory security rights.

In view of the ease with which security rights in generic categories of present and after acquired movables may be obtained, modern secured transactions regimes invariably have found it necessary to recognize exceptions to temporal priority in order to facilitate other business practices and policy objectives. In the interests of ensuring transaction finality in the market, for example, secured creditors and transferees who take physical possession of negotiable instruments, negotiable documents of title, and certificated securities are generally accorded a super-priority over even prior registered security rights.

Perhaps the most predominant exception to temporal priority is the special status accorded to creditors who finance the debtor's acquisition of new assets over prior secured creditors holding security over after acquired assets of the debtor of the same kind. The roots of this special priority lie in the practice of vendors to retain title to goods sold on credit pending payment of the full purchase price. The reservation of title protects the vendor by ensuring that any security rights granted by the debtor to other creditors never attaches to the goods.

As Rod Macdonald explains, while the principal controversy surrounding acquisition financing is conceptual and doctrinal, these apparently formalistic concerns can lead to different distributive outcomes. Functionalist regimes like Article 9 characterize a reservation of title by a vendor or financing lessor as giving rise to a security right for the purposes of secured transactions law and accord it a super-priority against competing secured creditors, including prior secured creditors. Consistent with functionalist logic, the same super-priority status is extended to lenders who finance the debtor's acquisition of assets from a third-party vendor. Other regimes find it difficult to displace fundamental property law distinctions between owning and owing and exclude reservations of title from the concept of security. In some of these regimes, similar functional outcomes are achieved by subjecting the vendor or financing lessor to the same creation, public registration, and enforcement rules that apply to a secured creditor and by recognizing within the secured transactions regime a special-priority security right in favour of lenders who finance the acquisition of assets. In other states, the rights of vendors and financing lessors are governed according to the strict logic of ownership, with the result that they may not be required to publicize notice of their reservation of title and their enforcement rights on default may be less constrained than those of secured creditors. In these traditionalist regimes, no special priority is recognized in favour of lenders who finance a debtor's acquisition of assets.

A more recent exception to temporal priority relates to security rights in financial collateral in the form of deposit accounts and securities credited to a securities account (intermediated securities). Article 9 and derivative regimes give super-priority to a secured creditor who has obtained "control" of these forms of collateral as against prior registered secured creditors, including secured creditors who finance the debtor's acquisition of inventory and assert a claim to money deposited to a bank account as proceeds of inventory.

Control is not a unitary concept, nor are secured creditors who have all obtained control ranked equally. If the secured creditor is an external lender, control may be obtained by entering into a control agreement under which the bank or intermediary agrees to comply with instructions originated by the secured creditor directing disposition of the funds or securities credited to the deposit account or securities account without further consent by the debtor. Alternatively, the secured creditor can obtain control by becoming the bank's customer or by having the intermediated securities credited to its own account. If the secured creditor is the depository institution or securities intermediary with whom the bank account or securities account is maintained, control vests automatically, and the bank or intermediary has super-priority even over other secured creditors who have obtained control (other than one who obtained control by becoming the bank's customer or having the securities credited to its account).

The special control regime for financial collateral represents a significant departure not just from temporal priority but also from the general publicity principle underpinning secured transactions law. Control does not "publicize" the existence of the security right to third parties in the same manner as the usual mechanisms for obtaining third-party effectiveness – public registration or physical dispossession of tangible assets. The bank or intermediary is not required to confirm the existence of a control agreement entered into with a secured creditor of the debtor or of a security right granted in its own favour.

As Rod Macdonald observes, a control regime, with its secret third-party effectiveness consequences and trump priority status for banks and securities intermediaries, raises policy concerns with respect to the transparency and efficiency of secured transactions and fair competition between secured creditors that are banks or intermediaries and the debtor's external secured credit suppliers. These concerns are presumably thought to be outweighed by the perceived benefits to the financial actors and financial elites in jurisdictions like the United States, whose economy has increasingly undergone "financialization" since the 1970s and where financial markets accordingly dominate over the traditional industrial and agricultural economics. In view of the global reach of the activities of financial actors situated in states with financialized economies, there is increasing transnational pressure on other states to adopt a like regime, and the ULGST indeed recommends this approach for deposit accounts. Rod Macdonald's insistence on the need for secured transactions reforms to be adapted to local social and economic conditions tells us that states where the industrial and agricultural markets still dominate may well choose a different distributional outcome.

Conclusion

Rod Macdonald's scholarship in the field of secured transactions offers a rich narrative of the multiplicity of local factors and interests that may produce different models of secured transactions law in general, and of distributive justice in particular, despite the best efforts of global norm entrepreneurs to promote uniform solutions. Of equal interest is his exposition of the dynamic nature of secured transactions law over time.

Article 9 was born in the mid–twentieth century, and the original iteration, with its emphasis on the facilitation of financing against assets such as inventory, receivables, and equipment, reflected the dominance of the industrial economy in the United States at that time. Article 9 has since undergone multiple iterations, with the most recent version reflecting the increasing dominance of the financial sector in the United States economy. More generally, from a regime based on general functionalist principles and organized around a mandatory public registration system for non-possessory security rights, Article 9 has become increasingly differentiated and complex, with specialized rules for special interest groups. That transformation over time bears strong witness to Rod Macdonald's insistence on recognizing the impact of the local context on the shape of secured transactions law and the consequent inevitability of pluralism in the regimes adopted by different states.

Whatever their policy differences on particular issues, however, one common thread runs through all modern secured transactions reform proposals at both the national and international levels: this is the expansion of the movable assets that may be made the object of a security right in favour of a consensual creditor to encompass virtually the entire potential insolvency estate of the debtor. In light of the distributional consequences of this expansion for unsecured creditors, it is appropriate to conclude with the following cautionary words from Rod Macdonald: "What is clear, however, is that if states do not wish to see national priorities in relation to non-adjusting and involuntary creditors to whom they wish to afford non-consensual security or a bankruptcy carve-out sacrificed on the altar of excessive creditor preferences imposed by organized economic interests under a principle of party autonomy, they will have to act. A failure of state-specific legislation will not make the desire for transnational reform of the law of proprietary security rights disappear."[8]

NOTES

1 Lynn M. LoPucki, "The Unsecured Creditor's Bargain," *Virginia Law Review* 80 (1994): 1,899.

2 Roderick Macdonald, "Article 9 Norm Entrepreneurship," *Canadian Business Law Journal* 43 (2006): 240–91.

3 Professor Macdonald's contributions to these initiatives are documented in his extensive curriculum vitae, available at http://www.mcgill.ca/law/about/memoriam/macdonald-roderick.

4 Available at http://www.uncitral.org/uncitral/en/uncitral_texts/security/Guide_securedtrans.html.

5 Macdonald, "Three Metaphors of Norm Migration in International Context," *Brooklyn Journal of International Law* 34 (2009): 652, citing in n. 135 the definition of *phronesis* in the *Stanford Encyclopedia of Philosophy Online*, "Virtue Ethics," http://plato.stanford.edu/entries/ethics-virtue.

6 Macdonald, "Three Metaphors of Norm Migration in International Context," *Brooklyn Journal of International Law* 34 (2009): 603–53.

7 For a discussion of the debate and citations to some of the literature, see Macdonald, "Transnational Secured Transactions Reform: Book IX of the Draft Common Frame of Reference in Perspective," *Zeitschrift fur Europaisches Privatrecht* (2009): 746–7.

8 Ibid., 782.

13

Law Reform and Distributive Justice: The Secured Transactions Scholarship of Rod Macdonald

JOHN D. MCCAMUS

INTRODUCTION

One of the most striking features of the legal scholarship of Rod Macdonald is its volume. The outpouring of books, law review articles, book chapters, law reform studies, and government reports he produced over the years of his academic career borders on the torrential. Even more impressive, however, is the range of subject matter subjected to his penetrating analysis. Very few scholars are able to combine detailed study and analysis of both public law and private law subjects and, further, to bring to bear on such a broad range of subjects a similarly broad range of theoretical perspectives. Depth of analysis is never sacrificed by Macdonald for breadth of coverage. His numerous articles on aspects of the law of secured transactions bear these attributes.

In his secured transactions scholarship, Macdonald demonstrates an enormous mastery of the details of personal property security law and an ability to illuminate its mysteries with a sweeping command of theoretical work. Macdonald was a legal scholar's legal scholar. Also on display in his work is his deep interest in and, indeed, affection for the civil law of Quebec. Sadly, however, what would no doubt have been a crowning achievement of his work in this field – a treatise on the secured transactions law of the Province of Quebec – remained unfinished at the time of his passing. Whether other hands will be able to complete this massive manuscript remains to be seen. A reading of his published work in this field, however, suggests not only the momentous achievement no doubt contained in the manuscript but the vast scale of the task in store for any who might be willing to tackle its completion.

Macdonald's work in the secured transactions field began when he was steeped in the common law and teaching in a common law university faculty. He was entirely familiar with the common law background that preceded modern secured transactions legislation and with the remarkable statutory reform of secured transactions law achieved in the United States through the medium of Article 9 of the Uniform Commercial Code (UCC). With his additional training in civil law, however, and his move to the McGill Faculty of Law, he began to focus his attention on the civilian law of secured transactions and, at the same time, the possibilities for importing into a civilian system the basic tenets and approaches of Article 9. The articles I have had the opportunity to review strongly suggest that Macdonald's thinking on these latter topics evolved over time, as I shall try to indicate.

Unsurprisingly, Macdonald's strengths as a secured transactions scholar in both common law and civil law enabled him to play a prominent role in attempts to reform the secured transactions law of Quebec and, in turn, of the law of Ukraine. In due course, Rod was appointed a member of the Canadian delegation to the UNCITRAL Working Group VI, Secured Transactions. In his secured transactions scholarship, Macdonald became an important voice and resource in international efforts to reform secured transactions law. Collectively, the papers I have had the pleasure of either rereading or reading for the first time for the purpose of this symposium distill the wisdom Macdonald gleaned from these various experiences with respect to such questions as the feasibility of exporting the Article 9 model to other jurisdictions, especially civilian jurisdictions, the essential elements of secured transactions regimes, the prospects for harmonizing such regimes across different legal cultures, and, further, the role of international initiatives in facilitating or encouraging reform of secured transactions law in particular national jurisdictions. Macdonald's papers reveal the work of a comparative law scholar at the height of his powers and a commercial law scholar of extraordinary talent.

In the present context, little would be served by attempting to summarize Macdonald's work in this field. The reader would be better served by consulting the original papers themselves. What I will attempt, however, is to identify the strengths of Macdonald's secured transactions scholarship that characterize his work and, in my view, distinguish it from other work in this field. Participants in this symposium have also been invited to indicate the manner in which some of Macdonald's ideas play out in their own research, and I will attempt to accomplish that in the final sections of this brief comment.

Penetrating Analysis of Foundational Ideas

Macdonald's private law scholarship reveals a remarkable ability to articulate and conceptualize an analytical framework for developing an in-depth understanding of the material or problem set under examination.[1] This capacity is very much in evidence in his work on secured transactions, as is his ability to articulate the fundamental considerations of public policy underlying complex bodies of legal doctrine. If asked to identify foundational considerations with respect to design of personal property security legislation, I suspect that most of us would reach for core issues manifest in the drafting of Article 9 – the need to devise a scheme that would embrace the various methods used by creditors to secure debt obligations through title arrangements and hence the need for a broad and subtle definition of the central concept of a "security interest," the need to develop a coherent and clear priority scheme that will meet with broad acceptance as to its fairness within the commercial world, the need to facilitate the acquisition of new assets by a debtor, and so on. For Macdonald, it appears that such ideas would be considered superstructure rather than basic structural foundations. Thus, in a paper prepared for his UNCITRAL colleagues,[2] Macdonald locates personal property security interests within the larger framework of security rights and provides a set of core ideas or principles underlying the secured transactions field. Macdonald identifies seven core principles and, in each case, a set of corollaries. It is not possible to do justice to this analysis in the present context. Nonetheless, it is possible to at least create an impression of the richness of Macdonald's analysis by providing an illustrative sample. The first and most basic principle together with its corollaries is as follows.

Principle One: Coherence with Public Policy and Legal Tradition

A regime of security on property is an adjunct to the regime of debtor–creditor relationships and should provide balance between the legitimate public policy goals of states as they are reflected in the regulation of basic concepts of status, property, and obligations and the principle of freedom of contract.

Corollaries:

1 *No impressment of physical persons.* A regime of security on property implies the affectation of property to ensuring the enforcement of obligations. It should not tolerate either direct enforcement against people – whether through slavery, debtor's prison, or the impressment of future and unearned wages – or indirect enforcement against persons through legislative provisions making the failure to pay a debt a criminal offence.
2 *Promotion of freedom of contract where possible.* A regime of freedom of contract, like a regime of private property, is a political choice that states make in order to achieve various distributional goals. Consequently, while freedom of contract should underpin this subset of the law of security on property, it must be well integrated into the overall logic of debtor–creditor relationships adopted by particular states.
3 *Regulating wealth redistribution.* A regime of security on property is necessarily wealth redistributing. Consequently, states should be entitled to establish the conditions under which different forms of wealth transfers as between classes of creditors (for example, secured, privileged, and unsecured) should be permitted.
4 *Not a stand-alone field of legal regulation.* The foundational logic of a regime of security on property should be consistent with other basic principles of debtor–creditor law in a given jurisdiction – notions of status, property, contract, civil liability, civil procedure, exemptions from seizure, execution, or judgments, and execution priorities.
5 *Integration with insolvency and bankruptcy regulation.* A regime of security on property should be cast so that it can be efficiently integrated into cognate legal regimes such as banking, negotiable instruments, interest regulation, and, especially, insolvency and bankruptcy regulation.

The remaining six principles identify various means of achieving "efficiency" in the design of the regime through comprehensiveness and functional analysis, by promoting party autonomy, through intelligible rules and internal coherence, and by maximizing realization value. Again, by way of illustration, the third principle reads as follows:

Principle Three: Efficiency through Functional Analysis

In principle, the same regime of capacity to grant security, eligible collateral, pre-default rights and obligations, secured creditors' recourses, and general theory of publicity of secured rights should apply regardless of the origin or form of the security right.

Corollaries:

1 *Overcoming acrobatic techniques to retain or transfer title.* Creditors who seek to use conditional rights of property and other devices such as trusts, leases, and consignments to achieve a security right should be subject to the same regime.
2 *Overcoming legislative subversion of the regime.* Except where a compelling public policy rationale can be advanced for differential treatment, the mechanisms of non-consensual security regimes should track those of consensual security.
3 *Preventing strategic choice of publicity regimes.* While publicity may be achieved in diverse ways – for example, possession or registration – and while the registries may be designed to be searchable in different ways – for example, by identifying the collateral or identifying the debtor – the *inter partes* and third-party effects of publicity should be the same regardless of the mechanics of the publicity regime.

There are a number of striking features of this analysis and the explanations that accompany each of the corollaries. While many observers engaging in such an exercise would similarly place considerable emphasis on the desirability of creating a regime that provides incentives for efficient conduct of various kinds, Macdonald, perhaps uniquely, places considerable emphasis on the redistributive nature of secured transactions regimes. Second, by locating secured transactions regimes within a broader context of political and legal regimes, Macdonald usefully emphasizes the historical contingency, as to time and place, of the particular implementation of these ideas contained in Article 9. Finally, the entire document could serve as an illuminating set of instructions for those who would tackle the challenging task of devising regimes of this kind. The instructions obviously are lessons learned as a result of Macdonald's personal involvement in such exercises in Quebec and Ukraine. Principle Three, usefully and perceptively, identifies a number of hazards that the architects of such regimes should attempt to avoid.

Colourful Use of Language and Metaphor

Macdonald's article examining the secured transactions law reform in Quebec and Ukraine is titled, with characteristic flair, "Article 9 Norm Entrepreneurship."[3] There can be little doubt that the expression "norm entrepreneur" and its application to enthusiasts of Article 9 itself is Macdonald's invention, as is the cheeky title for part 2 of the article, "Have I Got a Law for You ..." In his paper "A Model Law on Secured Transactions: A Representation of Structure? An Object of Idealized Imitation? A Type, Template or Design?"[4] Macdonald considers whether UNCITRAL, having developed a legislative guide, a document cast in more general terms than one would find in a common law statute at least, identifying the basic precepts to be embodied in a personal property security legislation, should take on a further project of adopting a "model" law for enactment across the various represented jurisdictions. Macdonald's answer, for which he offers persuasive support in the article, is that a model law was neither desirable nor feasible and, further, that the timing for such an exercise was, in any event, not optimal. In the opening paragraph, Macdonald begins his analysis by rehearsing the three senses of the noun-adjective "model" drawn from the *Oxford English Dictionary* and reflected in the subtitle of the article and then attracts the reader's attention by asking the following three questions that, as he claims, "spring to mind whenever one enters onto the terrain of law reform through model laws."[5] In Macdonald's view, these questions are:

1 Should we understand model laws as we understand "model airplanes"?
2 Should we understand them as we understand runway performers at a fashion show?
3 Or should we understand them as we would understand an architect's or an engineer's template?

I confess, without embarrassment, that these questions did not immediately spring to my mind. Macdonald goes on to add that the "[p]olysemic character of the word is manifest in current critical discussions about the utility and desirability of transnational model laws."[6] What might seem to the reader a somewhat dry and technical subject has come alive. I doubt that many, if any, could read the first paragraph of Macdonald's paper and then put it aside. It is impossible to do so.

In the paper "Three Metaphors of Norm Migration in International Context,"[7] we note in passing, and with pleasure, the concept of "norm migration." Macdonald identifies three metaphors of harmonization, transplantation, and viral propagation as metaphors that can usefully explain in turn the personal property reform projects in Quebec, Ukraine, and UNCITRAL. The first two metaphors are easily understood by those interested in cross-jurisdictional law reform. The purport of the third as a metaphor is less obvious, but it refers to the unplanned and self-perpetuating influence of models such as Article 9 of the UCC. With respect to each metaphor, Macdonald asserts the counterintuitive thesis that we could learn more about the lessons of these metaphors for such law reform activities by examining in greater detail their operation in their original homes of music, botany, and genetics, respectively. Doing so, in Macdonald's view, would lead one to be more sceptical of the transcendent role some would advocate for a North American legal artefact like Article 9. The reader is then treated to an examination of the logic of harmonization in music – there being no such thing as perfect harmony – then of the logic of transplantation in botany and the measures of its success, and, finally, of the transmission of viruses to human organisms as the origin of the metaphor viral propagation. On the latter topic, we are invited to compare Article 9 to the common cold and the AIDS virus. The Macdonald view appears to be that the propagation of Article 9 comes closer to AIDS than to the common cold. The viral propagation metaphor is perhaps the most difficult to explain, but one might consider as a homespun illustration the Canadian pandemic of conversion of the LLB degree to the American JD degree that has spread like a virus across many common law programs, including my own.

In the case of each of the three metaphors, Macdonald charmingly and interestingly matches the affinities between the role of these concepts in their home disciplines and their metaphorical use to explain various models of law reform. One comes away from the piece with a deep distrust of transplantation and something close to disgust for viral transmission. Indeed, in Macdonald's treatment, the Article 9 "norm entrepreneurs" begin to appear as the Donald Rumsfelds of global law reform – invading foreign jurisdictions at will, displaying great disinterest in and insensitivity to local conditions, and with no apparent or obvious exit strategy. Macdonald's affection for the civil law tradition is reflected in his defence of the particularity of civil law against the Article 9 norm entrepreneurs on the basis that "there are no conceptual features of the civil law tradition preventing the enactment of a functionally integrated secured transactions regime that achieves the same goals as Article 9 and does so in an equally efficient manner."[8] Along the way, the reader has experienced the great pleasure of engaging with a witty and brilliant mind.

A Willingness to Reconsider and Abandon Previously Held Views

It takes a large intellect to question, re-evaluate, and ultimately abandon strongly held views and preconceptions. Macdonald had a large intellect. In these papers, we see him gradually move away from a view, albeit gently expressed, that the basic functional approach taken to personal property security legislation in Article 9 and in its Canadian progeny, the provincial PPSAs, rests on a sound analytical and policy footing and that Article 9 is worthy of emulation.[9] Macdonald seemed disappointed with the rejection of some aspects of the Article 9 model in the Quebec law reform experience. By the time we get to 2009, however, and the paper "Transnational Secured Transactions Reform: Book IX of the Draft Common Frame of Reference in Perspective,"[10] Macdonald has reconsidered the validity of what he has come to call the Secured Transactions Theorem (STT) underlying the Article 9 approach. Again, the point is made colourfully. Adherents of the theorem are characterized in religious terms for their faith in the untested hypotheses of the theorem and their failure to provide any justification for its distributive effects. As he states, after reflecting on his work in Quebec and Ukraine, "I began to reconsider some canons of the STT faith. However, it was not until my seven-year experience with the Canadian delegation to UNCITRAL's working group ... that my tendency to heresy turned into full-blown apostasy."[11]

A Deep Commitment to Law Reform

As a member of the Ontario Law Reform Commission in the early 1990s, I became aware of Rod Macdonald's passionate commitment to reform of the law. Our chair, The Honourable Rosalie Abella, had appointed Macdonald as a scholar-in-residence to the Ontario commission. The spirited commission discussions engaged in by two leading members of the bar, Margaret Ross and Earl Cherniak, and the late and very distinguished political scientist, Richard Simeon, were much enlivened by Macdonald's contributions. Although I harbour the thought that this experience may have contributed to Macdonald's thinking on the process of law reform, it is nonetheless true, I am sure, that he contributed much more than he received. These papers provide a chronicle, in effect, of Macdonald's contribution to law reform in the personal property security field. Macdonald devoted much of his considerable energy and talent to law reform initiatives of one sort or another. His contributions were both institutional – in particular, his brilliant leadership of the Law Commission of Canada – and, as these papers indicate, his contributions to law reform efforts in the personal property security field were very substantial. As we have come to expect, Macdonald's contributions were both institutional and scholarly as he contributed much of value to the literature concerning the reform of legal institutions.[12]

Lessons for Restitution

Turning, then, to the question of how Macdonald's ideas and thinking play out in the context of my own work in my first academic passion, the law of restitution, I will briefly draw three lessons or admonitions from Macdonald that are manifest in his work in the personal property security field and attempt to apply them to restitutionary issues. First, beware transplants. Second, beware untestable or untested theories. Third, do not ignore distributive justice in the context of private law theory. I should indicate clearly that I do not contend that Macdonald would necessarily agree with the points I am about to make.

Beware Transplants

One Canadian restitution scholar appears to have taken the view that in *Pettkus v Becker*[13] in 1980, the Supreme Court of Canada overruled all of the traditional (and vast) common law of restitution or unjust enrichment and replaced it with a single rule based on a civilian "absence of juristic reason" analysis.[14] Surprisingly, and presumably unintentionally (for we can be sure that J. Dickson, who wrote the Court's opinion in *Pettkus*, had no such idea in his contemplation), the Supreme Court anticipated by more than two decades the similar suggestion made by the late Oxford Professor Peter Birks in his final work[15] that the English law of restitution be replaced (indeed, he improbably claimed that it had been replaced) by a principle drawn from German civil law that recovery should be granted in any case where there is an "absence of basis" for the defendant's enrichment. No such radical change has occurred in English law, we may note in passing, nor am I aware of the identity of any

English jurist or academic other than Birks himself who favours such a notion. One Canadian scholar, an admirer of Birks, contends that in *Garland v. Consumers Gas Co.*[16] in 2004, the Supreme Court completed the revolution begun in *Pettkus* and set the existing common law of restitution aside for a civilian future. I have argued elsewhere[17] that such views neither accurately record the substance of Canadian Supreme Court jurisprudence on point nor offer a plausible way forward for common law restitutionary doctrine. Such scholars would do well to read Macdonald's discussion of the difficulties inherent in the transplantation of legal concepts from one system to another. As Robert Stevens observes in a critique of the Birks proposal: "Comparative law is a dangerous business. Comparison of narrow legal rules may be misleading unless done in context as apparent inconsistencies may be explicable by more fundamental structural differences. Harmonisation of individual rules may increase rather than remove the dissonance between different systems and runs the risk of creating incoherence within individual systems."[18]

I regret to say that this risk has become very real in recent Canadian jurisprudence in this field. Some provincial appellate and trial courts have been successfully tempted by counsel to simply ignore the existing doctrine and "make up the law from scratch"[19] by purporting to apply what they believe to be a civilian doctrine with which they have little or no familiarity. Although the results in such cases are typically satisfactory, the analysis offered to explain the result often borders on the bewildering.[20]

Beware the Untestable or Untested Theory

As is the case in these articles, Macdonald was always quick to challenge theories that are untestable in the sense that they do not purport to explain data and those that, though testable, have not been tested. Thus, in his work on secured transactions, Macdonald eventually comes to challenge the untested theories that underlie the Secured Transactions Theorem. More generally, in my view, theories of private law, including those pertaining to restitution, should be approached with Macdonald's sense of scepticism. An interesting illustration of such a theory in the law of restitution again comes from the work of Professor Birks. Birks advanced the theory that unjust enrichment claims in the disgorgement measure such as claims for profits secured through breach of fiduciary duty, breach of confidence, tortious wrongdoing, and breach of contract are "parasitic" in the sense that restitutionary liability in disgorgement is secondary to primary liability in some other branch or field of law.[21]

Thus, disgorgement for tort, for example, can be granted only if all of the elements of the relevant tort can be established by the plaintiff. The alleged "theory," however, is inconsistent with the history of the doctrine and rests simply on an assertion that this must be true. It simply does not apply to or offer a coherent explanation for disgorgement for breach of fiduciary obligation, an area of the law in which disgorgement was the primary remedy and so remains to this day. The "theory" rests on an untestable and simple assertion that the parasitic theory must be true. It offers no explanation or justification for its unstated and central assumption that the rules imposing disgorgement liability must be the same as the rules imposing liability for compensatory damages. With Macdonald's scepticism as my guide, my conclusion is that the "parasitic" theory is groundless.[22]

The Importance of Distributive Justice in Private Law Theory

As is well known, one prominent Canadian legal scholar has attempted to explain much, if not all, of the law of torts as grounded on the concept of corrective justice.[23] He has more recently attempted to explain the law of restitution for unjust enrichment on this basis.[24] We would do well, in my view, to follow Macdonald's lead in at least considering whether elements of distributive justice should not hold some explanatory power in the context of private law theorizing. Thus, in the context of law of restitution, one might think that corrective justice provides the most amenable explanation for the simple and central case of the recovery of the mistaken payment. If, however, one probes more deeply for an explanation as to why most or many people would feel that the recovery of mistakenly paid monies is a just result, one might run into concerns about distributive justice. Why, after all, do we instinctively wish to allow recovery of a mistakenly made payment? It appears that the law (and the citizenry) abhors the accidental loss of wealth. "Finders keepers, losers weepers" never had much appeal, even in the schoolyard. One possible explanation for this is that we abhor the accidental loss of wealth for the same reason that we favour the possibility of its acquisition – that is to say, for the reasons that support the institution of private property. That institution, I suggest, cannot be easily or simply justified on the basis of corrective justice. Although identification of the most convincing justification for the institution of private property is not without contention, the leading candidates rest on elements of distributive justice.[25] If this is correct, even in this paradigm case of what might be considered an illustration of corrective justice, it may be that distributive justice provides at least part of the explanation for the widespread instinct to allow recovery in mistaken payment cases.

Conclusion

The contribution made by Rod Macdonald to our understanding of the law of secured transactions and of the challenges inherent in "norm migration" between common law and civilian jurisdictions has been enormous. It is deeply saddening, of course, that we have been deprived of the further contributions that he would doubtlessly have made to legal scholarship in these and other areas of the law. Although Macdonald's work was imbued with legal theory, a central hallmark of his writing, from which I will continue to draw inspiration, was his confident scepticism toward and critical assessment of untested and untestable legal theory. This, and his frequent reminders of the distributive aspects of private law doctrine, will, I am confident, be enduring aspects of the legacy of his legal scholarship.

NOTES

1 For an illustration of this aspect of Macdonald's scholarship and, indeed, my first encounter with it, see Roderick Macdonald, *Prospects for Civil Justice* (Toronto: Ontario Law Reform Commission, 1995) – an examination of fundamental considerations underlying the reform of civil process.

2 Macdonald, "Core Principles for a Regime of Security on Property," UNCITRAL Working Group VI – Security Interests" (typescript, 2002), http://www.mcgill.ca/macdonald-symposium/texts.

3 Macdonald, "Article 9 Norm Entrepreneurship," *Canadian Business Law Journal* 43 (2006): 240–91.

4 Macdonald, "A Model Law on Secured Transactions: A Representation of Structure? An Object of Idealized Imitation? A Type, Template or Design?" *Uniform Law Review/Revue du droit uniforme* (2010): 419–46.

5 Ibid., 419.

6 Ibid., 419.

7 Macdonald, "Three Metaphors of Norm Migration in International Context," *Brooklyn Journal of International Law* 34 (2009): 603–53.

8 Ibid., 649.

9 In his paper "Article 9 Norm Entrepreneurship," Macdonald describes the development of an Article 9–type regime for Quebec in 1978, the failure of the government to move on this initiative at that time, and the later work of a working group that rejected the initial proposal largely on the basis, it seemed, of special pleading by stakeholder groups, including the notarial profession. Macdonald describes each of the proposals of the working group and indicates that he had dissented from all of them. See "Article 9 Norm Entrepreneurship," 246.

10 Macdonald, "Transnational Secured Transaction Reform: Book IX of the Draft Common Frame of Reference in Perspective," *Zeitschrift fur Europaisches Privatrecht* (2009): 745–82.

11 Ibid.

12 For his most recent contribution, see Macdonald, "Law Reform for Dummies (3rd Edition)," *Osgoode Hall Law Journal* 51 (2014): 859–88.

13 [1980] 2 S.C.R. 834.

14 M. McInnes, "A Return to First Principles in Unjust Enrichment: *Kerr v. Baranow*," *Canadian Business Law Journal* 51 (2011): 275–90.

15 P. Birks, *Unjust Enrichment*, 2nd edn (Oxford: Oxford University Press, 2004).

16 *Garland v. Consumers Gas Co.*, [2004] 1 S.C.R. 629. And see M. McInnes, "A Return to First Principles in Unjust Enrichment: *Kerr v. Baranow*," *Canadian Business Law Journal* 51 (2011): 275–90.

17 J.D. McCamus, "Unjust Enrichment, 'Existing Categories' and *Kerr v. Baranow*: A Reply to Professor McInnes," *Canadian Business Law Journal* 52 (2011–12): 390–415. And see generally P.D. Maddaugh and J.D. McCamus, *The Law of Restitution* (Toronto: Canada Law Book, 2014) ch. 2, 3.

18 R. Stevens, "Absence of Basis Accepted, Unjust Factors Rejected," *Restitution Law Review* 12 (2004): 270.

19 The dangers of which were pointed out by Lionel Smith. See L. Smith, "The Mystery of Juristic Reason," *Supreme Court Law Review* 12 (2000): 240. Although Professor Smith's article was referred to in *Garland*, its advice was unfortunately unheeded. See *Garland*, para. 42–5 per J. Iacobucci. At the same time, however, it is possible to interpret *Garland* and subsequent Supreme Court of Canada decisions as not intending an overruling of all existing law on restitutionary claims. See the works cited in note 17. See also Smith, "Demystifying Juristic Reasons," *Canadian Business Law Journal* 45 (2007): 281–304. And see now *Bhasin v. Hrynew*

[2014] S.C.C. 71 at paras 67–9 (confirming that the unjust enrichment principle has not replaced the existing and detailed common law rules of the Canadian law of restitution).

20 For a recent illustration, see *Nishi v. Rascal Trucking Ltd.* (2011), 340 D.L.R. (4th) 284 (B.C.C.A.). On appeal, the Supreme Court of Canada reversed and held that the existing and well-established doctrine should be applied rather than the absence of juristic reason test. See [2013] 2 S.C.R. 438.

21 Birks, *An Introduction to the Law of Restitution* (Oxford: Oxford University Press, 1985), 328–32; Birks, *Unjust Enrichment*, 11–16.

22 For a more extended attack on the parasitic theory, see J.D. McCamus, "Waiver of Tort: Is There a Limiting Principle?" *Canadian Business Law Journal* 55 (2014): 356–60. See also D. Friedmann, "Restitution of Benefits Obtained through the Appropriation of Property or the Commission of a Wrong," *Columbia Law Review* 80 (1980): 504–8; J. Beatson, "The Nature of Waiver of Tort," in *The Use and Abuse of Unjust Enrichment*, edited by J. Beatson (Oxford: Clarendon, 1991), ch. 8.

23 E.J. Weinrib, *The Idea of Private Law* (Cambridge, MA: Harvard University Press, 1995).

24 Weinrib, "Restitutionary Damages as Corrective Justice," *Theoretical Inquiries in Law* 1 (2000): 1–38; Weinrib, *Corrective Justice* (Oxford: Oxford University Press, 2012).

25 Perhaps the most interesting symposium on the institution of private property remains J.R. Pennock and J.W. Chapman, eds, *Property: Nomos XXII* (New York: New York University Press, 1980).

14

Secured Transactions in Modern Times

MICHAEL BRIDGE

My theme for these proceedings is the law of secured transactions. As everybody knows, this has a close proximity to the subject of distributive justice, a subject that played a most prominent part in Rod Macdonald's academic journey. The themes I want to dwell upon on particularly are two. The first is the modernization of personal property security law. The second is what we might call fairness, which is perhaps just distributive justice under another name. I must acknowledge here my own particular debt to Rod Macdonald: it was through him that I became familiar with Lon Fuller's work on the subject.

Modernization

It is reasonably well known, I believe, that there has been an historical antipathy to non-possessory security. In the common law, for example, ownership is defined in the language of possessory entitlement.[1] The absence of credit and the existence of sumptuary laws resulted in equating the possession of things with their ownership. Hence, someone in possession of a thing who had alienated it, or had purported to grant a security right over it, displayed a false badge of wealth calculated to mislead those dealing with him. And the creditor or owner who permitted this display of false wealth was also complicit in the deception. The distrust of non-possessory security dates clearly and demonstrably from the sixteenth century.[2] It is fair to say that that hostility disappeared from common law systems and thinking rather more quickly than it did from the civil law. When the Northampton bootmaker, Mr Saloman, incorporated himself as a one-man company, which then granted him in his private capacity a debenture secured by a floating charge, the charge was effective.[3] This episode gave rise to the requirement that floating charges and certain other charges be registered in order to be opposable to third parties. The civil law was driven to treat the non-possessory pledge as a kind of deemed possessory device by fictitious means, and I think that evidences to a degree a certain uneasiness with non-possessory security that remains even to this day. Depending on the jurisdiction, pledges are more or less effective and extensive. Registration systems exist, often in plural and therefore less accessible forms, in numerous jurisdictions. Germany has survived without seeing any need to register.[4] In a closed system where the major players know each other and know what is going on, there is no need to open a window to the world.

My next point concerns the conviction that easy access to secured credit is beneficial to the development of commerce and thus to all concerned. We come now to the historic debate between trade creditors and banks. The bank says, "if we did not finance the business, you would not have access to this particular customer," and the trade creditor responds by saying, "our supply of trade credit to the customer is what keeps the business going and therefore able to pay down the debt that you have advanced to the customer." Well, in a chicken-and-egg argument, it is good to recall Samuel Butler's insight that a hen is only an egg's way of making another egg. I incline myself to the view that finance is needed to start the business rolling and that ultimately, easy secured credit does serve a critical purpose of building up business momentum. That does not mean that the bank should necessarily always and fully prevail. Article 9 of the Uniform Commercial Code (UCC) cannot be disregarded of course in any account given to modernization, and one can say that it resolves the debate or the discussion in terms of notions of transparency and rationality: transparency in the sense that secured credit, if not seen to be a matter of possession, should nevertheless be a matter of public record; rationality in terms of the obliteration of outmoded legalistic distinctions, notably that between retention title and security properly so called in the form of a charge or a similar type of security device. By facilitating once and for all security interests that extend to future assets and future supplies of credit, the trade supplier is accommodated and, with the super-priority of a purchase money financier accorded to the trade supplier,[5] a balance is attempted between the short-term credit interests of trade suppliers and the longer-term interest of financing banks.

Now, the Article 9 resolution of the matter is very much in terms of functionalism. If something looks like security, then it is security. Put differently, do not tell me what it is called, tell me what it does. But there is a certain reductive aspect to this. It results in a type of over-inclusion: the functional lens allows just about everything being seen as serving the purpose of security.[6] Consequently, it becomes difficult to know where to draw the line between what should be regulated as security and what ought not to be. You might say that functionalism, if carried to an excessive degree, imparts a type of new religiosity. I have certainly seen in the ranks of Article 9 advocates some degree of firm conviction that one must subscribe to the *ipsissima verba* of Article 9 in whatever manifestation it currently is in order to be a true advocate of modernized secured credit. I do not agree with that. In fact, I note the growing conviction that a differentiation can properly be drawn between title-based schemes and security in the narrow sense, and yet the acceptance of both forms still serves the cause of transparency and rationality.

This is evident in such instruments as the Convention on International Interests in Mobile Equipment (known as the Cape Town Convention)[7] and also the UNCITRAL Legislative Guide on Secured Transactions (which owes a great deal to Rod Macdonald's substantial involvement over a number of years).[8] The cause of freedom of contract can be served by permitting financiers and their contractual counterparties to structure their transactions either as secured credit or as title reservation. A modern system of secured transactions does not mandate, at least, the removal of freedom of contract in this area. It may do so where there is a non-assignment clause in a contract giving birth to a receivable. The conflict here between freedom of contract and the free circulation of assets is irreconcilable. I think we can thank Rod Macdonald, perhaps more than most people, perhaps more than anybody, for his firm view and belief that this distinction between title reservation and security properly so called can still be retained within a modernized personal property security regime.

Article 9 thinking nevertheless retains its utility within bounds, especially in cross-border initiatives, because it is a very powerful type of intellectual device for cutting through domestic historical legal dogma and opening up the field for international collaboration. Its influence, for example, is evident in the Draft Common Frame of Reference in Europe,[9] which has yet to come to practical fruition. Having said all of that, one has to note that developments in financial markets pose a very significant threat to transparency. I have in mind, from the perspective of a European, the EU Financial Collateral Directive,[10] along with the various national measures that have transposed it into national law and the various exemptions from filing and formal requirements, as well as the dispensation from compliance with fundamental insolvency rules, that are given where collateral is in the possession, or under the control, of the secured creditor. I find it rather difficult myself to see control as a form of true transparency or publicity. It seems to me very much an exemption from having to conform to such standards, but that is not something that the Article 9 community is likely to accept.

Fairness

In turning from modernization to fairness, let me start with the classic English case law approach, which regards security and reservation of title as a simple matter of contract. In the latter case, the parties to a contract of sale, for example, are free to determine when the property in goods, once identified to the contract, passes. There is no dogmatic rule that it must pass at the contract date or must pass on delivery.[11] That contractual intention, however, must fit the commercial steps the parties take and the commercial reality of their situation. This is why extended reservation of title clauses reaching out to new goods manufactured by the buyer, and to the proceeds of resale in the buyer's hands, routinely fail as reservation of title and are thus re-characterized as security. In fact, the whole law of English secured transactions is an extension of the notion of contract. Equity looks on that as done that ought to be done: a contract to give security is as good as security. And constantly we see – this is still present in English law – freedom of contract as the paramount consideration in the creation of security, which involves the denial of more or less any role for public policy and the belief that the unsecured creditors can be put to one side notwithstanding the principle of distribution so that secured creditor and debtor can work out their arrangements without any need to concern themselves with that third-party constituency.[12] To the extent that the bargain of creditor and debtor can be imposed upon from the outside, it has to be done in the form of legislation. Outside statute, to the extent that no such intervention takes place and creditor and debtor are free to strike their own bargain, this amounts to, in a bilateral world with case law and litigation, the disregard of distributive justice considerations.

How, then, do we achieve fairness by legislation? You might say that fairness can arise by accident if you make it difficult to attain secured credit by putting up roadblocks and chicanes and limiting particular types of security device to particular cases, like the special Italian security over Parma ham. Another obstacle is the notion of over-security, which strikes down a pledge or other security to the extent that the collateral taken exceeds the value of the debt it secures. The empirical reality is that secured creditors rarely recover the full amount owed. This type of philosophy is not a particularly satisfactory way of proceeding. An alternative approach, and this is the approach adopted in England, is to make it easy to take security but then to top-slice the security. Hence, legislative changes in England have created out of floating charge assets a fund in favour of unsecured creditors.[13] Moreover, the very powerful instrument of administrative receivership has been converted by and large into out-of-court administration and a directive imposed upon administrators, prior to distributing to secured creditors, to take into account the interests of both secured and unsecured creditors. I am not sure that outcomes are particularly different from cases formerly dealt with as administrative receivership, where the receiver was the agent of the distressed debtor but the servant of the creditor. It could be said that the legislative approach directing the cascading functions that an administrator must perform – first, salvaging the company, then, if this is not possible, striving for an outcome that takes account of the interests of all creditors before finally making a distribution[14] – is not a great deal more than a box-ticking exercise. And when we come to assessing the degree of fairness thus imparted into the system, we do have to wonder how we quantify the necessary degree of fairness. Can we do it in raw percentage terms, as a legislative instrument might direct, or is the achievement of distributive justice something that is altogether more nuanced and to be assessed only on a case-by-case basis? Well, it is very difficult to measure that kind of judicial discretion with legislative lawmaking. It is well known that many years ago now the Crowther Committee in England[15] thought that the needs of unsecured creditors could be satisfied by putting aside a 10 per cent margin. Questions have been raised about how this was arrived at and whether it was as the result of some profound discussion. This was not the case: it was a back-of-the-envelope calculation, as Roy Goode himself has recounted on numerous occasions. So I certainly support the need for distributive justice, but I am not quite sure how we get there and whether we have the right instruments to achieve it.

NOTES

1 Frederick Pollock and Robert Samuel Wright, *An Essay on Possession in the Common Law* (Oxford: Clarendon, 1888).

2 In England, see *Twyne's Case* (1601) 3 Co Rep 80b, 76 ER 809.

3 *Saloman v. A. Saloman & Co. Ltd* [1897] AC 22.

4 For useful guides to German, French, and other leading civil law systems, see H.C. Sigman and E.-M. Kieninger, eds, *Cross-Border Security over Tangibles* (Munich: Sellier, 2007) and *Cross-Border Security over Intangibles* (Munich: Sellier, 2009).

5 Uniform Commercial Code, Article 9-103, 9-324.

6 On the Daintree River in Queensland, I was once promised by the guide a sure sighting of a crocodile through binoculars. A crocodile had been painted on one of the lenses.

7 Convention on International Interests in Mobile Equipment 2001, sponsored by Unidroit.

8 UNCINTRAL Legislative Guide on Secured Transactions 2010.

9 *Principles, Definitions and Model Rules of European Private Law: Draft Common Frame of Reference (DCFR)* (2009), http://ec.europa.eu/justice/policies/civil/docs/dcfr_outline_edition_en.pdf.

10 Directive 2002/47/EC of the European Parliament and of the Council of 6 June 2002 on financial collateral arrangements.

11 Sale of Goods Act 1979, ss 179.

12 The best example is *Welsh Development Agency v. Export Finance Co. Ltd* [1991] BCLC 936.

13 Insolvency Act 1986 (as amended), s 176A.

14 Insolvency Act 1986 (as amended), Schedule B1 para 3.

15 Report on Consumer Credit 1971 (Cmnd 4596).

15

Un Guide pour les guides : où il sera question d'un chat, de lapins en chocolat, de dry martinis, et d'une Chevrolet…

JEAN-FRANÇOIS RIFFARD

Suivez ce chat !

C'est un chat.

Un drôle de chat. Comment s'appelle-t-il ? À quoi ressemble-t-il ? Nul ne le sait et ne le saura jamais. Est-ce d'ailleurs un chat ? J'en doute aujourd'hui. J'aurai dû m'en assurer avant de le suivre. L'intitulé de l'article – très étrange – que je proposai de lire m'y incitait pourtant fortement : il faut toujours s'assurer que l'on peut appeler un chat un chat ![1] Je ne tins pas compte de l'avertissement et décidai de le suivre en pénétrant dans les arcanes de cet écrit. Mais, peu à peu, ce chat se transforma en un lapin, et tandis que je le suivais, tout comme Alice, sans que je ne puisse jamais le rattraper, il me fit traverser le miroir. Au fur et à mesure de ma lecture, je découvris les secrets et délices de l'approche téléologique des sûretés. Mais l'étrange « cha-pin » poursuivit sa course et m'invita alors à pénétrer plus profondément encore dans son monde et à me confronter à la vision du Droit de celui que je ne connaissais pas encore : Rod Macdonald.

Encore des lapins (en plus en chocolat) !

Et c'est un monde à part, mais fascinant que je découvris alors. On a déjà insisté, et bien mieux que je ne pourrai jamais le faire, sur l'interdisciplinarité de Rod Macdonald et sur son attachement à replacer sans cesse le droit dans son contexte, ce qui fait de lui un des rares juristes humanistes au sens classique du terme. Vision salvatrice s'il en est, notamment pour les juristes privatistes français, qu'un collègue québécois avait pu un jour qualifier de « plombiers du droit » – le Québécois est taquin ! – soulignant ainsi une certaine propension à ne se satisfaire que de l'étude du droit positif et de la règle dans sa seule expression normative. Certes, la maîtrise de la technique et la connaissance des règles sont des prérequis indispensables. Mais Rod Macdonald nous a toujours invités à percer cette surface et à appréhender ce qu'il est convenu d'appeler, depuis R. Sacco, la dimension muette du droit.[2]

Cette approche, qui va plus loin que la simple transversalité des seules matières juridiques, a conduit ainsi nombre d'enseignants à revoir non seulement leur façon d'appréhender et de penser le droit, mais aussi, et surtout, de l'enseigner. En ce sens, il est possible d'affirmer que Rod Macdonald fut et restera un Guide pour les guides, un Guide pour ceux qui, comme lui, ont la lourde, mais passionnante tâche non seulement d'enseigner le droit, mais de le faire comprendre et aimer. Je fus conforté dans cette voie à suivre lorsque, toujours déambulant dans le monde de Rod, je rencontrai en 2010 un autre lapin, en chocolat celui-là ! Qui d'autre que lui, en effet, pouvait nous inviter à réfléchir sur l'architecture du droit à travers quelques interventions aux titres pour le moins déroutants tels que « La journée du droit des lapins en chocolat », « Hockey balle dans la ruelle », ou « C'est pas juste il m'a frappé le premier ! »[3] Certes, il s'agissait pour l'auteur de souligner à travers ces exemples la dimension normative du quotidien, permettant ainsi à tous, juristes ou non-juristes, de saisir et de comprendre à travers divers petits exemples tirés de la vie quotidienne les enjeux du droit. Mais ce faisant, il invitait surtout chacun d'entre nous à toujours penser de manière concrète, exercice salvateur s'il en est. D'ailleurs, sa technique a été reprise voire institutionnalisée dans au moins une école de droit en France, où l'habitude a été prise d'inciter les thésards à faire ce qu'il est désormais convenu d'appeler une présentation à la « Rod Macdonald », lors de laquelle ils vont exposer en quelques minutes aux étudiants de licence ou de master leur thème de recherche à partir d'un cas concret et sous une forme ludique. L'engouement a été immédiat.

À côté de cette inestimable contribution à la science de l'éducation du Droit, il est un autre aspect de l'œuvre de Rod Macdonald sur lequel je souhaiterais m'attarder quelques instants. Il s'agit de son apport au droit comparé et plus exactement à la recherche comparative.

Suivez le Guide… mais appliquez le bien!

Parmi tous ses écrits, il en est un qui à mon sens témoigne le mieux de son sens aigu des problématiques posées en la matière, et ce même si cet écrit est demeuré à ce jour méconnu, car non publié. Cette œuvre est un travail que Rod Macdonald fit circuler en 2004 dans le cadre de la négociation au sein de la Commission des Nations Unis pour le Droit Commercial International (CNUDCI) et qui allait devenir le Guide législatif sur les opérations garanties. Avec ce projet intitulé « Considerations Relating to a Possible Chapter on Implementation », il s'agissait pour lui de souligner la nécessité de prévoir un chapitre sur « la mise en œuvre du Guide ». Un mode d'emploi du futur Guide, en somme.

Pour comprendre l'apport de ce guide pour le Guide, il convient de le replacer dans son contexte. Depuis 2002, la CNUDCI s'était attelée à la rédaction d'un projet ambitieux, à savoir la rédaction d'un Guide législatif destiné à favoriser l'harmonisation du droit des sûretés réelles mobilières. Fidèle à la démarche fonctionnelle qui est la sienne depuis de nombreuses années, la CNUDCI a entendu proposer, à travers ce Guide et surtout les recommandations qui y sont contenues, un système complet, idéal et efficace de sûreté. Cette approche reposait sur le postulat que le droit des sûretés est un droit parfaitement unifiable,[4] à l'instar du droit commercial en général, puisque politiquement et socialement neutre. Il serait donc possible, à travers une simple approche pragmatique et fonctionnelle, de déterminer des règles objectives pouvant, quel que soit le contexte étatique, produire les effets les plus efficaces.

Très rapidement, Rod Macdonald mit en garde le Groupe de travail sur le caractère illusoire d'une telle vision. Quand bien même le Guide serait sur le plan substantiel parfait, il serait malhonnête sur le plan intellectuel de laisser croire aux législateurs que ce Guide puisse se suffire à lui seul. La transformation de ses recommandations, pourtant rédigées en des termes quasi législatifs, en une loi donnée nécessite un travail d'adaptation et de réflexion important. C'est sur cet aspect fondamental, mais pourtant négligé jusqu'alors que Rod a souhaité apporter, à la lumière de son expérience, un éclairage nouveau.

« Mieux vaut une Chevrolet qui roule qu'une Cadillac au garage! »

Vouloir créer un modèle parfait de droit des sûretés réelles mobilières, c'est bien; mettre en œuvre un régime qui fonctionne dans un contexte particulier, c'est mieux. Telle est la philosophie suivie par Rod Macdonald à travers son allusion imagée à la Chevrolet. Pour ce faire, il dégage trois thèmes fondamentaux : le préalable, le moyen et le suivi.

Le préalable : le receveur est-il compatible ?

Le phénomène d'emprunt législatif est un phénomène bien connu et il est commun d'utiliser pour le décrire la métaphore de la transplantation d'organes ou de plantes.[5] Afin d'éviter tout phénomène de rejet, il convient de suivre certaines précautions, lesquelles ont été synthétisées par le dédicataire de ces lignes en dix leçons – dix commandements devrions-nous dire – elles-mêmes regroupées autour de quatre axes : économique, juridique, social, et politique.

S'il est évident que les législateurs devront, dans leur travail de transposition du Guide, tenir compte du contexte économique (Leçon 1), et notamment des modes de distribution du crédit, ils devront surtout veiller à assurer une certaine compatibilité juridique entre le nouveau régime transplanté et le contexte receveur. À cet égard, Rod Macdonald insiste particulièrement sur le respect de deux points essentiels (Leçons 2 et 3), à savoir, d'une part, l'architecture générale et traditionnelle de l'ordre juridique et, d'autre part, les principes fondamentaux le structurant. En d'autres termes, et selon une terminologie chère à Pierre Legrand que n'aurait pas désavoué Rod, il s'agit de veiller au respect de la culture juridique propre à chaque ordre juridique et qui en fait sa spécificité. En prônant le respect des principes fondamentaux que sont pour lui, en matière de sûreté, les principes du droit de propriété et des contrats, Rod Macdonald nous rappelle la nécessité de veiller à ce que les recommandations essentielles du Guide législatif soient compatibles avec ce qui, selon L.J. Constantinesco,[6] constitue les éléments déterminants de tout ordre juridique.

L'exigence de compatibilité s'apprécie aussi au regard d'autres pans connexes du droit avec lesquels le texte adopté doit s'articuler. S'agissant du droit des sûretés, y a-t-il besoin de souligner la nécessaire collaboration – et non pas concurrence – qu'il doit entretenir avec le droit des biens, des procédures civiles d'exécution, ou celui des procédures collectives, à défaut de quoi il risque de rester lettre morte (Leçon 5) ? Une leçon que le législateur français aurait bien été inspiré de suivre lors de sa réforme inachevée de 2006 …

Le troisième axe développé est celui de la compatibilité sociale. La réussite de toute réforme, et cela dépasse bien évidemment le seul cadre de l'harmonisation, dépend de la prise en compte en amont des attentes concrètes des destinataires de la norme (Leçon 6) ainsi que de celles des institutions ou autres professions publiques ou judiciaires chargées de l'appliquer (Leçons 7 et 8).

Le quatrième axe se rapporte à l'adoption d'un texte harmonisé, qui suppose de respecter la culture politique de l'État de réception (Leçon 9). Appliqué au droit des sûretés, ce commandement conduit à voir dans le système des sûretés un moyen permettant au législateur de mettre en œuvre un programme de politiques sociales, notamment en diminuant le coût du crédit pour l'emprunteur, sans toutefois influencer les États quant au choix de ces politiques.

Enfin, la dernière leçon, très générale, sonne comme un avertissement : « Le mieux est l'ennemi du bien ». Tout système de sûreté étant nécessairement relatif, ce n'est pas parce qu'un système donné est, à tort ou à raison, considéré comme étant le plus efficace, voire le « meilleur » dans un ordre juridique donné, qu'il pourra être transposé avec le même succès dans un autre ordre. Chacun aura deviné ici que cette leçon était un petit caillou lancé, avec malice par l'auteur, dans le jardin des chantres – dont nous sommes, dans une certaine mesure ! – de l'Article 9 de l'UCC.

Car ne nous y trompons pas. Ce projet de chapitre sur la mise en œuvre n'avait pas seulement, dans l'esprit de Rod Macdonald, vocation à n'être qu'un guide pour les Guides. Il avait surtout vocation à éclairer les délégués et à attirer leur attention sur les dangers qu'il pouvait y avoir à suivre trop aveuglément un exemple existant. On a souligné par ailleurs le parti pris de Rod Macdonald quant à l'influence que devait avoir l'Article 9 sur les réformes du droit des sûretés au Québec ou à l'étranger. Sans doute, sa proposition de texte se situe-t-elle dans la droite ligne de cette position. Et même si le texte de notre Ami ne fut pas adopté, il est certain que son objectif a été, sur ce point, atteint, le texte final du Guide législatif marquant une distance raisonnable, voire une autonomie certaine par rapport au modèle américain. C'est dire une nouvelle fois l'impact important que Rod Macdonald a eu sur le texte adopté.

Les moyens : concept, termes et traditions

Après avoir invité les futurs législateurs à prendre en considération le contexte, Rod Macdonald s'attela à attirer leur attention sur les moyens et les difficultés concrètes qu'ils pourraient rencontrer lors de la transformation du Guide en un texte législatif final. Là encore, bon nombre de ses sages avertissements se sont révélés au fil du temps prémonitoires.

Nous n'en prendrons que deux exemples. Respecter l'architecture de l'ordre implique que le nouveau texte trouve sa place dans son ordonnancement. S'agissant du droit des sûretés, une difficulté va immanquablement surgir dans les ordres faisant une distinction entre droit commercial et droit civil. Les sûretés touchant aux deux domaines, le nouveau régime doit-il figurer au Code de commerce ? au Code civil ? ou être réparti entre les deux ? La question est délicate comme le démontre le – mauvais – exemple français. Pour avoir voulu ménager la chèvre – ou le lapin ! – et le chou, le législateur a choisi en 2006 de consacrer dans le Code civil un régime de gage de droit commun, lequel peut être avec ou sans dépossession et porter sur n'importe quel bien présent ou futur[7] ... tout en consacrant dans le code de commerce un gage spécial des stocks,[8] ce qui n'a pas manqué de faire naître rapidement un problème de cohérence, les praticiens s'interrogeant sur la possibilité d'écarter, par une disposition expresse, le régime spécial qui n'est manifestement pas d'ordre public afin de pouvoir appliquer le régime de droit commun. Très curieusement, la Cour de cassation a récemment prohibé une telle possibilité.[9] Faut-il y voir une volonté de la Cour de sauver le gage spécial – et donc une certaine topographie juridique aurait dit Rod Macdonald[10] – ou au contraire d'appliquer une politique du pire destinée à faire pression sur le législateur afin qu'il revoie sa copie et respecte l'exercice de planimétrie en la matière ? La question reste posée.

Le second exemple de conseils prodigués tient à la forme. Rod Macdonald se livra à un véritable plaidoyer pour l'adoption d'un texte aussi simple que possible – une autre pierre dans le jardin de l'Article 9 de l'UCC ? – rédigé dans un style clair, rigoureux, mais néanmoins compréhensible, autant de qualités dont manquent aujourd'hui cruellement les textes adoptés. Il aborda alors une question bien connue des comparatistes, qui est celle de la transposition – voire de la traduction – de concepts ou de termes spécifiques empruntés à un ordre juridique modèle. Ainsi, peut-on raisonnablement adopter le terme de « *Security interest* » alors que ce terme n'a aucun équivalent dans un système civiliste ? Mais le problème peut se poser aussi pour des expressions a priori moins problématiques. Ainsi, la notion de « commercialement raisonnable » peut-elle être retranscrite telle quelle dans un texte adopté par un pays de droit civil, lequel n'a aucune antériorité sur les contours d'une telle notion, lui préférant le standard de « bon père de famille » – du moins tant que ce dernier n'a pas succombé aux coups de boutoir des défenseurs de la cause féministe qui y voient un standard archaïque et machiste ? De même en est-il du « cours normal des affaires ». On ne peut alors qu'approuver Rod

Macdonald lorsque celui-ci milite pour une rédaction descriptive plutôt que l'adoption d'une terminologie existante, mais trop marquée, afin de laisser au législateur le soin de dénommer l'instrument adopté. La périphrase descriptive plutôt que la traduction arbitraire.

Le suivi : la phase d'acculturation et le traitement antirejet

Le troisième volet développé par notre dédicataire porte sur le phénomène d'acculturation. C'est là un aspect trop souvent négligé alors qu'il est fondamental. Il s'agit de vérifier que le texte proposé s'intègre parfaitement dans le contexte juridique et social qui le reçoit. Ainsi énoncée, on peut craindre que l'acculturation fasse double emploi avec les Leçons 6 à 8 exposées *supra*. Elle présente toutefois une différence essentielle. Alors que les leçons commandent de prendre en considération, préalablement à la réforme, le contexte et les attentes pour établir la norme, l'acculturation s'apprécie, quant à elle, en aval. Il s'agit de s'assurer que l'environnement judiciaire, pratique et politique accepte le projet devenu réalité et se l'approprie pleinement. C'est une sorte de phase de consolidation durant laquelle doivent être déployées nombre d'initiatives visant non seulement à promouvoir le nouveau texte, mais aussi à en tirer les premiers enseignements, que ce soit auprès des juges, de la doctrine, des enseignants, ou des praticiens.

Même s'il n'était pas dénué d'arrière-pensées politiques – légitimes – par rapport à l'approche adoptée dans un premier temps par la CNUDCI, ce travail de Rod Macdonald constitue un *vade-mecum* précieux pour ne pas dire indispensable pour le législateur souhaitant tirer profit du Guide. Il prend surtout tout son sens à l'heure où la CNUDCI a ouvert le chantier d'une loi modèle sur la question.

Pas de Guide pour les paresseux !

À la lecture de son projet de guide pour le Guide, il est aisé de comprendre pourquoi Rod fut pendant longtemps, sinon opposé, du moins tout à fait réservé quant à l'opportunité d'établir une loi type sur le sujet.[11] Parce que le droit des sûretés est trop intimement lié avec d'autres pans importants du droit civil, parce qu'il serait vain d'envisager un modèle standard de régime suffisamment neutre et universel pour être adopté tel quel par n'importe quel législateur dans le monde, l'idée même de loi type lui semblait illusoire, pour ne pas dire dangereuse. Dangereuse dans la mesure où le fait de proposer un produit fini clé en main serait de nature à inciter les législateurs, malgré la présence de commentaires, à incorporer telle quelle la loi type sans prendre en considération l'ensemble des aspects développés par Rod Macdonald. Alors que le Guide offre une marge de manœuvre au législateur dans la mise en œuvre des recommandations, lui permettant ainsi de respecter ses traditions juridiques en ajustant celles-ci aux conditions locales, la loi type, en raison de sa standardisation, le lie, augmentant ainsi les risques de rejet absolu.[12]

Ce danger apparaît d'autant plus réel que l'élaboration de cette loi type a été justifiée par le fait que nombre de pays en voie de développement n'ont pas les ressources nécessaires pour tirer profit du Guide et pour s'atteler à l'ensemble des problèmes attachés à sa transposition, d'où leur attente d'un produit fini prêt à l'emploi, lequel est un leurre. On ne peut que regretter un tel choix alors que d'autres solutions existaient. Parmi elles, une était chère à Rod : l'éducation à travers une assistance qui aurait pu – dû ? – être fournie au législateur par la CNUDCI ou d'autres organisations afin de l'aider à tirer la substantifique moelle du Guide législatif et à rédiger par lui-même un texte adapté à ses besoins.

La CNUDCI n'a pas suivi cette voie et le Groupe de travail a entrepris depuis décembre 2013 ses travaux en vue de l'élaboration d'une loi type. Gageons que les délégués sauront néanmoins tirer les enseignements de Rod Macdonald et auront à cœur de garder à l'esprit ses conseils. C'est peu dire que, même s'il a suivi avec attention et jusqu'à son dernier jour l'évolution de nos travaux, la présence de Rod nous a manqué et nous manquera. Ses conseils nous manquent. Sa sagesse nous manque. Nos « consultations informelles » pour reprendre la terminologie CNUDCIenne, autour d'un dry martini – on ne soulignera jamais assez l'apport du dry martini à l'avancée des travaux du Groupe VI – nous manquent. Mais c'est aussi et surtout son sens de l'humour qui nous fait défaut. En exergue de l'ouvrage qui lui est consacré figure une de ces citations dont Rod avait le secret : « Un vrai nœud papillon n'est jamais tout à fait droit ». « Pas plus que ne l'est une cravate ! » pourrait lui répondre un certain président français, lequel pourrait légitimement se sentir visé par ladite citation ! Je vous l'avais dit, le Canadien était taquin !

NOTES

1 Roderick Macdonald, « Faut-il s'assurer qu'on appelle un chat un chat ? Observations sur la méthodologie législative à travers l'énumération limitative des sûretés, "la présomption d'hypothèque" et le principe de "l'essence de l'opération" », dans *Mélanges Germain Brière* (Montréal : Éditions Wilson et Lafleur, 1993), 527–94.

2 R. Sacco, *La comparaison juridique au service de la connaissance du droit* (Paris : Economica, 1991).

3 Macdonald, *Lessons of Everyday Law/Le droit du quotidien* (Montréal Kingston : McGill-Queen's University Press, 2002) (édition bilingue).

4 Sur le concept d'unifiabilité, voir Marc Ancel, *Utilité et méthode du droit comparé* (Ides Edition, 1971), 82 et s.

5 Macdonald, « Three Metaphors of Norm Migration in International Context », *Brooklyn Journal of International Law* 34 (3) (2009) : 603–53.

6 L.J. Constantinesco, *Traité de droit comparé. Tome 2. La méthode comparative* (Paris : Economica, 1983).

7 Code civil, art. 2333 et 2339.

8 Code de commerce, art. L 527-1 s.

9 Cass. Com. 19 février 2013, Bulletin 2013, IV, n° 29. La cour de renvoi est toutefois entrée en résistance contre cette solution : CA Paris, Pôle 5, Ch. 9, 27 février 2014.

10 Roderick Macdonald et Isabelle Deschamps, « Planimétrie et topographie en droit des sûretés », dans *Les mutations de la norme, le renouvellement des sources du droit*, Collection Études juridiques (Paris : Economica, 2011), 177 et s.

11 Macdonald, « A Model Law on Secured Transactions : A Representation of Structure ? An Object of Idealized Imitation ? A Type, Template or Design ? » *Uniform Law Review/Revue de droit uniforme* (2010) : 419–46.

12 Macdonald et Deschamps, 138 et s.

16

Contextualizing Governance

KIRSTEN ANKER

Rod Macdonald was so prolific and wrote on so many topics that it is possible to drive for miles and still stay within the same province, as it were. Before I was asked to present the texts for this panel on "Contextualizing Governance," I had read many of his articles on legal education and legal pluralism, but not being a "governance scholar," I had not crossed the border to these texts. I realize now that I should have! There are many familiar themes, of course, but the fact that they are presented in a new context, teasing out new problems, helps me to understand, in a deeper way, his other writings.

I can't do justice in this forum to the complete arguments of these five texts or to their inevitable complexities, the thickness of ideas and cross-references, but will merely try to evoke them, to bring them to life, around five themes. Their explicit topics include various combinations of public administration and regulation, rule of law, accountability, instrument choice, and economic development. However, to allow me to convey some of their arguments collectively as well as to make a few higher-order points about Rod's approach, I have chosen the themes of context, governance, means and ends, form, and play.

Context

Rod affirms, "It is impossible to write about administrative law without anchoring the discussion in real aspirations and real problems."[1] Historical and cultural contexts are important to all these pieces, particularly to ensuring that administrative law principles are not presented as timeless and absolute. But in the role given to context, I also hear echoes, first, of an approach to hermeneutics like that of Lon Fuller in his critique of formalism: context is essential for words to mean anything, and it is through an iterative process of testing propositions against a variety of specific situations that we come to see what we really meant.[2] Second, I hear echoes of an approach to knowledge that was mentioned in Harry Arthurs's opening remarks: *phronesis*, or practical wisdom, in which actionable knowledge comes from lived experience rather than from abstract decontextualized principles.[3] In Rod's texts, attention to context becomes not just a research methodology but a theory of administrative law.

I want therefore to start by giving some context for these five texts on governance.

"Understanding Regulation by Regulations"[4] is the earliest of the texts, a research paper produced in 1984 for the Commission on the Economic Union and Development Prospects for Canada (a commission headed by a different "Macdonald"). The title suggests one of Rod's basic arguments, namely, that it is strange that regulations – or delegated legislation – are seen as the only kind of regulation rather than one of a subset. The objective of understanding regulation is a pragmatic one for the commission – to open up options for public policy – but the piece has the larger didactic purpose (could it be otherwise?) of proposing a theory of law and government to counter the orthodox one.

"The Acoustics of Accountability: Towards Well-Tempered Tribunals"[5] was published in 2004 but draws on papers written while Rod was president of the Law Reform Commission in the 1990s. The published text addresses a central and eastern European audience and is concerned with providing a pragmatic counterpoint to the American model of accountability via judicial review of "due process," namely, one based on the Canadian experience with regulatory agencies and tribunals.

"Call-Centre Government: For the Rule of Law, Press #"[6] was a paper given at a conference on the work of prominent Canadian public law scholar John Willis in 2004. Rod's theme is "lawyer's values and civil servants' values," which had been the title of Willis's critique of the 1969 report of the McRuer Commission on Civil Rights. The ensuing debate between Willis and McRuer had typified the poles of administrative law thinking in the twentieth century: the former advocated broad discretion guided by expertise and rational decision-making, and the latter advocated the legalistic model of *ex ante* rules governing the exercise of administrative discretion, the propriety of which is overseen by courts.

"The Swiss Army Knife of Governance"[7] comes from a 2005 interdisciplinary conference on the twentieth anniversary of a study by the Economic Council of Canada, "The Choice of Governing Instruments."

The collection posits a shift from instrument choice to governance – as Rod makes clear, a shift from thinking about pure means, as distinct from their policy objectives and in terms of their efficiencies, to a more complex understanding of combinations of networks of state and non-state actors in which means and ends – instrument choice and policy goal – are in a feedback loop relationship.

"Rabbits, Ravens, Snakes, Turtles: Analyzing the Political Economy of Aboriginal Communities from the Inside Out"[8] is a paper contributing to a large team research project on Peuples Autochtones et Gouvernance or Indigenous Peoples and Governance at Université de Montréal that is exceptional for being both interdisciplinary and committed to engagement with indigenous communities. Overarching themes of the project include the social, cultural, economic, and political conditions that shape current and future definitions of indigenous self-governance. This paper, written by Rod along with his former student Thomas McMorrow, articulates the links between identity, property, economy, and governance and asks whether Aboriginal economic development depends on adopting forms of identity, property, and governance that developed alongside a market economy in Europe. Its specific political context is a raft of piecemeal legislative reforms since the mid-1990s that allow Indian bands to introduce taxation and develop their own land codes and registry systems outside of the Indian Act.[9]

Let me turn now to Rod's specific arguments about context in "Call-Centre Government." Tracing the development of three national policies in Canada from nationalization to welfare statism to multiculturalism, he shows that the various government tools in use can only properly be understood in relation to the goals of these policies – direct instruments like Crown ownership of railways, immigration laws, and tariffs suited policies aimed at providing physical and symbolic cohesion and developing Canadian industries, for instance.[10]

The "Understanding Regulation" text places similar importance on historical context, this time on the expansion of government regulatory activity in Canada since 1945, in order to be able to "understand regulation." There are political science explanations for this: highly visible "command and control"–style regulations give "more bang for the buck" with marginal voters. There are economic explanations: regulations are justified where they are the most efficient. And finally there are legal explanations: the rule of law requires simple, permanent, and accessible statutes, which would be compromised by the complex, evolving, and technical aspects of law as administered; politically neutral legal experts can translate the political objectives of statutes into detailed rules via delegated legislation. But all these rationales seem out of touch with the empirical functioning of regulations and of regulation, and so does the focus on the criminal law rule/penalty/enforcement package. Why, he asks, should a statute imposing product safety warranties be seen as an example of regulation but the creation of a small claims court (improving consumer access to judicial remedies) or provision for class action (which facilitates private enforcement of rights) not be so characterized?[11] The lines that are drawn exclude from the concept of regulation, for example, the common law and informal norms within bureaucracies that shape the exercise of discretion, positive interventions such as subsidies, and even the maintenance of institutions, like private property, that make the market possible in the first place.

But sometimes the institutions of private property do become obvious as an instrument choice. In "Rabbits, Ravens, Snakes, Turtles," Rod and Thomas McMorrow consider proposals for introducing private property on Indian reserves. As the authors put it, Aboriginal development is often conceived of as developing a modern trading economy. Historically, though, "Aboriginal" and "modern" have been in opposition. So recent reforms aimed at revenue-raising, investment security, lower transaction costs, and greater accountability in band councils purport to be bringing the benefits of a modern economy but do so by municipalizing Indian reserves from the outside in. The assumption seems to be that establishing this modern form of good governance combined with instruments of private law is a prerequisite to a successful economy. Again, though, on-the-ground context shows that the First Nations adopting these reforms are the ones that have spent the least amount of time under the Indian Act and thus have stronger forms of traditional governance. It seems that "modern" might have to learn to deal with "Aboriginal" in order to achieve effective economic development from the inside out.[12]

Rod's concern with context in these pieces is partly in tracing historical developments in a given political setting in order to denaturalize certain orthodoxies in administrative law or policy strategies. It is also related to an interest with the way things work in practice: once we are interested in effects of governmental action or inaction in general, the given theoretical landscape, the categories and strategies that are assumed, are often shown up as incongruous, artificial, or just hot air.

Governance

Rod's interest in viewing the big picture through the details of the everyday explains somewhat his choice of the word "governance" to capture these studies of administration. I'm not sure I heard the word a single time in my undergraduate years, and the general impression students get in law schools is that we lawyers take the prior existence of law and legal institutions largely for granted; our job is to interpret and apply it. Thinking about design, about the function of governing, comes as an afterthought, reactively and in a piecemeal fashion in response to flaws we discover in the way the law is written or works.

The clearest explanation for Rod's choice of this terminology is in "Acoustics" in which he advocates changing the metaphor according to which independent regulatory agencies are discussed from "governments in miniature" to "governance in miniature." The first lens, "government," highlights the fact that agencies often carry out a combination of legislative, executive, and administrative functions. It tends to focus on the formal rules that govern the operation of agencies and thus to advocate judicial review as the means for ensuring accountability by correcting errors. Because of the focus on separation of powers implied by "governments," these errors are characterized as resulting from agencies exceeding the limits of their authority, from lack of impartiality or independence, or from failure to grant parties due process.[13]

In contrast, the second lens of "governance" directs our attention to the range of activities undertaken in the process of governing. It locates accountability in personnel, in institutional design, and in organizational culture. It is usually more likely that these sites are responsible for "failures" of accountability, which represent not so much misuses of power but more so errors resulting from, for example, inadequate training in the conventional meaning of a statute or an inappropriate application of unofficial policy (such as cutting back on spending) to the case at hand. Recruitment, education, and internal administrative processes are the best remedies for those kinds of errors. The usual gut response to the problem of accountability is to impose tighter and tighter formal constraints from above. Not only does this ignore the real effects of the presence of tacit institutional norms, but it also focuses decision-makers' attention on correct and risk-averse decisions rather than on the substantive mandate of the agency. Any energy for reform, says Rod, is best directed to developing, refining, publicizing, and promoting a healthy and client-responsive culture. Because of the role informal norms in organizations play in the concrete way that decisions get made, the shift to "governance," in short, is in imagining agencies not as little governments but as little legal systems.[14]

The idea of responsiveness, in fact, goes to the heart of an understanding of governance as concerned with citizen agency and empowerment, something Rod identifies as inherent to Canada's "third national policy" on public administration. In "Call-Centre Government," he sees in citizen agency a further reason for suspicion of the command and control version of governance.[15] As a technique of governance, top-down rules perceive citizens as passive recipients. The way that a choice of governance model or tool already commits governments to particular views of their mandate and of their clientele reflects, of course, the interdependence of political goals and legal means – third theme.

Means and Ends

The paper "Call-Centre Government" focuses on the way that system design, and, in particular, the continuum of choices offered up by lawyers' values and civil servants' values, determine how problems are conceptualized and addressed. For the classic rule-of-law lawyer, a focus on *ex ante* rules, individual rights, and formal adjudication of disputes drives conflicts toward pre-established forms and taxonomies, gives little scope to clients for bottom-up construction of their own problems, and frustrates parties' search for empowerment. It also tends to pathologize human relationships: just as in "if you only have a hammer, everything starts to look like a nail," "if all you have is a right, every issue looks like an infringement or an abuse."[16] And if explicit *ex ante* rules are the only tool you have, then the only way to conceive of constraining discretion or ensuring accountability in decision-makers is to enact increasingly detailed directions and protocols. In contrast, civil servants' values, at their best (in his view), are related to public service; their means are things like mission statements and logos that provide a focus for institutional cohesion and identity, staff retreats, customer feedback and responsiveness to it, informal bureaucratic culture, and structures for internal oversight of budgets, personnel, and decision-making.[17]

Form

"The Swiss Army Knife of Governance" provides an even more pointed analysis of the interdependence of means and ends in the context of instrument choice. But I really cannot go any further here without talking about the Swiss Army knife metaphor and thus about Rod's own means in using images and allegories. If you look at them, the titles in this session on governance are among the more unusual ones – acoustics, rabbits, and telephone call centres feature alongside the Swiss Army knife. Acoustics are the properties of a physical space that determine how sound is transmitted, and this points us to Rod's argument about the importance of the internal conditions of administrative tribunals in transmitting a "well-tempered" organizational culture of accountability. The rabbits, ravens, snakes and turtles all have reproductive places – nests, warrens, and so on – that provide metaphors of connectivity, perspective, and autonomy in the question of Aboriginal political economy. But the Swiss Army knife (SAK) and the call centre provide by far the most elaborately developed metaphors of this selection of texts.

Let me give you a sampling of how ends and means work in a feedback loop:

1. When your SAK contains several tools that might work for a job for which none are specifically designed, you might have certain presumptions or habitual preferences as to which tool to use – I would use a knife to carve my boyfriend's name into a tree – but only by using can we tell whether our preference will be optimal or whether, in practice, something less obvious might work better – the knife keeps folding up, but the corkscrew gives me a really firm grip and a stable pointy thing.
2. If you have boy scout camping in mind, you might wonder why you need a corkscrew (although see the first example). But the fact that there *is* one shows how instrument design can be responsive to changing cultural practices – epicurean adult camping, for example – and may even cause us to rethink the place of the SAK as a useful household tool.
3. If we become too dependent on our SAK, we may seek to use our impressive array of specialized tools when actually something simpler – even just our fingers – would do.[18]

In "Call-Centre," the comparison that I referred to between lawyers' values and civil servants' values is played out in analogies with different types of "customer service" phone systems. We all know call centres: we pass through a number of stages of keypad or voice-recognition options that channel our inquiry into more specific categories and either end up accessing an automated message – if the category is something like branch opening hours or address – or a customer service representative. We all know how frustrating this can be: the categories don't match our needs, the system sends you round in circles or gets you stuck somewhere you don't want to be, it is difficult to talk to a live person, and when you do, they talk to you in a predigested script or are unable to help at all. It may seem, says Rod, that the call-centre analogy is one of civil servants' or administrative servants' values run amok: "the perfect technology for irresponsible, unaccountable, and anonymous exercises of anonymous discretion; they privilege the system over the individual and make a fetish of proper procedures and rules."[19] But the exploration of the call centre experience actually allows him to associate some of its flaws with the lawyerly approach: top-down pre-categorizations of problems, predetermined solutions, and a system serving its own logic rather than its clients.

Alternative call-centre design – "contact centres" or backroom call centres – provides an illustration of civil servants' values. Contact centres use a variety of media options, including live navigation of websites, in order to increase interactions with clients and to introduce them to tools that will enable them to be self-reliant. Backroom call centres are maintained within an organization rather than outsourced, their operators have an incentive to maintain good relationships with other parts of the organization, and they are service- rather than information-oriented.[20]

These extended metaphors are evocative and powerful. But as a choice of writing style or form, what do they tell us about the relationship between Rod Macdonald's own means and ends: if the medium is the message, what is the message here?

It is, of course, the point that many have been making here that law is not an isolated sphere of human activity. Rod approached his subject matter as a vehicle for thinking about being human: law is a way of being alive. So the aptness of these metaphors is not an accident but a result of patterns of thinking, doing, and being that repeat over different spheres of human activity.

We know that Rod took form seriously. After reading a paper[21] in which I had analyzed the use of an Aboriginal painting as evidence for a title claim and argued that in order to work as a deed of ownership or a map, it had to be considered as law – that is, in its aesthetic representation of place, space, humans, and entitlement as a normative form – Rod stunned me by responding that if judges really took the canvas seriously as law, they would render their judgments in painting. Another time, at a faculty retreat, we were asked to use plasticene to represent a core idea from one of our teaching topics. The rest of us did our best, but in presenting our models back to the others, we lamely fell back on propositional explanations. Rod forged ahead with an elaborate model of secured transactions – it even had moving parts – and resisted the urge to translate back into rational discourse, saying that this would undersell the significance of the exercise.

Playfulness

But the commitment to form – the kooky titles, the guitar-playing, and the interpretive dance – goes beyond merely representing something in a different way. There is a kind of playfulness to it, and that is my final theme. Abandoning familiar forms can be vertiginous and also risks making us appear ridiculous, but only if we take ourselves too seriously. When, like children, we become playful, we look at everything with curiosity, excitement, and joy. Playfulness is perhaps the perfect antidote to instrumentalism – it is about exploration, an immersion in experience, an abandonment of an investment in outcomes; it is the journey and not the destination. The kind of playfulness we see in these titles, in Rod's method of the everyday, in his delightful manner of asking you questions that turn your world upside down, speak to this immanent childlike quality.

Influence

It was through Rod's writing on legal pluralism that I first got to know him: "Metaphors of Multiplicity,"[22] "Critical Legal Pluralism,"[23] "Against Nomopolies."[24] I found in these writings one of the most complete descriptions of the colonizing legal orthodoxy – not just the state, positivism, or the unity of law but the chirographic prescriptivism of explicit and reified rules. For the laws of indigenous peoples – my field of study – these are all important. Indigenous law is law outside of the state, non-centralized, frequently unwritten, infrequently objectified. Letting go of prescriptivism is one of the hardest challenges, I think. One of my favourite quotes is from Blackfoot scholar Sakej Henderson, who says, "You *can* talk about Indigenous law as rules, but it's like trying to understand an opera by reading the flute score."[25] This recognition of indigenous law "as something" (or the reverse, recognition of something as indigenous law) has been one of my preoccupations, and rather than try to work out what indigenous law really is, I have concentrated on looking at processes and contexts in which parts of life come to be identified as law, the transformative effects of translation, and so on. But there has always been this nagging problem that merely accounting for this constitutive process does not tell us what we should do and in particular does not provide an answer to the question that my students are always interested in: what should judges do, how should they go about recognizing indigenous law without assimilating it into a colonial category, or, how can a judge be a critical legal pluralist?

But I had a bit of a revelation moment reading these governance texts, because the point made in them about acknowledging agencies as mini-legal systems is not about the formal recognition of specific aspects of the internal law of those agencies but about taking in the whole organizational context, its purpose and the means available, and the needs and capacities of participants and users. Of course, the shift away from courts and litigation and the problem of formal recognition is old-hat now in Aboriginal law, but frequently negotiation is seen as the political alternative. In contrast, I can see that it will be useful to stop thinking about the problem as one of recognition and start thinking about it as one of governance, to stop thinking about the pathology of the clash of Aboriginal law with state law, or to articulate a better top-down rule for consultation on resource development, for example, and start thinking about how to construct healthy institutions, relationships, and processes. This is probably not news to some, and it sounds obvious now that I say it, but it demonstrates how Rod's work continues to influence me.

I have often wondered what a more explicitly intercultural version of his critical legal pluralism would look like. As with attack on the colonial orthodoxy or Republican consensus, much legal pluralist theory seems to be concerned with opening up theory to the possibility of alternative sources of normativity and concentrating on challenging aspects of orthodoxy that stop us from seeing them. Given that a judge of the Supreme Court asked counsel, in the recent Tsilhqot'in Nation hearing, how Aboriginal peoples could have had laws that entitled them to the land when they didn't have courts,[26] I think there is still work to be done in that direction. But making space is one thing, and engaging with indigenous or other traditions on legal theory itself is another. I wonder, for instance, what practitioners of indigenous law would make of the focus on humans as the source of law, on agency, or on governance as presented in these texts. I look forward to finding out.

However, in the end, any account of Rod's influence on me based on his scholarship in a narrow sense would be – well, it would be like only reading the flute score of an opera. I count it as a privilege that I have had a chance to experience the full sensory performance, and for that, I thank him.

NOTES

1 Roderick MacDonald, "Call-Centre Government: For the Rule of Law, Press #," *University of Toronto Law Journal* 55 (2005): 453.

2 Lon L. Fuller, "Positivism and Fidelity to Law: A Reply to Professor Hart," *Harvard Law Review* 71 (1958): 666–7.

3 Aristotle, *Nichomachean Ethics* (Book VI), translated by W.D. Ross (Kitchener: Batoche Books, 1999), 94–5.

4 Macdonald, "Understand Regulation by Regulations," in *Regulations, Crown Corporations and Administrative Tribunals*, edited by Ivan Bernier and Andrée Lajoie (Toronto: University of Toronto Press, 1985) , 81–154.

5 Macdonald, "The Acoustics of Accountability: Towards Well-Tempered Tribunals." (Speech to the 14th Annual Conference of the Council of Canadian Administrative Tribunals, Ottawa, 31 May 1998) (typescript).

6 Macdonald, "Call-Centre Government."

7 Macdonald, "The Swiss Army Knife of Governance," in *Designing Governments: From Instruments to Governance*, edited by Pearl Eliades et al. (Montreal: McGill-Queen's University Press, 2005), 203–41.

8 Roderick Macdonald and Thomas McMorrow, "Rabbits, Ravens, Snakes, Turtles: Analyzing the Political Economy of Aboriginal Communities," in *Gouvernance autochtone: reconfiguration d'un avenir collectif*, edited by Pierre Noreau (Montreal: Thémis, 2010), 211–35.

9 Indian Act, RSC 1985, c I-5.

10 Macdonald, "Call-Centre Government," 454–9.

11 Macdonald, "Understand Regulation by Regulations," 101.

12 Macdonald and McMorrow, 228–35.

13 Macdonald, "Acoustics of Accountability," 7–8.

14 Ibid., 18–22.

15 Macdonald, "Call-Centre Government," 456–9.

16 Ibid., 476.

17 Ibid., 489.

18 Macdonald, "The Swiss Army Knife," 226–33.

19 Macdonald, "Call-Centre Government," 469.

20 Ibid., 463–9.

21 Kirsten Anker, "The Truth in Painting: Cultural Artefacts as Proof of Native Title," *Law Text Culture* 9 (2005): 91–130.

22 Macdonald, "Metaphors of Multiplicity: Civil Society, Regimes and Legal Pluralism," *Arizona Journal of International and Comparative Law* 15 (1998): 69–91.

23 Martha-Marie Kleinhans and Roderick Macdonald, "What Is a *Critical* Legal Pluralism?" *Canadian Journal of Law and Society* 12 (1997): 25–46.

24 Roderick Macdonald and David Sandomierski, "Against Nomopolies," *Northern Ireland Legal Quarterly* 57 (2006): 610–33.

25 James Henderson (Sakej), "Comprehending First Nations Jurisprudence" (Paper presented at the Indigenous Law Journal Conference, Indigenous Law and Legal Systems: Recognition and Revitalization, University of Toronto, 27 January 2007).

26 *Tsilhqot'in Nation v. British Columbia*, Supreme Court of Canada, Webcast of Hearing, 07/11/13 http://www.scc-csc.gc.ca/case-dossier/info/webcasts-webdiffusions-eng.aspx, 106:30-112.07.

17

Tools of the Trade: Three Propositions on Governance

ERIC H. REITER

The very idea of law must be autobiographical.[1]

A preliminary disclaimer: I am not a scholar of governance, or, I should say, the categories into which my work tends to fit or be fit are not labelled "governance" as such. But as Rod argues persuasively in these five texts on governance – and in the others considered during this symposium – it is *all* about governance, just as it is *all* about legal pluralism or *all* about substantive or distributive justice. Separating out a theme is hard, or even counterproductive, because all the other themes connect to it, challenge it, enrich it. As is always the case with the best scholarship, Rod's work tends to resonate with whatever one is working on at the moment. A passing remark about legal subjectivity casts new light on one's thinking about mediation; a puzzling passage in a text read years before springs to mind and launches a train of thought that helps one reconfigure a lecture in a more compelling way; and dozens of other such "aha!" moments that arise often when one least expects attest to the powerful creativity of his work.

How do we read these five texts? Confronted with a list (on the website for the original symposium, they were listed more or less in reverse chronological order), do we start at the beginning of the list, abiding by the order imposed on them by others? Do we scan the titles looking for subthemes and follow them? Do we – or I should say does a historian like myself – reorder them into strict chronological order and start at the beginning? Apparently banal choices like these actually matter a great deal – a point Rod makes in various contexts – but they should get us thinking, not paralyze us. They underscore right at the beginning the issue of governance, how our choices shape our outcomes, how procedures influence substance, and so on. I opted for the historical method and imposed a chronological order on the texts, thinking they would perhaps reveal something of the development of Rod's thought. They certainly do that, but they also take the reader on an autobiographical excursion, revisiting ideas, rethinking cherished beliefs, challenging assumptions. I played a background role in the writing of one of these texts, but all of them speak to moments of my own development as a lawyer, as a teacher, as a socio-legal scholar, and beyond, with his insights mapping out a continuing conversation with him and with myself.

I will avoid allegory, which inevitably would be a pale imitation of Rod's masterful use of the genre, but I would like to adopt a Macdonaldian organization to my remarks and present and argue three propositions arising from the texts, propositions that stand for three key insights about governance and about law that I draw from them and that have been helpful to me at different times. Not helpful in a "tool choice" way – I do not reach for Rod Macdonald for certain jobs, for Pierre-Basile Mignault for others – but helpful as suggestions, the puzzling out of which has led me in productive directions. A mere three propositions pale in comparison to Rod's call centre from hell with *seventeen* governance options before the editors of the *University of Toronto Law Journal* balked[2]; one wonders what riches the director's cut of "Call-Centre Government" might hold! The insights gleaned from our texts loosely follow three points in my autobiography, from my first encounter with Rod as his research assistant in 2002, to his formal supervision of my graduate work, and since then to his ongoing role as mentor, whether in person or via his writings.

Proposition 1: Fashions come and fashions go, but Lon Fuller remains the Urtext *for thinking about governance.*

When Rod hired me in 2002 as research assistant on what would become "The Swiss Army Knife," my first job was to go off and read Fuller. I had known Fuller's "Speluncian Explorers" and *Morality of Law*, but he had me explore rarer bits of Fuller's oeuvre: "Means and Ends," "Mediation: Its Forms and Functions," the "temporary edition" (whatever that means) of *The Problems of Jurisprudence*. Fuller's ideas on social ordering provided the gravitational pull to bring together various separate fields of governance studies, from alternative dispute resolution to instrument choice to legal process. But Fuller is more than just one possible choice: his work is the natural centre because his fundamental optimism about the perfectibility of society provided the necessary foundation for understanding Rod's view of governance.

Fuller remains under-read and under-cited and most under-read by the very people with most to learn from him. But engagement with Fuller runs through all of Rod's work – never as an authority, cited to close debate, but as a source of ideas, as an antidote to legal positivism, as a breath of Texas realism. In particular, Rod's development of certain themes from Fuller in these articles underscores the deficiencies of the instrumental view of law, which misses the "circles of interaction" between means and ends, between institutions and people, between law and life. Governance involves *systems* in which choice of means shapes ends, in which desired ends constrain means, but ultimately in which substantive outcomes are what matter.

Proposition 2: Scholarship and teaching are interrelated, and both must draw on the experience of real life.

Our texts here develop a variety of allegories and extended metaphors. Rod's antidote to the highly formalized, conceptual view of administrative law or choice of governance instruments is the teacher's approach – to present lessons or situations for the reader to consider and work out for herself or himself. This puts a heavy onus on the reader. Rod was of course able to write in an expository register with remarkable clarity when the forum so demanded. But more often, he chose to write allusively, metaphorically, allegorically. This should not be mistaken for mere playfulness, although that was certainly part of it. The intellectual journey is paramount, and key points are too important to risk to a dry exposition that might cause a listener or a reader to tune out. An allegory, however, stands out and challenges the reader to join in, to contribute in the production of meaning.

The Swiss Army knife allegory is an example of this. "Tool choice" scholarship, whatever its virtues, can be arid, conceptual, lifeless – the reflection of the dismal science on which it draws. Rod's solution is to take the image of "tool choice" literally – an actual tool, a Swiss Army knife – and so to move a lifeless discussion into the realm of real life. And that is precisely the point: because there is no bright line between "law" and "life," there is no bright line between how we assess policy options in a governance situation and how we decide which blade to use or whether to buy a Victorinox Swiss Champ or a Wenger Highlander. We might turn around Holmes's dictum that the life of the law has been experience: Rod's work shows us that the law of life is experience.

Proposition 3: The "traditional view" (that is, "lawyer's law") misses the richness of law in society because it sells society short.

In our five texts, Rod demonstrates an enviable command of a variety of disciplines: sociology, history, philosophy, and beyond. In the earliest text, "Regulation by Regulations" from 1985, we find him as a pioneering voice for legal pluralism and the socio-legal approach in opposition to a centralist or monist view of law. His remark that "almost every recipient of governmental largesse performs a semi-public regulatory function" is for its time a bold assertion of legal pluralism and the dynamism of individual agency, even though I suspect that in latter days he would surely have removed the qualifier "almost."[3] His insights into law and society have shaped my own socio-legal world view. Here, briefly, are three points drawn from these texts that I have found particularly instructive.

First, Rod's focus is on substance over form – on looking to interrelationships rather than taking the lawyer's usual approach of distinguishing, categorizing, and labelling, which are just different ways of saying "separating." It is not hard to find examples today of our governments or our organizations approaching problems by "throwing law at them," making specific rules to try to effect specific ends, an approach that confuses law as means with law as end. This takes us back to the problem I posed at the beginning – the problem of the order in which to read five texts is just an example of the categorization dilemma law often presents. Categories facilitate, but they also set up walls that obscure. Labels impose an external order whose seeming naturalness makes us forget that categorization is a governance choice.[4] This in turn obscures, even prevents, the situational thinking that gives law its vitality.[5]

Second, and related, is the issue of discretion. Throughout these texts, Rod develops the key argument that the problem is not too much *discretion*, but too much *law* – or more precisely, too much *ex ante*, one-size-fits-all rule-making – which in the administrative context hampers the creativity and smart exercise of discretion that organizations need to thrive. The point of governance is to recognize and have confidence in people as "law-creating" rather than merely "law-abiding," as he put it in

"The Swiss Army Knife."[6] The problem, put bluntly, is not too much discretion but too little, or, more accurately, too little smart discretion. Here we venture onto ground that could be seen as somewhat dangerous, at least for a lawyer, as threatening to supplant the rule of law with ad hoc discretion. This is to miss the point, however. Rod's view of governance is not to supplant the rule of *law*, to take us back before *Roncarelli v. Duplessis*[7] to an era of administrative cronyism, but rather to supplant the rule of *rules*, the fetishism of micromanagement via written norms. We must, in other words, understand his point about discretion in the context of his legal humanism, which brings me to my last point.

Third, and finally, in all these texts we see a profound optimism about governance because of Rod's profound optimism about people. This reflects Rod himself, his intellectual connections to Lon Fuller, as well as a healthy scepticism of economics as a framework within which to understand governance, law, and human relationships generally. Across these texts he develops the idea that life brings experience, experience brings wisdom, and all three together bring the capacity for creative and situational thinking. Governance means letting people do what they're capable of doing, providing a minimal framework within which experience, wisdom, creativity can come forward and flourish. And law, then, as Rod noted on more than one occasion, becomes facilitative, symbolic, aspirational.

NOTES

I was Rod's research assistant in 2002, and he supervised my LLM from 2002 to 2004.

1 Martha-Marie Kleinhans and Roderick A. Macdonald, "What Is a *Critical* Legal Pluralism?" *Canadian Journal of Law and Society* 12 (1997): 46.

2 Macdonald, "Call-Centre Government: For the Rule of Law, Press #," *University of Toronto Law Journal* 55 (2005): 473n57.

3 Macdonald, "Understanding Regulation by Regulation," in *Regulations, Crown Corporations and Administrative Tribunals*, edited by I. Bernier and A. Lajoie (Toronto: University of Toronto Press, 1985), 103.

4 Roderick Macdonald and Thomas McMorrow, "Rabbits, Ravens, Snakes, Turtles: Analyzing the Political Economy of Aboriginal Communities," in *Gouvernance autochtone: reconfiguration d'un avenir collectif*, edited by Pierre Noreau (Montreal: Thémis, 2010), 214–15.

5 Macdonald, "The Acoustics of Accountability: Towards Well-Tempered Tribunals" (Speech to the 14th Annual Conference of the Council of Canadian Administrative Tribunals, Ottawa, 31 May 1998) (typescript), 21–2.

6 Macdonald, "The Swiss Army Knife of Governance," in *Designing Government: From Instruments to Governance*, edited by Pearl Eliadis et al. (Montreal: McGill-Queen's University Press, 2005), 238.
7 *Roncarelli v. Duplessis* [1959] SCR 121.

18

Inspiring Governance through Law: Rod Macdonald's Jurisprudence of Hope[1]

THOMAS McMORROW

My aim in this paper is to highlight and expand upon what I see as a central theme in Roderick Macdonald's scholarship. I call this the imperative of "inspiring governance." By "inspiring governance," I mean: governance that inspires (while being inspired by) each individual's quest for meaningful, creative engagement in the collective undertaking of building a just society. "Inspiring governance through law" means enabling individuals to experience their implication in, and responsibility for, the continuous challenge of constructing norms, structures, and processes that foster each human being's self-directed pursuit of the good. In this paper, I begin by discussing how Macdonald frames the governance endeavour. Next, I highlight the distinctive, human agency–focused manner in which Macdonald conceives "governance through law." Following this, I discuss the paradoxical relationship between "governance through law" and the "exercise of human agency" that Macdonald's work exposes. I argue that Macdonald's endeavour to foreground the problem of facilitating human agency in his legal research reveals a "jurisprudence of hope" whereby pursuing one's life in the law may be understood as a way of striving for justice in the world.

Governance

Depending on how the phrase is grammatically construed, the theme of our panel, "Contextualizing Governance," may be interpreted in two different but, I would argue, inherently connected ways. To hold both significations in one's mind at once means that whether one is referring to a concept, institution, process, or method of governance, the challenge is not just of viewing governance in context but of pursuing governance in a manner that is sensitive to context.

Consider how the problems Macdonald addresses in each of the articles assigned to this panel become restated in a wider context through his treatment of them. In "Call-Centre Government: For the Rule of Law, Press #," the debate between "lawyers' values" and "civil servants' values" in administrative law is resituated in light of the question of how the design of normative architecture influences administrative accountability and is explored through a careful examination of call centres and their allegorical significance for public administration. In "Rabbits, Ravens, Snakes, Turtles: Analyzing the Political Economy of Aboriginal Communities," the question of reforming the property law regime prescribed under the Indian Act is presented as tributary to the relationship between the political economy of First Nations and the flourishing of indigenous legal traditions, as illustrated through the metaphor of several animals' habitats. Furthermore, in "The Swiss Army Knife of Governance," the role of instrument-choice theory in identifying approaches to contemporary governance challenges is appraised in light of the limitations of a strictly instrumentalist conception of governance as illustrated through a detailed analogy between using "the tools of governance" and using the tools contained in a Swiss Army knife. In "The Acoustics of Accountability: Towards Well-Tempered Tribunals," measures for ensuring the independence and impartiality of regulatory agencies are reframed in relation to a study of the existential conditions for accountability along with an encyclopedic rendering of the various external structures and processes supporting an ethos of personal accountability among administrators. Finally, in "Understanding Regulation by Regulations," the role of delegated legislation in market regulation is represented through a detailed analysis of how the ends and means selected by governments when choosing to employ a particular form of subordinate legislation reveals insights into to the nature of regulation itself.

These examples of Macdonald's scholarship illustrate the idea of "contextualizing governance" in both descriptive and normative senses of the term. There is a vital relationship between how Macdonald imagines what the place of governance is and what it should be. As researcher, writer, and teacher, he demonstrates sensitivity to context in bringing governance to light while showing as witness, activist, and advocate of justice that the same thing is indispensable to bringing light to governance. Macdonald offers an account of governance with both descriptive and prescriptive elements, because every purposive human endeavour may be characterized in such a manner to highlight both dimensions: "Descriptively, governance is taken to be the iterative endeavour of identifying goals and objectives, designing policies, selecting processes and instruments, deciding particular programmes, targeting sites and systems, and identifying actors by and through which human aspirations and actions may be rendered into achievements and accomplishments. Prescriptively, governance is taken to be the endeavour of identifying and managing both aspiration and action in a manner that affirms and promotes human agency."[2]

In other words, governance is about getting things done but getting them done in a particular manner. On the one hand, the objective of governance is to render "human aspirations and actions ... into achievements and accomplishments."[3] On the other hand, the way in which the project of governance is carried out ought to both affirm and promote human agency.

The challenge of governance is not simply that of getting people to do what they are told. Governance is a more complex undertaking than one-off or even repeated direction by one who governs, for it involves facilitating self-direction among those whose actions one purports to govern. Such a concept of governance displays the notions of "is" and "ought" as intertwined and indicates the influence of Lon Fuller's work on Macdonald's thinking.[4] In his essay "Irrigation and Tyranny," Fuller evinces an ironic sympathy for the tyrant: that is, the one who looks to bend the creative energies of his subjects completely to his will.[5] Fuller argues that exercising tyrannical control amounts to a Sisyphean task. By pushing human beings around as if they were a collective, inert, boulder-like mass, the tyrant will discover that the moment he stops applying his muscle, his efforts roll back in his face. Describing and achieving governance means attending to the interplay of purposes belonging to both governor and governed.

On the one hand, to be governed is to have things chosen for us; on the other, through being governed, we are afforded choice. The possibility of human agency, liberty or freedom, does not just turn on the absence of constraint; on the contrary, meaningful human decision-making presupposes the existence of constraint. Thus, Fuller observes, "Language imposes on us a sometimes unwelcome allocation of choice; if it did not, we would be unable to talk."[6] Every governance endeavour prescribes limits to the exercise of human agency; paradoxically, it is precisely the existence of limitations that makes human agency possible.

Governance through Law

If governance is the iterative endeavour of translating human aspiration into achievement in a manner that fosters human agency, then "governance through law" refers to a particular symbolic modality for its performance. Governance through "economics," through "religion," through "love" – each of these presents a different lens, highlighting distinct points of emphasis. Any form of human interaction may be imagined through every one of these frames. Layering these frames can grant a deeper, more textured view of a particular governance endeavour. Done self-consciously, each frame can bring into sharper relief aspects of each other as well.

According to Macdonald, what makes law distinctive is "the manner by which human interaction is held up for assessment in the mirror of rules."[7] Specific behavioural conventions, co-ordinative social institutions, and the political state act in tandem to provide sets of reference points to which human beings may advert in order to avoid sifting through more numerous and allusive forms of justice claims.[8] Law, in this sense, performs the function of surrogate: legal norms serve as shortcuts for identifying what justice requires. In this way, however, every normative claim (whether it is explicitly legal or not) is a hypothesis of just action; recognizing the potential heuristic value of all law is to implicitly acknowledge each human being's capacity and responsibility to reject those hypotheses of action that do not resonate with one's own idea of what justice requires.[9]

Law's influence on how human beings understand their normative commitments is potentially quite pervasive. Consider, for example, the role of legislation in labelling activities in which citizens engage. Macdonald points out that the widest normative implications of law lie in how it contributes to the ways in which we describe our reality: "Parliament is involved in deciding the deeper meaning of events in the world ... It is actually making decisions about the symbolic construction of human agency. It is deciding how it wishes citizens to symbolise the kind of interaction with others ... Choices it makes about the legal classification of the everyday events of human interaction have much to teach about who it believes citizens are and what it believes they ought to aspire to be."[10]

Notwithstanding this example of the role statute may perform, it is important to recognize that Macdonald does not equate "rules" with explicitly legal, institutionally enacted, canonically formulated norms alone. Legislation represents one instantiation of legal normative symbolism; adjudicative decisions, custom, and inferential norms constitute other forms in which law is expressed and interpreted. Recognizing the diversity of sites and modes in which the meaning of law is dialogically constructed, Macdonald rejects the imputation of "a common logical structure, namely the explicit, propositional form associated with legislative enactments" to law itself.[11] For this reason, he rejects an a priori, formalist conception of law that automatically privileges patent legal normativity and reinforces a hierarchy of norms and normative orders based on institutional pedigree.[12]

Recognizing law as plural – seeing that its sources and instantiations are not only explicit and formulaic but implicit and inferential too – means that the challenge, according to Macdonald, is for both "official institutions to replicate the wisdom of unofficial social symbolisms, and unofficial social symbolisms to replicate the democratic and social egalitarian values we ascribe to our official processes."[13] At the same time, justifications for ascribing wisdom to unofficial social symbolisms or values such as democracy and equality to official processes should not be taken for granted. What law is as well as what law should be must both be "argued for."[14]

When governance is understood to involve facilitating self-directed human interaction, the endeavour to rule appears destined to fail to the extent that it ends up extinguishing rather than liberating the creative energies of the ruled.[15] Such an insight may very well arise when adopting other frames of analysis as well. Still, Macdonald notes: "To see any particular incidence of human interaction through the lens of law is a choice – a choice we make to put issues of justice and the quest for the good front and centre in thinking about the quality and character of that interaction."[16]

Recognizing this as the purpose of legal inquiry leads to thinking beyond official legal institutional processes while at the same time exploring how and why a personal and collective commitment to justice ought to animate every undertaking of governance through law. Governance through law is not merely a matter of official state law-makers claiming authority over, and securing behavioural conformity from, legal subjects.[17] Rather, governance through law involves institutions, norms, processes, and concepts (regardless of their provenance) being recognized as legitimate and attracting commitment from the human beings they purport to govern. "Governance through law" represents a distinct way of understanding and pursuing the iterative, dialogical activities of governance.

Inspiring Governance through Law

Macdonald distinguishes "governance through law" from "control by force" or "rule through *diktat*."[18] In his view, neither an appeal to coercion nor a one-way projection of authority captures the endeavour.[19] For Macdonald, governance through law is a normative project,[20] proceeding through ethical argument rather than turning on threat of harm.[21] As such, it is necessarily an unpredictable undertaking. By affirming rather than eliding the active role the "subject" of law plays in interpreting "state" law and in constructing legal normativity generally, the more the prospects of any specific governance endeavour appear to be left to chance. What is more, from this perspective, all governance through law is aspirational governance – aspirational because it is rooted in a faith in each human being's capacity for exercising agency. For aspirational governance to succeed, it must be "inspiring governance" – that is, governance that inspires, while being inspired by, the goal of fostering human agency.

To inspire is "to breathe life into." Inspiration takes many forms. Since consciousness of a fact is by no means a necessary condition of its existence, one may be inspired without knowing it. Much of governance – the primary modalities of its animating force – consists in "structures and processes."[22] To the extent that human beings experience their implication in, and responsibility for, contributing to the conditions under which the decisions affecting them are made, one may say that such structures and processes inspire while being inspired by governance through law. A vision of governance through law, framed by a conception of each natural person as an ethical being, makes room for interrogating the justice of any claim to govern. I argue that Macdonald's writings on governance emphasize the imperative of pursuing ways of thinking and doing governance that foster the meaningful implication of everyone it affects. It means thinking beyond official legal institutional processes and at the same time exploring how and why a personal and collective commitment to justice ought to animate every undertaking of governance through law.

At the risk of stretching the metaphor of inspiration, what I mean more precisely is the matter of making "breathing room" rather than providing the oxygen itself. When it comes to diagnosing unaccountable public administration, Macdonald argues that conscious maladministration and deliberate politicization are symptoms, not causes. Macdonald demonstrates that the challenge of achieving accountable public administration is foremost a question of institutional design.[23] Failures in the design of administrative structures and processes provide a breeding ground for these kinds of abuses by frustrating the possibilities for effective and legitimate governance in the first place. Accountable public administration depends above all on creating the optimal conditions in which to exercise discretion. Thus, when an administrative agency is prescribed an impossible mandate, addled by a dysfunctional appointment process, burdened by unduly formalistic standards, or lacking an adequate internal normative structure, its prospects for achieving "good governance" are pre-emptively damaged.[24] The challenge, therefore, is not just one of preventing abuses of discretion but of enabling the proper uses of discretion.

Presenting the problem of administrative accountability in this manner shifts the focus away from exclusive concentration on the external mechanisms charged with checking the excesses of administrative power toward the conditions necessary for the legitimate exercise of that legislatively delegated power.[25] While the role played by external oversight institutions – whether it be an auditor general, an ethics commissioner, an ombudsman office, any one of a number of specialized independent oversight agencies, or the courts themselves – may be a necessary component of ensuring the impartiality and independence of public agencies, it is not in and of itself sufficient for ensuring administrative accountability. That is because the conditions under which independent regulatory bodies fulfill their objectives are, in a fundamental sense, intrinsic to those administrative agencies themselves.

By way of analogy, consider Canada's Olympic women's hockey team. The work of this group is subject to a variety of formal and informal oversight bodies, including the International Ice Hockey Federation, the International Olympic Committee, the Canadian Olympic Committee, and Hockey Canada – not to mention fans, friends, and families. Conditions of eligibility, qualifications for participation, standards of performance, and rules for playing are all shaped in one way or another by the actions of these bodies. It was not, however, members of these formal or informal oversight agencies who would take the ice in Sochi. Nor does the mechanical discharge of one's accountability to each of these oversight groups translate into what members of the team do every time they lace up their skates to play against an opponent. It is the iterative decision regarding what kind of player – and therefore what kind of person – one wants to be that constitutes the nexus between governance through law and human meaning-making.

The Paradox of Governing Human Agency through Law

To think about law as a way of symbolizing any governance endeavour is to imagine law as a language of interaction, affording human beings a creative role in the construction of normativity. The logic of a command/obey conception of human action wrongly casts normativity as a kind of independent, pre-existing life-instruction manual.[26] To recognize the role of law in providing baselines for human interaction, rather than instructions to be followed by automatons, is to acknowledge that the meaning of law is mediated by and through the ways in which human beings interact. Unlike Newton's Laws, legal normativity does not exist outside or prior to the human capacity to create it.[27]

But of course that does not mean that the manner in which each person's actions are symbolized under the governance of rules is of one's own unfettered invention. Each person may have his or her own manner of speaking, but that is not the same thing as having one's own language. Whatever use such a private language might have, it would not serve the purpose of engaging in meaningful intersubjective communication with others. Conventions as to spelling, punctuation, and syntax – not to mention the meaning of words – govern how each individual communicates. On the other hand, to reduce language to mere compliance with semantic and grammatical conventions is to forget that the purpose of a language is to facilitate intersubjective communication; without this animating purpose, a language is dead. Similarly, conflating governance through law with achieving compliance with laws ignores the extent to which law, like language, is a resource on which human beings draw to serve their purposes.

While placing this primacy on human agency, Macdonald nonetheless admits that participation in governance structures may be either voluntary or coerced.[28] But how does this acknowledgment of a coercive dimension to governance square with a vision of governance in general – and "governance through law" in particular – as agency-enhancing?

The profound asymmetry in power evidenced, for example, in the relationship that citizens bear to the state appears to preclude the very possibility of individual participation in governance structures being voluntary. As Leslie Green notes, even where genuine popular control of governments obtains, that control is not individual but collective in nature.[29] Only by organizing in groups and sustaining significant transaction costs may individuals exercise control over the state.

Whereas Macdonald presents legal subjects as creative actors – indeed, "law-makers"[30] – Green insists that individually, citizens are nothing more than "law-takers." By distinguishing between the modern state and the "the family, tribe, neighbourhood, or other face-to-face communities," Green appears to acknowledge that individual will can or does shape how interactions within "face-to-face communities" are governed. Green is able to conclude confidently that "[t]he actual limits on the authority of law ... reflect the collective rather than the individual will," because he defines law as the normative outputs of the political state.[31] This account of law is different from Macdonald's. For the latter, law is that language through which governance may be symbolized not just at the state level but within each site of human interaction. Moreover, law is not the property of legal officials or even legal academics. Each human being has a right of ownership in the common property of legal normativity.

Macdonald does not deny the disparities in power that various governance relationships present – be those relationships to the state, an institutional religion, one's family, or the market – but he locates in the activity of law the possibility of re-describing, reimagining, and re-forming those dynamics. If the truth is that law only tracks power, then such transformative potential is foreclosed. If, however, law permits power to be confronted with uncomfortable truths, then the possibility of realizing more just ways of ordering these interactions persists.

Self-governance is an aspiration whose fulfillment (as with all human aspirations) may only be accomplished partially, finitely. Its possibility to be expressed in one form depends on its abnegation in another. Positing the individual as the irreducible site of law furnishes only one side of the equation, but so too does ignoring the extent to which governance through law is interactive and not uniquely situated in terms of the citizen's relationship with the state. Exposing the paradoxical relationship between law and human agency, Macdonald does not offer a solution. What he does do is offer a nuanced, sophisticated way of imagining that paradox as well as its implications for how human beings pursue governance through law.

Rod Macdonald's Jurisprudence of Hope

Human motivation is complex, and it is a considerable understatement to note that human decision-making processes do not always reflect self-directed, reason-based, other-regarding deliberation. And yet every appeal to reason is predicated on a belief in each human being's intellectual and moral capacity to recognize such an invitation and respond to it. Hope that people are both willing and able to partake in the kind of honest, self-reflective, intersubjective communication in which all normativity is rooted grounds the ambition to achieve governance through law. But what if the endeavour to elaborate structures, norms, institutions, and processes whose vitality depends on conscientious participation meets with disinterest, disaffection, distemper, and dissimulation? In the words of Samuel Beckett: "All of old. Nothing else ever. Ever tried. Ever failed. No matter. Try again. Fail again. Fail better."[32]

When the Grand Inquisitor in Dostoevsky's *The Brothers Karamazov* mocks the Christ figure he is interrogating for relying on the conscience of individual human beings to embrace him lovingly rather than employing the powers of miracle, mystery, and authority to make them follow him, he asks incredulously: "Is the nature of men such, that they can reject miracle, and at the great moments of their life, the moments of their deepest, most agonizing spiritual difficulties, cling only to the free verdict of the heart?"[33]

To assume that human beings will only be moved to act by extrinsic force is to despair of their potential for agency and to foreclose the very possibility of governance through law. The rationale of the Grand Inquisitor, framed as it is by the will to power, is not unfamiliar. Whether it is because of the Grand Inquisitors one has encountered in the world or those within oneself, the project of governance through law may seem aspirational indeed. A disjuncture between aspiration and achievement will no doubt yield disappointment, but whether disappointment leads in turn to cynical resignation or to active perseverance depends on hope.

Onora O'Neill writes: "Hope … is an orientation to an uncertain future which attends not to what is likely, but to what is possible. So long as we have incomplete knowledge of what is likely, we have reason to take serious account of what is possible for us, and to act in the light of hope."[34]

At the opening of the symposium, Harry Arthurs observed that "Rod – in his work as in his life – engaged with reality as a thoroughgoing optimist." I think that whether Macdonald was an optimist or a pessimist is the wrong question. Optimism concerns one's attitude to the probable. Macdonald's writings do not just ask what is likely but what is possible. By imagining law as a purposive human endeavour, one that may be expressed through a variety of symbolic modalities, Macdonald identifies the question of how human beings govern their actions in fact as fundamental to legal inquiry.

Central to his conception of governance through law is the idea of law's purpose as the facilitation of human agency. The answer to the question of what it means for a human being to exercise agency defies any neat, singular formulation. For Macdonald, the tasks of conceiving and performing governance as a collective undertaking are inextricably linked to the intensely personal, iterative activity of discovering what it means to live virtuously. It is in the course of "everyday life" (with all the experiences of monotony, frustration, and suffering as well as occasions of joy, accomplishment, and insight the "everyday" may evoke) that strivings for justice, truth, and understanding take place. To make the pursuit of truth and justice the purpose of a life in the law is to be at once clear-eyed and visionary, daring and practical, hardworking and imaginative.

As Rod once remarked to a group of graduate students, "If law does not allow you to do the things you aspire to do and be who you aspire to be, what you need is a better philosophy of law."[35] In Macdonald's research, this has meant demonstrating what it might mean to rethink "our attitudes and our expectations about who owns law, what it can realistically accomplish, and how it can be most effectively deployed to promote a more just society."[36] In my view, inspiring governance through law means bearing witness to a jurisprudence of hope. It means recognizing that to ask what justice requires of law is to ask what we demand of ourselves.

NOTES

1 I wish to express my gratitude to Richard Janda and the other organizers of the symposium, the members of the panel "Contextualizing Governance," the rest of the participants in the symposium, especially the Macdonald family, and the following individuals for their comments on various drafts of this essay: April Bateman, Suzanne Bouclin, Kate Glover, Philipp Kastner, Michael McMorrow, and David Sandomierski. For his example, as a scholar and, more important, as a human being, my heartfelt thanks to Rod.

2 Roderick Macdonald, *The Governance of Human Agency* (Background Document for the Special Senate Committee on Illegal Drugs, 2002), http://

www.parl.gc.ca/Content/SEN/Committee/371/ille/library/background-e.htm: paragraph 2.

3 Ibid.

4 See Lon L. Fuller, "Human Purpose and Natural Law," *Journal of Philosophy* 53 (1956): 697–705; see also Kenneth I. Winston, "Is/Ought Redux: The Pragmatist Context of Lon Fuller's Conception of Law," *Oxford Journal of Legal Studies* 8 (3) (1988): 329–49.

5 Fuller, "Irrigation and Tyranny," *Stanford Law Review* 17 (6) (1965): 1,021–42.

6 Fuller, "Freedom as a Problem of Allocating Choice," *Proceedings of the American Philosophical Society* 112 (2) (1968): 101–6.

7 Macdonald, "Triangulating Social Law Reform," in *Dessiner la société par le droit/Mapping Society through Law*, edited by Ysolde Gendreau (Montreal: Thémis, 2004), 124.

8 Ibid.

9 What may sound like a warrant for anarchy is in fact the foundation of civil disobedience. Macdonald conceived law as a symbolically multifarious, intersubjective, communicative activity. Law encompasses a wide variety of expressive forms, issuing from a plurality of sources, whereby human beings derive a sense of obligation about how to act. "The 'bad man' will not be choosing between accepting or rejecting the legislative hypothesis; the 'bad man' will also be choosing among legislative hypotheses, and by so doing providing an indication of which hypothesis carries the most weight until someone comes up with a better alternative": Macdonald, "The Fridge-Door Statute," *McGill Law Journal* 47 (2002): 32.

10 Macdonald, *Governance of Human Agency*.

11 Macdonald, "On the Administration of Statutes," *Queen's Law Journal* 12 (1987): 504.

12 Martha-Marie Kleinhans and Roderick Macdonald, "What Is a *Critical* Legal Pluralism?" *Canadian Journal of Law and Society* 12 (1997): 31–2. See also John Griffiths, "What Is Legal Pluralism?" *Journal of Legal Pluralism and Unofficial Law* 24 (1986): 1–55; Sally Falk Moore, "Law and Social Change: The Semi-Autonomous Social Field as an Appropriate Object of Study," in *Law as Process: An Anthropological Approach* (Boston: Routledge, 1978), 54–81; Sally Engle Merry, "Legal Pluralism," *Law and Society Review* 22 (1988): 869–96; Brian Z. Tamanaha, "Understanding Legal Pluralism: Past to Present, Local to Global," *Sydney Law Review* 30 (2008): 375–411.

13 Macdonald, "Justice Is a Noun but Access Isn't a Verb," in *Expanding Horizons: Rethinking Access to Justice: Proceedings of a National Symposium* (Ottawa: Department of Justice Canada, 2001), 4.

14 Robert S. Summers, "Professor Fuller's Jurisprudence and America's Dominant Philosophy of Law," *Harvard Law Review* 92 (1978): 441.

15 Hope glimmers in human appreciation for the economy of action: "The way to be comfortable is to make others comfortable. The way to make others comfortable is to appear to love them. The way to appear to love them is to love them in reality": Jeremy Bentham, *Works*, published under the supervision of Sir John Bowring (1843, etc.), 71, cited in Fuller, "Freedom as a Problem," 106.

16 Macdonald, *Lessons of Everyday Law* (Montreal: McGill-Queen's University Press for the School of Policy Studies, Queen's University, and the Law Commission of Canada, 2002), 7.

17 See Roderick Macdonald and David Sandomierksi, "Against Nomopolies," *Northern Ireland Legal Quarterly* 57 (4) (2007): 611.

18 See Macdonald, "Call-Centre Government," 459–69.

19 It is an interactive process that proceeds through reason-based justification rather than an act of domination achieved through the cultivation of fear. Law is a form of symbolic communication. Communication implies interpretation as well as expression. It implies the cooperation, therefore, of more than one mind. A reaction resulting from contamination by fear is not the same thing as an action arising from intersubjective communication, for it can take place without any mind present at all.

20 The distinction reflects H.L.A. Hart's argument about the difference between conceiving law "as an affair of rules" versus "a set of commands–backed-by-threats" turning on the difference between the internal and external points of view, as well as the difference between having a sense of obligation rather than merely feeling obliged: H.L.A. Hart, *The Concept of Law*, 2nd edn (Oxford: Oxford University Press, 1997), 82–91.

21 Evan Fox-Decent argues that since there are many instances in which consent to state authority is either impossible or impracticable, the state's authority does not repose in an accumulation of each citizen's individual grants of trust but in the state's trustworthiness to act in their best interests. The title of his article captures the idea: Evan Fox-Decent, "The Fiduciary Nature of State Legal Authority," *Queen's Law Journal* 31 (2005): 259–310. In seeking to explain "the state's legal authority to announce, administer and enforce law," the focus is on state action, but the state is only one kind of a plurality of would-be legal authorities; moreover, to conceive the construction of legal normativity as interactional as well as not strictly emanating from the state is to recognize that announcement, administration, and enforcement do not of themselves law make.

22 Donald Kettl, "The Future of Public Administration," *Journal of Public Affairs Education* 5 (1999): 127.

23 Macdonald, "Call-Centre Government," 449.
24 Ibid., 494.
25 Macdonald, "The Acoustics of Accountability: Towards Well-Tempered Tribunals" (Speech to the 14th Annual Conference of the Council of Canadian Administrative Tribunals, Ottawa, 31 May 1998) (typescript).
26 It is this simplistic logic that in turn gives rise to the idealization of legalism and the perpetuation of its absurdities.
27 See Macdonald, "The Fridge-Door Statute," 19–20. The idea of law providing baselines for self-directed human interaction is one that Macdonald draws from the writings of Lon L. Fuller; see *The Principles of Social Order: Selected Essays of Lon Fuller*, edited by Kenneth Winston, *passim* (Oxford: Hart Publishing, 2001); *Rediscovering Fuller: Essays on Implicit Law and Institutional Design*, edited by Willem J. Witteveen and Wibren Van der Berg, *passim* (Amsterdam: Amsterdam University Press, 1999).
28 "At one and the same time, human beings express their agency through their acts of self-governance, and through their voluntary or coerced participation in governance structures that they share with others and that channel the occasions for exercising that human agency": Macdonald, *Governance of Human Agency*.
29 Leslie Green, "Law, Legitimacy and Consent," *Southern California Law Review* 62 (1988–89): 801–2.
30 Macdonald and Sandomierksi, 611.
31 Green, 801–2.
32 Samuel Beckett, *Worstward Ho* (London: John Calder, 1983).
33 This paragraph, including the Dostoevsky quote (Fyodor Dostoevsky, *The Brothers Karamazov*, New York: Random House, 1950, 303) is reproduced from my dissertation: Thomas McMorrow, "Critical for What? Legal for Whom? Examining the Implications of a Critical Legal Pluralism for Re-imagining the Role of High School Students in Education Law" (DCL thesis, McGill University, 2012), 90. Belley's identification of Macdonald's legal thought with the Christian anarchism of Dostoevsky as reflected in the story of the Grand Inquisitor led me to draw out this quotation: Jean-Guy Belley, "Le pluralisme juridique de Roderick Macdonald: une analyse séquentielle," in *Théories et émergence du droit: pluralisme, surdétermination et effectivité*, edited by A. Lajoie, R.A. Macdonald, R. Janda, and G. Rocher (Montreal: Thémis, 1998), 57–68.
34 Onora O'Neill, "Is Hope a Virtue?" (Trinity College Chapel Sermon, Cambridge University, 1 January 2012), Trinity College Chapel Archive of Preachers and Sermons, http://www.trinitycollegechapel.com/media/filestore/sermons/O%27Neill%20Hope310110.pdf: 8.

35 Roderick Macdonald, oral communication, recalled to the best of my abilities, to participants at DCL retreat at the Faculty of Law, McGill University, 16 October 2009.

36 Macdonald, "Justice Is a Noun," 3.

19

Beyond Judicial Review: Governance and Public Administration in Rod Macdonald's Theory of Administrative Law

NICOLAS LAMBERT

Introduction

Between the late 1980s and early 1990s, Rod Macdonald's administrative law scholarship turned decisively from conventional questions such as procedural fairness and federal court jurisdiction to a more exploratory, open-ended inquiry into the nature of good public administration and the role of law. His change in orientation also brought with it a new focus on economics and legal sociology but also some overarching critiques of legal thinking. He almost appeared disenchanted with the discipline of law itself. As Rod notes:

> Largely under the impulse of the Charter, high-level conceptual analysis remains the preferred discourse of many public law scholars, whose rather narrow conception of law and legal normativity leads them to mischaracterize their subject field as "administrative law" rather than "judicial review of administrative action."[1] … I make this claim advisedly, since so little recent writing in the field of judicial review in common law in Canada has sought to reorient the field by taking up the challenge launched by René Dussault & Louis Borgeat … It has focused, rather, on finding linkages between traditional doctrines of judicial review and review of administrative action under s. 7 of the Charter.[2]

The few short lines, the latter of which were written in footnote, could sum up Rod Macdonald's final thoughts on the direction of Canadian administrative law. However, the claim is not new and has been noted, in one way or another, over the past century.[3] Already at the turn of the last century, F.W. Maitland noted that legal education did not in fact teach public law as it was practised in government.[4] S.A. de Smith underscored, in the opening lines of his textbook, that judicial review of administrative action was simply one small part of administrative law.[5]

Today, these words are viewed by some as eccentric, if not irrelevant. What became problematic, and is now controversial for the administrative lawyer, is the idea that public administration can be studied on its own, as a field of legal inquiry, independently from judicial review.[6] Symptomatic of this attachment is that even when administrative lawyers turn away from the courts, their focus remains fixated on the judicial elements of public administration: administrative tribunals, procedure and administrative independence, and impartiality. This point is so fundamental – one might even say part of the common law tradition itself – that Rod never took it on as a point of law, head-on, but turned directly from "judicial review of administrative action" to "public administration." The line between the two thus remains uncertain; their juxtaposition brings them physically closer while accentuating a difference in theory if not ideology.

However, the "law and administration" movement remains a minority critique. The difficulty is that it only offers an indirect rebuttal of the judicial review fixation while making law and administration an either/or choice. The result is a juxtaposition of law and public administration, not an integration of administrative action into the legal realm itself. The purpose of this paper is to add support to Rod's criticism along with some words on how the "law and administration" movement could broaden its contribution inside the classroom and beyond.

Public Administration as a "Remedy" to Administrative Law

Many in the legal profession would characterize Rod's change of focus as going from administrative law to governance and public administration. Insofar as it is concerned with the activity rather than the institution of government, "governance" has reoriented public administration so as to provide a continuous cross-sectional view of "collective" action, from core governmental activities to the numerous private linkages that straddle the fringes of public administration. At this level, "governance" fits well into Canadian administrative lawyers thinking, because it does not draw any bright line between public and private activity. At the same time, "governance," or even public administration, are rarely mentioned in Canadian administrative law, for the simple reason that the object of study in Canadian administrative law is not good public administration but good judicial review.

Rod himself did not see the study of administrative action as "legal" in the conventional sense: he opposed "contextualized governance" to what he termed "call-centre government," namely, one where matters were directed from the top down and fell magically into place through a Weberian hierarchy. Drawing on positivist juridical parallels, he viewed conventional "rule of law" modes of legal thought along similar lines: idealized, mechanized, and sanitized models of decision-making with little to do with the everyday administrative decision-making body. He thus insisted on putting more thought into institutional design and adapting it to circumstance, thereby allowing legality to flow from the bottom up rather than seeing matters as preordained, hence the term "contextualized governance." In this sense, he viewed each tribunal as having its own internal law based on its own unique circumstances.

The divorce between law and administration was solemnized by textbooks implicitly portraying lawyers more as pathologists than physiologists of government. There would be no lacuna in legal education, because "government action" is not what "law" is about. As Rod notes, Canadian administrative law increasingly demonstrates a tendency to feed on itself, turning faster and faster into smaller concentric circles, maintaining an appearance of specialization while teaching more and more about less and less. The focalization on judicial standards of review, their nature, their application, and the proper methodology of judicial review is a case in point. If "control" is the only hammer in the administrative lawyer's toolbox, all problems have now become nails, not only in the courtroom but in the classroom as well. However, Rod was never able to pull the two together and at times also seemed attached to the "control" rationale for administrative law. The fundamental disagreement, as he put it, was about responsibility for oversight procedures. In his words: "[T]he central problem of contemporary governance is less a 'conflict of values' between public servants and the legal profession than a disagreement about how best to pursue public policy according to law. It is a disagreement about the design of oversight procedures for public agencies arising because of the Diceyan-Rule-of-Law assumption that there can only be one administrative law – that propounded by courts."[7]

Moreover, he also leaned back into the "values" debate while leaving it out of law, framing it as a matter of governance and public administration: "Governance and public administration are about the substantive goals that states and other public bodies pursue."[8] In this respect, public administration would remain a matter of substance, while administrative law remained a matter of control and oversight. Visibly, this dichotomization does not change much; Dicey himself did not see administrative discretion as legally relevant; law for him was merely a matter of oversight, albeit judicial. Thus, even in the progressive "law and administration" movement, administrative action remains a matter of policy, while control – be it judicial or administrative – remains one of law.

Rod's practical solution to the judicial review fixation was the study of "administrative process," a course that he developed and taught at McGill. However, we question whether this course was more of a compromise and actually went as far as he advocated in his later writings. Already, the term "process" neutralizes the substantive aspects of the inquiry while suggesting that we are not dealing with "law" proper. Second, the administrative process school, in its antagonism to the "rule of law" ideology, rejects any judicial involvement in the definition of administrative goals and objectives. As a result, case law is implicitly rejected as one of its sources. Third, one wonders where the line between administrative law and public administration can be drawn when each individual tribunal's internal law becomes part of the inquiry, as suggested by Rod. Last, from a normative perspective, policy debates on good governance should not be equated with primary or substantive administrative law, even in its critical elements. There is an immense wealth of knowledge to be gained from public administration literature, although the task of the "law and administration" movement is to integrate administrative policy discussion into existing legal frameworks, not to work in splendid isolation from one another.

Substantive versus Remedial Administrative Law

Any clarity in the tangle comes with the realization that governance scholars and lawyers seem to leave one another the task of understanding and critiquing contemporary public administration on its own terms. Moreover, in the common law world, public administration has always been viewed as separate from law, although it is difficult to imagine one without the other. Indeed, for Max Weber, the grandfather of modern public administration and himself a lawyer, public administration was the optimal form of collective organization through hierarchy and competency.

One must remember that when it first presented itself in North America, administrative law shared much with public administration as we understand it today.[9] However, over the coming decades, administrative law curricula turned to meet the immediate needs of private practitioners – thus the turn from primary, institutional, and relational portrayal of the law to its secondary remedial template of legal action through the courts (i.e., judicial review of administrative action). As a result, much of the theorizing in administrative law is pushed off to the courts. The governmental habit of turning to lawyers only when there is a problem, of using lawyers to justify government action, is the institutional reflection of legal education itself: one in which law students are trained as pathologists, not physiologists or even anatomists of government institutions. Some have noted a convergence of "law and administration,"[10] although we would not be so optimistic without understanding its conceptual antecedents.

The difficulty is that existing categories in administrative law provide no easy way out of the focus on judicial review. Contemporary administrative law's *summa divisio* between substantive and procedural review is a case in point. This distinction carries little consequence on its own while suggesting that substance refers to statute, procedure to the common law. Its value, however, is that it teaches by example. Students are not required to understand every aspect of public administration. However, it distorts the inquiry and focuses too much on contention when the substantive goals of government should be given more attention. In fact, what administrative lawyers should give credence to is not substantive or procedural review but substantive law, on the one hand, and its sanctioning by the courts, on the other. This in fact is the distinction that Rod seems to refer to in his writings, although it is rarely given credence in public law, Anglo-American in particular.

The value of the distinction lies in understanding that remedial administrative law cannot condition the meaning of substantive rules with remedial rules; it can only describe their operation. This is especially true in the case of statute. As a result, there can be no substantive value in "reasonableness," "jurisdiction," or "correctness" lest courts themselves add to the meaning of statute. This simple observation, however, has been lost for many administrative lawyers searching for the administrative "holy grail," i.e., a substantive definition of jurisdiction and reasonableness. At the same time, we question the value of these discussions on the terms suggested. Yet for lawyers who thrive on ambiguity, there is always a reward in falling back into these debates. As Upton Sinclair said, "It is difficult to get a man to understand something, when his salary depends on his not understanding it."

Moreover, the law and administration movement has at times appeared critical of law as an institution itself, thereby giving credence to the idea that law cannot be made but through the courts.[11] Indeed, by not distinguishing substantive law from its sanctioning by the courts, theories of "judicial" administrative law appear to be hostile to public administration, while public administration theories appear anathema to law itself, or at least to judicial review. The correlation is exemplified in Harlow and Rawlings's dichotomy between "red-light" and "green-light" theories of administrative law – the former exemplifying the focus on judicial control and the latter the permissive penchant for public administration. In both cases, however, the "light" remains the courthouse.[12] The question of how much academics should focus their energies on judicial review (answer: part) is thus confused with the question of how much actual judicial review should be exercised by the courts. This last question is irrelevant if all agree that substantive law should condition the scope of judicial review.

Thus, in not fleshing out substantive law from its sanctioning in courts (e.g., standards of review), even progressive administrative lawyers inescapably fall back onto "control" as a bedrock for administrative law while portraying administrative action as policy-based. Substantive administrative law becomes a normative inquiry into how public administration should be exercised (i.e., governance), thus leaving values to the administrators, oversight to the lawyers. Public administration and governance scholars, for their part, point to the same academic blind spot. While public administration and administrative law seemed to grow out of the same "seed" of political science, governance and public administration have veered off into a more idealized form of public administration, "good governance" in particular. Meanwhile, the description and critique of administrative behaviour has become more economic than juridical.[13] The result is a theory of public administration that is disconnected from reality, incapable of foreseeing the institutional quagmires into which contemporary governance has legislated itself.

At the same time, it bears mentioning that while administrative lawyers know little about public administration, those who are supposed to know the law (public administrators) have no formal administrative law education, nor are they allowed in most Canadian universities to gain one. In the end, when contemporary legal academics encourage interdisciplinary research, what they mean is the privilege of lawyers to look beyond the law school, not for outsiders such as public administration students to take part in administrative law discussions in the law school itself. If administrative law has not changed in the century since the words of F.W. Maitland, we suggest that this may have something to do with the problem.

Conclusion

The study of "governance" is not anathema to administrative law, although the solution to administrative law's focus on remediation is not the juxtaposition of judicial review and public administration or governance. Rather, it is the recognition of a substantive branch of administrative law focusing on the objectives of administrative action itself. This is probably the vision that Rod sought to articulate, although as with many in the "law and public administration" movement, he faced an uphill battle and criticized the focus on judicial review in cultural rather than legal terms. However, to be fully overcome, the focus on judicial review must be attacked on its own terms, as a matter of law, not merely as the wrong attitude. If a reptile analogy is permitted, one could say that the way out of a python's bite is not by trying to pull out (thereby deepening the wound) but, first, by going deeper into the animal itself.

That being said, if anything has proved true, it is that what shapes administrative law is less the shape of government that exists today than the model of education that existed when administrative law first reared its head in Canada. To this extent, if anything is to change in administrative legal thinking, it cannot only come from academic journals but from legal educators and reformers such as Rod not only talking the talk of law reform in law journals but walking the walk of law reform through legal education itself.

NOTES

1 Roderick Macdonald, "Call-Centre Government: For the Rule of Law, Press #," *University of Toronto Law Journal* 55 (2005): 456.
2 Ibid. [reference omitted].
3 Mario Bouchard, "Administrative Law in the Real World: A View from Canada," in *Judicial Review of Administrative Action in the 1980s*, edited by Michael Taggart (Auckland: Oxford University Press, 1987), 179.
4 "Do not imagine that English law is exhausted by those departments of it that you can study here – the law of crimes, the law of property, torts, and contracts, and that part of constitutional law which is concerned with king

and parliament. No, there are vast departments of law lying outside these boundaries; some of them belong to constitutional law, others perhaps be called administrative law; for the most part, they are statutory and of recent creation, the work of the last fifty years; but their importance is very great": Frederick W. Maitland, *The Constitutional History of England* (Cambridge: Cambridge University Press, 1908), 505–6.

5 "Judicial review of administrative action is inevitably sporadic and peripheral. The administrative process is not, and cannot be, a succession of justiciable controversies": John Evans, *De Smith's Judicial Review of Administrative Action*, 4th edn (London: Sweet and Maxwell, 1980), 2.

6 Karl Llewellyn, "A Realistic Jurisprudence – The Next Step," *Columbia Law Review* 30 (1930): 455, describing administrative action as "law."

7 Macdonald, "Call-Centre Government," 452–3.

8 Ibid., 453.

9 See, for instance, Frank Goodnow, *Comparative Administrative Law* (New York: Burt Franklin, 1903).

10 Carol Harlow, "Law and Public Administration: Convergence and Symbiosis," *International Review of Administrative Sciences* 71 (2) (2005): 279.

11 Harry Arthurs, *"Without the Law": Administrative Justice and Legal Pluralism in Nineteenth Century England* (Toronto: University of Toronto Press, 1985).

12 Carol Harlow and Richard Rawlings, *Law and Administration* (Cambridge: Cambridge University Press, 2009), 1.

13 Donald F. Kettl, *The Transformation of Governance – Public Administration in Twenty-First Century America* (Baltimore: John Hopkins University Press, 2002).

20

The Governance of Human Communities

RICHARD JANDA

The governance of any human community – and perhaps that of non-human communities as well – can be contextualized in its propensity for abuse of power, corruption, and endless tragedies of the commons. When we encounter these phenomena, crying out as they do for justice, we begin to find it astonishingly naive to contextualize the governance of any human community in its propensity for giving, self-sacrifice, and interdependent collective action. To put this in biblical terms, the knowledge of evil occludes the perception of good. There is consequently an almost irresistible intellectual temptation to acknowledge what is dysfunctional and pathological in us and to seek to channel and control it toward the production of some lesser evil. Thus, why not acknowledge self-interest and greed and orient it toward stable markets and competitive consumption? Why not invent separations and distributions of power that can keep our own need for authority in check? Why not give each of us the shield of personal rights to fend off the havoc that might otherwise be wreaked upon us and by us? I call this the posture of fatalistic narcissism, and Rod Macdonald taught me to resist it with every juridical fibre available to me.

It is no mean feat to construct an entire body of thought around an indefatigable, practically minded, and demonstrably successful appeal to our better selves even as we confront the worst abuses of which we are capable. A crucial aspect of Rod's thought that serves to defeat fatalistic narcissism is its disciplined insistence that every human encounter is a setting for open-ended justice claims. For many jurists, but not for Rod, the formalism of treating like cases alike serves to give shape and orientation to legal inquiry. Indeed, it is a core and deeply unsettling insight in his work that formalism, which in small doses seems to protect us from our worst selves, in fact, through its acceptance of fatalistic narcissism, ultimately releases them. Of course, as he insisted almost ad nauseam, this formalism begs the question as to what is truly alike, since nothing ever is, except in one respect: every human encounter carries the possibility of a higher aspiration.

However, when we ask ourselves what prospects for future research are held out by a writer, we are really asking: how truly radical is his or her thought? Conventional wisdom can hold out no prospect for future research, because it can only produce the confirmation of what is already known. To borrow a metaphor used by Hoi Kong, it is true that small departures from conventional wisdom can shine light into hitherto unseen corners of our collective experience by applying the tried and true with some slight variant.[1] But as Rod might put it, what exactly is the point of doing the umpteenth study of how to apply the Charter of Rights and Freedoms?

If, perhaps precisely because you detect in Rod Macdonald a certain diffident social democrat and are therefore unpersuaded that he is a radical thinker, consider the encounter between him and two perennial Latin maxims. One is on the wall of McGill's Moot Court Room: *honeste vivere, alterum non laedare, suum cuique tribuere*. Even now, when I read those words, I feel a certain dignity descend upon me and can be persuaded that if I just cleave to them, I cannot go astray. I do not want to go as far as saying that for Rod these words were an affront. But if I go through the exercise of reading them immediately after rereading his work, they come to seem dull and unambitious. To live honestly is only to begin to live as a fully engaged citizen. To do no harm is to have not yet taken on the burden of discovering the good one can do for others. To render to each her due – that talisman of justice – only begins to open up the vista of what can fully be enabled for her.

Consider a second maxim that has come to be embedded in the unconscious of generations of students of the common law: *stare decisis et non quieta movere*. When I repeat the exercise of contemplating those words after rereading his work, I feel rising in me a certain impatience and frustration. How can I possibly allow myself to stand on my decision? At most, I should give it honest continuing appraisal, account for the harm I might do in departing from it, and ensure that I am not about to deprive someone of what is due if I abandon it. This is perhaps what is meant by giving it the status of a default rule. But governance, as Rod conceived it, is all about a continuous fluid appraisal of our needs, latent capabilities, and transformative potential. *Stare decisis* is a waxworks that purports to leave things in undisturbed calm when we know it can melt in the presence of a little heat.

Rod's thought may indeed cast asunder words that have been engraved on stones for many a year, but for his thought to have prospects also means that something could be built on it in place of those ancient words. The pose of critique, fashionable at times even in law schools, does not hold out prospects for future research if the deconstruction it accomplishes leaves only rubble in its wake. After all, what's really to choose between endlessly reproduced conventional wisdom and unrelenting critique? They are simply obverse forms of monomania that have been on display at least since Parmenides proclaimed the persistence of the One only to be countered by Heraclitus's dictum that one cannot step into the same river twice.

So let's be frank here together. Who among us has not smirked a bit thinking that Rod's endless fascination with cottage docks and packages of Smarties lacks gravitas in the face of the Holocaust and climate change? Who among us has not given way to the temptation to see in his work a custom-made cabinet of curiosities filled up with vim and vigour but destined ultimately to be cupboarded away like some discarded law commission? I dare say that he himself on occasion gave way to that temptation, wondering whether all of his efforts were not mere ephemera in the face of our overwhelming capacity for amnesia, indifference, indolence, and greed. These forces eat away at us like a cancer.

Therefore, let me take you on a brief trip to the dark side of Rod Macdonald's thought. The articles this panel has under consideration are in fact quite open about its existence. "Call-Centre Government" channels intense frustration with the mind-numbing quality of the collective idiocy that over here is called bureaucratic rationality and over there is called customer service.[2] "Rabbits, Ravens Snakes, Turtles," under the guise of yet another Macdonald paean of praise to the richness of human experience, peers into an abyss that has been created by the persistent afterlife of colonialism in Aboriginal communities.[3] "The Swiss Army Knife of Governance," with all the gleam of the smooth and shiny tools on display, begins by invoking the Tower of Babel – a recurrent image for Rod – that monument to failed communication, one huge, toppled Habermas.[4] Into "The Acoustics of Accountability" erupts what deeply troubles and dramatically unsettles him: agency capture, partisan politics, subverted independence, rent-seeking and bribe-taking.[5] And what is "Regulation by Regulations," a piece that has had transformative significance for me, if not a *cri de coeur* against what Harry Arthurs has called the Washington Consensus and John Whyte has decried as market fundamentalism?[6] Rod is not a happy camper here.

Virtually all of us, when we look at the Gorgon's head, turn into stone. To be petrified is to be utterly immobilized with fright. Rod long had a rare, unusual form of double vision with which he could behold a terror at the same time as turning entirely away from it. Who has not felt that Rod had eyes in the back of his head?[7]

I cannot help but invoke a "Rod story" to illustrate my point. This is not hagiography – it is my effort at rigorous application of his scholarly methodology. Every experience is material for writing.

A number of years ago, I arranged a meeting for the two of us with the dean of music to pursue the possibility of intersecting our two faculties, building on Macdonald's long-standing efforts to weave legal inquiry into the entire fabric of the university. It had taken a bit of doing to convince the dean that such a meeting made sense, and finally the day arrived when the efforts were about to pay off. I remember that day vividly. It was in 2001, September 11 to be exact.

A phone call from my wife had me glued to the radio in my office. I was petrified. I couldn't stop listening. I needed to find a television. Then I remembered our meeting, almost too late. I phoned Rod, who was expecting me in his office, and I said:

Rod, have you heard?
Yes, where are you?
I can't believe it.
When are you going to be here?
Rod, I don't think I can do this meeting.
[Long pause]
Janda – can you do anything for New York?
No.
Does your fixation on the news change anything?
No.
Get over here now, we have a meeting.

I followed his order. That was Rod, on the battlefield.

I have revisited that exchange periodically over time. It was one of my vivid "Rod" moments. I have never quite fathomed its meaning, even to this day. At the time, it un-petrified me. It braced me back to life. But I was left with unease about it as a lesson in governance. I felt as though I had been brought to play my instrument, cued by the conductor's baton, there in the middle of Teresienstadt. What sense could this make?

It was only recently that I came to understand the nature of the meeting Rod had cajoled me into attending. It *was* the meeting to do something about what was petrifying me. Reflecting on remarks made at this symposium, permit me to express some intemperate anger at Harry Arthurs and John Whyte, and maybe even at Les Green and Denise Réaume,[8] which in fact, as you will see, is really anger directed at myself, rebounded from the anger Rod had expressed on September 11.

That lightweight, magic realism, with all its elaborate incantations of procedural fairness, accountability, and virtue, is deathly serious and represents the only thing we can fortify to confront the evils that petrify us. If you want to give way to power, if you want to bemoan an evil you can do nothing about, stand aside, because you have nothing to offer. If you believe that these incantations are but baubles and trinkets about to be swept aside by the surge of history while Gaia, the goddess earth, finally takes its revenge on the ravages we have done against her, just go, take a front row seat, and wait for the apocalypse.

I have not learned all the magic that lies in Rod's incantations. But I think I know one of the spells. It's in the piece that changed my scholarship many years ago, and I suppose, since it was written under the editorial direction of Andrée Lajoie, it was destined to bring me into a kind of magic circle with her, Rod, Guy Rocher, and Pierre Noreau: "Understanding Regulation by Regulations." There is much to the piece, but the spell in question is there in plain view, though it bursts upon the reader so suddenly and with so little elaboration that its deep significance seems to have been missed. We all know the Coase Theorem and Arrow's Theorem, but how many of us recall, let alone teach, Macdonald's constant. It is simple and elegant: "the sum of regulation in any given economy is a constant; what vary are the degree of centralization of regulation and its instrumentalities."[9]

As I look back upon it, I think one way of describing my own work and its future trajectory is that it is an effort to elaborate Macdonald's constant.

From what is Macdonald's constant derived? Everything we have spoken about at this symposium. The regulation of any given economy is the sum of all human endeavours to steer it. It is the alignment and misalignment of our agency.

Our economy is ubiquitously capitalist, with the gift economy that runs in counter-cycle to it more often than not misaligned and drowned out by the price signal. However, the sum of regulation is a constant. To the degree that the economy can be decentralized toward constitutive human agency and if human agency can be instrumentalized toward gift, the sum of regulation will remain a constant and capitalism will be transformed. Yes, Rod acknowledged instrumentalism – he spoke at length of choice of instrument. The instrumentalism he rejected is one that fails to acknowledge the means–ends complex. The end in view is to overcome the power that petrifies us.

Think therefore on Macdonald's constant.

NOTES

* To Annalise Acorn, with deep thanks and affection.

1 See Hoi Kong's contribution to this volume.

2 Roderick Macdonald, "Call-Centre Government: For the Rule of Law, Press #," *University of Toronto Law Journal* 55 (2005): 449–95.

3 Roderick Macdonald and Thomas McMorrow, "Rabbits, Ravens, Snakes, Turtles: Analyzing the Political Economy of Aboriginal Communities," in *Gouvernance autochtone: reconfiguration d'un avenir collectif*, edited by Pierre Noreau (Montreal: Thémis, 2010), 211–35.

4 Macdonald, "The Swiss Army Knife of Governance," in *Designing Government: From Instruments to Governance*, edited by Pearl Eliadis et al. (Montreal: McGill-Queen's University Press, 2005), 203–41.

5 Macdonald, "The Acoustics of Accountability: Towards Well-Tempered Tribunals" (Speech to the 14th Annual Conference of the Council of Canadian Administrative Tribunals, Ottawa, 31 May 1998).

6 Macdonald, "Understanding Regulation by Regulations," in *Regulations, Crown Corporations and Administrative Tribunals*, edited by I. Bernier and A. Lajoie (Toronto: University of Toronto Press, 1985), 81–154.

7 As my colleague Daniel Boyer points out, continuing the metaphor in the same direction, for many of us Rod's work functions like Perseus's shield.

8 Leslie Green and Denise Réaume both intervened during the symposium. Leslie Green's remarks came during the panel on "Pluralizing the Subject" and can be found at http://bcooltv.mcgill.ca/Viewer2/?rid=9a0608e6-50cf-4f24-9d35-b1afd28bc2f5, at 59:38. Denise Réaume's remarks came during the panel on "Kaleidoscopic Federalism" and can be found at http://bcooltv.mcgill.ca/Viewer2/?rid=ed9db6bc-da20-4d40-b7a2-bdec41fa42b2, at 1:36:04.

9 Macdonald, "Understanding Regulation," 145.

21

Rod Macdonald's Society of Friends

JEREMY WEBBER

Those of us who know Rod Macdonald's writing on legal education or saw his interaction with students will have been struck by the moral tenor of his exhortations concerning legal education: his insistence that the study of law – indeed law itself – is about coming to know oneself, one's most fundamental values, one's commitments, one's life.

So, how are we to understand what Macdonald was doing in those exhortations? How did he conceive of the nature of our search for ourselves and our lives in the law?

I will engage with Macdonald's thinking and teaching under three headings. The first two are entirely familiar, but the third is insufficiently recognized – although I believe that when it is perceived, it is central to an understanding of all that Macdonald did and indeed central to his appeal. It is also the aspect of his thought that is least understood – perhaps it was even the least understood by Macdonald himself. It is therefore one aspect to which we need to bring our most concerted attention.

The three headings are: Pursuing Virtue, Embracing Pluralism, and the least understood dimension, the Gift of Prophecy.

Pursuing Virtue

In a recent article, Rod Macdonald and Tom McMorrow say: "The inherent challenge of legal education is not simply to produce lawyers or law professors who lawyer or profess law ethically, but to enable people to grow in virtue through their study of law."[1] This is characteristic. Macdonald insisted, above all, on the primacy of substantive value in all his descriptions of legal analysis and indeed life.

Nowhere is his emphasis on substantive value more obvious than in his frequent invocation of Robert Samek's conception of the "meta phenomenon." He summarizes the meta phenomenon as "the displacement of ends by means, of substance by form, of thought by reflex, of people by process, of interaction and relationships by unilateralism and individualism."[2] He begins one of his essays with the following passage from Samek: "The meta phenomenon is the human propensity to displace primary with 'secondary' concerns, that is, concerns about ends with concerns about means. The latter come to be perceived as primary, and distort the former in their own image. The new primary concerns are in turn displaced by the new secondary concerns about the means to be adopted to achieve the new ends, leading to another shift in the focus of consciousness. The new secondary concerns come to be perceived as primary, and so on."[3]

This does not mean that he was wholly dismissive of procedure. Macdonald had the most acute institutional sense I have ever seen. He knew the value of participation, knew the processes and ethics of leadership and engagement that foster participation (although he typically valued informal over formal processes), read people like nobody else that I have ever met, and knew what is necessary to move an institution toward decision. Moreover, his primary area of law was, initially, administrative law.

But he always insisted that the main purpose of any process is the affirmation and instantiation of substantive value, the cultivation of virtue, the perfecting of relationship, and the achievement of ends that are good in themselves. Procedure was always a means to these objectives. He definitely was impatient with the displacement of substance by process. He realized, however, that the nature of substantive value is often veiled – glimpsed only through a glass darkly – and thus an object of aspiration rather than accomplishment. Hence the emphasis, in all that he did, on activity – on *pursuing* virtue, on *coming to learn* who one is, on "a continual and creative rediscovery of ourselves."[4] And that of course is the role of process in his thought: it is about how we come to know who we are, how we come to *be* who we are.

Embracing Pluralism

But Macdonald was also a pluralist. He devoted his life to affirming that law is made in our daily encounters, including our most intimate encounters, and that means that law is generated from the most intensely local milieus upwards throughout all society. Indeed, in another article that invokes the meta phenomenon in the context of law reform, he combines that notion with his commitment to pluralism: "To focus only on official law reform ... is to displace the primary (the law as lived and generated, relived and regenerated, by those to whom it evidently speaks) by the secondary (the law as written and made, rewritten and remade, by those who claim a special authority to do so). It is also to focus on the most visible and explicit of existing legal artifacts without recognizing their artificiality."[5]

He was alert to the fact that in these local interactions, we continually encounter difference, contrasting claims, imperfect understanding, and differences of language. Indeed, we encounter that diversity inwardly as we seek to reconcile our own plural identities as teachers, as researchers, as administrators, as members of a community, as parents, and as seekers after the deepest truth. In his view, the quality of our legal relations, indeed of our moral lives, is determined by how we manoeuvre among those contending identities and relationships.[6] As he says in the introduction to "Office Politics," "it is in the recognition of intimacy and vulnerability and in the reconstitution of ourselves through our relationships with others that we understand why merely formal conceptions of authenticity are inadequate to capture fully the meaning of institutional life."[7]

One sees that theme abundantly in his two masterpieces – in the range of voices in "Office Politics," which are never fully resolved in a canonical interpretation, and in the inevitable partiality of language in "Legal Bilingualism."[8] Pluralism plays two essential roles in Macdonald's work. (1) It makes the local the arena in which the essential action is. It is out of practical interaction, which in Macdonald's view is always emphatically local, that true normativity arises. And (2) it emphasizes our perennial encounter with difference and our consequent need to develop relationship, interpretation, attention, and skills of engagement and integration as essential attributes of law.

But are we caught, irredeemably, within plurality? Can we break through that plurality to truth? Or, to put those questions with more of an edge: What stops the plurality of voices from blowing any sense of normativity apart so that difference overwhelms any possibility of harmony? What stops everything from spinning out of control? If two crucial themes in Macdonald's work are the primacy of questions of substantive value on the one hand and the inevitable plurality of voices on the other, what allows the whole to remain together?

This brings us to the last theme. It was alluded to in the conference out of which this volume emerged when several speakers noted that Macdonald was fundamentally "optimistic." But I think the last theme has more substance than that. It has more structure than a mere sense of optimism suggests. It is integrally built into the foundation of his theoretical approach. For one thing, treating Macdonald's approach as merely optimistic fails to make room for the fiercely critical dimension of his scholarship to which Richard Janda called our attention at the conference. I deal with Macdonald's approach under the last heading.

The Gift of Prophecy

I have always been struck by Macdonald's commitment to the establishment of harmony:

- in his prescriptions for social interaction, in the way he conducted arguments, or even in his chairing of faculty meetings, where he often tried to mollify and cover over conflict, where he insisted that we already hold a set of commitments that resolve our disagreements, where he suggested that there is an emergent truth around which everyone can converge;
- or in his approach to legal pluralism, where he was confident that harmony *already* exists within the fabric of our social interactions and he attempted to bring that immanent harmony to light – indeed, it often seemed, to speak that harmony into being.

Harry Arthurs has referred to this phenomenon as "magic realism."[9] To me, it is that Macdonald speaks in a quintessentially prophetic mode. He deploys appeals that are like those of a prophet: he calls us to reflect upon ourselves; he exhorts us to attend to virtue. And in those appeals he often uses devices that allude to an underlying and ineffable truth that cannot be spoken. He uses parables; he speaks in poetic terms; he makes statements that have an impact like a Zen koan, impossible to understand discursively but that speak to us nevertheless.

This mode of speaking is more than simply a description of what happens to be the case. It is more even than a prediction of a future state of affairs. That is why the notion of optimism understates what Macdonald is doing. Rather, he is pointing to an underlying truth, seeking, through its identification, to call it into being, even against obtuse or malevolent opposition. He is speaking in an exhortative rather than merely descriptive mode.[10]

When in faculty meetings he spoke, for example, of the implicit and inferential norms that govern the interactions of the Faculty of Law, he did not mean that, merely in fact, there were implicit norms that the faculty customarily followed. He was saying that there was a normative order that accorded with the *best* sense of how this faculty might interact, with the best sense of what this faculty is. He asked us to recognize those norms as the ideal embodiment of this faculty and to make our conduct accord with those norms. That is why moral reflection, reflection into the deepest nature of ourselves, is integral to legal process. The process of articulating the norm is an attempt to invoke what we are truly meant to be and to exhort us to bring ourselves into alignment with that truth.

In "Office Politics," for example, one has a clear sense that there is, in that welter of voices in the memos, a truth that is struggling to manifest itself. One hears at points, in some of those memos, a voice that is clearly that of Macdonald.[11] Don't get me wrong: he is utterly faithful to the allegory. No one voice completely gets it. The truth always needs to be completed by additional voices. Moreover, there is always an element of self-reflection, of the possibility of error, of the need to expose oneself to questioning – both relentless questioning internally and the questioning of others – in everything that Macdonald wrote. But one has the distinct sense in Macdonald's work that error is possible in relation to a truth that pre-exists the conversation. And that truth is not merely a descriptive truth but a more fundamental truth about what we are meant to be.

That truth is also evident in Macdonald's treatment of the realm of practice – of the inarticulate realm of practice – in "Legal Bilingualism." Macdonald emphasizes that norms exist before they are articulated in language. The norms are not dependent on being spoken to exist. Indeed, he thinks of the true norm as existing beyond language and of linguistic formulations as only approximating that norm, a norm that he also clearly conceives in the singular, not the plural.[12] This also means that the norm is not consciously made by the parties. It emerges before they know that norm. They discover it. In fact, correct me if I am wrong, but in "Legal Bilingualism," doesn't the pluralism appear only at the level of language? Isn't the underlying norm something that is common, which exists as a norm before the parties seek to put it into words?

Note the consequences of this for the specific character of Macdonald's legal pluralism. He genuinely affirmed pluralism. He believed deeply in the multiplicity of voices. But he thought of those voices as existing in relation to a harmony that lies beyond the parties themselves. In an important sense, the harmony already exists, ingrained within their interaction. The parties' task – our task – is to draw it out. The norm is not merely the product of the parties' deliberate action, working through their institutions.[13]

Moreover, this foundational harmony is not contingent. That is why the language of "optimism" misses an essential point. It is not just that harmony might appear. It is not even merely that he hoped it would appear. Rather, he had confidence that, at an immanent level, woven through our Fullerian practices (not on some separate supernatural plane) it already exists and our task is to identify it and to instantiate it in our lives and our institutions.

This involves a distinctive conception of responsibility – a responsibility to reflect continually upon what that essential harmony might be and upon what our relationship to it should be. Macdonald did believe that that responsibility is distributed to each and every one of us. He embraced an emphatically democratic conception of the prophetic role in which we each have things to reflect upon and contribute. He envisaged a true society of friends. That underlies his approach to pedagogy, where he sought to exhort people, to provoke people, or to cajole them to seek after that fundamental truth. But that truth is not the product of their own will or even of their own intellect. It is something outside of themselves that they are charged with pursuing.

This prophetic dimension of Macdonald's thought accounts, I believe, for much of its appeal:

- its emphasis on a harmony existing in principle but achieved in practice through relationship: the substance of our hopes, the fulfilment of our trust;
- its calling of us back, continually, to attend to the affirmation of that good, to pursue virtue;
- and the collective conduct of that pursuit, through the exercise of an emphatically individual moral and intellectual responsibility in the society of friends.

Let me conclude by quoting a passage to which Macdonald alludes, indeed which at one point he paraphrases, in "Legal Bilingualism":

> whether there be prophecies, they shall fail; whether there be tongues, they shall cease; whether there be knowledge, it shall vanish away.
> For we know in part, and we prophesy in part.
> But when that which is perfect is come, then that which is in part shall be done away.

> When I was a child, I spake as a child, I understood as a child, I thought as a child: but when I became a man, I put away childish things.
> For now we see through a glass, darkly; but then face to face: now I know in part; but then shall I know even as also I am known.[14]

A genuine vein of religiosity runs through Macdonald's work. It is a secular religiosity, without a personal god, affirming the pursuit of virtue in a society of individuals who bear their equal share of truth. And it finds its consummation in the faith that there is an order that lies within human interaction, which can be perceived and affirmed if only we have the knowledge, insight, and perseverance to do so.

NOTES

1 Roderick Macdonald and Thomas McMorrow, "Decolonizing Law School," *Alberta Law Review* 51 (4) (2014): 724–5.
2 Macdonald, "Who's Afraid of the Cyber-Law-Journal?" *Queen's Law Journal* 36 (2) (2011): 347.
3 Macdonald, "Access to Justice and Law Reform," *Windsor Year Book of Access to Justice* 10 (1990): 287, quoting from Robert A. Samek, *The Meta Phenomenon* (New York: Philosophical Library, 1981), 4.
4 Macdonald, "Curricular Development in the 1980s: A Perspective," *Journal of Legal Education* 32 (1982): 590.
5 Macdonald, "Recommissioning Law Reform," *Alberta Law Review* 35 (4) (1996–97): 878.
6 Martha-Marie Kleinhans and Roderick Macdonald, "What Is a *Critical* Legal Pluralism?" *Canadian Journal of Law and Society* 12 (1997): 46; Macdonald, "Custom Made – For a Non-chirographic Critical Legal Pluralism," *Canadian Journal of Law and Society* 26 (2011): 323–7.
7 Macdonald, "Office Politics," *University of Toronto Law Journal* 40 (1990): 421.
8 Ibid.; Macdonald, "Legal Bilingualism," *McGill Law Journal* 42 (1997): 119–67.
9 See Harry Arthurs's contribution to this volume.
10 For these two modes in legal scholarship generally, see Jeremy Webber, "Legal Pluralism and Human Agency," *Osgoode Hall Law Journal* 44 (2006): 192–4; Webber, "The Past and Foreign Countries," *Legal History* 10 (2006): especially 6–11.
11 And not merely – or even chiefly – the memos that are said to emanate from Macdonald (e.g., Macdonald, "Office Politics," 468–70). See especially Paul Willard's memo, 455–60, which paraphrases Macdonald

extensively, "Pour la reconnaissance d'une normativité juridique implicite et 'inférentielle,'" *Sociologie et sociétés* 18 (1) (1986): 47–58.

12 See, for example, Macdonald, "Legal Bilingualism," 161: "The act of interpretation will always be an attempt to apprehend the legal norm of which the text is a contingent formulation. This point might be misunderstood as a claim that meaning is radically constructed and that the indeterminacy of language fatally compromises the very project of law. It means no such thing ... The language of legislation is a point of access for apprehending, constructing and translating a legal norm; it is never the norm itself." See also 126, 128, 149, 164–6. At other points (e.g., 141–2, 153, 155–6), Macdonald seems more accepting of an open-ended process of construction through interpretation.

13 As I would tend to characterize the situation: Webber, "Legal Pluralism."

14 1 Corinthians 13: 8–12, paraphrased in Macdonald, "Legal Bilingualism," 164.

22

If It's Not Impossible, It's Not Worth Doing: Rod Macdonald's Vision of Legal Education

ROSALIE JUKIER

"If it's not impossible, it's not worth doing." I have chosen these words as the title for my paper on Professor Rod Macdonald's vision of legal education, for two reasons. The first is that this is a direct quote from Rod Macdonald, one he used when he spoke at Harvard University's Law School and presented McGill's transsystemic law program to its faculty.[1] The second, and more important, reason is because this expression exemplifies the man himself. It speaks to his whole life and career, one that by any standards is impossible to most, but to Rod, one that in its sheer and audacious impossibility was the only one worth doing.

Andrée Lajoie, emeritus professor at Université de Montréal and long-time friend, colleague, and collaborator of Rod Macdonald, recently published a biographical monograph entitled, *La vie intellectuelle de Roderick Macdonald: un engagement.*[2] This publication project itself attempts the impossible in that it aims to capture the entirety of Rod Macdonald's multi-faceted career in a single book. Moreover, it seeks to give the reader insight into the man himself, the beliefs that forged the path of his life, and the extensive contribution he has made via his scholarship, his teaching, his mentorship, and his public service.

The success of Andrée Lajoie's book is that it is not merely a dispassionate summary of Rod Macdonald's life and work. The book is peppered with interesting biographical data and is brought to life by extensive quotes from numerous interviews with Rod Macdonald himself, as well as from those who have worked and collaborated with him in the Faculty of Law at McGill University, at the Law Commission, and in the broader academic community. Professor Lajoie also includes excerpts from Rod Macdonald's publications, another challenging task, because it is difficult to know even where to begin to sift through the reams of words and pages he wrote in his three books, 140 articles, and eighty-eight book chapters (many of them quite lengthy) to find the right quotes that describe or exemplify the point being made. For all this, Professor Lajoie should be applauded and thanked.

However, an inevitable consequence of trying to capture such a prolific and influential man and thinker in a single volume is that many readers will complain of inadequate coverage of their "favourite" aspect of Rod Macdonald's creative and ground-breaking thinking. Given that his work spans numerous weighty topics that include, to mention just a few, legal theory and legal pluralism, access to justice, security on property, constitutional law, and administrative law, these complaints are somewhat unjustified. They are, however, understandable because Rod Macdonald's research has influenced each of us in such profound but unique ways.

In this paper, I would like to highlight a scholarly contribution that was not only given less prominence in Lajoie's book but that often got eclipsed by his paradigm-shifting research in other areas of law, namely, Rod Macdonald's important scholarship on legal education and theory of legal pedagogy.

When one thinks of Rod Macdonald's contribution to legal education, the natural impulse is to focus on his influence as a pedagogue and mentor to his students and his colleagues, many of those colleagues being former students. As Andrée Lajoie correctly describes him in her book, Rod Macdonald was "avant tout professeur." And as a professor, he advanced a distinct vision of teaching as an agent for social change, developed unconventional, challenging, and creative methods that shaped his pedagogy, and lived his belief that we don't teach "stuff," we teach who we are. Moreover, during his term as dean of the Faculty of Law at McGill from 1984 to 1989, he made significant contributions to legal education through the curricular reform that he advanced in his decanal capacity.

What is, however, often under-recognized is Rod Macdonald's important influence on legal education and pedagogy in his scholarship – the influence of which surpasses both the curriculum at McGill and the students and colleagues with whom he interacted directly. Rod thought deeply about all aspects of legal education, from the power of mentorship[3] to how curricular choices evidence deep philosophical decisions.[4]

His important scholarship on this subject enables the world to benefit from his philosophy of legal education and his wisdom concerning what it really ought to be about.

It is worth noting that legal education, as a scholarly pursuit, is not something Rod Macdonald undertook only after decades of experience teaching thousands of students. In fact, a glance at the long list of publications that make up his curriculum vitae confirms that Rod Macdonald actually began his scholarly career with an academic interest in legal pedagogy, publishing his very first articles on legal education in the late 1970s.[5] One can also not help but notice that his three most recent articles, one appearing in print posthumously, are also on legal education.[6] Constituting bookends of his academic career, this topic was obviously a lifelong academic and personal interest of his. And interestingly, although he refined and developed his views over the almost four decades he engaged with it, he really did not change his mind about much! Many of the seeds of his important contributions can be found in one of his earliest publications on the topic, an article he wrote in 1979 entitled "Legal Education on the Threshold of the 1980s."[7]

What exactly did Rod Macdonald, in his research on legal pedagogy, teach us? What follows is my understanding of some of his most important teachings and those that have influenced me as a pedagogue and an aspiring scholar of legal pedagogy.

First and foremost, he taught us that our view of legal education is far too narrow if we think it occurs only in the classroom dispensed only by law professors. Rather, he taught us that it occurs both inside and outside the law faculty, formally and informally, in a variety of sites and through a variety of media and that we should rejoice in "the implicit, the inferential, the tacit, the underground [because there, we] truly discover where change is occurring."[8] He lived his belief in the pedagogical power of hallway conversations, encounters in coffee shops, and shared rides home on the bus.[9] He found, and taught us to find, important lessons of law from interactions with the unlikeliest of legal sources, ranging from piano teachers to one's own children. And, unsurprisingly, he challenged the exclusive use of traditional sources, such as state-enacted law and appellate court decisions, in teaching materials, quipping, "what effect, if any, do appellate decisions have on the way ordinary people live their lives"?[10]

Rod Macdonald also taught us to challenge the traditional dichotomy of legal education, what he termed "the perennial chestnut" of "'practical' as opposed to 'theoretical' education," a dichotomy that has plagued so much of the debate concerning the nature and role of legal education.[11] He exposed the falsity of this dichotomy by explaining rationally, and poetically, that "[a]bstract, theoretical knowledge is [simply the] canvas on which students of law learn to paint."[12] Moreover, he maintained throughout his academic writing that legal education can, and should, prepare our students for a multitude of careers and that the "goal is not to stigmatise certain career choices, but rather to value all careers and thereby confront every student ... with the challenges and responsibilities attendant upon the ethical deployment of legal knowledge in any type of practice."[13]

These were important lessons for me when, together with a doctoral student at McGill, I embarked on writing about legal education as it pertains to graduate study in law. My co-author, Kate Glover, and I used Rod Macdonald's conception of legal pedagogy to posit that undergraduate and graduate legal education should not be polarized and siphoned off into separate silos where, inevitably, much of the conversation about legal education excludes graduate study. Viewing them in separate spheres only serves to perpetuate the tug of war Rod identified between legal practice and legal theory, mapping graduate studies onto legal academia and theory and undergraduate studies onto legal practice and the profession. Instead, we proposed conceiving of the law faculty in a holistic sense, as an integrated whole, with a single but broad mission: that of cultivating jurists. Thinking of legal education as forming jurists avoids pigeonholing law graduates into categories of academic, theoretician, practitioner, or policy-maker. It evokes a calling that transcends the practising bar and the academy, one that incorporates contribution to society and legal thought, intellectual reflection, and creative and critical thinking and one that is shared across graduate and undergraduate legal education.[14]

For Rod Macdonald, the law faculty (and he always deliberately referred to it as a "law faculty" rather than as a "law school") was not only an intellectual community but also a community of learners where professors learn as much from their students as students do from their professors. Rod Macdonald lived that philosophy every day of his teaching life. Aiming to elicit not only class participation but genuine dialogue, he knew that the best teachers learn from their students. In his words, "true *teaching* involves qualities, skills and actions that are the exact opposite of the notion that equates teaching with authority and the one-way projection of expert knowledge from teacher to learner."[15] It is profoundly telling that in one of his later articles on legal pedagogy,

"Everyday Lessons of Law Teaching – Le quotidien de l'enseignement juridique," he features sixteen "teachers" from whom he has learned and includes several of his students in that list.[16]

Many aspects of Rod Macdonald's scholarly life were defined by his challenging of the status quo and perceived orthodoxy. Legal pedagogy was no exception. He challenged all the "isms" – the instrumentalism, pragmatism, formalism, and professionalism of legal education long before this was popular. In so doing, he also taught us the importance of being provocative, a trait that came quite easily to him. If we had any doubt, he sometimes proudly told us that in his written texts, saying openly, "I mean deliberately to be provocative."[17] After all, who but Rod Macdonald would have had the nerve to write in a journal article in 1979, at an incipient stage of his academic career, that he wasn't quite sure that teaching the law of contracts was preferable to teaching the law of bumble-bees,[18] bemoaning, years later, "[w]hy, in heavens name, do the labels put on subjects by practitioners and treatise-writers a century ago continue to drive the way we, as university law teachers, organize our curriculum?"[19] Rod's call to provocation was deliberate. It was to teach us the dangers of complacency, the reality of contingency, and the importance of instability. Only through what he called "destabilizing the known" can we "imagine the world differently."[20]

Rod Macdonald was always far ahead of his time when it came to ideas about legal pedagogy. Although it is a hot topic in law faculties today, Rod was a pioneer when he began to stress the importance of interdisicplinarity. He recognized early on that law courses "have a non-legal meaning [and that] their boundaries are defined by non-legal factors."[21] He taught us that "to see any particular incidence of human interaction through the lens of law is simply a choice," law being but one lens through which to analyze and solve human problems.[22]

Through this notion of law as a means of solving human problems, Rod Macdonald taught us his most important lesson – what legal education should really be about. Inspired by Lon Fuller, who, in Rod Macdonald's words, "saw law as a human project, a human accomplishment, and a human aspiration that emerges from ongoing patterns of human interaction and the reciprocal adjustment of human expectation,"[23] he conceived legal education as being, at its core, learning how "to attend to the complexities of human beings in interaction with each other,"[24] stating that we should teach how law could be "a facilitator of human interaction"[25] and "about finding social outcomes that help solve human problems [rather than] perfecting abstract concepts to solve legal puzzles."[26]

He stressed that teaching law is not about teaching "the" law but rather "focus(ing) on the goals we seek to achieve through law"[27] and that the "pedagogical propeller" of a law course had to be its "commitment to questioning orthodoxy's privileged place in the creation and perpetuation of legal knowledge."[28] Ultimately, he taught us that legal education is about self-discovery. And that the "who" (who we are and who we become) is more important than the "what" (what we teach or what we learn).

Remarkably, despite being extremely critical, even at times mocking, of traditional conceptions and practices of legal education, he managed to inculcate in us a sense of optimism. Instead of leading us down the path of cynicism, which would have been relatively easy, he told us that not only are we are fortunate to be law teachers but that teaching law is actually a way of being alive![29]

Rod Macdonald's thinking on legal education and pedagogy ultimately evolved into his conception of the virtuous life. There is much to say about his concept of virtue, and many papers in this collection rightly focus on it.[30] Rod Macdonald himself summed up what pursuing virtue meant – "a morality of duty and responsibility in our relationships towards others and a morality of aspiration and virtue in our expectations of ourselves."[31]

To many, this may sound impossible, but as Rod has taught us, "if it's not impossible, it's not worth doing."

NOTES

1 Roderick Macdonald, "If It's Not Impossible, It's Not Worth Doing: The Challenges of Trans-systemic Legal Education" (Presentation at Harvard University Law School, 23 November 2004).

2 Andrée Lajoie, *La vie intellectuelle de Roderick Macdonald : un engagement.* (Montreal: Thémis, 2014).

3 In "Post-Charter Legal Education: Does Anyone Teach Law Anymore?" *Policy Options* 75 (February 2007): 83, he writes, "How law professors teach and what they teach mightily shape the attitudes, ambitions and aspirations of their students. These aspirations will then influence how students understand law for their entire careers."

4 See, for example, his discussion of curricular reform in "Legal Education on the Threshold of the 1980s: Whatever Happened to the Great Ideas of the 60's?" *Saskatchewan Law Review* 43 (1979): 39–62.

5 Of note are articles such as "Law Teachers and Their Jurisdiction," *Canadian Bar Review* 56 (1978): 710–23; "Law Schools and Public Legal Education," *Dalhousie Law Journal* 5 (1979): 779–90; and "Legal Education on the Threshold of the 1980s."

6 Macdonald, "Everyday Lessons of Law Teaching – Le quotidien de l'enseignement juridique," *Canadian Legal Education Annual Review* 6 (2013): 1–14; Roderick Macdonald and Kate Glover, "Implicit Comparative Law," *La Revue de droit de l'Université de Sherbrooke* 43 (1/2) (2013): 123–92; and Roderick Macdonald and Thomas B. McMorrow, "Decolonizing Law School," *Alberta Law Review* 51 (2014): 717–38. This last article appeared in print in August 2014 after his death in June 2014.
7 Macdonald, "Legal Education on the Threshold."
8 Macdonald, "Still 'Law' and Still 'Learning'?" *Canadian Journal of Law and Society* 18 (1) (2003): 21.
9 Macdonald, "Everyday Lessons of Law Teaching," 6.
10 Macdonald, "Legal Education on the Threshold," 48.
11 Ibid., 50.
12 Macdonald, "Does Law Have a Place in the Modern University? Or Every Great University Needs a Legal Studies Programme." (London School of Economics Law, Society and Economy Working Papers 4/2012, 2012), www.lse.ac.uk/collections/law/wps/wps.htm.
13 Macdonald, "Everyday Lessons of Law Teaching," 4.
14 Rosalie Jukier and Kate Glover, "Forgotten? The Role of Graduate Legal Education in the Future of the Law Faculty," *Alberta Law Review* 51 (4) (2014): 761–87.
15 Macdonald, "Everyday Lessons of Law Teaching," 3.
16 Ibid.
17 Macdonald, "Post-Charter Legal Education," 76.
18 Macdonald, "Legal Education on the Threshold," 54.
19 Macdonald, "Still 'Law' and Still 'Learning'?" 15.
20 Macdonald and Glover, 130.
21 Macdonald, "Legal Education on the Threshold," 44.
22 Macdonald, *Lessons of Everyday Law* (Montreal: McGill-Queen's University Press for the School of Policy Studies, Queen's University, and the Law Commission of Canada, 2002), 7.
23 Macdonald, "Let Our Future Not Be behind Us: The Legal Profession in Changing Times," *Saskatchewan Law Review* 64 (2001): 16.
24 Macdonald and McMorrow, 725.
25 Macdonald, "Legal Education on the Threshold," 59.
26 Macdonald, "Let Our Future Not Be behind Us," 26.
27 Macdonald, "On Teaching Law Transsystemically," *inFocus*, Faculty of Law, McGill University publication, spring-summer 2007: 4 (on file with the author).
28 Macdonald and Glover, 140.

29 Macdonald, "Everyday Lessons of Law Teaching," 12.
30 See, for example, papers in this collection by David Sandomierski and Blaine Baker.
31 Macdonald, "Everyday Lessons of Law Teaching," 12.

23

Pursuing Virtue: Human Potential, Citizenship, and a Research Agenda for Legal Education

DAVID SANDOMIERSKI

Rod asked that this panel on his works on legal education be called "Pursuing Virtue." I can think of three reasons why he might have suggested the title. First, perhaps he wanted us to talk about *his* notion of virtue as we might interpret it from his writings. Second, he potentially wanted us to talk about our *own* notions of virtue, as inspired by his influence. And third, perhaps he chose the title – pursuing virtue – because it is the *act of pursuit* that matters most and that, rather than urging us to any specific definition, he is inviting us to engage in our own reflections on what virtue means.

I'm going to hedge my bets and discuss all three possibilities.

Rod's Notion of Virtue

This discussion focuses primarily on his piece "Curricular Development in the 1980s: A Perspective."[1] Written first in 1979,[2] it could equally be called a "prospective" – not only because it purports to look forward to the decade ahead but because the ideas in that article also foreshadow his subsequently developed theories of law. What would later crystallize into concepts of legal and moral agency are latent in this early work on legal education. Teasing out his notion of virtue here can help us to understand the roots and foundations, indeed the soul, of Rod's longstanding and enduring commitments.

Rod's writing, teaching, and mentorship all embody a belief that legal education has the capacity to maximize and realize human potential. This commitment to human potential, I suggest, has three pillars.

The first pillar could be labelled "Discovery." For Rod, all we need to know, we have within ourselves. He frequently told his colleagues and students aspiring to teach law that the essence of what you teach is not the subject matter but rather "oneself." Law, and life, is autobiographical.[3] So, to teach, we must understand ourselves; we must apply the "logic of discovery,"[4] that he said legal study should inspire about law, to ourselves.

He exhorted us that as legal educators, we are agents of our own learning and teaching.[5] We have a responsibility to "discover or rediscover the values that underlie"[6] our practices, to "assert control over what we believe and what we teach."[7] We must get to know our own theory of life and legal knowledge that underlies what we do. If we do the hard work of discovering what we believe – if we pursue the "continual and creative rediscovery of ourselves"[8] – we will imbue the activity of law-teaching with meaning.

The second pillar of Rod's commitment to human potential may be called "Diversity." In "Curricular Development," he calls for "diversity in all aspects of law school activity."[9] He valued – indeed, revered – the diverse range of talents, learning styles, and skills of everyone in the room. He frequently refers to the Kolb learning cycle, encouraging law students and teachers to reflect explicitly on their learning styles.[10] This reflects a phronetic,[11] particularistic concern with individual talents. It celebrates our humanity. It also celebrates his particular conception of law.

The idea that the lawyer acts as an "architect of social institutions"[12] – that the lawyer's job is to navigate a range of diverse modes of social ordering – implies that legal education ought to cultivate a set of diverse skills. This range of legal skills is commensurate with a pluralistic, limitless range of human capacities. This is one reason why a "nonpositivistic curricular structure" has "primordial" importance.[13] Exploding the sites and modes of legal inquiry maximizes the range of human capacities we value in legal education, promoting a virtuous circle whereby *more* graduates are *more* capable of accessing *more* of their own talents in the service of enhancing society through law.

The third pillar of Rod's faith in human potential could imperfectly be called "Divinity." I don't mean this literally, of course – though there are plenty of religious references and metaphors in his work.[14] Rather, what I mean is that his commitment to human flourishing is inflected with a commitment to "substantive justice,"[15] ethics, and human goodness (all manifestations, no doubt, of virtue).

Not only did Rod insist that virtue should be the aim of legal education, but he believed that humans, left to their own devices, will tend to achieve it. He writes that human beings *autonomously* "develop ... decision-making institutions [and] deploy them justly."[16] Thus, his concern with agency does not only reflect a descriptive claim about the nature of law; embracing legal agency will facilitate (indeed, dignify) people's intuitive grasp of justice and also likely yield a substantively just result.[17]

At the same time, he demanded that *human* law teachers "face up to their personal ethical theory,"[18] that they develop their own "philosophy of knowledge and reform,"[19] and that they "become self-consciously aware of the implications of what they are doing."[20]

For Rod, legal education is not "so far from God."[21] Rather, he both believed in our goodness and, like a divinity might, exhorted us toward it.

Discovery, Diversity, Divinity – pillars of an abiding faith in human potential.

My (Evolving) Notion of Virtue

My current doctoral work examines how first-year contract law professors conceive of their role as educators. What are their goals for their students, and why are these goals important? What visions of lawyer, professional, citizen, and person are embodied by (or tacitly present in) the particular approaches to teaching contract law? Reformulated in the terms of this panel, what are professors' various conceptions of virtue, and what are the particular elements of their pursuits?

In earlier iterations of my project, I described my inquiry as one into the "citizenship" mission of Canadian law schools. I employed the concept of citizenship, while acknowledging its limitations, because it captures the notion of the individual, the unit who exercises agency, engaged in society. I meant, as I imagined Rod might have when *he* periodically used that term, to shear the term of its stately connotations.[22] I took from Rod a faith in the power of Latin and of etymology, interpreting *citizenship*'s root, *civitas*, to refer more closely to the notion of the public sphere than to the nation-state. "Citizenship," I felt, could serve as a meeting place for the dualities of self and other, and of agency and structure, that infuse the inquiries into the meaning and purpose of legal education. "Citizenship," I thought, could capture a broader range of virtues for legal education than might other terms, such as "lawyer" or "professional."[23]

I see now that his naming of the panel is meant to be disruptive. Is it the conception of *citizenship* or the pursuit of *virtue* that I have been investigating all this time? Which term is more capacious, more celebratory of human potential, more central to my inquiry? Was Rod's naming of this panel meant to get me to reconceptualize my dissertation? Directly, I doubt it. Yet indirectly, the title of the panel is, I suspect, designed to nudge us off our comfortable perches, to disorient us just a little, and to set each of us off in a slightly different direction. His simple gesture of naming this panel, like so many of his many other metonymic interventions, invites me to re-examine "citizenship" as an animating theme for my doctoral research.[24]

The Pursuit

This leads me to the third question. Perhaps the oblique and allusive naming of this panel is akin to a judo move, calculated to throw all of us off balance while we try to wrestle with an unwieldy concept – with the hope of enlisting everyone in the room to restore the balance. If it really is the *pursuit* that Rod is inviting us to engage in, let me expand the invitation by suggesting what the pursuit of virtue may imply for a future agenda of research into legal education.

First, I think we need empirical work to discover and name the aspirations of legal educators – to try to "discover or rediscover"[25] the latent notions of virtue that underlie our current practices. "Everything we need to know, we have within ourselves," and scholarship can help identify, synthesize, and ultimately argue for a diverse range of virtues in legal education.

We need such research to understand what possibilities and constraints for legal education flow from the interplay of agency and structure. What do legal educators aspire toward, if asked to dream uninhibited? And how do "tradition, university politics, the expectations of the bar, government funding priorities, the wishes of students, materials of study available,"[26] in Rod's 1979 terms, affect, impede, or enable these aspirations?

Second, we need empirical work on students' experience and how it matches up with the imagined aspirations. We need both point-in-time and longitudinal studies to understand students' and graduates' conceptions of law, legal knowledge, and civic and professional identity. While there are some excellent projects and data sets out there – the *After the JD* project[27] and *Law School Survey of Student Engagement*[28] come to mind – these largely succeed at capturing surface phenomena, such as jobs actually obtained or activities actually pursued while in law school. I believe we need new empirical techniques to dig deeper, to discover how and whether notions of virtue in legal education are influencing students' ways of viewing the world and their role in it.[29]

The third major gap is sustained inquiry into the process of curricular reform. Rod writes that "thoughtful curricular debate is a law school's primary heuristic device."[30] I suspect that many of the implicit, powerful norms and values about the mission of legal education often only surface at the moments of inflection when a change to the curriculum is proposed or takes place.

Wouldn't it be great if researchers had access to this wealth of intellectual capital so that they could tease out the fundamental values, which otherwise are mooted under a cone of silence? Rod gave us "Office Politics."[31] In fact, he gave it to us twice.[32] Who among us will write "Curricular Politics" or, more aptly, "Curricular Virtue"?

Fourth, the sociology of legal education could be further deployed to explore the informal norms and underlying values of the law school. We need more pieces like Desmond Manderson and Sarah Turner's coffeehouse article.[33] But we also need to understand how other participants in legal education conceive of virtue. How, for example, do career development officers imagine the deployment of human potential after graduation? How do admissions officers interpret human potential before admission? How do adjuncts and legal writing teachers and student TAs conceive of their mission?

A Prospective

These are just examples of scholarship that would help us to *understand* the incidence and content of virtue. After we have articulated and developed these latent notions, the necessary next step will be to make much better arguments than we currently do for the broader social value of legal education.

Rod's thinking invites us to conduct at least two distinct intellectual processes. The first is to probe beneath surface phenomena to understand the values, commitments, and philosophies that underlie what we do. The second is to reject "conventional mythology"[34] – to challenge existing frames of debate, questioning the "shibboleths of the legal Academy."[35]

In the contemporary debate on legal education, both are sorely needed. We are in a rather depressing iteration of the "perennial"[36] debates about theory and practice, control over curriculum, and a shifting legal marketplace. Law schools are under attack for their "broken economic model"[37] and their failure to "train for the marketplace."

We can deploy the pursuit of virtue as a judo move in this debate. We can take this preoccupation with "value" and turn it on its head and show that there is an enduring, broadly conceived social value to studying and teaching law. If there is a crisis in legal education, it is only the result of a temporary failure of imagination and boldness. By heeding Rod's deliberately ambiguous invitation, I believe we can turn the great balance wheel and reaffirm, honour, and continue his relentless faith in the greatness and goodness of the collective enterprise.

NOTES

1 Roderick Macdonald, "Curricular Development," *Journal of Legal Education* 32 (1982): 569–90.
2 The paper is a revised version of speech given to the Canadian Association of Law Teachers in 1979 and originally published as Macdonald, "Legal Education on the Threshold of the 1980's: Whatever Happened to the Great Ideas of the 60's?" *Saskatchewan Law Review* 39 (1) (1979): 39–62.
3 On the continuity between everyday life and law and the fact that the processes and modes of formal law inhere in daily life, see Macdonald, *Lessons of Everyday Law* (Montreal: McGill-Queen's University Press for the School of Policy Studies, Queen's University, and the Law Commission of Canada, 2002), 3–12.
4 Macdonald, "Curricular Development," 579.
5 On his commitment to agency, see, e.g., Roderick Macdonald and Jason Maclean, "No Toilets in Park," *McGill Law Journal* 50 (4) (2005): 721–87 (in the specific context of legal education); Roderick Macdonald and David Sandomierski, "Against Nomopolies," *Northern Ireland Legal Quarterly* 57 (2006): 614–5 (on "legal agents"); Macdonald, "Three Metaphors of Norm Migration in International Context," *Brooklyn Journal of International Law* 34 (2009): 603–53 (on moral agency).
6 Macdonald, "Curricular Development," 573.
7 Ibid., 578.
8 Ibid., 590.
9 Ibid.
10 See, e.g., Macdonald and Maclean, n90 (discussing "helping students develop a self-consciousness about how they learn"); Macdonald, "Compendium of Themes" (Legal Education Seminar, McGill University, 2006) (asking aspiring law teachers to "locate" themselves within the Kolb typology). On the Kolb cycle, see generally www.learningfromexperience.com.
11 On Rod's commitment to *phronesis*, see Macdonald, "Three Metaphors," 652 (in respect of moral agency); Macdonald, "Does Law Have a Place in the Modern University? Or Every Great University Needs a Legal Studies Program" (London School of Economics Law, Society and Economy

Working Paper 4 2012), www.lse.ac.uk/collections/law/wps/wps.htm (as a requirement for a great university); Macdonald, "Unitary Law Re-form, Pluralistic Law Re-Substance: Illuminating Legal Change," *Louisiana Law Review* 67 (2007): 1,138–41 (as essential for the understanding of the total normativity of a situation for which "white light" serves as metaphor).

12 Macdonald, "Curricular Development," 583. Rod borrows this term from Lon Fuller, the subject of his 1975 LLM thesis (Macdonald, "Prolegomena to a Theory of Legal Relevance" [LLM thesis, University of Toronto, 1975]). Angela Swan, his thesis supervisor, underscored at the symposium that the concluding section of that thesis is extremely prophetic of his future thinking in legal theory.

13 Macdonald, "Curricular Development," 588.

14 See, e.g., Macdonald, "Legal Bilingualism," *McGill Law Journal* 42 (1997): 119–67 (using the "paradox" of the Tower of Babel to understand and problematize the concept of legal bilingualism); Macdonald, "Custom Made – For a Non-chirographic Critical Legal Pluralism," *Canadian Journal of Law and Society* 26 (2011): 301–27 (developing both the notion of "Legal Evangelicalism," 303ff., and contrasting the preoccupation with "the word" in law to the similar preoccupation in religion, 310).

15 Macdonald, "Curricular Development," 587.

16 Ibid., 584.

17 Indeed, Rod writes elsewhere that implicit or everyday law may be *more* likely than formal law to achieve substantively just results (Macdonald, *Lessons of Everyday Law*, 6–7).

18 Macdonald, "Curricular Development," 588.

19 Ibid., 589.

20 Ibid.

21 Harry Arthurs, "Poor Canadian Legal Education: So Near to Wall Street, So Far from God," *Osgoode Hall Law Journal* 38 (3) (2000): 381–408. This piece is part of Arthurs's significant oeuvre of works on legal education that seeks to highlight the structural limitations placed on Canadian legal education by the forces of globalization, political economy, and the legal profession. See Arthurs, "The Political Economy of Canadian Legal Education," *Journal of Law and Society* 25 (1) (1998): 14–32; Arthurs, "The Tree of Knowledge/The Axe of Power: Gerald LeDain and the Transformation of Canadian Legal Education," Osgoode Hall Law School Comparative Research in Law and Policy Research Paper Series 8, no. 6, Paper no. 25 (2012). Despite Arthurs's emphasis on structure, it is important to emphasize that he rejects "fatalism and determinism" (Arthurs, "Poor Canadian Legal Education," 407). In the keynote speech at the

symposium, Arthurs signalled the long-standing difference of opinion between himself and Macdonald: for Arthurs, Macdonald's emphasis on agency disregards the notion of power. In a powerful riposte, Richard Janda rebutted the claim, characterizing Macdonald's assertion of agency as a deft way of acting in the face of terror.

22 See, e.g., Macdonald, "Custom Made," 308.

23 See David Sandomierski, "Educating Lawyers, Cultivating Citizens, and Re-enchanting the Legal Professional," *Alberta Law Review* 51 (4) (2013): 739–60.

24 I am grateful to Evan Fox-Decent, in his comments to me after the symposium, for the additional nudge in this direction.

25 Macdonald, "Curricular Development," 573.

26 Ibid., 570.

27 See generally American Bar Foundation, "AJD and Related Publications," http://www.americanbarfoundation.org/publications/AftertheJD/AJD_Publications.html.

28 See generally Law School Survey of Student Engagement, http://lssse.iub.edu/about.cfm.

29 One example of a novel empirical study is Elizabeth Mertz's work on legal epistemology using linguistic anthropological methods. See Mertz, *The Language of Law School: Learning to "Think Like a Lawyer"* (New York: Oxford University Press, 2007).

30 Macdonald, "Curricular Development," 569.

31 Macdonald, "Office Politics," *University of Toronto Law Journal* 40 (1990): 419–76.

32 Roderick Macdonald and Jonathan Widell, "Office Politics (Again!)," *Canadian Journal of Law and Society* 20 (2) (2005): 1–26.

33 Desmond Manderson and Sarah Turner, "Coffee House: *Habitus* and Performance among Law Students," *Law and Social Inquiry* 31 (3) (2006): 649–76.

34 Macdonald, "Curricular Development," 571.

35 Ibid., 590.

36 Ibid., 585.

37 See, e.g., Brian Z. Tamanaha, *Failing Law Schools*, part IV (Chicago: University of Chicago Press, 2012).

24

Character-Building at Multiple Sites of Justice: Administration and Teaching as Texts, Scholarship as Ethical and Political Action

BLAINE BAKER

The title of this session of last winter's Macdonald symposium, "Pursuing Virtue," might be said to be simultaneously intriguing, inspiring, and elliptical. Rod coined the names for that symposium's panels, and, as I have done with a significant portion of his other writing, I am going to edit the title of this session by substituting for it an insight largely gleaned from the papers assigned for this panel. Readers can identify essays that I refined with blue pencils for Rod, because textual negotiation with him typically resulted in the retention of two or three mixed metaphors rather than seven or eight in the first couple of sentences, their main themes are generally set out before those papers' halfway points rather than later, and subtexts or buried themes have normally been reduced in number from double to a single digit. Rod appears to have thought that assaults on the conventions of literary style are, for the most part, hortatory. I am therefore not bashful about moving Rod's prose around, even when it is only a couple of words in the name of a conference session.

"Pursuing Virtue" could have been cast as "promoting the collective good," "practising wisdom," "cultivating decency," "aspiring to citizenship," or "building character." Those alternative titles might have made this panel's theme more accessible without changing its thrust. "Building character," a slightly pedestrian translation of "pursuing virtue," has special resonance, because much of Rod's sense of the human spirit and its capacity developed from summers spent as a camper and counsellor at Kirk Wipper's Camp Kandalore in Ontario's Haliburton Highlands. Time spent playing music with others, as well as sharing home and cottage maintenance tasks, seem to have been other important incubators for Rod's insights into the human spirit's plurality and potential. Indeed, those activities were also fertile sources of illustrations for his published work.[1] In any event, Rod's summer-camp influence is apparent in papers discussed elsewhere at last winter's symposium.[2] Insofar as disciplinary and even topical fences are few and far between in his writing, the impact of unbounded, camp-like wilderness spaces can arguably be seen across Rod's scholarship.[3]

Unlike McGill University's patriarch, James McGill (who canoed because he was keen to rendezvous with his Native fur-trading partners as regularly as possible), summer-camp paddlers do not generally canoe as a means to an end. Nor are sports like archery usually undertaken in camp settings because the archers are competing for membership on a Canadian Olympic team. Nor are crafts practised by artisanal campers because they hope to market their creations at the prestigious One-of-a-Kind Craft Show. Summer-camp activities are typically ends in themselves, they normally involve close and continuing relations with other campers and counsellors, and they often foster ethical strength or a distinctive temperament. Rod said much the same about the pursuit of virtue in law-school settings. He characterized that pursuit as an activity in which means and ends are conjoined and as one in which norms are constructed and understood through social interaction. Pursuit was also said to be an activity in which attention to the pluralism of communities and the self, embrace of the implicit character of norms, and optimism about the human spirit's capacity for introspection are fundamental constituents.[4]

Facilitating the pursuit of virtue is not the only thing that faculties of law or their sibling academic departments do. Most people can probably agree that university and other students should be challenged and changed by their learning experiences but emerge from them confident of themselves. Students should also finish those studies sure-footed in their understandings of the skills and information that were presented to them in learning settings and sensitive to the limits of the professional and other cultural traditions they appropriated through their formal and informal education. But virtue, wisdom, decency, citizenship, and character can be said to be matters of pervasive and critical presence in legal education, largely due to the social and economic privilege that follows that training's completion in many North American jurisdictions and to the self-regulating character of most local bars. Shading into the impact that Rod's scholarship has had on others working in university committee rooms, in classrooms, and at academic writing desks, it bears recollection that, when McGill's Faculty of Law set out twenty years ago to restructure its private-law curriculum, there was significant professorial opinion to the effect that the teaching and learning of skills (including the skill or state of mind called citizenship) should be as prominent in the new program as that of legal information. That meant that there should be planned, course-to-course, and year-to-year "skills progression" and that the teaching of doctrinal topics as platforms for the acquisition of skills and the pursuit of virtue should be justified not on the basis of the volume of library space occupied by that doctrine but on the grounds that particular topics were especially suitable springboards for engagement with skills and for introspection. Skills were thought to include everything from legal issue-spotting, to doctrinal synthesis, to the criticism and deconstruction of norms, to memorandum of law and appellate-brief writing, to legislative and document draftsmanship, to negotiation, to mediation, to reconciliation, to arbitral decision-making, to scholarly and popular writing about law. And virtue was thought to have to do with transformations of temperaments rather than with sets of rules. Rod's influence was a significant part of that current of opinion in an ambitious institutional reform. Law-school calendars typically highlight the introduction of new courses and programs that emerge from a "constant review" of those schools' curricula. Consistent with his own writing, however, Rod said that thoughtful curricular debate is a law school's primary heuristic or autodidactic device and that the processes of collective self-reflection and renewal that underlie curricular reform are therefore more important than reforms' results (however divisive that debate may be). Yet a keen companion interest in autonomy also led him to look for the development, from course and program revision, of a consuming and protective institutional identity.[5]

Perhaps obviously, the promotion of a shared good, the practice of wisdom, the cultivation of decency, an aspiration to citizenship, the building of character, or the pursuit of virtue in a law-school or other community setting will not be easy. But Rod provided modest guidance in published, role-modelling, and casual forms on how that project might proceed. Fostering among members of a teaching and learning community an appreciation of context and a sensitivity to human agency's omnipresence, in the materials of study and in the community itself, is an important step in that direction. That is so, he said, because citizenship is about the links between individuals and their communities, membership in any group is about robust participation in its public space, and virtue is about a commitment to the common good. Each community's norms are thus mystically "crafted" through interaction with a diversity of others at a range of sites and most profoundly expressed implicitly or symbolically. Means and ends are necessarily conjoined in that process, and the relevant morality is one of aspiration and optimism rather than one of fact or risk aversion. It is probably appropriate to suggest, at least as an aside, that his action-oriented but non-conformist Quaker background was reflected in that emphasis on relationships rather than on individuals, on processes of becoming rather than on states of being, and on the contextual or interpreter-contingent character of norms' meanings. Those touchstones of learning were identified by him as techniques for the uniquely important achievement of self-knowledge and might therefore be called "look-in-the-mirror" or "self-confrontation" exercises.

Rod was consistently supportive of the context-rich character of my own written work, almost all of which has had to do with modern legal history. While I valued that encouragement, contingency, human agency, and "everyday" law have had an important place in my scholarship primarily because I write history. And as long as there are historians, Rod and his fellow-travellers are not likely to achieve a monopoly in respect of contextual, pluralistic, or informal legal studies.[6] But the work that he did around motifs such as normative pluralism, contingency, and inference is none the less distinctive, weighty, and compelling. By contrast, the influence of Rod and his academic writing on my teaching has been large in palpable and intangible ways. Perhaps ironically, "before-and-after-Rod's influence" pictures of my classroom work could be provided by the other members of this panel, all of whom I taught. For them to make that comparison, Alison Harvison Young, Jeremy Webber, and Stephen Toope would have to contrast their early-1980s experiences of me (before I had much to do with Rod) with David Sandomierski's quarter-century-later experience of me (after I had extensive exposure to Rod). In any case, course-outline seeds planted by Rod became my Administrative Process course that is built around "worms'-eye" rather than "birds'-eye" views of state action. It emphasizes the interactive relations of bureaucrats with each other and with their regulatees, the range of hard, soft, and implicit forms in which administrative norms can be expressed, and especially inter- and transsystemic comparisons among delegated governments-in-miniature or sites of bureaucratic justice. I did something similar in course development with a "legal process" class in the 2013–14 academic year. Earlier teachers of that course like Lorne Sossin and Ayelet Shachar had begun to make Macdonaldian ambitions felt by using private-law processes as scaffolding to teach dispute pre-emption and settlement skills in tandem with inquiries into ethical lawyering. Experience with the Administrative Process class helped me to refine that new course along the lines of problem avoidance and problem-solving writ large, of which Rod would presumably have approved. Touring diverse sites of justice and multiple legal processes can be intellectually and spiritually liberating. It can also help to move law-school conversations away from the logic of justification and toward that of discovery. Similarly, the relational aspect of bilateral contracts became an increasingly large component of my Contracts and Contractual Obligations courses as time advanced. And multilateral contracts took on a belated role alongside those other types of transactions. Some of my growth on that front is attributable to Angela Swan, who produced a series of published casebooks for those kinds of courses that opened the classroom door to reflections on the priority of human relations rather than legal artefacts in commerce. Swan also supervised Rod's graduate studies at the Faculty of Law at the University of Toronto in which several of this panel's subthemes were anticipated. But most of my evolution in the Contracts classroom has had to do with sometimes Delphic missives he "let fly" by way of conversation, example, or scholarship about the multiple redistributive sites of contractual justice, the ubiquity and subtlety of implicit, privately embraced commercial norms, and the "commonwealth" of each little legal system that is called a contract.

It was gratifying to see 250 or more attendees at last winter's Macdonald symposium who were reading, speaking, and thinking about Macdonaldian themes like the production of fairness, pluralized subjects, kaleidoscopic federalism, the priority of distributive justice, contextualized governance, and the pursuit of virtue. Indeed, many of those participants were doing so at that gathering despite the fact that they had been through the texts chosen for that celebration several times before. No doubt the exploration of those themes by Rod, and their refinement by others who have followed him, are academically notable legacies. Their exploration may not now be complete, and their articulation may not be perfect, but those themes' treatment might be perfectible. Perhaps most important is the sheer sense of ambition, imagination, and dynamism that his texts extrude. The artistic, political, and intellectual leadership that his scholarship represents is probably its most significant feature. The fact that that writing was done at all, sometimes in strategic, provocative, and even outrageous ways, is a point that therefore deserves emphasis.[7]

Similarly, Rod's administrative leadership has had a demonstrable impact on such diverse communities as the Royal Society of Canada, the Law Commission of Canada, the Canadian Institute for Advanced Research, McGill's Faculty of Law, and the *Canadian Journal of Law and Society.* I know more about his involvement in the last two than I know about it in the first three, so I will draw on my experience with McGill and the *Journal* in what follows. Like Rod's writing, which has been treated here more like an expression of leadership than as a vehicle for the delivery of information or for the display of ideas, his pilotage of a law school and a scholarly journal appears to have had, and presumably will continue to have, significant impact on members of those communities and on future managers of them. Nearly unbounded energy and a willingness to contribute time, the patience to work with people at their best and their worst (with the apparent recognition that communities have to make the most of the members they have rather than dream about different human resources), and an ambition for institutions and other groups that verges from time to time on implausibility were the hallmarks of his formal and informal leadership. Sometimes mercurial, occasionally frenetic, at times indiscreet, often brilliant, and almost always contagious were characteristics common to his intellectual, managerial, and household work habits. It therefore seems appropriate to treat his facilitation or pursuit of collective and individual virtue in the boss's office and the classroom as a kind of text at the same time that his scholarship is being treated as political, ethical, and pedagogic action.

Rod did not seem to intend either pedagogical, managerial, or scholarly leadership to lead to indoctrination of, or imposition on, others. His repeated recognition of that "colonization" potential is, arguably, a first step toward its deflection. More to the point, his animating premise appears to have been that both words and actions are texts that necessarily engage speakers, writers, and actors with their explicit and implicit rationality that, in turn, draws those listeners, readers, and observers into a "noematic" circle that is mutually constitutive and reconstitutive of the participants in it. The acceptance of that premise, played out more modestly in other dimensions of local life like bilingualism and multiculturalism, helps to pre-empt at the inception of any group ethos the possibility of interpersonal domination.[8] Leadership, in that scheme of things, consists of acting like a good shaman, or a good facilitator, or a good deflator of false conscientiousness.

An anecdotal but modestly prescriptive conclusion seems appropriate, drawn from a Dean's Office reception at McGill's Faculty of Law shortly after my arrival there in the early 1980s. Guests were milling around, saying, "Hello Mr Dean, hello Mr Dean, hello Mr Dean" (a distinctive McGill salutation that has lifelong currency), and I turned to then-Professor Macdonald to ask what that was about. He gestured to one of the guests and explained that he was Percy Corbett, who was dean of McGill Law in the 1930s, and he signalled another, who was Law Dean–Designate John Humphrey during the 1940s, and then he gestured to Frank Scott and Max Cohen, who were McGill law deans in the 1960s, and he finally pointed out Dean John Durnford from the 1970s (he did not need to introduce me to the host, current Dean John Brierley). Fifty years of institutional leadership were thus in attendance at that reception, and there is at least an indirect sense in which Rod "stood on those forerunners' shoulders" to produce the two and a half dozen examples of his written work that provided the basis for last winter's Macdonald symposium (although he might have resisted that suggestion of enablement on the basis of his belief that none of us should allow ourselves to be unduly influenced by tradition). Former McGill law deans whom I knew, like Corbett, Durnford, and Brierley, were very interested in decency, but more was at work in Rod's intellectual and ethical development than their attenuated influence. The University of Western Ontario law school that I attended was sometimes anarchistic, and that quality was shown from time to time to be a strength. The Columbia Law School where I did graduate work was mostly patrician, and that quality was also shown much of the time to be a strength. The University of Chicago Law School where I did more graduate work was decidedly utilitarian or instrumental in orientation, and that quality ultimately became an important part of the school's brand. It seems unlikely that Rod could have produced the scholarship on which this panel and its larger symposium was based, the bulk of which was conceived and written at McGill, in predominately anarchistic, patrician, or utilitarian environments. A good description of precisely how he stood on his predecessors' shoulders, and sometimes on those of his McGill contemporaries, would therefore be helpful. What was it about being part of the legacy of an established institution, and part of an organic community in which conversations occurred about the production of fairness, kaleidoscopic federalism, pluralistic subjects, the pursuit of virtue, and the contextualization of governance, that helped to make Rod's scholarship, teaching, and management possible? Answers to those kinds of questions might help the McGill community of which he was part determine just what kind of light is, in summer-camp parlance, "under its bushel" and deserving of fuller exposure and comprehension. If that community is going to reach its stride as a place where faculty and students alike grow in virtue and other relational practices through law study attuned to a multiplicity of normative sites, the institution will probably have to lift that bushel and expose the light that somehow helped Rod's work happen. In that process, something may also be learned about such other like-minded but understudied twentieth-century McGill law school "citizens" as Walter Johnson, Dorothy Heneker, and Robert Warden-Lee. And a closer linkage might be discovered between that school's interleafing of norms, cultures, ethnicities, and languages and the ways in which Canadian federalism (McGill law school writ large, in his view) could be constructively re-imagined. Indeed, some of that re-imagining was attempted in the constitutionally oriented sessions of last winter's symposium.

Rod understood the pursuit of virtue to be a vocation of most communities, not just law schools or the groups that cluster around formal and informal sites of justice. Extrapolation to that pursuit in other interactive settings from observations made here would therefore be another suitable way to bring forward the five essays that have been the focus of this commentary.

NOTES

1 See, e.g., Macdonald, *Lessons of Everyday Law* (Montreal: McGill-Queen's University Press for the School of Policy Studies, Queen's University, and the Law Commission of Canada, 2002); Roderick Macdonald and Clarisse Kehler Siebert, "Orchestrating Legal Multilingualism," in *Jurilinguistique: entre langues et droit*, edited by Jean-Claude Gemar and Nicholas Kasirer (Montreal: Thémis, 2005), 377–406.

2 See, e.g., Macdonald, "The Swiss Army Knife of Governance," in *Designing Government: From Instruments to Governance*, edited by Pearl Eliadis et al. (Montreal: McGill-Queen's University Press, 2005), 203; Roderick Macdonald and Thomas McMorrow, "Rabbits, Ravens, Snakes, Turtles: Analyzing the Political Economy of Aboriginal Communities," in *Gouvernance autochtone: reconfiguration d'un avenir collectif*, edited by Pierre Noreau (Montreal: Themis, 2010), 211.

3 And was theorized by him in "Transdisciplinarity and Trust," in *Transdisciplinarity: Recreating Integrated Knowledge*, edited by M. Somerville and D. Rapport (Oxford: EOLSS Publishers, 2000), 61–76.

4 See, e.g., Macdonald and McMorrow, "Decolonizing Law School"; Roderick Macdonald and David Sandomierski, "Against Nomopolies," *Northern Ireland Law Quarterly* 57 (2006): 610–33.

5 See generally Macdonald, "Curricular Development in the 1980s: A Perspective," *Journal of Legal Education* 32 (1982); Macdonald and McMorrow, "Decolonizing Law School."

6 For indications that Rod understood that point, see, e.g., Macdonald, "The National Law Program at McGill: Origin, Establishment, Prospects," *Dalhousie Law Journal* 13 (1990): 211–363; Macdonald, "Understanding Civil Law Scholarship in Quebec," *Osgoode Hall Law Journal* 23 (1985): 573–608.

7 See, e.g., Macdonald, "Office Politics," *University of Toronto Law Journal* 40 (1990): 419–76; Macdonald, "Understanding Regulation by Regulations," in *Regulations, Crown Corporations, and Administrative Tribunals*, edited by Ivan Bernier and Andrée Lajoie (Toronto: University of Toronto Press, 1985), 81–154.

8 See, e.g., Macdonald, "Legal Bilingualism," *McGill Law Journal* 42 (1997): 119–67; Macdonald and McMorrow, "Decolonizing Law School."

25

Closing Remarks: Absence Makes the Heart Grow Fonder

DESMOND MANDERSON

Introduction

When I was invited to offer some closing remarks for this important symposium, which encompassed for the first time the full extent of Rod Macdonald's contributions to legal scholarship, I was daunted. Not just because of the responsibility it placed on my shoulders but because I was unable to be at the symposium in person. Speaking from Australia via Skype, I would therefore be in the somewhat invidious position of bringing together the themes of the meeting without actually having listened to most of the other presentations. As the convenor of the conference, Professor Richard Janda, dryly observed, "Well, it wouldn't be the first time."

Yet as so many of the other contributions to this collection attest, the breadth and impact of Rod Macdonald's scholarship across forty astonishingly productive years is surely undoubted. Macdonald's work is quite remarkable for its diversity, ranging from questions of security law, corporate law, access to justice, and constitutional law to questions of legal pluralism, sociology, and pedagogy. Regardless of its ostensible subject matter, this work is always presented in a fluid and entertaining style. Macdonald is never obscure, never jargonistic, never pretentious, and his essays always percolate with new ideas and flashes of insight. Sometimes we forget how rare these qualities are in academic writing and how valuable they are. At the same time, Macdonald – and again, regardless of the subject matter in question – is invariably a deep thinker. He is never content to stay on the surface of existing assumptions or legal rules or procedures. His analyses almost without exception move quickly to first principles and to the underlying assumptions and purposes of governance and, at the same time, to the social experiences, as he so suggestively put it, of "everyday law." Thus, his work drills down in two different directions at once: to the foundations of our thinking and to the bedrock of our existence. This movement, both toward underlying philosophy and toward underlying sociology – toward theory and practice at the same time – is likewise a rare combination. It has the effect of allowing the reader to engage with Macdonald's ideas on many different levels, just as the accessibility of his writing entices and encourages this engagement.

There is a famous mathematician named Paul Erdos who is known for his exceptional network of scholars and his unstinting collaborative generosity. Everyone, it is said, has an "Erdos number," like a degree of separation, depending on whether they have collaborated with Erdos, collaborated with a collaborator with Erdos, and so on. I think the same could be said about the work of Rod Macdonald. He has been everywhere, talked to everybody, and contributed to everything: an exceptional teacher, a generous and prolific collaborator. Perhaps in the future we will all be given M numbers to identify our place in the rapidly expanding universe of those who have been touched by his oeuvre. Examples of Macdonald's reach could be multiplied almost indefinitely. I might quickly just mention two brief instances from my own recent experience. At a conference on law and the humanities, Richard Mohr, an Australian sociologist, presented a paper (with Nadirsyah Hosen) on the complex relationship between food culture, legal regulation, and the topography of the street, which was dedicated to Rod Macdonald, not because of any specific work he had published but because of the breadth of his pioneering scholarship on legal pluralism. "Wherever we went," Mohr said, "we found that Rod Macdonald had been there before us." The next week, I was at a presentation by Terrance Halliday on global legal financial regulation. A very different subject, you would think, from the question of street food in inner Sydney. Halliday remarked that he had only ever seen "legal pluralism in action" once. The global working group of UNCITRAL was struggling to find a framework for international secured transactions across very different legal systems. The Canadian representative singlehandedly presented a way of reframing the problem and finding an innovative resolution to it. That person was, of course, Roderick Macdonald.

But for the purposes of this volume, and in order to provide a perspective not previously covered by the many other essays here, I wish to briefly observe a couple of overarching features of Macdonald's output. These features relate not so much to his substantive contributions to legal thinking but to the form and method of his legal imagination. They amount to an important and original contribution to the very idea of legal scholarship.

Institutional Thinking

Rod Macdonald was, of course, an exceptional contributor to institutional life. No one that I have ever met has thought as clearly and as cleverly about how to develop and change institutions. At McGill University, he was dean of the Faculty of Law and set the agenda for years to come. So too at the Law Commission of Canada, of which he was the founding president, and at the Royal Society of Canada, where he breathed new life into that august place and articulated new roles for it. But I think Macdonald quickly understood and as quickly touched the institutional dynamics of every place he spent time in. This sensitivity to the importance of institutional life for all of us, and to its dynamics and transformational potential, makes his work distinctive and practical rather than simply theoretically interesting. It is what connects his scholarship to that of Lon Fuller and Mary Douglas rather than to that of H.L.A. Hart or, for that matter, Peter Goodrich.

What is radical, however, in Macdonald's approach is the way in which he consistently inverts the question of institutional structures. He is not interested in how institutions control action but rather in how individuals modify institutions. With this radical move, he reconceives institutions of all kinds as sites of empowerment and finds within them – or invites us to find within them – spaces for creative development and expression. In "What Is a *Critical* Legal Pluralism?" Macdonald and his co-author make the claim that human beings, as legal subjects, are "law-inventing not law-abiding"; "the very idea of law," they continue, "is autobiographical."[1] Significantly, then, and throughout Macdonald's work, he does not ignore institutions but turns them inside out.

This inside-out approach to the structure-and-agent problem, a perennial one in twentieth-century social theory, can be seen to run like a golden thread throughout his central intellectual commitments. Let me identify just two. First, and in his work for the Law Commission of Canada in particular, in the white papers and discussion papers he produced there, and in the series of short but incisive meditations collected in *Lessons in Everyday Law*,[2] Macdonald understands institutions as vectors for the achievement of intimate human purposes. The far-reaching proposals he generates in relation to personal relationships, aged persons, and drugs, for example, all proceed from the initial assumption that these human needs – for love, dignity, and experience, one might say – are constitutively fluid by design and that, therefore, the institutions destined to recognize and cater to them must respond not to the outer form but to the inner need. Of necessity, therefore, Macdonald views legal and social institutions as themselves dynamic and constitutively fluid. No doubt this puts a new spin on an approach to institutional structures, which are normally conceived as inflexible and dogmatic. But by reframing *both* human relations and institutional and regulatory structures as fluid and purposive, Macdonald suddenly reframes old and sterile debates. The question is no longer about "marriage" as such but about underlying human needs for intimacy. The question is no longer about "illicit drugs" but about underlying human motivations. Governance becomes – and the implications of this move still take the breath away – the means not of preventing or regulating behaviour but of fulfilling human aspirations better. In this light, new relations and new questions suddenly come into focus, and ideological and historical artefacts become all but irrelevant. Macdonald, in this way, does not just respond to social issues but transforms the ground on which they are to be argued. The move is powerful both intellectually and strategically.

Second, and throughout his essays on legal pluralism, constitutional governance, and access to justice in particular, is his impatience with the idea of formal rules.[3] Macdonald was in this regard a close successor to Lon Fuller, to whose work in legal pluralism he adds new sociological and historical depth and a more complex understanding of virtue. Formal or positivist reasoning is inadequate to do justice to the complexity of social experience and is incapable of giving space to the dynamics of a society. The better the social life, the less it will have recourse only to formal processes and positivistic interpretations. The more adequate the institutional structure, be it a university faculty, a government agency, or a court system, the more willing it will be to let its interpretations be shaped by a complex and flexible understanding of individual social experience and far-reaching social purposes.

Macdonald's claims for the poverty of formalism and the richness of purpose – seen very clearly in works such as "Vieilles gardes" – are refreshing and in some ways incontrovertible.[4] Yet there is also, it must be said, a certain anarcho-individualism here, which is at the same time the most vulnerable point of his project. I think it is fair to say that Macdonald never offers a coherent approach to the workings and structures of power as they impinge on human freedom. The old guard he describes seems implausibly benign. In another essay, he writes, in relation to whether a musician is or is not "francophone," for example, that law "cannot trump the self-ascription of identity." That simply cannot be right. Identity is not just a matter of personal opinion. In fact, I would go so far as to say that that is really the least of it. Throughout most of human history, identity is not so much a matter of who you think you are but rather how other people choose to describe you. These labels and their legal implications are not in the least minor, as we well know; they are the heart of identity-formation within a society and the heart of oppression too. As Hunt and Wickham say, in relation to their critique of Foucault's theory of the juridical, law is certainly not everything, but it is nonetheless a site for the *condensation* of the practices and forces of power that affect our life, including our self-understanding.

Formal Thinking

Ironically perhaps for someone so opposed to formal conceptions of justice, questions of form and style lie at the heart of Rod Macdonald's writing and are one of the central features that make his scholarship so distinctive. But perhaps this is not in the end so surprising. Macdonald did not see legal forms as necessarily constraining but rather (as we have seen) as a vector capable of eliciting imaginative responses to the human condition. Legal institutions and forms are like canoes: narrow but highly mobile vessels for human creativity. And this is precisely how he understood forms of writing. By inventing new imaginative forms of scholarly writing, one could discover new ideas and tap new sources of creative thinking. So Macdonald's imagination was released and stimulated by formal invention, just as he thought that societies could be released and stimulated by the formal structures around them and as he believed that new forms could release new human potential.

Informal law, as it is sometimes called, is not by any means the *absence* of form but merely its more subtle and implicit arrangement. Macdonald's favourite literary genre was poetry (for the rambling novel he had no time) – and no surprise. Poetry, for example in the work of W.H. Auden or Louis MacNeice, manifests in the best possible light how formal constraints can be creative, not merely limiting. And this is the critical stylistic message that imbues all his work. I am only surprised that Rod Macdonald never wrote an essay in the form of a haiku. This would have been the ultimate summation of his theoretical and methodological principles.

On occasion, it has to be said, his commitment to formal and stylistic imagination got in the way. Like the great sociologist Boaventura de Sousa Santos, a kindred spirit if ever there was one, Macdonald was at heart a structuralist: someone for whom taxonomy was both an abiding virtue and an ever-present vice. De Sousa Santos argues that the use of silence is an important tool of informal mediation in the *favelas* of Brazil, but he can't resist telling us that there are in fact ten different kinds of silence, all of which he lists.[5] So too, in an article like "The Swiss Army Knife of Governance,"[6] Macdonald offers the reader five theses in relation to three issues in relation to four historical periods, followed by nineteen more theses and three more ideas. The formal structure of such an article is a somewhat unwieldy mechanism.

Macdonald's use of formal and structural devices, largely unfamiliar territory within the legal academy, as a means of creating new understanding is nonetheless often used to the most powerful effect. In "Office Politics,"[7] for example, he exemplifies the nexus between institutions and forms in a truly exceptional and sustained feat of creative writing, using only the epistolary form and writing in more than a dozen different voices. Written immediately after he completed his term as dean, Macdonald's essay is therefore *about* normative pluralism within institutions and *about* the relationship between institutional commitments, intellectual commitments, and personal commitments; the design of the essay exemplifies and manifests these ideas on a formal level as well as talking about them on a substantive level. He raises the question of the relationship between personal, institutional, and intellectual commitments through a form that is more layered and complex than a discursive discussion of the issues could ever be. And at the same time, the formal structure of a series of letters and memos by different fictitious professors (though clearly drawn from life!) allows him to refuse the complacency of easy answers. "Office Politics" raises multiple dimensions of these problems, multiple possibilities for how to respond to them, and does so with a subtlety and generosity that is vanishingly rare in legal academia. He achieves in this essay an almost perfect marriage between form and content.

Just as Rod Macdonald was essentially a formal thinker (a thinker about the relationship between form and law, always experienced *through* the relationship between form and law) so too was he essentially a metaphorical thinker (a thinker about the relationship between metaphor and law, always experienced *through* the relationship between metaphor and law). One recalls Auden, for whom the essential move is away from thinking about what law "is" and instead toward thinking about what law is "like." Macdonald never, ever told us what law is. But over and over again he tried to explain what law is like: a Swiss Army knife, a call centre, an early bible, the game of cricket, the colours of the rainbow, modalities of light, and so on.[8] Here too, of course, there is a danger, never entirely avoided, of over-larding the pudding. In "Kaleidoscopic Federalism,"[9] he comes dangerously close to saying that "federalism" is a metaphor for federalism. In another essay,[10] he informs us that the elephant is Canada's albatross. Perhaps this metaphorical peril is run more often in relation to constitutional law, because it seems to be hard to say what Canada itself really "is" and much easier to try and work out what Canada is "like." Like truth, Canada is a mobile army of metaphors.

But there is no doubt that in Macdonald's work – as in the relationship between law and language in general – metaphors do a huge amount of the heavy lifting. They dramatically change our perspective. They are capable of generating new connections, new distinctions, and new paradigms for action and thought. Even the perilously balanced piles of metaphors employed in some of his essays provide opportunities for destabilizing conventional thought – even, as he would happily admit, his own thought. "Custom Made"[11] addresses this question directly. Macdonald explicitly refuses to reduce one metaphor to the terms of another. He argues that this is part of his commitment to the heterogeneous and finally incommensurable pluralism of our personal lives. In a moving fashion that is to be found right across Macdonald's work, the personal experience of plurality in our intellectual and linguistic lives is intimately connected to our conceptions of law. Life, as Louis MacNeice says in one of Macdonald's favourite poems, is "incorrigibly plural."[12] And law is one part of that lived and fertile plurality. What could be more incoherent and resistant to analysis? And at the same time, what could be more true?

In this regard, and again perhaps with a conscious irony, the use of metaphor in and across his work brings us full circle. For we can see here an underlying thesis that law is not "like" life: it "is" none other than life itself. Macdonald's metaphors are in the end *metonyms*, aspects of a greater whole, which we only glimpse one fragment at a time but in each glimpse find the refraction of the blooming whole. This is not just an argument for deploying metaphors. It is an argument for caring about law.

Original Thinking

Ultimately, Rod Macdonald's greatest contribution has been to offer his readers and his students and his colleagues and his friends not so much a blueprint for legal research but a model of it: the former to be followed as instructions, as a prescription; the latter to be observed as an example and as an inspiration. He does not give us a recipe book; he serves us dinner. Macdonald's body of work provides us with a rich source of models for a stunningly ambitious vision of what would be involved in the conduct and vocation of citizenship and scholarship in the modern world. For Macdonald, if scholarly writing is not clear – and inventive – and insightful – and relevant – then it is not worth the ink. Can it be all these things at once? Macdonald shows us just what can be achieved. And this ambition and this achievement is so far beyond the run-of-the-mill scholarship that we encounter every day, let alone what was produced forty years ago, that one blushes at the temerity or the courage, however one wishes to label it.

Rod Macdonald often told the story of his first semester in law school. When he was asked by one of his senior professors what he planned to do with his degree, he replied that he was going to be a professor. To which his teacher replied that there was no place for Macdonald in legal academia. For Rod Macdonald, the moral of the story is: how wrong they were. And there is no doubt that his resentment at this slight, and his determination to prove it mistaken, was one of the driving forces in a driven life. But I submit that the truth is otherwise. The real moral of the story is: *they were right*. Look at the vast majority of the work being done and published by leading law journals circa 1970, in Canada as well as in other jurisdictions such as Australia. With certain wonderful exceptions, it is startling to note just how narrow and legalistic its focus, how pedantic its style, how casuistic its concerns, how modest its ambitions, and how obsequious its attitude to legal authority. This secure and cloistered intellectual world had no place for a writer like Rod Macdonald – no place for his creativity, his ambition, or his iconoclasm. He didn't fit.

Macdonald's response to this challenge is instructive, particularly since it is of a piece with his whole approach to scholarship, to legal institutions, and to law. Rather than cutting his academic coat to fit the institutional cloth with which he was faced, he transformed the institutions around him to fit his academic vision. In everything he has done – in his life as a teacher, an institution builder, and a legal scholar – he has shown that institutional structures are not inflexible. With enough determination and vigour, they are capable of facilitating rather than inhibiting personal self-realization. They become changed in the process. To the extent that legal scholarship today bears little relationship to what was being published forty years ago, scholars like Macdonald – and obviously not him alone – have been responsible for the change. But the process of institutional development is never finished. Liberating that transformative potential remains inherent in the academic vocation and challenges all of us, in our different ways, to do likewise. In that sense, one of his finest pieces, "Custom Made," exactly summarizes the position as he saw it and acted on it. Law is not just made by custom – but custom-made for each of us, all the time. This is true of academic life, judicial life, and scholarly life too. It is by no means the whole truth, but acting as if it were reaps extraordinary dividends.

Quite apart from the specific legal and social arguments he developed over the course of his career, Macdonald stands an exemplar and a model for all of us. He does not tell us what to think so much as how to think and the importance of following our own path in the thinking. His work is enduring testimony to the importance and powers of self-realization in institutional life. The personal is not just the political but the intellectual – and vice versa. An institution (a government, a constitution, a law faculty, or an academic essay) is like a poem – its formal constraints, which are by no means simply given but invented and reinvented each time, are the very *means* of our self-expression.

This is a lesson that is, I think, increasingly important in twenty-first century life. In academic journals, in white papers and government reports, in commissions of inquiry and non-government documents, I am not sure that the framework in which academics, activists, and thinkers act is much less constrained than it was when Macdonald started to write. There is no doubt more room on the margins than before, but the mainstream social and intellectual debate about law, society, and governance seems even more reductively instrumentalist, and institutionally and structurally conservative, than ever. I am acutely aware that my own absence from the symposium out of which this collection sprang is now immeasurably compounded by Rod Macdonald's own absence from our lives. Though his inimitable voice is now stilled, his remarkable example still stands before us, inciting us through the years. For students and scholars in particular, the scope and intensity of Macdonald's "legal imagination" reminds us above all that the term need not be and must not become a contradiction in terms.

NOTES

1 Martha-Marie Kleinhans and Roderick Macdonald, "What Is a *Critical* Legal Pluralism?" *Canadian Journal of Law and Society* 12 (1997): 46.

2 Law Commission of Canada, *Restoring Dignity: Responding to Child Abuse in Canadian Institutions Executive Summary* (Ottawa: Law Commission of Canada, 2000), http://publications.gc.ca/collections/collection_2008/lcc-cdc/JL2-7-2000-1E.pdf (with S. Zimmerman et al.); Law Commission of Canada, *Beyond Conjugality: Recognizing and Supporting Close Personal Adult Relations* (Ottawa: Law Commission of Canada, 2001); Roderick Macdonald, "Perspectives on Personal Relationships" (Opening address to the Conference on Domestic Partnerships, Queen's University, Kingston, 22 October 1999); Macdonald, *Lessons of Everyday Law* (Montreal: McGill-Queen's Press for the School of Policy Studies, Queen's University, and the Law Commission of Canada, 2002).

3 Macdonald, "Three Centuries of Constitutional Making in Canada: Will There Be a Fourth?" *University of British Columbia Law Review* 30 (1996): 211–34; Kleinhans and Macdonald, 25–46; Macdonald, "Kaleidoscopic Federalism," in *The States and Moods of Federalism: Governance, Identity and Methodology*, edited by J.-F. Gaudreault-DesBiens and F. Gélinas (Montreal: Blais, 2005), 261–283; Macdonald, "Unitary Law Re-form, Pluralistic Law Re-Substance: Illuminating Legal Change," *Louisiana Law Review* 67 (2007): 1,114–60; Macdonald, "Custom Made – For a Non-chirographic Critical Legal Pluralism," *Canadian Journal of Law and Society* 26 (2011): 301–27.

4 Macdonald, "Les vieilles gardes : hypothèses sur l'émergence des normes, l'internormativité et le désordre à travers une typologie des institutions normatives," *Le droit soluble [:] contributions québécoises à l'étude l'internormativité* , edited by Jean-Guy Belley (Paris: Librairie générale de droit et de jurisprudence, 1996), 233–72.

5 Boaventura, de Souza Santos, "The Law of the Oppressed: The Construction and Reproduction of Legality in Pasargada Law," *Law and Society Review* 12 (5) (1977): 29–38.

6 Macdonald, "The Swiss Army Knife of Governance," in *Designing Government: From Instruments to Governance*, edited by Pearl Eliadis et al. (Montreal: McGill-Queens University Press, 2005), 203–41.

7 Macdonald, "Office Politics," *University of Toronto Law Journal* 40 (1990): 419–76.

8 Macdonald, "Swiss Army Knife"; Macdonald, "Call-Centre Government: For the Rule of Law, Press #," *University of Toronto Law Journal* 55 (2005): 449–95; Roderick Macdonald and Thomas McMorrow, "Rabbits,

Ravens, Snakes, Turtles: Analyzing the Political Economy of Aboriginal Communities," in *Gouvernance autochtone: reconfiguration d'un avenir collectif*, edited by Pierre Noreau (Montreal: Thémis, 2010), 211–35; Macdonald, "Three Metaphors of Norm Migration in International Context," *Brooklyn Journal of International Law* 34 (2009): 603–53; Macdonald, "Unitary Law Re-form."

9 Macdonald, "Kaleidoscopic Federalism."

10 Macdonald, "Three Centuries."

11 Macdonald, "Custom Made."

12 Louis MacNeice, "Snow," in *The Collected Poems of Louis MacNeice*, edited by E.R. Dodds (London: Faber and Faber, 1966), 30.

PART TWO

Lessons from Rod Macdonald's Everyday Life

26

Un grand Québécois

PIERRE NOREAU

Roderick A. Macdonald, professeur à la Faculté de droit de l'Université McGill, a consacré sa carrière à comprendre le phénomène juridique. Sa thèse essentielle a consisté à démontrer et à documenter l'idée que le droit dépasse largement les seules limites de la loi, que par sa nature même, le droit se compose et se reconstruit perpétuellement, se combinant à bien d'autres formes de normativité, parfois implicites, parfois « inférentielles». Il a démontré que chacun de nous apprend spontanément à faire jouer entre elles ces différentes normativités et que cette diversité des formes de la normativité est une condition de la légitimité du droit. Le professeur Macdonald a largement fait la preuve que, dans tous les espaces sociaux que nous traversons, les habitudes, les diverses formes d'autorité, et les traditions non écrites font que nous ne nous référons pas constamment à la loi pour établir les orientations et les raisons de notre conduite personnelle. Dans la perspective développée par Roderick A. Macdonald, chacun de nous est, par conséquent, le siège de son propre ordre juridique. Certaines règles non écrites sont ainsi plus importantes que plusieurs des lois fondamentales de notre pays. Pourquoi faisons-nous la file au cinéma ? Pourquoi nous assoyons-nous toujours à la même place à table ? Pourquoi, en classe, alors que nous étions étudiants, nous sentions-nous indisposés lorsqu'un collègue occupait le pupitre où nous avions pris l'habitude de nous asseoir ? C'est en scrutant les replis de la vie quotidienne que Roderick A. Macdonald a tenté de comprendre les contours du phénomène juridique, et, après lui, plus aucun juriste n'a pu aborder le droit comme un simple ensemble d'énoncés couchés sur papier par un législateur impersonnel. Le droit est le produit d'un mouvement continu entre ce que nous nommons la loi et ce que nous en faisons… Elle trouve appui sur mille autres références normatives et idéelles. C'est la perspective ambitieuse développée par Macdonald : le droit est une forme particulière de la vie sociale.

Par sa simplicité même, la description qui précède montre que Roderick A. Macdonald est réellement l'auteur d'une œuvre. On reconnaît d'ailleurs la valeur de cette œuvre à sa stabilité, à sa cohérence, et à sa longévité. Elle tire sa pérennité de ce qu'on ne peut plus s'en passer après l'avoir fréquentée. Roderick A. Macdonald est un des principaux penseurs de la théorie contemporaine du droit. Il a cependant tiré l'essentiel de ses propositions d'une très fine analyse de la société québécoise, qu'il a su traduire dans des perspectives dont la portée est quasi universelle.

Au plan de la personnalité, deux grands traits ont traversé la vie et l'œuvre de Roderick A. Macdonald: la modestie et l'audace. Modeste, Roderick A. Macdonald n'ayant jamais fait grand étalage de sa véritable contribution au développement du droit contemporain, c'est à nous qu'il revient de le faire aujourd'hui. On lui doit en effet la conduite de plusieurs dizaines de recherches, la publication de centaines d'articles, de livres, et de chapitres de livres, ainsi que la tenue d'un nombre incalculable de conférences scientifiques et d'autant de conférences publiques, toujours écrites dans un style accessible qui a fait sa réputation de grand communicateur. Au plan institutionnel, il a été doyen de sa faculté; il a présidé le Groupe de travail sur l'Accès à la justice qui devait conduire, en 1992, à la tenue du Sommet de la justice; il fut président-fondateur de la Commission du droit du Canada. Il aura présidé le comité-experts dont le rapport allait conduire à l'adoption, au Québec, de la première loi canadienne sur les poursuites-bâillons, et il œuvrait encore quelques jours avant son décès comme commissaire au sein de la commission Charbonneau. Il a œuvré au sein du comité-conseil de la commission Bouchard-Taylor sur les accommodements raisonnables. Il a présidé la Société royale du Canada. Dans son esprit, cependant, sa contribution la plus importante aura été d'accompagner les centaines d'étudiants qui ont eu le très grand privilège de le connaître comme professeur à tous les cycles de la formation universitaire et dans plusieurs universités.

Au plan intellectuel comme au plan de sa production universitaire, Roderick A. Macdonald a par ailleurs fait constamment preuve d'une grande originalité et d'une grande audace. Cette audace s'est exprimée tant sur le plan de l'écriture que sur le plan de l'inspiration. Mais ce goût pour l'originalité n'a jamais été gratuit. Il a toujours servi la nécessité de transmettre une idée: trouver la forme pédagogique qui fait comprendre. Faut-il inventer un conte, écrire une nouvelle, un poème, une chanson, ou un article scientifique, l'important a toujours été de savoir communiquer sa compréhension des choses.

L'œuvre de Roderick A. Macdonald est elle-même fondée sur une certaine vision du monde. Il n'a jamais abordé la vie comme un lieu qu'on habite ou un bien (un don) que chacun possède en propre, mais comme un bien commun qu'on partage. On comprend immédiatement que cette conception du monde suppose une certaine éthique de la relation. Il a toujours entretenu avec ses étudiants et les autres membres de la communauté intellectuelle et juridique des rapports simples et égalitaires et, pourrions-nous dire, presque « fraternels ». Cette qualité de relation a traversé toute sa vie intellectuelle, une vie intellectuelle qui n'a eu de sens qu'en tant que forme particulière de sa vie personnelle.

Il m'apparaît impératif de rappeler la contribution de Roderick A. Macdonald au développement de notre collectivité. Il fait partie de ces personnalités exceptionnelles qui vivent la situation paradoxale de participer intimement à leur propre société et de la transcender en même temps. Engagé de multiples façons dans le débat collectif, il a toujours défendu l'idée que les collectivités devaient trouver dans leur réalité leur propre mouvement. Aussi s'est-il constamment défini comme un membre actif de sa propre communauté. Il a toujours fait confiance au mouvement social, à la société civile dans son ensemble et au sens civique de ses concitoyens. Parallèlement à ses projets universitaires et aux engagements importants qu'il a souvent accepté de prendre tant au Québec qu'ailleurs au Canada, il a lui-même participé au développement d'organisations plus petites, acceptant souvent de prendre des responsabilités au sein d'organisations communautaires, municipales, ou régionales, notamment dans le domaine de la santé et des services sociaux. En plus d'avoir contribué au développement du droit québécois, il a constamment plaidé en faveur de l'accès à la justice et a défendu la nécessité d'une approche plus humaine des services publics. Il n'a jamais hésité à prendre publiquement parti pour ce qui lui apparaissait juste, même lorsque son point de vue tranchait avec celui de la majorité. Ce faisant, il a témoigné d'une conception fondamentalement démocratique du débat public et de la participation civique. Tous ceux qui ont côtoyé Roderick A. Macdonald peuvent témoigner avoir rencontré, au moins une fois au cours de leur vie, un véritable humaniste, et chacun d'eux a pu avoir le sentiment d'être, un instant, parfois au détour d'un échange furtif, la personne la plus importante du monde. Je rappelle ici ces faits avec la plus grande simplicité, car elle correspond à la façon unique dont Roderick A. Macdonald a toujours su exprimer aux autres ce qu'Aristote appelait « l'amitié civique ».

Je veux conclure cet hommage sur une dernière dimension qui m'apparaît au moins aussi importante que toutes les autres. Roderick A.

Macdonald a été toute sa vie un grand Québécois. Au-delà de l'immense réputation qu'il a acquise dans les universités canadiennes, le professeur Macdonald a surtout été l'un des principaux artisans du rapprochement entre les communautés universitaires de langue anglaise et de langue française et entre la Faculté de droit de McGill et la Faculté de droit de l'Université de Montréal. Il a été de toutes les initiatives qui ont permis qu'une véritable tradition intellectuelle émerge au fil des années au sein de la communauté juridique québécoise, en tirant notamment avantage de l'interaction entre nos deux traditions juridiques, et par extension, entre deux modes de pensée. C'est ainsi que Roderick A. Macdonald peut être considéré comme un des pères du transsystémisme au Québec. Sa grande maîtrise du français et sa très grande compétence juridique en ont fait, à sa façon, un spécialiste du Québec et du droit québécois (particulièrement du droit civil) au Canada et à l'étranger. Dans ce sens, il a extraordinairement servi le rayonnement du Québec et du droit civil, tant au plan canadien qu'au plan international, où il a souvent agi comme expert dans différents domaines : du droit des sûretés jusqu'au droit constitutionnel. Plus encore, il a formé une nouvelle génération de juristes qu'on retrouve aujourd'hui dans un très grand nombre d'universités, partout dans le monde. Ils poursuivent des idéaux qu'il a lui-même servis.

C'est parfois un honneur pour un individu d'en honorer un autre. Roderick A. Macdonald a été un homme de son temps, profondément engagé dans sa société et inspiré par elle. Il nous a rendus plus fiers de ce que nous sommes et de ce que nous tentons de réaliser ensemble dans les domaines juridique et académique. En ce sens, il fait partie des quelques individus qui, au Québec, doivent nous servir de modèle. Les hommes et les femmes comme lui fixent à la fois l'instant et l'avenir de cette société.

27

The Turn to Critical Legal Pluralism: The Contributions of Roderick Macdonald

SALLY ENGLE MERRY

It was the mid-1990s when I first heard about critical legal pluralism. At the time, legal pluralism was an interesting idea but was generally understood as a static concept, primarily descriptive. Its focus was on recognizing forms of law outside the state and challenging the view that all law was centralized in states. It was an approach that tended to valorize what was called "folk" law and often criticized legal scholars for "legal centralism," the view that the only form of law was that of the state. In the 1970s and 1980s, the burgeoning interest in alternative dispute resolution, typically coupled with a critique of state law, fed into this perspective.

Yet this theoretical view of legal pluralism led to fights about whether non-state law was really law. Ultimately, many scholars decided that this was a rather dry, definitional debate. There were clearly normative codes, modes of decision-making, and enforcement mechanisms outside the state, but they were also clearly different from state law. At this point in the development of the concept, it seemed to have stalled. Yes, there were multiple legal orders that coexisted, but so what?

In the hands of Roderick Macdonald, legal pluralism became something more, something more interesting and vibrant. Rod recuperated the idea of legal pluralism by redefining it as "critical legal pluralism." What did that mean? From my perspective, he drew on critical legal studies perspectives with his focus on power, on forms of legal subjectivity, and on the transformative processes by which legal orders are formed by litigants and everyday use. Not only are there multiple legal orders, but individuals experience themselves as embedded in a multiplicity of orders, and these orders shape each other. This is a far more interesting and productive approach to understanding legal pluralism than the simple assertion that multiple legal systems, codes, and practices coexist in a single social field.

The introduction of a critical perspective shifted legal pluralism from a static and primarily descriptive model focusing on the existence of multiple legal spheres to a more dynamic one that highlights the agency of everyday actors in constructing legal orders. This turn in the theoretical concept of legal pluralism has contributed to the development of a vibrant and expanding field of analysis that incorporates state and international law as well as community forms of law. It was important in my own efforts to conceptualize the way human rights law intersects with national law and local community practices, leading me to focus on the way international human rights law is appropriated and redefined in local contexts.

In Rod's important article in 1997 in the *Canadian Journal of Law and Society*, "What Is *Critical* Legal Pluralism?" he articulates this dynamic approach clearly: "it is possible to see in legal pluralism a concern with how manifold legal norms emerge, change, and negate or reinforce one another in social situations not derived from, tributary to or purportedly structured by State action."[1] In a subsequent article in 2011,[2] he argues that habits and practices create norms; they are not simply based on texts. He advocates what he calls "panjuridism": the idea that "law is everywhere, and that the relationships between its different forms, processes, sites and orders can best be explored through 'ideal-type' formal and functional taxonomies."[3] One contribution of the legal pluralist perspective is to "valorize otherwise suppressed normative orders and normative discourses."[4] As these quotes show, Rod is clearly focusing on the implications of uncovering and recognizing non-state legal orders for understanding power relationships, challenging the exclusive power of state law.

His critical legal pluralist perspective is deeply concerned with the nature of legal subjectivity, the transformative capacity of individuals, and the role of knowledge. Rod argues that legal subjects conceive of themselves as subjects within multiple legal orders. They are not determined by these orders but "possess a transformative capacity that enables them to produce legal knowledge and to fashion the very structures of law that contribute to constituting their legal subjectivity."[5] The critical approach, he says, focuses on the role of legal subjects in generating normativity. Legal subjects, he says, are "law inventing," not merely "law abiding."[6] They carry multiple identities in a single field and move through a series of legal fields, none of which is necessarily normatively homogeneous.[7] He emphasizes that subjects construct legal orders rather than simply being controlled by them. Thus, critical legal pluralism radically reshaped ideas of legal pluralism as a set of static, homogeneous legal orders nicely arranged in levels and replaced this layer-cake model with a focus on knowledge, power, and the possibility of transformative legal subjects. This focus on the way narrating subjects construct law is a project that Rod appropriately represents as emancipatory.[8]

This new perspective on legal pluralism had institutional as well as intellectual consequences. In 1995, Rod invited me to join a Canadian Institute for Advanced Research program he had created to study critical legal pluralism, called the Program on Law and the Determinants of Social Ordering. We spent two or three years in regular meetings thinking through the meanings and significance of a focus on critical legal pluralism. It was a great group and a very productive set of exchanges for me. Rod was always a most inspiring and generous leader of discussions and explorations of the range of ways we might conceive of legal pluralism and use it to enhance our analysis.

Critical legal pluralism inspired me to explore different forms of legal pluralism. I had already worked on the better-known form of legal pluralism produced by colonial law in a study of the introduction of American law in Hawai'i in the nineteenth century, but in conjunction with this turn to critical legal pluralism, I began to study another kind of legal pluralism created by the transnational sphere of human rights law. This was an internationally based form of law yet, at the same time, one whose power rested largely in the extent to which individuals adopted its broad perspectives and appropriated them for social movements. How did it intersect with state law? What was its relationship to local forms of ordering? Here the inequalities of power were subtle and complex. I found patterns of vernacularization: local appropriations of global concepts and approaches, refashioned to fit with other existing ideas. For example, in a city in western India, a women's organization seeking to promote women's human rights used the device of making kites adorned with an anti-sex-selection logo for the annual kite-flying contest. When the kites fell to the ground, residents of the city would see this message opposing female foeticide, a widespread practice in the region. In the same organization, women who experienced domestic abuse were encouraged to stand up for themselves as a way of asserting their human rights. A women's organization in Beijing developed an alternative program to the state system of protecting women's rights by using a human rights framework to respond in a more holistic way to the women's problems. Noting the link between social work approaches and human rights, the organizers of this program enacted their understanding of human rights by paying attention to the feelings and concerns of litigants instead of simply focusing on what the state had, or did not have, to offer. In some situations, human rights ideas were creatively merged with existing systems, as in the creation of special women's courts, or panchayats, in India, called *nari adalats*, to handle cases concerning domestic violence, divorce, and dowry. Everywhere, I found legal subjects reconstructing legal orders out of the pieces of other legal orders, not always free to do as they liked, of course, yet still with some real agency. This is not a simple layer-cake model of legal pluralism but one continually redefined by crossings, by travels among countries, from villages to Geneva and New York and back again, and by mergers and reconfigurations of existing legal and normative forms and practices. These processes reveal the possibilities of change, despite unequal power relations, as well as areas of inflexibility that resist change. I think this is what Rod meant by critical legal pluralism.

I associate the concept of legal pluralism, particularly in the legal academy, in particular with McGill's Faculty of Law. I suspect this is in part because of the recognition of diversity within the legal system, given Quebec's legal history. It is also clearly the result of Rod's influence on the law faculty during his many years of service and leadership. In developing and expanding this highly productive way of thinking about law, Rod helped to foster a recuperation of this theoretical framework. It has a growing influence. For instance, at both Yale Law School and King's College Law School, University of London, legal academics are teaching courses and talking about legal pluralism. At the 2013 meeting of the Law and Society Association, I chaired a very well-attended panel on Paul Berman's new book, *Global Legal Pluralism*. Once an obscure theory that explained the relationship between clans in Papua New Guinea, under Rod's intellectual power and leadership it has been transformed into a central concept for socio-legal research. Along with many others, I have benefitted enormously from his deep intellect, extraordinary generosity of spirit, and abiding curiosity and care for the world.

NOTES

1 Martha-Marie Kleinhans and Roderick Macdonald, "What Is a *Critical* Legal Pluralism?" *Canadian Journal of Law and Society* 12 (1997): 29.

2 Macdonald, "Custom Made – For a Non-chirographic Critical Legal Pluralism," *Canadian Journal of Law and Society* 26 (2011): 301–27.
3 Kleinhans and Macdonald, 33.
4 Ibid., 34.
5 Ibid., 38.
6 Ibid., 39.
7 Ibid., 40.
8 Ibid., 46.

28

A Tribute to Rod

H. PATRICK GLENN

In this short tribute, I'd like to do essentially three things. First, I'd like to talk not about what Rod has done, a very large subject, but what he has not done, or more precisely the ways of writing about law that Rod has not followed. Second, I'd like to talk about that feature of Rod's work that has most influenced me. Finally, I'd like to engage in the fundamental privilege of senior faculty members to reminisce, back to the 1970s and 1980s when Rod was a recent arrival at the McGill Faculty of Law.

What Has Rod Not Done?

When Rod came to the faculty in the 1970s, John Rawls had just published an important volume on the theory of justice, and the coffee room of the faculty reverberated with Kantian and non-Kantian claims, the debate on the distinction between analytic or synthetic statements, and other such important issues. Rod was the most important participant in this debate. He had mastered it all, and I expected for a few years that Rod would eventually write something that showed definitively that Emmanuel Kant was wrong or that he would articulate a true distinction between analytic and synthetic statements. Rod never did this, however, and I eventually came to the conclusion that he shared, in some measure, the sentiment expressed recently by Aharon Barak, the former Chief Justice of Israel, in the *Harvard Law Review*. Chief Justice Barak wrote that contemporary movements in law, and he extended his remarks to include positivism, legal realism, and natural law, were all inadequate to capture "legal reality," itself "too complex to be adequately captured by any one of these schools of thought."[1] Likewise, Rod was not capable of capture as a writer in any school or movement of legal thought and writing. As Harry Arthurs has said, his work is *sui generis*, though perhaps a one-person category of being, as Arthurs has suggested, "magical realist" might come close to describing Rod's overall position.[2]

How Rod's Work Has Most Influenced Me

I think Rod influenced me most by his ability to breathe life into legal situations or legal problems. His was an unparalleled ability to open the full range of debate that is possible on any legal problem. This is a talent for *unpacking*, to reveal the hidden presuppositions or biases in even the most simple-looking propositions. It was this pan-legal exercise of the imagination across fields that was Rod's major achievement. He did not simply say that it should be done. He did it.

Rod also greatly influenced me, however, in his explicit battle against reification. Both the civil and common laws reify *à outrance*, and this process of reification is what inevitably creates boundaries and exclusion. The real culprit, however, would be the underlying reification and not the ensuing boundaries and exclusion in themselves. It is a reification that extends widely across public international law, private international law, and domestic law. The preference Rod expressed is that of avoiding "essentialist reification," as he once described it. His expressed preference is that of "meaning" as opposed to "institutions" and that there should thus be a "dynamic of law emerging in the dialectic between legal orders."[3] I wish I had written that.

Reminiscences

In the 1980s, I had a great argument with Rod about whether the superior courts of justice of the common law world had an inherent power of judicial review. I maintained they did not. Rod, to my surprise, did not agree and offered a vigorous defence of current common law dogma, at least in the Commonwealth. We argued for days, in the coffee room, in our offices, up and down the stairs. I wanted to argue, because I knew Rod knew it all in matters of administrative law, which he was then teaching. Eventually the debate subsided. Years later I came to the conclusion that Rod was willing to argue with me because he knew that I didn't know it all and that I should be aware of all that I was up against in case I wrote on the subject. I still don't know whether there was any real disagreement between us or whether it was all in the manner of formulation of the problem. I do know, however, that Rod had the imagination to appear unimaginative as a means of providing assistance to a colleague in evident need, and for that I will always be profoundly grateful.

NOTES

1 A. Barak, "Foreword: A Judge on Judging: The Role of a Supreme Court in a Democracy," *Harvard Law Review* 116 (2002): 21.
2 See Harry Arthurs's contribution to this volume.
3 Martha-Marie Kleinhans and Roderick Macdonald, "What Is CRITICAL Legal Pluralism?" *Canadian Journal of Law and Society* 12 (1997): 35.

29

Scholarship as Activism

KIM BROOKS

People get into my head. Sometimes, it's deliberate. I conjure a refraction of the person, a refraction with sufficient definition for me to ask a question and listen for the response. Sometimes, it's inadvertent. The person is pesky. He'll intrude on the edge of an idea.

Either way, imagine Rod Macdonald. Standing there in my head, staring with inquisitive blue-grey eyes, bow tie just noticeably askew, jacket with sleeves that are unquestionably too short because of his improbably long arms, and enormous hands, gesticulating, fingers spread apart.

This is what it has been like for me, coming to know Rod a little. A mix of deliberate and inadvertent, sometimes welcome, sometimes unwelcome intrusions into my brain. What follows are some concrete illustrations of these mental interventions as a prism through which to view the relationship between scholarship and activism in Rod's work.

I met Rod when I was a law student in Vancouver and he was a visiting professor at UBC, teaching two courses. His public lecture at UBC that visiting year is not listed on his seventy-six-page, apparently still not comprehensive CV. But I think it ultimately became his *UBC Law Review* piece, "Three Centuries of Constitutional Making in Canada: Will There Be a Fourth?"[1] His talk followed closely behind Quebec's 1995 referendum. My recollection is that somewhere in the middle of the talk, Rod queried whether Quebec sovereignty would ever be achieved, resolved, and put to rest. Then he challenged us to stop asking that question and to redefine the territory from which we observed constitutionalism practices: that instead of being preoccupied about "when" the question of Quebec sovereignty might finally be resolved, we should simply accept Quebec sovereignty as a conundrum that provides the terrain from which we should explore other constitutional dilemmas.

What I learned from that talk, in the first year I was exposed to Rod's unbounded mind, was that sometimes, when a puzzle seems frustrating – so much so that I get impatient and just wish we could stop asking its motivating questions – the best move is to embrace the puzzle as your geography. Take it as the space you live within, not as the question you answer. Take, for example, the intractable problems of inequality. Sometimes, as someone who cares about material distribution, I think I can't possibly attend one more conference or workshop or session where we rail against inequality. I wish that we could make the world equal or, if not, just declare it to be so and get on with other things. Even for a day. And then I conjure up Rod, standing there looking small for once, in contrast to the oversized lecture hall in the now demolished UBC law building: a lecture hall with no windows, abysmal acoustics, and an enormous set of mounted speakers that dangled, only half-attached, to the concrete bunker walls and that were never working. And on the days I am plagued by the complex problems of the world, I think: how can I build a lighthouse on this painful, rocky ground, climb the stairs, and stare out from a new place with the aid of a beam? Equality, and distributive justice, are the questions we live, not the questions we answer. And I am liberated, by Rod's unbounded mind, from my own frustrations and impatience.

When I arrived to teach at McGill in the summer of 2007, my interactions with Rod became more frequent. In Rod, I met a colleague with an unprecedented curiosity and appetite for engagement. Try something out, if you haven't. Send Rod a paper. Rod will read it, often within a couple of days. He will be the first person to get back to you, and his email will apologize for his delay in responding. A trail of his reflections will track down the margins of your work. (I must confess that sometimes I think about just cutting out those reflections, putting *them* into a paper, and submitting them in lieu of my paper. They are inevitably better.)

In a recent exchange, Rod writes, in a little bubble on the side of my inconsequential musings: "We should question everything, ask 'what if' about everything, respond to what seem like wild ideas from students and outsiders."

Perhaps not oddly, this is what Rod says when he comes into my head uninvited. He forces himself upon my brain, leaning in with those enormous hands waving, demanding, "Is this the question to be asking? What other questions might be asked? What questions are you avoiding? What answers have you assumed? Why do you care about the answer, anyway?"

Activism is, I think, most fundamentally about the project of being motivated to engage in the world. Rod's scholarship and activism live symbiotically. Rod performed scholarship in all manner of forms: cases and materials, essays, monographs, translations, government reports, research studies, unpublished musings, journal articles, songs, editorial projects, chapters, case comments, conference agendas, research grant applications, book reviews, review articles, pamphlets, newspaper and magazine articles, columns, annotations, headnotes, legislation, research proposals, faculty reports, parliamentary briefs, emails, and conversations. No matter the form, his scholarship brings him into our heads and changes the way we think and act in the world. Ultimately, when you read Rod, in my experience, you will be left with him, gesticulating wildly with those long arms, in your head. This, it seems to me, is scholarship intersecting activism.

NOTE

1 Roderick Macdonald, "Three Centuries of Constitutional Making in Canada: Will There Be a Fourth?" *University of British Columbia Law Review* 30 (1996): 211–34.

30

Rod Macdonald : *Point de bascule*

NICHOLAS KASIRER

Un des thèmes évoqués par Andrée Lajoie dans sa superbe ode à Rod Macdonald est sa contribution à la vie institutionnelle du droit. Il y a lieu, certes, de saluer son apport à diverses facettes de la vie publique. Je m'attarderai quelques instants sur la manière dont les universités ont été marquées par le professeur Macdonald. On pense à l'Université York, où il a fait ses premiers pas en sociologie et en droit ; à la section de droit civil de la Faculté de droit de l'Université d'Ottawa, où, avec un français approximatif au départ, il a décroché la médaille d'or ; à l'Université de Toronto, où il a fait ses études supérieures sur Lon Fuller ; à l'Université de Windsor, où il a commencé son enseignement ; aux différentes facultés au Canada et ailleurs, où ses étudiants ont pris place comme professeurs ; et encore aux douzaines d'universités où il a professé à divers titres depuis presque 40 ans. Vous m'excuserez si je m'arrête particulièrement sur la marque qu'il a laissée sur l'Université McGill, où il enseigne depuis 1979, et sur sa Faculté de droit, qui a, envers Rod Macdonald, une immense dette d'honneur.

At its best, this faculty – like all universities – is a gloriously free and infinite space. And like all universities, McGill is shaped by human strengths and frailties – as a social space, the faculty is occasionally messy, pretty much ungovernable, and, if only because its student body is in constant flux, it suffers from an incurable (and no doubt healthy) form of triennial amnesia. Historians of the Faculty of Law at McGill have found it easiest to write in the register of anecdote – say, the antics of the class of '22 or the strike of '71 – and, with some good success, of hagiography, inventing the occasional luminary to light up one era or another of the faculty's past. A good historian of the faculty would be quick to say that in a university – especially an ancient one like McGill – it is unlikely that a single person can bring about change and less likely still that a single moment in one person's academic career could serve as an epiphany, or a turning point, or a *point de bascule* in its intellectual life.

Well, I'm no historian. I think there *was* a moment that changed this faculty forever. Summer 1981. Rod Macdonald became associate dean (academic) of the Faculty of Law, appointed by a great dean who was turning the corner in a long and occasionally thankless mandate. Formally, Rod Macdonald would take charge of teaching and learning in the faculty. Informally – no, perhaps "inferentially" is the better word, knowing what was to come – Rod Macdonald was given the opportunity to reinvent Law at McGill.

It was a surprising and visionary appointment – bringing Rod Macdonald to the Faculty of Law and putting him in a position of influence were among the crowning achievements of Dean John Brierley's fabled career as a scholar and administrator at McGill. When Rod arrived to teach administrative law, civil law security on property, and common law wills in 1979, he was already stripped for more climbing – wildly imaginative, no unearned claims to his loyalty, ready to sing and paddle, matched with Shelley. In a word, Rod was already what only the best can be: free. His work of rethinking McGill began in earnest as he matched courses to teachers in 1981. The project was simple: make law-teaching a university pursuit at McGill and champion those who believed law had its place in the world of ideas. The faculty had somewhat complacently told itself that it had been an early home to full-time law-teaching, thanks to Walton, Lee, Scott, Corbett, and others. Not true. The *prise de la Bastille* came late to McGill: I date it from Rod's associate deanship and the extraordinary, pyrotechnical deanship that followed. That deanship seems so inevitable today. It was not. That brave appointment matched anything of brilliance that the principal of the day has managed before or since (and I am including, in that list of the signal achievements, his own happy appointment to Rideau Hall).

Rod would be quick to say he had help and he had setbacks, but the fact remains that he changed forever recruitment of students and teachers from the top down and from the bottom up; that he had a hand in recasting nearly every course in the faculty; that no administrative structure or administrative process was shielded from his fair-minded gaze; that he established, almost alone, the research-intensive ethic that has defined the faculty ever since. Every sentient candidate for a professorial appointment understood, sooner or later, that this place did its best to keep up with Rod's aspiration for the university – for all universities – as a place to be free and *engagé*, to be *libre* and engaged, all at once.

And he wrote. During the associate deanship and the deanship of the 1980s came the most innovative works on the civil law and administrative process published in Canada in twenty-five years. Awestruck, his colleagues read during those heady years *Pour une reconnaissance d'une normativité implicite et inférentielle*, as well as the early drafts of "Legal Bilingualism," the epistemological history of the national program at McGill, "Custom Made," "Office Politics," and more. Some smaller works from that firecracker period deserve to reread – like the entry on the civil code in the *Canadian Encyclopedia* or his soaring tribute to the Université du Québec in the preface of *Le droit dans tous ses états*. And while we are at the heavy task of toting up the scholarship, let's add the dozens of unpublished reports sent to various corners of the university and other institutions, which gave voice to his originality and courage as a thinker. It all came so fast and furious: for his colleagues and friends, reading alongside Rod was a happy source of intellectual exhaustion. Come with me, he wrote. We dropped our old books and followed.

With all that superbly scholarly noise, this faculty was an endlessly exciting place. From the time of Rod's associate deanship starting in 1981, the faculty was just simply never the same. For all the glories of Frank Scott and Percy Corbett and F.P. Walton and R.W. Lee, none of the great and good souls who led the faculty had made it a personal project to reinvent the place *comme si la faculté n'avait jamais réellement existé auparavant*. In a thousand ways and a thousand settings, studying and teaching law at McGill became a proper quest for virtue; the law took shape as a limitless inquiry into how human beings endeavour to organize the chaotic sources of legal knowledge, and the curriculum became an examination of the forms, sounds, and colours of the institutions of public and private life. In Rod's law faculty there is no room for smugness or self-satisfaction, no sacred cows, nothing off limits. Students, teachers, and administrators are busy looking inwards and outwards at once, engaging with difference behind and beyond themselves, acquiring practical wisdom and questioning practicality as a limit on wisdom, holding the implicit up for scrutiny, and showing the explicit to be a weak account of power deployed and weakness suffered.

As successive principals and provosts at McGill have learned, from about 1981 on, Rod's Faculty of Law has been a special site for observing what a university can aspire to be when it dares to break the mold, why universities must be anti-instrumental, why strategic planning is unstrategic, why learning must be self-reflexive if it is to be anything of value, why the scholarship that matters is *libre recherche scientifique* that has, as its first mission, to insert itself in the dialogue between teacher and student.

The time has now come for all of us to strip with Rod for more climbing. We pause alongside Professor Macdonald, breathlessly doing our best to keep pace with him on the way up. It is time for this faculty and this university to say how much we need Rod Macdonald to stand again, as Frank Scott wrote, on new frontiers. If studying law is a way to be alive, as Rod often said, then the Faculty of Law is a glorious place to feel alive, providing a way of knowing the world for thousands of grateful people, like me, marked by the great genius of this kind man.

31

Shifting Paradigms

YVES-MARIE MORISSETTE

Macdonald Deanship

I was Rod Macdonald's successor as dean of the Faculty of Law at McGill University, and I believe that being the dean after Rod Macdonald was immeasurably easier than it might have been before Rod Macdonald.

The reason for this is simple: in five years, he transformed the place, not only academically – that's obvious – but also in several other subtle and profound ways. To cite just one example, during his deanship the faculty became a small, thriving political community where students had much more of a say in the general unfolding of things and where, consequently, they also had more responsibilities, which, Rod Macdonald would tell you, is in itself a rich educational opportunity. That was typical of his thinking. Reality is all of a piece, and there is no "upstairs or downstairs." In the short period of his deanship, between 1984 and 1989, the faculty underwent a massive institutional reboot, the effects of which continue to be felt twenty-five years later.

Access to Justice

Throughout his career, Rod Macdonald had a keen interest in access to justice, a fact that is well documented in Andrée Lajoie's book, *La vie intellectuelle de Roderick Macdonald: un engagement.*[1] Indeed, in what is otherwise a truly overwhelming list of publications, there are no fewer than twenty-four titles of articles, monographs, or reports of Rod's that deal directly with the topic of access to justice.

But the point I would like to make is more specific. Two pieces in this list are especially noteworthy: his "Theory of Procedural Fairness," published in the *Windsor Year Book of Access to Justice* in 1981,[2] and his contribution on "Access to Justice," published in 2010 in the *Oxford Handbook of Empirical Legal Research*.[3] These texts are like bookends. The first appeared not long after Rod came to McGill, and it is an essay in pure jurisprudence. It astonished me at the time: it had never occurred to me that one could talk about law in such a manner, at once so original and so powerfully eloquent. It posits an all-encompassing theory of "fairness" very broadly conceived and fairness as a crucial component of justice. The second text first asserts that any normatively defensible account of justice must take seriously the conceptions of justice that citizens themselves hold and must therefore push reflection beyond concern with official dispute-resolution processes and institutions. It then presents as critical and as exhaustive a survey of empirical research about access to justice as one could hope to read.

Rod Macdonald had a way of conducting a discussion that consistently shifted the paradigm. He and I taught administrative law side by side for many years. When he was done with rethinking that field, administrative process and judicial review of administrative action replaced administrative law in the faculty, and they opened a much broader window on justice and administrative action. The law's irrepressible proclivity for narrow self-absorption had been successfully resisted and defeated in this part of the curriculum, as it would in several others under his leadership.

The remarkable thing is that Rod did all this with equal ease at both ends of things: both the jurisprudential and the empirical ends.

Oliver Wendell Holmes wrote somewhere that he hated facts, and, according to one biographer, he was fond of saying to an esteemed colleague: "Brandeis, don't confuse me with facts." Mastering theory and paying constant attention to facts, to the reality of the matter, are characteristics of Macdonald's one-of-a-kind scholarship and, in particular, of his work on access to justice. It is a gift to us all, and there is only one word to describe it: it's remarkable.

NOTES

1 Andrée Lajoie, *La vie intellectuelle de Roderick Macdonald: un engagement* (Montreal: Thémis, 2014).
2 Roderick Macdonald, "A Theory of Procedural Fairness," *Windsor Year Book of Access to Justice* 1 (1981): 3–34.
3 Macdonald, "Access to Civil Justice," in *Oxford Handbook of Empirical Legal Research*, edited by P. Cane and H. Kritzer (Oxford: Oxford University Press, 2010), 492–521.

32

Rod Macdonald: A Man of Virtue, a Teacher of Virtue, and a Friend of Virtue

ROSALIE SILBERMAN ABELLA

I have been a student of Rod Macdonald's ever since I came to McGill to teach in 1988. Over the next five years, teaching a different course every year, I came to see that bringing me to McGill was part of Rod's plan called "Educating Rosie."

My first class was advanced administrative law. I suppose that Rod thought that since I was chairing an administrative tribunal, I might as well learn some administrative law and, as every professor knows, teaching is the best way to learn.

The next year, he asked me to teach a class on advanced jurisprudence with him. I had never taken a course in jurisprudence, let alone taught one, but I had been a judge for thirteen years, so I thought I knew what jurisprudence was about. I was wrong. In the first class, Rod and I sat at the head of a long seminar table around which sat about twenty third-year students. His opening words were "How do you know this is a table?" Not "Hi, how are you, welcome to the class." Nope. Just "How do you know this is a table?" And for the next two hours, I watched as Rod and the students debated how they knew it was a table. As I recall, my own philosophical contributions were along the lines of "Are you kidding me?" "But it looks like a table," or, the philosophically unanswerable, "Isn't this what tables are supposed to look like?" I was pathetic.

I thought that because I was entering Macdonaldland, I was going to learn how to use multi-syllabic, incomprehensible words, like epistemological, instrumentalism, deontological, or polycentrism. But tables? When the class ended, I said to Rod, "I don't think this is for me. I've been a judge for a lot of years, and this isn't what we do. Who owns the table, maybe, but *why* is it a table, never."

"Don't give up," he said. "Next class we start with the readings, and it'll all come together for you." And it did. So we started our journey through Christopher Stone's "Law, Language and Ethics" with the classic Brod/Kafka metaphor, and I started my journey into understanding what a judge was. More importantly, I came to understand the "why" of judging. By reading and discussing wonderful judgments, terrible judgments, progressive philosophers, restrictive ones, I came to sort out my ideas of what makes a good judge.

Through a legal imagination that included imagining the academic potential of non-academics like me, Rod actually unbound not only how I imagined law but how I imagined myself *in* the law. He taught me that justice is the aspirational application of law to life, that the status quo is only the beginning of the inquiry, that law and the public interest should have a good working relationship, and that virtue and fairness are law's biological parents.

He also showed me how the legal imagination takes off from many legal runways – the ones travelling to public law, private law, legal systems generally, and legal education in particular.

And underlying this magnetic gift Rod had of opening our minds to imagining new ways of thinking, and our hearts to understanding why we should, was his sheer decency. This man was many things for which we should be grateful, but above all, what we cherish is that he was a "mensch" – a good man. A preternaturally brilliant, prolific, and inspiring one, but a mensch all the same.

A man of virtue, a teacher of virtue, and a friend of virtue. How lucky McGill was to have him in its midst, and how lucky the rest of us were that McGill shared him with us so generously.

33

The Value of Pursuing Virtue

ALISON HARVISON YOUNG

When I was invited to speak at the Macdonald symposium on Rod's conception of pursuing virtue and its influence on my life, my first reaction was one of intimidation. I am a trial judge, called upon to decide cases on the basis of evidence and the law, "to call 'em as I see 'em." If I were to start discussing the pursuit of virtue in my next set of criminal reasons, I might expect a complaint to the Judicial Council or an appeal!

But as soon as I started reading Rod's work on this subject, and I began with "Decolonizing Law School,"[1] I was immediately relieved and somewhat taken aback. I was relieved, because the work is much more familiar than I had expected, and taken aback at the extent I have internalized these values in my work throughout my legal career.

In considering the influence of Rod's values, I adopt Blaine Baker's working reference to pursuing virtue[2] as "promoting the collective good," "practicing wisdom," "cultivating decency," "aspiring to citizenship," or "building character," and those alternative titles might have made this panel's theme more accessible without changing its thrust.

The value of "pursuing virtue," as expressed in Rod's work, began early on when I was a first-year law student in Rod's personal property class, and it now runs so freely in my veins that I have taken it for granted in many ways. I cannot separate the impact of his "work" in the narrow scholarship sense from the influence that his teaching, mentorship, leadership as my dean, colleague, mentor, and friend has had and continues to have. And separating out these influences, I now understand, would not be consistent with his view of virtue as expressed through his work.

Rod has inspired me in his roles as a teacher, colleague, dean, and friend and always as a mentor. But I must emphasize that none of this influence has been neatly sequential. Rather, it is a story of iterative influence and converging circles.

I start with my time as a law student. I had the great good fortune to begin law school in the fall of 1979 during Rod's first term as a professor at McGill. I entered the faculty at the age of twenty-six, with a three-year-old in tow. I thought I did not belong, because I did not fit the usual profile of a law student. Rod reached out to me as a student and gave me opportunities (beginning with hiring me as a research assistant and planting the seeds of graduate school and an academic career) that changed that perception for me. Rod saw my pre-law life script and the obvious fact that it stuck out from the typical law student's pre-law chronology of life events as an advantage that *added* to the mix, rather than as an "other" that merited polite tolerance. Years later, as a member of the faculty admissions committee, this was a perspective that I always remembered.

Under Rod's leadership, social and disciplinary diversity became a more explicit part of McGill's admissions policy and one that I had the opportunity to participate in as a member of the admissions committee for some years. Obviously, this reflects the broader and fundamental notions of pluralism and diversity that run through his work.

Continuing with my life at McGill, I turn to my teaching career and my first term teaching as a young prof at McGill. At that time, Rod was dean and suggested that we co-teach Foundations to the entire first-year class during the first term to give me a chance to get up to speed to teach in the second term. I was impressed with his kindness and generosity. It did not take me long to see it a little differently. Rod took "co-teaching" very seriously. It did not mean that we divvied up the classes and he showed up occasionally. He was in the classroom for every single class that term. After the first class, we went to the tearoom for coffee, and he said, "that was great ... you only made three major mistakes," and it went on from there. One of the students in that class who, somewhat surprisingly, went on to take other courses from me, commented that the students noticed how my hands shook less near the end of the term.

This was quintessential Rod. Co-teaching for Rod never meant a way of stretching thin resources. It meant enriching the classroom environment and the teachers as well. The students in that Foundations class saw their dean – a senior, brilliant, and challenging teacher – mentoring a young, inexperienced, and newly minted lawyer. This young law professor, and the students in that class, learned first-hand about engagement and mentorship and the sheer joy of teaching and learning from our students.

"Office Politics"[3] was published about the time I joined the faculty. It is a piece that has inspired me in many ways. First, it influenced my own work and thinking about administrative law and the complex, dynamic, and human nature of institutions and decision-making. Second, it illustrates the power of the allegory and the elegance of the simple example to develop complex ideas, a technique Rod had mastered. Third, it is great fun and essentially so human. Despite the disclaimer about all the characters being fictional, some of us greatly enjoyed recognizing certain colleagues, or at least their styles, in the memos.

Rod's work influenced my academic work significantly, where common themes in my own work considered the relationship between social and legal orders,[4] and the limits of traditional legal constructs, in the context of addressing complex and emerging aspects of new reproductive technologies.[5]

After a decade as a member of the McGill's Faculty of Law, I left to serve as dean of the Faculty of Law at Queen's University. From that perspective, "Office Politics" had renewed significance for me. I discovered that the same characters and the same styles of justification exist in every academic institution! Most recently, a new senior judge was appointed to our court, and one of his first vexing jobs was to deal with office allocation issues for both newly appointed and retiring judges, and the issues raised by the various players manifest very similar characters, patterns, and institutional conundrums. In short, there is a universality to the lessons of "Office Politics" that I did not fully appreciate twenty-five years ago.

As a dean, I became more conscious of Rod's influence, because it was a priority for me to build on the dominant model of diversity and to expand and enrich the academic/intellectual environments. As Rod's work clearly flags, such change is effected mainly through student and faculty recruitment. To use a simple example, if you have an appointments committee made up of people who all have graduate degrees from Utopia University, there will be a natural tendency to value similar applicants more highly than those with different credentials.

I almost reflexively sought out and built on different disciplinary links, tried to encourage graduate work (on the part of prospective faculty members and students alike) in a wide range of areas, attempting to bring in a wider range of political and ideological orientations with a view to providing the opportunity "for students to learn law in a multiplicity of sites and concomitantly, become more diverse sites of normativity themselves."[6] In short, I tried to encourage a multiplicity of intellectual, social, political, and economic identities. Doing this requires the promotion and fostering of the values that must precede the actualization of the creation. That is, one must both lead and persuade the led to buy into those values.

Pursuing this virtue in the Rod sense means building an alternative to a cosy, comfortable environment where faculty tends to have similar credentials in similar disciplines from similar institutions and the students are colonized to those views. Actively promoting different perspectives is tough work and tough for administrators and leaders. Often, like the devil in Milton's *Paradise Lost*, "cosy" looks really good.

The point is that both the creation and encouragement of the virtuous law school and mediating the rich identities that blossom as a result are continuous and interactive processes that are hard work and great preparation for real citizens with legal educations. Rod saw this as active work falling on all members of the community: "When 'doing law' is understood as contributing to how principles such as peace, justice, equity, legitimacy, responsibility, etc. are understood and practiced both within and beyond the walls of law school – then each member of a law school community, and each member of society, is potentially teaching, learning, and doing law all the time."[7]

Finally, I turn to the influence of Rod's work on me and my work as a judge over the past nine years. Again, it has proved to be surprisingly relevant, given that one cannot miss the fact that the judicial function is not at the top of the food chain according to Rod's pluralistic vision, which took issue with what he saw as the "hegemony of adversarial adjudication."[8] But the nature of deliberation invokes, or should invoke, a richness of considerations and identities and influences on the part of both the judge and the judged, which a good judge must always recognize, mediate, and negotiate. This is true whether one is engaged in the most basic sort of fact-finding (e.g., is a witness's testimony logically consistent internally?) or whether one is engaged in Charter interpretation concerning fundamental human rights or interpreting statutes with significant social and political repercussions.

Moreover, being a judge, and trying to be a good judge, is not just about the adjudicative function. It is also about the institutional life and role, which is something else that pervades Rod's work. For me, this means mentoring law clerks, teaching at "new judges' school," participating in programs for advocates, discussing tough cases with colleagues, trying to be a good institutional citizen and, within appropriate limits, participating in the broader community. It also means trying to reconcile it all with being a mother and grandmother, partner, caregiver for an elderly mother, and someone who tries to read non-law books and have some sort of cultural, social life. I am still juggling almost thirty-five years after Rod first taught me in law school. Rereading his work has reminded me that a rich life is about mediating identities and that all these identities feed on and reinforce the others.

This juggling is essential to, and not a distraction from, the messy plurality of the not-always-harmonious identities that constitute life, or at least a life that tries to pursue virtue. That is what I think "the wisdom of a judge" should mean. It does not drive particular results, but it is an ever-present mediator of the process of judging and of "deliberation." It is a much richer process than an impoverished model of adjudication consisting of the "smart" and merely analytical application of rules to the evidence.

This brings me full circle, back to the question of how Rod's work has influenced me. The question is actually not how Rod's work *has* influenced my work, but how has it *not*. That would have been a much shorter answer.

NOTES

1 Roderick Macdonald and Thomas B. McMorrow, "Decolonizing Law School," *Alberta Law Review* 51 (2014):717–38.
2 See Blaine Baker's contribution to this volume.
3 Macdonald, "Office Politics," *University of Toronto Law Journal* 40 (1990): 419–76.
4 E.g., Alison Harvison Young, "Reconceiving the Family: Challenging the Paradigm of the Exclusive Family," *American Journal of Gender and the Law* 6 (1998): 505; Young, "This Child Does Have 2 (Or More) Fathers ..: Step-Parents and Support Obligations," *McGill Law Journal* 45 (2000): 107.
5 Alison Harvison Young and Angela Wasuna, "Wrestling with the Limits of Law: Regulating New Reproductive Technologies," *Health Law Journal* 6 (1998): 239.
6 Macdonald and McMorrow, 17.
7 Ibid.
8 Macdonald, "Curricular Development in the 1980s: A Perspective," *Journal of Legal Education* 32 (1982): 584.

34

Rod Macdonald: The Perfect Graduate Student

ANGELA SWAN

There are two great and enduring joys for me in teaching law students. The first is that, with respect to undergraduate students, I never leave a class without knowing more than I knew when I went in. With graduate students, every meeting is a chance to engage with an inquiring mind in a person willing to work hard and, for me at least, a great source of new ideas, opportunities to revise old ideas, and simply to see things more clearly or in different ways. The second joy lies in seeing my students join me in the profession as practising lawyers (and judges) or in teaching.

Rod Macdonald was my graduate student in 1974–75. At that time, H.L.A. Hart was the dominant figure in Anglo-Canadian jurisprudence, and at our initial meeting Rod expressed an interest in doing something on Hart and English positivism. I suggested that, instead, he look at Lon Fuller and, in particular, at Fuller's *The Morality of Law*.[1]

The importance of Fuller is that he saw law as having a purpose: it was *for* something; it was for him, "the enterprise of subjecting human conduct to the governance of rules." This point of view struck a chord with me, because it helped me make sense of my principal courses, Contracts and Conflicts, the latter, I may add, being particularly in need of being asked, "What is it for?"

Rod and I met regularly, I think once a week, for that academic year, and every week Rod brought me new publications of Fuller's. He claimed at the end of the year that he had tracked down everything that Fuller had ever published. The bibliography at the end of his thesis is convincing evidence of his very thorough scholarship.

Fuller's jurisprudence was, in my opinion, greatly influenced by the fact that he was a great scholar of the common law. His paper, with his student William Perdue, on "The Reliance Interest in Contract Damages,"[2] is still an important part of every first-year contracts course in Canada. This influence meant that Fuller's jurisprudence had to be useful; it had to speak, not just to the legal philosopher, but to the practising lawyer and judge.

Fuller acknowledged the importance of the concrete case, what I call the "discipline of the concrete case." No legal theory is of much use if it does not help in the concrete case. Rod's work has explored many areas of the law, and it is obvious that his principal focus has been in making the law work, on making it forward the goals of those who both use it to do things that, were the law not as it is, could not be done and advise their clients on what to do to achieve their own goals. Rod has acknowledged the importance of Fuller to his thought and research, and I think that Fuller is responsible for the great utility that Rod's work has.

Rod's thesis was entitled, "A Prolegomenon to a Theory of Legal Relevance." Although perhaps less popular now, the words "prolegomenon" and "prolegomena" were very popular in the 1970s. The thesis is now in the Library of the Faculty of Law of McGill University. I would like to end by quoting two passages from Rod's thesis.

> In the first place, Fuller, by attempting to draw out the implications of viewing law as the "enterprise of subjecting human conduct to the governance of rules" commits himself to examining the explicit and implicit elements of this endeavour. Such a task leads him to the conclusion that there are many differing forms of social order which conventionally are included within the realm of "law ... "[3]

> Applied to the problems of legal relevance, this thesis immediately shows a different orientation than legal positivism: the question of elaboration and application of rules can be dissected and subjected to evaluation – the formal aspects of law are seen not as being characteristic of law, but in terms of the facilities which they provide for human aspiration; why some rules are more determinate than others (due to factors such as lack of enforcement, ambiguity, misinterpretation, etc.) becomes a central issue; again, the question of justice, rather than being considered a meta-legal problem, is shown to pervade all aspects of law – legal ideals are studied not as values

> imposed by external ethics but as criteria which result from the needs and functions of the law in all its varied forms; finally, the problem of "social control" and coercion, which constantly lurked in the background of positivist theories, is digested whole by Fuller – the authority of law is seen to derive not from its sanction, but from its integrity.[4]

I think that what Rod said here prefigured both the great lawyer and teacher he was to become and the ideas that informed his scholarship.

NOTES

1 Lon L. Fuller, *The Morality of Law* (Fredericksburg: Yale University Press, 1964).

2 Lon L. Fuller and William Perdue, "The Reliance Interest in Contract Damages," *Yale Law Review* 46 (1936): 52, 373.

3 Roderick Macdonald, "Prolegomena to a Theory of Legal Relevance" (LLM thesis, Faculty of Law, University of Toronto, 1975), 179 [references omitted].

4 Ibid., 180 [references omitted].

35

Producing Fairness at the Law Commission

SUSAN ZIMMERMAN

I was a student of Rod's at McGill in the early 1980s. When he was appointed president of the newly created Law Commission of Canada in 1997, I became his director of research. As both professor and boss, Rod challenged accepted wisdom and the traditional ways of approaching problems.

At the Law Commission, Rod crafted a logo that reflected the activities of the commission as he conceived them: observing, listening, posing questions, and proposing solutions. He applied his methods right from the start, and I am proud to see that one of the texts selected to illustrate the first theme of this symposium, "Producing Fairness," is the executive summary of the first major work produced by the Law Commission of Canada. It's a reference from the minister of justice on child abuse in Canadian institutions, a daunting topic that Rod chose as the commission's first initiative. The work reflected his characteristically fresh take on a seemingly intractable problem – namely, how to address the harm caused by the physical and sexual abuse of children in institutions operated, funded, or sponsored by government. Unbounded by traditional legal concepts like jurisdiction, Rod conceived the work as a reflection on the nature and impact of the harm inflicted on individuals and communities, regardless of who was responsible in a strict, legal sense.

Rod was equally unfettered by political and bureaucratic constraints. Ottawa was a new world for Rod – and Rod was a new phenomenon for Ottawa! It was fascinating and endlessly instructive to see how he navigated this new territory, with the same fearlessness, integrity, and intellectual rigour he always applied in the more familiar terrain of academia.

The result was *Restoring Dignity: Responding to Child Abuse in Canadian Institutions*,[1] a work grounded in the principles of fairness, respect, accountability, and reconciliation. It provided concrete guidance for approaches to redress, which included fact-finding, engagement, apology, and compensation. Typical Rod, it combined deep thinking paired with clear directions for action. Elements of this ground-breaking work were eventually mirrored in the federal government response to abuse in residential schools: a formal apology, compensation, and consideration for the needs of communities and peoples. In the eyes of some, the response did not go as far as it could and should have, but that shortcoming cannot be traced back to the report of the Law Commission.

Through his work at the Law Commission, Rod was able to reframe public policy discussions. When it came time for the commission to consider same-sex marriage, he cast the issue as part of a broader reflection on relationships of dependence. Rod painted on a bigger canvas. His greater breadth of vision often lifted a debate from tired, fixed positions to higher ground, where it was possible to identify and build upon common interests.

For me, Rod's example of observing and listening first in order to pose the right questions and only then propose solutions has served as an excellent foundational approach to the practice of law in many spheres. Public service can be one of the most challenging and important ways to make the law come alive and to ensure it is relevant and responsive to the people it is supposed to serve. In my current position, I develop and implement policy on research ethics and integrity for Canada's research agencies. My daily work involves crafting policy and promoting responsible conduct of research in Canada's academic research community. Hardly a day goes by without my work being informed and inspired by the lessons I learned with Rod.

NOTE

1 Law Commission of Canada, *Restoring Dignity: Responding to Child Abuse in Canadian Institutions, Executive Summary* (Ottawa: Law Commission of Canada, 2000), http://publications.gc.ca/collections/collection_2008/lcc-cdc/JL2-7-2000-1E.pdf (with S. Zimmerman et al.).

36

Three Ideas for Reimagining Law and Institutions

COLLEEN SHEPPARD

I first met Rod in 1988 when I came to Montreal looking for a teaching job. Rod was the dean of the Faculty of Law at the time. I was seven months' pregnant when he hired me – a decision that I think attests to his human agency in acting institutionally to advance gender equality.

When I arrived at McGill, I was and I still am deeply committed to understanding formal law as a mechanism that can contribute to societal change and social justice. That commitment might be seen to be at odds with Rod's theoretical engagement with legal pluralism, particularly radical legal pluralism. And although I continue to view formal legal reform as critically important, Rod's work has had a significant influence on my thinking about how to do this. I want to highlight three ideas in Rod's scholarship that have profoundly influenced me. These ideas are explored in many of Rod's articles; in these short remarks, I highlight three texts that I found particularly interesting.

The first encounter I had with Rod intellectually, before I had the chance to meet him in person, was through his 1982 article "Postscript and Prelude: The Jurisprudence of the Charter – Eight Theses,"[1] an article I found fascinating. It provides a brilliant introduction to the idea that formal legal change is not enough and that we need to think about changing culture and changing society rather than simply changing laws. Indeed, that larger project is critically connected to the impact of any formal legal reform, such as the introduction of the Canadian Charter.

The second text that had a significant influence on me was his 1993 article on Aboriginal justice, which he did for the Royal Commission on Aboriginal Peoples.[2] In his article, he maintains that access to justice is about accessing justice rather than accessing courts. Rod explored this broader conception of access to justice in numerous articles and reports.[3] Yet I find his discussion of it in the context of Aboriginal justice particularly poignant and compelling. Rod's expansive ideas about access to justice extend responsibility for ensuring justice far beyond the confines of the courtroom to the relationships and decision-making contexts and practices of everyday life and diverse communities.

The third article I want to highlight is one that he co-authored with Martha-Marie Kleinhans entitled: "What is a *Critical* Legal Pluralism?"[4] The lens of legal pluralism has elucidated the importance of being attentive to the intersection between formal law and informal institutional norms.[5] Critical legal pluralism adds an insistence on non-essentialism, recognition of the diversity of norms within institutional contexts, and the possibility of conceiving of law as an "emancipatory practice."[6] These ideas are critical to understanding the dynamics and realities of systemic inequality and help to explain its persistence even in the face of formal legal norms endorsing equality. They also open up pathways for reconceptualizing the role of human agency and institutional change. Indeed, critical legal pluralism resonates with what I have called "inclusive equality"[7] – a conception of equality that incorporates attentiveness not only to the substance of equality but also to the procedural and institutional mechanisms for creating it.

NOTES

1 Roderick Macdonald, "Postscript and Prelude: The Jurisprudence of the Charter – Eight Theses," *Supreme Court Law Review* 4 (1982): 321–50.
2 Macdonald, "Recognizing and Legitimating Aboriginal Justice: Implications for a Reconstruction of Non-Aboriginal Legal Systems in Canada," in *Aboriginal Peoples and the Justice System* (Ottawa: Royal Commission on Aboriginal Peoples, 1993), 232–74.
3 See, e.g., Macdonald, "Access to Justice and Law Reform," *Windsor Year Book of Access to Justice* 10 (1990): 287–338; Macdonald, "Access to Justice in Canada Today: Scope, Scale and Ambitions," in *Access to Justice for a New Century*, edited by J. Bass, W.A. Bogard, and F. Zemans (Toronto: Irwin Law, 2005), 19–112; Macdonald, *Jalons pour une plus grande accessibilité à la justice : rapport du Groupe de travail sur l'accessibilité à la justice* (Québec: Ministère de la justice du Québec, 1991) (with Pierre-E. Audet).
4 Martha-Marie Kleinhans and Roderick Macdonald, "What Is a *Critical* Legal Pluralism?" *Canadian Journal of Law and Society* 12 (1997): 25–46.

5 See also Macdonald, "Metaphors of Multiplicity: Civil Society, Regimes and Legal Pluralism," *Arizona Journal of International and Comparative Law* 15: 69 (1998). In my own work, I have explored the intersection of equality and legal pluralism: see, e.g., Colleen Sheppard, "Equality Rights and Institutional Change: Insights from Canada and the United States," *Arizona Journal of International and Comparative Law* 15 (1998): 143; Sheppard, "Equality through the Prism of Legal Pluralism," in *Dialogues on Human Rights and Legal Pluralism*, edited by René Provost and Colleen Sheppard (New York: Springer Press, 2013), 129–44.

6 Kleinhans and Macdonald. See also Susan Sturm, "Second Generation Employment Discrimination: A Structural Approach," *Columbia Law Review* 101 (2001): 462–3.

7 Sheppard, *Inclusive Equality – The Relational Dimensions of Systemic Discrimination in Canada* (Montreal: McGill-Queen's University Press, 2010).

37

Intellectual Oxygen

ANNALISE ACORN

One of the questions I ask my students to think about when they're reading an article or book is: "Does this contribute to the kind of scholarly culture that you want to be a part of?" And, nudging them in the direction of my own sense of a desirable scholarly culture, I add, "Does this piece of scholarship nurture your intellect? Does it enliven your imagination? Does it invite you to think more adventurously about justice? Did you find in it any vivid insight about law and the human condition?"

If I had to pick one legal scholar whose work inspires a resounding "yes" in me to all those questions, it is Rod Macdonald.

Take Rod Macdonald's book *Lessons of Everyday Law*.[1] This book sets out to bridge the cavernous real world/academic divide and succeeds by combining original, personal, and immediately recognizable stories and images with rigorous legal theoretical analysis. Rod was a wonderful exemplar of Einstein's maxim: "Everything should be made as simple as possible but no simpler." This book dumbs nothing down, but it is unfailingly engaging and insightful. Kids dividing a chocolate bunny informs a fascinating analysis of distributive justice. A ski-hill disagreement with his son about Celsius or Fahrenheit on a "darn cold" day is a springboard to an analysis of the illusion of perfect rationality in legal categories. The canoeing C-stroke versus "five-stroke loop around" renamed the "windy day C-stroke" (and Huck Finn's strategy of calling a shovel a jackknife) facilitates a penetrating analysis of legal fictions.

Every chapter is a gem that reveals Rod's sensitivity and acuteness of perception, his inventiveness in constructing conceptual frameworks to illuminate those perceptions, and the guts he has to deliver both observation and concept without a jot of academic pretention.

Rod sees law in so many of its social hiding places – the lineup for the bus, kid's arguments for staying out later on Halloween, the naming of professional sports teams. His clear-sightedness there is key to his gift for shedding light on law in all the old familiar places: courtrooms, legislatures, and administrative tribunals.

Rod's work exemplifies George Orwell's rules of good writing – in particular, "never use a stale image." And the implication of that rule: use images. The richness of his metaphor of law reform as fixing the dock at the lake after every winter's ice damage is dazzling.

Somebody, I think it was Wittgenstein (but it could have been anybody), said that the academy is an oxygen-deprived environment. Without the intellectual oxygen that Rod and his work have given me at crucial moments in my life and my career, I would not have survived.

NOTE

1 Roderick Macdonald, *Lessons of Everyday Law* (Montreal: McGill-Queen's University Press for the School of Policy Studies, Queen's University, and the Law Commission of Canada, 2002).

38

The Joy of Doctoral Studies

KATE GLOVER

I am a doctoral student at the McGill Faculty of Law, and I was lucky to have Rod as my supervisor. It would be easy for me to go on (and on) about the influence of Rod's texts – as well as their context and subtext – on my doctoral research. But in the spirit of the theme "Pursuing Virtue," I have chosen to focus instead on two lessons from Rod's scholarship on legal education that shape my everyday work of being a doctoral student and of trying to decipher the nature of the doctoral process in law.

Lesson One: Live the Process

The first lesson starts from the idea that "imitation is the sincerest form of flattery." And the lesson is that the saying is wrong. From Rod's work, we learn that a student's imitation of her teacher, including a doctoral student's imitation of her supervisor, is a deep breakdown of the learning process. The process should never be one of blind replication or impersonation. Rather, it should, like all legal education, create the conditions for deep self-reflection, for each student to become her own law teacher, for the pursuit of personal conceptions of virtue, and for each student to make her life her own. It should be, like law, autobiographical.

Lesson Two: Process as Life

The second lesson is reflected in an email that Rod sent me, which read: "If, as a teacher, you are not so nervous that you have to visit the washroom before every class, you have become stale, and should probably start looking for another job." In my view, this lesson equally applies to the exercise of doctoral studies. My doctoral studies should make me nervous, every day. And, when they fail to do so, there is again a breakdown of the process. The nerves come with confronting my own views about law, asking the hard questions at every step, and unlearning everything I thought I knew. But this unsettling is also a motivator – it fuels the drive to keep learning, seeking, discovering, and striving.

Finding Joy

I spoke to many doctoral students during the course of the symposium. The common theme of those conversations was that engaging with Rod's work is a reminder to be daring, optimistic, and virtuous in our doctoral studies. At the same time, it is a reminder for us to be ourselves and to pursue the questions that get under our skin, regardless of our perceptions about what will lead to a job, what is traditionally studied in a law faculty, or what defines the hot topics of the day.

From all of those students, and certainly from me, thank you, Rod, for all the lessons we learned from you, and for making us nervous but for inspiring us to find the joy in it.

39

Law and Time: A Transversal Theme in the Work and Life of Rod Macdonald

H. WADE MACLAUCHLAN

I would like to explore the transversal theme "Law and Time" as it relates to the work and life of Rod Macdonald. Let me invoke Rod's example by starting with the informal. Implicit normativity and human and institutional relationships were at the foundation of Rod's work across a broad range of subject areas.

The two days of the symposium on Rod's legal imagination were like "old home week," giving us the opportunity to reconnect with old friends whom we might not have seen for years but also the opportunity to meet people for the first time who *seemed* like old friends because of mutual connections through Rod. These reunions include customary observations about how we haven't changed a bit with the years. And that's generally true, if you're prepared to look beyond the obvious, which Rod insisted that we do. A very important lesson that we've all learned from Rod is to give a compliment. That was an essential feature of his optimism and generosity. While optimism and generosity are big and admirable concepts, they don't fully capture what it meant when Rod took an interest in us, or gave us feedback, or encouraged us, or told us that we could do better. At the highest level, what Rod did as an encourager, mentor, and true friend is about citizenship –a remarkable, irrepressible citizenship. In more intimate terms, it's love. We need more of both citizenship and love. And we have Rod as our exemplar.

This brings me back to "time." Was there anyone at the symposium who had not, at some point or at many points, asked: "Where did Rod find the time?" The time to tackle big and diverse questions; to write and read and think, productively and constructively; to truly cross and eradicate boundaries; to build new collaborations and disciplinary movements; and to do all of that in a way that would never be called "generalist." Rod went deep.

On top of that, in addition to his own amazing productivity, Rod found and made time to encourage and push each of us in our own way. And he made priority time for his beautiful family. As a reminder of how Rod managed time and kept himself grounded notwithstanding all of the things he had on his plate, it is noteworthy that over three-plus decades, he walked from his home in Westmount to McGill on most mornings and back again in the evening.

Comme nous sommes à Montréal, je vais citer un penseur montréalais qui est presque aussi renommé que Rod Macdonald, c'est-à-dire Pierre Elliott Trudeau. Trudeau a dit que « l'élément essentiel en politique est le *timing* ».

Trudeau aside, you may wonder why I am introducing a new term and broadening the scope of inquiry. That is to say, is it necessary to speak about "timing" when my topic is "Law and Time?" The best defence for broadening the scope of inquiry or adding a note of complexity is, quite simply, that this is what Rod Macdonald would do. You can't just talk about law and time. You have to think about timing. You can't look at this simply as a question of chronology. Let's bring in context, externalities, and implicit norms, considerations and influences.

Timing was an essential ingredient in Rod's scholarship. Before Rod, the concept of pluralism was different, if it was thought about at all. Federalism was not spoken of with such vigour. That would certainly be sometime prior to the last First Ministers' Conference, which was held in November 2008. Think of it: conversations and context change. This is especially true when there is no conversation.

The point here is that Rod Macdonald chose his timing, and more precisely he created his timing: here at the McGill Faculty of Law, at the Law Commission of Canada, and most notably and above all in his diverse and insistent scholarship.

Rod always looked across time, asking probing and sometimes quirky questions about historical context and legal evolution. He brought a historically grounded and contextualized approach to his work on Quebec civil law, on federalism, secured transactions, administrative law, legal education, and legal philosophy.

As Rod himself often did, I am going to draw upon music, and a singer, for a final thought about time. Maria Callas, the magnificent Greek opera star who, like Rod, had an impressive range, once said: "An opera begins long before the curtain goes up and ends long after it has come down. It starts in my imagination, it becomes my life, and it stays part of my life long after I've left the opera house." As we think about "Law and Time" and reflect on Rod Macdonald's great contributions and friendship, we do so with assurance that it will carry on long after we have left the opera house.

The printed program for the symposium, reproduced as the cover of this book, features an image that we might, at first glance, believe to be a representation of the earth seen from far aloft. However, as we look more closely, we see that the image is titled "Pothole." This work by Shelley Freeman, Rod's wife, is a reminder of the need to see things at a down-to-earth level and to see them in multiple perspectives. It is also a reminder of the great influence that Shelley has had on Rod.

The symposium held in Rod Macdonald's honour reminded everyone of the many ways and the innumerable occasions that Rod made time for us. That was Rod's ultimate resolution of law and time: to make time for others, in the hope that we'll make good use of it.

PART THREE

Lessons from Rod Macdonald, in His Own Words

40

A Conversation with Roderick Macdonald

ANDREA MUBI BRIGHENTI

November/December 2004

On Life and Environs

AB: *It would be nice to begin this conversation by talking a bit about your personal experience and then move to more conceptual questions. Indeed, in your essays you often try to draw lessons from lived experience and everyday life. So, where did you grow up, and what were your first studies?*

RM: I was born in a small farming town in Ontario, of about 800 to 900 people, just northeast of Toronto, which is where my mother's parents lived. When it was time for me to be born, my mother went to live with her parents because my father was frequently working out of town. So I happened to be born in Markham, even though at that time my family had already moved from the rural area into a suburb of Toronto, which is where I grew up.

I went to a neighbourhood public elementary school in a new suburb that was created from farmland between 1946 and 1949. The elementary school had been built in 1952. I began school in 1954, and I was there until 1961. Then I went to the local public high school, which was only about half a kilometre from my house, from 1961 to 1966. I had a pretty normal suburban childhood. Only a couple of things stand out. First, I started going to summer camp in 1956, and that turned into a passion. I spent parts of every summer (and from 1964 onwards all summer) at camp until I got my first law teaching job in 1975. In addition, I was always interested in sports, although I was far from being a good athlete. I played on school teams in soccer and softball (in elementary school) and cross-country running, track and field, basketball, and swimming (in high school).

During my Grade 8 studies, the last year of elementary school, I was named as a page boy (the guy who runs messages for the elected members during the sittings, brings water, updates their binders of law and Hansard, and stuff like that) at the provincial legislature in Ontario. So I was out of school for six months, and we had a private tutor. We were thirteen boys from all over Ontario, and it was the first time I really got to interact with people from different socio-cultural backgrounds.

When I was twelve and my brother was fourteen, we built airplanes, big airplanes, with twelve-metre-length wings, and we flew them. We climbed up a hill and launched them, sometimes with younger neighbourhood kids as pilots, by pushing them over a cliff. We also built rockets. Some of them actually worked, but our science club came to an end when one exploded – seriously injuring a friend. I had always done very well in maths and sciences, and it was generally thought at that time that if you wanted a career in sciences, you had to read German, because a lot of scientific papers in physics and chemistry were written in that language. So in Grade 10 my parents thought I should learn German. I took an extra class in German and made some very good friends. There were only about eight boys in the class, and six of us still keep in regular contact. This year we all got together for a reunion. Besides the science courses, I also studied Latin, French, and history.

I don't know why, but at the end of high school I decided that science was boring. Despite the fact I was recruited for science programs in established universities (I had managed to graduate with an 80 per cent average – in 1966 this would have put me in the top 5 per cent of the class), I decided to go to a new university – York University – to study liberal arts. In first year, I took courses in English, French, social sciences, humanities, economics, political science, logic, natural sciences. However, in later years I never really took advanced seminars in a particular discipline; I just had a broad base. I did follow a couple of upper-level history courses, a few political science courses, and two sociology courses but do not feel that I acquired a disciplinary field. That's why I say I am a bit of an autodidact.

When I finished my BA in 1969, I really wanted to be a university professor. By that time, there had been a huge expansion in Canadian universities, but in Ontario most of the posts had been already taken – usually by Americans who were political refugees and draft dodgers from the Vietnam conflict. My undergraduate adviser told me that the chances of finding a job in the liberal arts were pretty slim. While there were more chances in political theory and Canadian history than in other fields, I was advised not to pursue a PhD but to look for a field where universities were still hiring Canadians.

So I wound up enrolling in the law faculty at York University – Osgoode Hall. From the first day I embarked on legal studies, I knew I was not there to be a lawyer, I was there to be a professor. It was pretty terrible the first year. I was not interested; I had mediocre grades. It is true that the teaching was pretty traditional, but I had some very good teachers: in fact, the real problem was that I was a bad student. It wasn't until my second year, when I met Shelley, my future wife, that I reconciled myself with the fact that if I was ever to get a job as a law teacher, I would have to get better marks! By my last semester, I managed to reconcile myself to law and wound up with three As, one B+, and one B (a lot better than the two Bs, one C and two Ds in my first year). Funnily, it turns out that I spent all my education to that point (elementary school, high school, liberal arts, and law from 1954 to 1972) studying at institutions with an address on Keele Street in Toronto!

I also decided that if I wanted to have a chance of making a life together with Shelley (who was an anglophone Quebecker), I would have to improve my French and be able to teach civil law as well as common law. So after I graduated from Osgoode Hall with a common law degree, I went to the University of Ottawa and studied civil law entirely in French. I was there for two years. At that time, I guess I was a bit more serious about things. I got the prize for standing first in civil law courses, and I applied to the University of Toronto for a master's program. I was accepted and found a fabulous supervisor, a wonderful person, John Swan.* Researching for my master's thesis was my first exposure to Lon Fuller. The thesis was a 140-page work on different approaches to finding the frontier of law, of legal relevance. The great consequence of that was that Professor Swan told me to take the opportunity to read – to build intellectual capital – and not just to write. It was terrific advice. Even now I can conjure up references and connections and understandings that I first encountered during my LLM year.

Then I applied for a teaching position. Most faculties wouldn't even look at me because when hiring Canadians, they preferred Canadians who had a graduate degree from the US or from England. So I went to the University of Windsor, which turned out to be a very fortunate move. I had a fabulous, supportive dean and great colleagues. At Windsor I became involved with law and poverty work, with community legal

* Now Angela Swan.

education, and with access to justice – activities that have remained preoccupations throughout my teaching career.

Who were the most important reference persons for your intellectual life during that time?

Other than my parents (my father, an engineer, was an encyclopedia of information and a meticulous craftsman; my mother was more spontaneous, intuitive, athletic and always saw connections across disparate fields) influences I felt were my Grade 3 teacher (Nancy Laurenson – an exchange teacher from New Zealand), my Grade 7 teacher (Doreen Henley – who also later became the tutor for the page boys at Queen's Park), my Grade 10 and 12 Latin teacher (Charles Brubacher), and my Grade 9 and 13 English teacher (Gregory Schultz). At university, the most significant person in my undergraduate studies was a professor of humanities, Brayton Polka. I was actually never a student of his. He was the senior tutor at the residence where I lived and where I ultimately became a floor don, and, more than anybody else, he encouraged me to think about teaching as a career. I also felt a personal affinity to a history professor – Jack Granatstein – who though not an intellectual mentor, taught me a lot about discipline, hard work, and scholarship.

At my first law studies at York, there wasn't really a person in the faculty who made much of a difference to me. The funny thing is that they were almost all very fine professors whom I was too immature to appreciate. The person at that faculty I got most close to afterwards was Harry Arthurs, who was the associate dean when I was a student. He later became dean at Osgoode and president of York University – but I never met him at that time. He is the person I have been interacting on a scholarly level the most with since the early '80s. When I went to Ottawa, there was one professor, Alain-François Bisson, whom I liked and came to admire because he was a questioner and a rigorous scholar. During my graduate studies, I was fortunate to have studied with John Swan. As I said, most of my professors were very good, but maybe I wasn't a particularly good student.

As a professor, I have to acknowledge the important impact of my first dean at Windsor – Ron Ianni – and the dean at McGill who hired me in 1979 – John Brierley. Both were outstanding leaders, and Brierley was also an incredible intellectual and scholar. Contemporaries who have shaped my understanding were my friends Robert Wolfe (from the School of Policy Studies at Queen's University) and Ralph Simmonds, whom I met at U of T, taught with at Windsor and McGill, and who is now a judge on the Court of Appeal of Western Australia. As well, many students over the years (of whom several are now colleagues) were among my best teachers.

Besides canoeing, I know your other passions are music and carpentry. What do you find exciting in music? What was the period of your life in which you played most?
I am, here also, an autodidact. I had a couple of years of piano lessons when I was six or seven. By the time I got to Grade 10, I guess I was thirteen or fourteen, my parents gave me a guitar and ten lessons as a Christmas present. So I started to play popular stringed instruments – ultimately, banjo, dobro, mandolin, autoharp, etc., as well. Well, we are talking about the time when Bob Dylan and others were appearing on the scene. I also wrote poetry at that time, most of which was pretty mediocre stuff, but some not so bad. I would often perform my own songs at clubs to make money to support my university studies. I played the standard mid-'60s folk-type music, but I also went on to play a bunch of instruments that were common in country-western bands, because there was much demand for bar bands. What sometimes happened is that I was a pick-up: a band would have a booking, and someone in the band would get sick, and I'd be called to replace him. I had more or less given all this up by the end of the 1960s and was only an occasional performer after that.

Who are your favourite artists/writers?
Leonard Cohen was certainly a contemporary poet who really spoke to me when in high school. I also really like Wallace Stevens and Sylvia Plath. There was a group in England in the '30s that comprised Spender, Auden, Betjamin, C. Day Lewis, and so on. Collectively, their poems appealed to me because of their political orientations. Of that group the one who has come probably to speak loudest was Louis McNeice – particularly because his politics were more personal and more subtle. Ever since my teenage years, I have been fascinated by T.S. Eliot's *Murder in the Cathedral.* I was much more interested in that than in *The Waste Land* and the other works he is usually cited for.

As far as singer-songwriters are concerned, I especially like Phil Ochs, Buffy Sainte-Marie, Tom Paxton, Joni Mitchell, Tim Hardin, Eric Anderson, Neil Young, Steve Goodman, Jerry Jeff Walker, Kris Kristofferson – and, of course – Bob Dylan. Among later writers whose music I found attractive were Gordon Lightfoot and John Denver. Some of Woody Guthrie's stuff appeals, as do the Weavers, Pete Seeger, Cisco Houston, Goebbel Reeves, and Jimmie Rodgers.

Apart from the possibility of listening to music while you do carpentry work, what is it that makes carpentry self-rewarding and gratifying? Is it more important to build new things or to fix the old ones?
I suppose you don't want an epistemological discussion on what is old and what is new. What I like doing most of all with carpentry and construction is solving puzzles. Building is solving puzzles. There are as many challenges in figuring out how to reposition a wall or a window, or fix a roof, as there are in building something new, say, building a cabin from scratch. The ideas of encountering a problem and thinking about how to solve it are the same when building something new and when fixing something up. Executing the performance successfully is what I find is giving a sense of accomplishment. I do electrical work, plumbing, carpentry, but not concrete. I also would build rock walls as well as docks. It's fun to work with different kinds of material, because every material has its own limitations and its own possibilities and this requires additional creativity. I mentioned that I enjoy playing sports. I also like canoe tripping, hiking, rock climbing – generally being outdoors. I never had summer jobs in the city with law firms when I was a student; rather, I always had employment at summer camps.

On Theory, Concepts, Themes, and Refrains

From your work, a very thick concept of agency transpires. How was this concept forged through your life experiences?

I think this probably comes from my childhood and my relationships with my family. I'm sure that I was a real pain to my elder brother, whom I much admired (and therefore whom I constantly copied – in building airplanes and rockets, in athletics, in interests in outdoor life at camp) – but with whom I was extremely competitive. I carried a sense that my mother (whose attention I craved) liked my brother best. As for my sister, I think she got visited with unfair comparisons to me. I'm convinced she was actually smarter than me, but I had a better memory and could therefore do "school things" more easily, was a boy at a time when the world was even more stacked in favour of men than it is now, and was more willing than she was to defer strategically to authority.

I also think that I was not a very good son to my parents as long as I lived at home. I chafed under their discipline because my friends seemed to have much more freedom than I did. My parents had quite Protestant (in my mother's case practically puritan) views of one's role in life. I was strong-willed and argumentative. My mother felt that the way to control me was to constantly elevate her expectations of me – nothing I ever did elicited from her a comment that I had done well or that I merited congratulations. In the last year of her life (when she was dying of a brain tumour and therefore was going through quite a change of personality), she frequently reminded me of how much I had disappointed her.

As a result, I think I grew up with a sense that one had to develop a strong sense of oneself in order to resist the demands of others – be these demands of parents or society generally. Concomitantly, I came to see that there could be a sense of powerful affirmation of oneself in the decision to subsume one's conduct to the rules of another. Very early on, I saw structures as potentially liberating so that rather than thinking about following patterns of others as surrender, I came to see the power of adopting a structure as a conscious act of will – of asserting the possibility of not choosing to follow: every decision of "doing what authority (parents, the summer camp boss, the dean, the state) wants" was a decision that was *my* decision. In my adolescence, I came to see that I was never doing what the dean wanted, I was always doing what I wanted in choosing to do what the dean wanted.

I can think of at least half a dozen times – at summer camp, in the university, working at the Law Commission – where I have said, "I have chosen to do what you wanted loyally and without complaint, not because I felt I had to but because I chose to; now I choose not to, because you are wrong; if you don't like it, then fire me, but don't expect me to do something I think, for good reason, that I ought not to do simply because you are in authority." When people talk about Nazi orders or soldiers in Vietnam simply following commands, I have often wondered whether I would be the kind of the person who would do evil because the commander says "do it." And I don't really know. We never know what we would actually do until we confront the situation. But I know how I would think about it, and to the extent I can think about it, I can't imagine myself doing evil just because the commander says "do it." In my life so far, just because the commander has said "do it" has never been a good enough reason for me: the reason for acting has to be independent from what the commander wants. The commander's command would always be a factor in the decision to act, but it would never be determinant.

As far as I can judge, this is what I believe. And it is this belief that probably grounds my idea of human agency. To be truthful, I don't know this for sure, and I certainly don't know what the theological origins or even implications of this view are.

Is agency about free choices within a system or about changing the structure of the system of choices?
I have not thought about this before. Let me try to give a kind of Kantian answer about the proof of intentions. I presume that one might be able to exercise agency as I conceive it within a system, but you don't know whether you are really exercising agency or whether you are just being significantly determined by the system itself. You could well be exercising agency, but there's no way to tell that, because there is no counter-hypothesis. So when I say to the dean that I'll do what he wants, but only because I choose to do so, it is not easy to figure out the character of my actions. This is even true when you explicitly say that you will not do what the dean wants. Perhaps resistance within the system is agency; perhaps it is just co-optation by hegemonic power.

But if what you're doing is taking on the system, contesting it, asserting the new as against the system, then you are exercising agency, and you know that you are doing so. This is what I meant by a Kantian answer. It is like Kant's claim about moral behaviour: if you are doing something that is in your own interest, you may well be acting morally, but you never know, but you know for sure that if you do something that you believe to be right and that is against your interest, then you are acting morally. I do not deny that agency can exist within structures, it's just that – whether we accept or contest authority, when we acknowledge the legitimacy of the authority as authority (even when it is wrong) – we never know for sure if we are exercising agency. So if you are looking for an instance of agency you can be sure of, it would be in contesting a system – in contesting not just orders, decisions, and actions but in contesting the legitimacy of the authority of the system itself, whether this is a political system or an intellectual system.

One of the main dichotomies in your thought about law is the distinction between the two legal domains or legal dimensions of the explicit and the implicit. You argue extensively for the importance of the implicit over the explicit …
Well, let me interrupt here. I'm still working on this puzzle, but as I get older I'm not quite sure that this explicit/implicit dichotomy is the right way to frame my epistemological concern. At one point I used to talk about the difference between formulated and inferential artefacts of human knowledge as a complementary dimension. So you could have a relatively formulated but implicit artefact. It seems to me that normativity or the sense of knowledge that we have of it is, at its most fundamental level, both inferential (non-formulated) and implicit. It is central

to the way we think. Somewhere I came to call this the "tacit." So one could imagine, in terms of normativity, that the standard everyday legislation is explicit and is formulaic. What is produced by judicial decision-making, in the way we develop notions of precedent, is also explicit in the sense of textual and institutional but is inferential. And what we typically associate with practices and custom is unwritten (implicit) but is pretty recognizable – it has a kind of formulaic character to it. These three forms are different from each other, but they all share this feature: each has a sense of limitation built in (whether institutional in the case of the explicit, or ontological in the case of the formulaic, or both in the case of most of the artefacts through which we organize and understand our lives). The tacit, which is a fourth type of artefact, is ineffable. It has no limitation. Puzzling about these two overlapping dimensions of human accomplishment first opened my eyes to the tacit; thinking through the implications of such a conception of law and human knowledge has occupied a large part of my reflection for the last twenty years.

Why do you think the implicit, and especially the tacit, have been rejected and under-theorized for so long?
A tradition of the book is a tradition of text, and most Western law – whether it be civil law or common law – is a tradition of the book. So whether the text is a legislative text or a judicial text, it has a character of explicitness attached to it. And it is taught: law is taught, as opposed to learned in the living. One of the things I tried to reflect on in my little collection *Lessons of Everyday Law* is that there are no rules that are thoroughly explicit. Even the point of "the lesson" is never explicit. Why then are jurists so prone to explicit? Well, it's easy to find, easy to identify. Techniques for the interpretation of words are much more widespread than mechanisms that we have for interpreting actions. And since so much of thinking about law today has become instrumentalized, then our attention is focused on artefacts that we can identify, elaborate, and deploy for instrumental purposes. Recipe-book jurisprudence is the curse. More than this, the "turn to post-modernism" is no salvation. Deconstruction is simply reconstructed instrumentalism that depends on language, on text, and on dissimulating power through language.

Do the dynamics of explicit and implicit involve a matter of control over expression too?
Ernst Cassiser and Suzanne Langer were both interested in the way human beings communicate other than by language. When you are in a system that privileges language, and discursive language in particular – as opposed

to poetry and other modes of communication – one can pretend that one is in control, because one can pretend that the language empowers one to capture all human experience. As Wittgenstein said in the *Tractatus* (I paraphrase), "if I can't say it, I can't think it, and if I can't think it, it isn't" – and as a corollary, "if I can think it, I can express it clearly."

But I think the challenge of Michael Polanyi, who is another person whom I found very interesting, is that if you can think it, you can attempt to write it down, but your expression of an idea will always be inadequate. The writing it down will always be an incomplete expression of the tacit, and the very act of writing or attempting to seize it generates new tacit knowledge that you were unaware of at the time that you were doing it. So you can see the regress: if you can drag it back to the explicit, this only means really regenerating another tacit somewhere else.

At least since the beginning of the '90s, you have been exploring legal issues through the use of metaphors. Is it just the case to remember family relationships, scouts experiences, dramas, Gospels, house objects, and, more recently, music and hockey? What is the rationale for this project?
Well, generally, the metaphor (unlike the simile) assumes that there is a distance between the objects of our knowledge – the distance is not comparative; it is not the reach for a general category that we can deploy to organize the likeness as in a simile. The one term of a metaphor is a way of invoking or understanding the other, but they are really different knowledges. The metaphor exists because there is a distance. The stories in *Lessons of Everyday Law*, the story of "Office Politics," and the other stories I deploy may be allegorical, but they are not (as I intend them) *metaphors* of law. They are not metaphors, because these stories *are* law. It's not as if there is analogy of what goes on in the family *as* what goes on in law, because what goes on in the family *is* already law. An allegory is a story which is meaningful on its own but by which there is also something else to be learned. An allegory has a parabolic character.

Are all of them allegories?
That is hard to answer. Let me start by distinguishing allegories, such as that in "Office Politics," and metaphors, such that invoked in "The Swiss Army Knife of Governance." The Swiss Army knife is a metaphor of law and governance, while office politics is itself law and governance. In other words, a Swiss Army knife has no agency itself; the metaphor arises because the knife is more than instrumentalized; the Swiss Army knife has at least some agency attributed to it.

In addition to metaphors like the Swiss Army knife, there are more difficult cases like "The Fridge Door Statute." Here we have at one level an object like a Swiss Army knife – a metaphor of law (especially for those who see law as just the product of the political state). But at the same time, fridge doors are used within families as normative constructs. The fridge door reflects all the messages posted on it; therefore, unlike the Swiss Army knife, the fridge door is a site of normativity itself.

And what about the call centre, an image which you adopt to talk about governance and government?
The interesting thing about the call centre, and the "Call-Centre Government" article, is that it seems to imply yet another category of figure of speech: the call centre is a mode of governance that not only governs call centres but that is deployed by governments as a means of organizing law. As a structure of human interaction, it is a simile, a metaphor, and an allegory all at once. So it is not just metaphorical in the way the fridge door is metaphorical. The fridge door is both a metaphor and a site of governance; the call centre is directly a site of governance in its own way. Therefore, here there is no need of imagining allegories; I am just trying to draw attention to the ways in which governance and government take place today.

However, the interesting point is that, while people may be willing to see some governance in a call centre, they do not usually think about it as a form of government – lest they think governments as types of call centre …
You are right. As I mentioned, the call-centre idea has two features: in one dimension it is government, a mode of governance in itself, while in another dimension it is an instrument of governance which governments deploy. At one and the same time, it is an instrument and the government structure itself, the site of governance.

When did you begin this kind of research in metaphoric and allegorical styles of exposition?
During my reading for my master's thesis in 1975, I was impressed with Fuller's 1968 essay "Two Principles of Human Association." The use of an anecdote from his youth struck me as a powerful way of starting a reflection, because there he was able to show how his own experiences as a child were directly connected to problems he encountered throughout his life as a jurist. I thought no more about this until after the birth

of our first child in 1982. Like all parents, I was always reading her fairy tales and other bedtime stories – Shelley was much better than I, and like A.A. Milne with Winnie the Pooh, she invented stories every evening. These evening encounters led me to realize how much law could be found in these fairy tales, how successful they were in conveying ways of understanding normativity.

The first text I wrote using personal stories was shortly after the birth of our second child. In a 1985 essay called "Pour la reconnaissance d'une normativité implicite et inférentielle," I wrote very briefly (and elliptically) about three personal events: a singing group I was involved in in the 1960s, the phenomenon of old guards at summer camp, and the process of office allocation in the law faculty. That was also the first time I intentionally wrote an article that adopted a law and society perspective as well. Interestingly, apart from Fuller, most of the legal writing I had read up to that point was either doctrinal analysis of fields of law or high-level legal philosophy that presupposed the irrelevance of practice to understanding law.

To your mind, is the use of allegories and metaphors more a way of enlarging the views of lawyers and legal scholars, or is it more a way of figuring out the actual characteristics of the object "law," i.e., is the use you make of these tools more pedagogic-heuristic or more epistemologic?
I don't think that the primary interest is in what we might call the pedagogical point. Ask yourself as a scholar, "Why do you do research? Why do you bother to puzzle through problems?" I believe that you are doing this for yourself; you are doing it to understand, to make sense of your world. In this sense, a legal article or a book is like a fine piece of literature: no matter what it is written for, it can still have a meaning and an impact which goes far beyond what the author may have thought or intended. I don't think I have written anything self-consciously to say to another: "Look here, dummies, this is it." Writing like that appals me.

Allegories also came with different genres and styles in your theoretical production. Alongside briefs, you have been writing laws, poems, short stories, songs, epistolary collections, fridge sticks, sport comments, études, and even call-centre menus, all of these on law and legal topics. How was the reception of your writings: have you ever been criticized for your theoretical project?
Surprisingly, not – if by criticized you mean *critique*. Some people obviously reject everything I do straight up without engaging with the text.

Here is an example. When I first delivered "Office Politics" at a conference, one very smart co-dean of mine, who later became president of the University of Toronto and who is a fine legal scholar in his own right, came up to me afterwards and said: "Rod, this is crap. What is it? What is your point? I just don't get it."

Concomitantly, a real weakness of the intellectual tradition in Canadian legal scholarship is that people who are happy that I do what I do are uncritical about it. I've never been taken on for the epistemology: as I say, I've been rejected by some but without any proper argument on the substance of the paper. Likewise, with many of those who read what I do and find it interesting and are enthusiastic about it, there is a kind of "immaturity" in the sense of lack of a critical tradition. Maybe only such a tradition would make it possible for people to feel comfortable in saying: "I like 'Office Politics,' and I like the way you have presented it. But there is a problem – in two senses: substantively, you are assuming 'x' and 'y,' which are demonstrably unsustainable, for the following reasons; and procedurally, the allegory does not work, because you assume that 'a' is like 'b' and that the ontological perspective is transferable. Well, it is not, and here is why." But so far I never had to defend anything that I have done on its epistemological or ontological ground from such a critique.

Is it because the inner logic of your works is cogent, or is it because people have not explored them far enough to find their shortcomings?

Again, this is a tough question. I may be seen as complaining about the lack of a critical tradition in Canadian legal theory. But this is a mixed blessing. Intellectual traditions tend to produce "schools" – and schools are deadly for genuine inquiry. A school of legal theory means you've entered into a common way of thinking; even as opposition, it means that you keep saying something which looks like it is critical but in fact only reinforces all the standard premises of the position you are critiquing. One of the reasons that it took so long for people to read Fuller intelligently is because he did not get into a first-order debate. For years, people wanted to reduce his thinking into the box of "natural law" so they could fit him into the existing schema. Only now is the richness of his thinking being appreciated.

Compared to the complexity of trying to engage with Fuller's position, the legal realist versus analytical positivists debate is really simple. Both camps of schools see the reality of law as essentially power, and the only question is "is this power in the hands of legislators or in the courts?"

And the same can be said for adherents to the critical legal studies perspective: they accept that the object of their critique is state law. These various internal debates can rage happily for decades, because people actually agree on the most important thing.

But when someone like Fuller comes along and says, "your whole understanding of law is wrong" and "law is fundamentally implicit and it's about the architecture of interaction," there is initially not much of a debate, because people don't get it. At that point, either you buy Fuller completely and try to find intellectual allies with whom you can engage in a truly critical discussion of his ideas, or you reject his perspective by just saying, "not for me." I think this is what happened with some of my own stuff, because I refuse the premises that most academics agree upon. People either just rejected me from where they stand, or they said, "you're right" rather than actually trying to work on or contesting or developing my premises.

Would you agree that Fuller was your main intellectual mentor?
I never met Fuller personally. When I went to the University of Toronto, my graduate supervisor – John Swan, who taught contract law and who had encountered Fuller through the teaching of contracts – encouraged me to read Fuller's work other than the standards: "The Reliance Interest in Contract Damages," "The Speluncean Explorers," "Positivism and the Separation of Law and Morals," *The Morality of Law*, "The Forms and Limits of Adjudication." I xeroxed or purchased everything he ever wrote and every article or book review critical of him. By working through this material, I started to feel that he was puzzling about the kind of questions in law that seemed to me the most interesting to puzzle about.

How would you describe the main similarities and differences between Fuller's approach and your own?
Fuller had a very strong concept of human agency and had a deep preoccupation with individualism and liberty. For this reason, he was often considered to be a conservative thinker. This image was not helped when he served as chair of the Professors for President Nixon organization in the lead-up to the 1960 US presidential election. But this view is paradoxical. True, he did write about non-state legal institutions probably more than anybody else in the Anglo-American tradition in the twentieth century. He asked questions about what we commit ourselves to when we adjudicate or when we ponder or make a rule and so on. But he was actually quite ecumenical about state action. If he did not like regulatory agencies, it was because they were trying to use command and control

regulation and adjudication as a process of ordering to accomplish social tasks for which they were unsuited. In largely forgotten essays now, he also provided strong justifications for government regulation but using other tools such as property, voting, markets, and contract.

In other words, he and I share the concern with thinking about legal processes and instruments and means–ends complexes. His image of the lawyer as architect strikes me as infinitely better than the realist image of the lawyer as social engineer. In the end, Fuller was limited mainly by the fact that he was an auto-didact who never sorted out all the pieces of his intellectual universe so that people could more easily see the coherence to his theoretical perspective.

So far, I see more similarities than differences ...

There are differences in emphasis. Fuller was more preoccupied with what he called freedom than with justice. Fuller's concept of freedom is very close to my understanding of – or to what I try to puzzle with through the concept of – agency, the capacity of human beings to make choices. But I am probably more interested than Fuller was in a theory of justice, a theory of the good.

Fuller was exploring the way human beings manage institutions for the achievement of purposes that were respectful of other human beings as agents on the assumption, I guess, that generally if you enhance those conditions, good consequences will result; therefore, he was not as concerned with directly thinking about consequences. Perhaps I'm more concerned with power and unequal distributions of power and resources and unequal outcomes. It is a difference in stress.

I remember once being asked – when I was writing my first essay on procedural fairness – whether I would choose equality over liberty. I naively answered, equality. Now I think I would answer that freedom is the precondition to justice but that without the aspiration to justice, freedom is not worth having.

The difference of symbolic forms and the multiplicity of symbolic languages is also an important point in your thought. When we move from one system to another, how much can we really carry with us? This question, if you prefer, can be also read: is it more important to be able to translate from one system to another or to master different systems at the same time?

The reason why we are brought to aspire to draw, write poetry, be a sculptor, build things, be a musician, dance is not because we are trying to translate our experience from one symbolic system to another symbolic system but because we recognize that the richness of our lives is enhanced by multiplying and extending the range of ways in which we can communicate and share ideas and experiences with others in multiple symbolic ways. So the multiplicity of symbolic languages is not instrumental, is not directly meant to achieve an end.

I don't learn French because I want to speak English better: that is inevitably a consequence, but that's not the aim for doing it. "Orchestrating Legal Multilingualism" does not mean that the object is to perfect that translation of knowledge from one symbolic form into another. Rather, it is about attempting to keep as many of these expressive modes alive and in communication with each other. It is about seeking them out in one's own life, about looking for multiple symbolisms in which to apprehend and understand the complexity of one's own being.

Well, what you are saying makes me think that the distinction upon which I based the question was somehow a false distinction ...
Maybe not. Some people think it's very important. Some people instrumentalize relationships, other people are interested in interdisciplinarity. But the ultimate reason for multiplying symbolic discourses and for engaging passionately in the exercise is not instrumental. It is because human beings are symbolizers.

*The image of law in the Western legal tradition has been unquestionably dominated by the verbal understanding (*lógos*). You have been questioning the idea that law is only or primarily a creature of language. In this vein, I think, Desmond Manderson – one of your former students who is now a professor – has written under your supervision a doctoral thesis that is now a monography on the aesthetic dimension of law.*
Desmond and I have a different take here, because to me it's not clear whether Desmond sees aesthetics as normative. His thesis is about the aesthetic dimensions of law, as if there is a separate law, which we can analyze in aesthetic terms. I think I would position myself by saying that aesthetics is an alternative normativity. The aesthetics of law is part of what constitutes law as law: it's not something you can do to law, it's what law is. If you think of logic, for example, it would seem funny to say "logical dimensions of law," because implicit in our understanding of law is that there is a degree of logic in it. That comes with the term. Likewise, aesthetics is not an external critique of law, because laws and judgments are aesthetic in themselves.

In general, then, how do you see all the five sensorial dimensions interact with the disembodied, conceptual dimension of law?
Well, what do we know? We know that we have a preoccupation with language, *lógos*, and that as a result, our understanding of that which is law is framed around language and especially written text. But if you acknowledge that much of the business of law is interactive and behavioural, then what are the analytical tools that we have that allow us to understand behaviour as a site of law? They are the analytical tools of sight, sound, smell, of senses. They become the mode of apprehension of the normativity of action.

It seems to me that in your recent "Orchestrating Legal Multilingualism," you suggest that sound and music are a mode of apprehension of normativity but also that what goes on in organizing, training for performing, performing, and then listening to any kind of sonic material raises normative problems and problems of personal commitment. So, if we are to overpass the simple simile that music is like law, e.g., that their structures are similar, should we say that making music is making law and vice versa?
Absolutely. Art and music are not things out there that could be looked at in some kind of legal analysis. The performance of them is law.

Let's try to move these reflections into a concrete example. You used these background ideas in your thread of research on access to justice, fairness, and property. Recently, you have prepared a paper for a Quebec conference on autochtony and governance where you try to imagine what a legal infrastructure for Aboriginal economic modernity could look like. This is also a topic you are going to develop further. What do you argue for?
One thing that capitalist economy tends to produce is a multiplication of forms of property – perhaps even an entropy – as our understanding of value becomes dissociated from objects: the idea of property is increasingly dematerialized. In the Western legal traditions, we started with a conception of property which was largely about land and objects. Gradually, we have come to understand value in the utilities of property – in its usages. What that suggests is that it is possible for the Aboriginal people to maintain a vision of property, especially land, that is consistent with collective ownership but at the same time to deploy the increasingly sophisticated dematerialized units of property to achieve their social purposes. My paper was an argument that you don't have to go through

a stage of private property of land in order to get to a decomposition of possibilities of ownership: the economic exploitation of the various possibilities of ownership in land can be divorced from ownership of the land itself.

Can the different conceptions of property be made transversal to different societies?
That is a question that is directly raised by the work of Étienne LeRoy: do you have to find analytical categories of property which are outside any existing regime of allocation of rights? His answer is "yes, the only way you can talk about Aboriginal conceptions of property is to use a vocabulary and concepts rooted in something other than existing systems." I don't know. I think if First Nations want to join a trading economy, there are certain things they will have to do, and the question is: is there a way of imagining to have these things done that does not undermine their view of collective identity and collective ownership?

The answer to that question surely has to be: let's look at what you can do with the latest capitalist property concepts, let's see how many of those can be related to that subtext in a way that lets you participate in a global economy without at the same time undermining your root conception of sovereignty of the land. You don't get there by going up to a level of abstraction and then asking what's the equivalent Aboriginal concept, because that is not going to get them to any viable regime. That's just a great scholarly pastime. It has analytical merit, but it's not pragmatically a workable mechanism for engaging with modernity.

The paper to which you refer was actually a small part of a general project of modernity commissioned by the Assembly of First Nations of Quebec and Labrador for instrumental purposes – improving the conditions of those living in First Nations territories. I did not set out to write an abstract piece of legal theory, although the paper ended up developing a few key theoretical concerns; I tried to write a paper that stays relatively close to the pragmatic purpose asked of me by the Assembly of First Nations.

An Aboriginal economic modernity would certainly change the Aboriginal society. But would it also change the mainstream society and, if yes, to what extent?
That is actually the same issue that all European and North American countries address when we talk about immigration. Immigration will generally change a society if there is enough of it that the receiving society

has to account for it as a phenomenon. There is no doubt that engaging with economic modernity and its institutions will change Aboriginal society. Mediating and accommodating that change will be the largest governance task for First Nations leadership over the next fifty years.

What about Aboriginal conceptions influencing mainstream society? In other words, is there enough land, money, people, resources in Aboriginal communities that they can not only carry on to the Western conceptions but move those conceptions to their own purposes? I don't think so. Rather, what would happen is that people operating in the capitalist model would see things going on in the Aboriginal community and say, "hmm, that's interesting, let's use this idea." The impact it is likely to have is the demonstration of ideas that are attractive enough that people will want to borrow them. The impact will not be like the immigration phenomenon, where 500,000 Italians have actually changed the way life in Toronto works, whether people who were then living in Toronto wanted their style of life to change or not.

Talking about migration, your argument about the relationship between migration and legal pluralism is for a radical enlargement of the concept of migration, which overpasses the classical geographical and geopolitical meaning of the term.

The problem with classical analyses of migration is that they think that the phenomenon of migration is essentially one of "movement of people" and the movement of peoples across "state boundaries." I would say this classical phenomenon can be modified in two ways. The first is to consider that *geographically* sometimes people migrate because boundaries move: they stay in the same place but boundaries move, and therefore here we have a reflexive phenomenon. The second is to consider migration that happens when you view a change not just in geography but in commitments, in what you believe in: changing school, changing religion, getting married, changing jobs. This shows that migration can be thought as a phenomenon of intellect as well as a phenomenon of space.

Let me put it this way: my theory of migration is like the evolution of my theory of legal pluralism. The first stage is the idea that the only boundaries that count are those of the state and you can have at most interstate relationships. Then you have a social scientific theory of legal pluralism, which strives to identify social spaces other than states. This corresponds to a theory of migration that recognizes movements such as rural to urban, from centre of city to suburb, changing neighbourhoods within a city, changing the place of employment. But then we move to a radical legal pluralism, which says: every time you change a normative universe, that's migration. The two fields are now one field: changing religion from Catholicism to Protestantism, passing from feeling an attachment for the Montreal Association for the Blind to an attachment for the Cystic Fibrosis Foundation, changing from an attachment for the soccer league to an attachment for playing baseball. All of these are migrations. That's how my idea of migration tracks my idea of legal pluralism.

Therefore, the idea of change should be put at the conceptual centre. I wonder what is the role of institutions in social and personal change. For instance, what did your empirical research on the small claims court teach you on the issue of access to justice? In a recent piece, you talk about a circumstance in which, as a citizen, you were tempted to resort to that institution, but because of your previous scholarly knowledge, you refrain from doing so.

I'm not a litigious type. It would really take me a lot to sue somebody. In the great divide between "fleers" and "fighters," I'm a fleer. But the access to justice had an important impact on my reflection about legal institutions: the sense of disempowerment and disengagement is deeply personal to the agent. There are not a lot of institutional responses that can produce equal empowerment. I'm very fortunate, because I have the advantages of time, of intellect, of financial resources, of knowing whom to call to navigate through all the bumps of everyday human existence. But despite that (and referring to the article you mentioned), an unresponsive service-department call centre can drive me crazy just like any other person. Most people in such situations just give up, they just can't cope with that. Of course, a very small minority grab a gun and wreak violence. But most just resign themselves to the fact that they "don't matter."

That's the lesson of access to justice. The small claims courts helps, but in fact it can only help those who can already help themselves. There is a certain level of something ineffable (confidence? energy? money? will power?) that you must have before you can get an institutional machine started. At the same time, it is not for me to say that the disempowered actor might say: rather than empower me, just give me thirty dollars a week for the next four weeks so I can buy four cases of beer. Does that make a better life? I don't know, that's surely not for me, but some might want that.

On Academic Life and Intellectual Engagement with/in the Present

You were appointed dean of the Faculty of Law here at McGill when you were only thirty-five. At about that time, and as a result of that experience, you also wrote "Office Politics," a caustic paper about under-the-table informal ways in which all the actors in a law faculty – ranging from the students to professors, as well as secretaries and the administrative staff – interact with each other in pursuing their own agendas, be they more particularist and devoted to immediate self-advantage or be they more universalist and devoted to some theorized or fancied "justice." But in the story, the dean himself was an actor, exercising what undoubtedly was a position of power. How was your experience with exercising power?

I often felt that I did not have any power at all. Actually, the range of action that a dean has is not that great – and that is a good thing. Institutions and procedures are meant largely as prudential constraints, as fail-safe mechanisms. My experience was one of coming to the conclusion that those exercising institutional authority may have the capacity of setting terms, developing aspirations, getting people to engage with certain kinds of themes, rather than the directive power of saying "you do" or "you don't do." I was very concerned as dean to prevent people from arguing with each other. As I've mentioned, one of the defects I suppose that I have as a person, or parent, or colleague is that I hate conflict. I can't stand it. I would rather walk away from such situations. This certainly compromised my capacity to induce recalcitrants to do what they should be doing. But in the end, I think more people perform better under a regime of condign sanctions than under a more coercive regime of punishments and explicit rewards.

How did the perpetual discordance between theory and practice come out during your academic experience?

I've never been able to figure out what the difference between theory and practice is. I suppose I can give some examples, but I don't know how useful these will be. One might say: being practical means navigating around the world as seen in the way that everybody else thinks the world looks like, while being theoretical means thinking that there may be other ways to think about the world that could help us navigate. But, presumably, to live in the world you both have to live in the world and try to change it. This is the lesson I take from the Eleventh Thesis on Feuerbach once again. If you want to change it, you can't just dream a different world: the point is to change it while living in it. On the other hand, it is very difficult to imagine anybody in a kind of reflective position being satisfied with the way the world is. I remember that when I was told the following as a joke, I did not think it was funny. There is an old expression in English: "that is a good idea in theory, but it won't work in practice." The joke is that a person criticized some proposal by saying: "that is a good idea in practice, but it won't work in theory." I don't find this funny. I find it true. Our actions and ideas have to work in practice and in theory. If they work in practice but not in theory, odds are that we are living in a false consciousness about what really "works" in practice.

Since 1995, you have been F.R. Scott Professor of Constitutional Law. In your inaugural lecture, you made a distinction between the "constitution according to Frank Scott" and "Frank Scott's constitution," where the former is more the concrete, historical, written achievement and the second is more aspirational. What is the legacy of F.R. Scott, and how do you see it related to the work you have been doing so far?
Like with the Vanderlinden piece on legal pluralism, I was given a topic and an occasion: this was an inaugural lecture meant to celebrate my accession to the chair and the career of the person for whom the chair was named. Since I was the first-ever chairholder, I felt that I had to talk in detail about the person and his ideas. However, however great he was as professor and scholar, he was not a very lovable person. So I made that distinction and spoke first of the "constitution according to Frank Scott" in the paper in order to allow those who knew what he really thought to see that I was projecting onto that what I thought he should have thought, trying to find some things in what he said that were closer to the view of what I believed that he should have said. Obviously, therefore, the aspirational content of "Frank Scott's constitution" was actually my own aspirational content, but the convention of the form of an inaugural lecture obliged me to put the point as I did!

Another figure who was very important for Canada was Pierre Elliott Trudeau. You are now a Trudeau Fellow appointed by the Trudeau Foundation. What are your thoughts about him?
My reaction to Trudeau is similar to my reaction to Scott. There is a lot of good in what Trudeau did over time. He was, undeniably, a great Canadian. But if you ask me, "given his overall legal and constitutional

theory, do you agree with him or not?" the answer is no, I don't. That doesn't mean that some of the things he did as prime minister were not terrific and worthy of praise. But I do not share his underlying legal theory. He was a classic legal republican, and I am not. He was a legal centralist (a statist), and I am not. He was an instrumentalist, and I am not.

However, federalism and bilingualism are two themes that both Scott and Trudeau dealt with at length. So you are dealing with the same issues, but from a different perspective ...
Exactly. For me, federalism – especially as I develop it in "Kaleidoscopic Federalism" – is a manner of thinking about legal pluralism, and bilingualism – especially as I develop it in "Orchestrating Legal Multilingualism" – is a manner of thinking multiple identities. I don't think either Scott or Trudeau conceived the state that way.

You mentioned Vanderlinden, to whom you dedicated another recent essay of yours. What is your relationship with him?
I met him first in 1993, although of course I had read his articles and books before. We are colleagues working on similar types of things and derive insights from each other's works, but we are not close collaborators on any specific project.

I would now like to move to your teaching experience. I was impressed by the fact that you remember the names of all your undergraduate students, which is no small number. From what I have seen, not many profs judge their relationship with their students exciting or even inspiring for their own research ...
I taught baseball and canoeing when I was a youth myself and was a Beaver leader after I had spent all those years at summer camp. In much of my life, I have been involved in positions where I was interacting with people who were my junior in the "discovery of stuff." But I never thought I was really that much smarter than anyone else. What you – as teacher, instructor, or coach – have is experience, insights, engagement. I'm fortunate to have been given a good memory, so I accumulated over time lots of experiences and relationships and reflections. And I remember those with whom I was interacting as part of recalling these experiences, relationships, and reflections.

I enjoy new experiences, and as part of that I find people fascinating. Actually, I haven't met many very boring people in my life; people always have very insightful things to say if you just keep your ear open to them.

When I ask questions in casual conversations, I am always amazed by how much I wind up learning. The university is an institution where you have this unique opportunity to get paid to interact with other people and learn from them!

You have been called an "instigator." Do you see teaching as an instigation to think?
Well, one thing I perhaps do too much is I find it very hard just to think about the specific issue on the table. Once a friend said to me, "the problem with you is that we can be talking about ashtrays and in two minutes you jack the conversation up into the scientific discovery of fire ceramics." I can't seem to stick for long at the basic level of an inquiry. So maybe I'm instigating in the sense that I'm constantly trying to explore the broader implication of things.

You said you haven't met many boring people. What are boring people like?
Boring people are those who have no sense that their own life is interesting. If you've no perception that there is anything interesting in what you're doing, and who you are, then you're boring.

I have appreciated your "Tips on Applying for an Academic Position," where you explain a lot of informal mechanisms young people applying for academic jobs should be aware of. Thinking about it, I realized that in Italy most of that knowledge – although actually quite simple in essence – is sort of kept secret and revealed only to the select few.
That's interesting because, although I would not presume to speak for Italy, I don't think that people here would say these mechanisms or tips are *kept* secret. What probably accounts for the fact they are not well known is that until now, nobody has taken the trouble to write about them. It's the implicit law. This unwritten law is not written down until someone feels the *need* to write it down. I felt that need, because I have seen the uncertainty of a lot of people who were entering the job market. Informally, personal mentorship seemed to be lacking. So I thought that it would be worthwhile to write something that would get people to think what are the kinds of things that would be important for them to keep in mind.

At McGill you have recently launched a new program for training law students in both civil and common law at the same time, based on what

you call a "transsystemic approach." How would that approach work on the field, when your students are lawyers?
This is a kind of metaphor of knowledge too: the more you know about more things, the better you can do any particular thing. So, if somebody would ask in what ways students trained in transsystemic education would be better than somebody else, they are going to be better only to the extent that to know more and to think about things having more reference points and more experiences is better than having less.

But do I think there is something magic in transsystemia? No. I don't even like the word "transsystemia," since it presupposes systems. For much the same reason I don't like the expression "international law," since it presupposes that the central artefact is national law. Our sense of the new teaching program is that law is like language, is like disciplines. Do you speak a better English because you speak French? Absolutely. Are you a better economist if you also happen to be trained in sociology? Absolutely. I think the drive to specialization, to positivizing knowledge is destructive, and to the extent that the transsystemic project moves in the other direction, that's its primary value.

What's the relationship between teaching and researching?
I think it's easier to talk about (and to see) how doing research with your students can be part of the teaching experience. Engaging with your students in having some of them as research assistants is a pedagogical opportunity: unless you totally instrumentalize your research students. Every professor who has ever worked with graduate students or undergraduate summer research students knows that in research is teaching, in both ways: you teach them, and they teach you. Of course, it's harder to see the ways in which the oral performance of the teaching function in the classroom is research. But I think it is in at least two ways.

First, in the context of the class, if you are a responsible teacher, you can only teach who you are. You won't just transmit other people's information about constitutional law or contracts as if you were somehow aside from or separated from what it is that you are teaching. That's not teaching – that is indoctrination. The exercise of teaching means mediating between who you are and the "expected understandings" of what the subject matter is in a way that is novel and insightful. And that necessarily produces chain reactions of ideas, since every class, every group of students, and every student has a different "expected understanding." The mediation of your own understandings and those of your students necessarily plays into the things you think about in the other work that you do at the research level.

Second, once you decide that the classroom should become an interactive endeavour, you give up the one-way projection of authority and magisterial structure of omniscience and (to be frank) the lazy professor's way of simply mollifying people by making the "information absorption" task merely passive. The interaction with your students will take the class in directions that you've never seen before and never heard before. The conversation with your students therefore becomes the implicit engagement of your students as research assistants, and you are together exploring new dimensions of ideas. There is rarely a class I teach that I don't come out of it with at least one idea I had never thought of directly before. And in the course of a semester there are probably four or five times when classroom observations, or postings on a discussion board, or hallway conversations with students do have a major impact on what you are thinking about. Students don't get a chance to see this, because they don't know what you didn't know beforehand, but when they take an advanced course that builds on an earlier course, then they can see how a previous classroom experience changes how you think about certain questions. That's another way that the teaching exercise feeds the research endeavour.

On Canada, the World, and Law Reform

I would now like to ask some questions about Canada and its society. You have described Canadian constitutional history as an ongoing hockey match between anglos/canadians and francos/habitants. Every polity is plural and conflictual. Here, however, the conflict is not only on the ordinary politics (laws) but also on the extraordinary politics (constitution). The problem is that usually extraordinary politics is thought to set out the rules of fair play to be applied in ordinary politics. In the absence of clear fair-play rules, in your judgment has there been a sufficient degree of fair play so far here?

The short answer is no, but the long answer is yes. I say this because Quebec is not Northern Ireland and Canada is not Zimbabwe. Actually, there is broad agreement on the framework, and where there is disagreement, it is not that there are no points of discussions, and it's not that there are thirty-eight opinions. There are two understandings, they reflect two well-developed political theories, they engage with each other on particular issues. The fact that the framework has been contested means that you have to be more careful about ordinary politics, and we have seen in Canada a couple of times that people made matters worse by forgetting that ordinary politics is a politics of negotiation, of compromise. When you move to extraordinary politics and constitutional challenges, where there are definitive winners and definitive losers, fair play is impossible. Fair play is only possible when more important than win or lose is to get to an agreement.

The issue of First Nations, or – as you suggest – the First People, is also a constitutionally historic chagrin in Canada. What is the point of the debate according to you?
There are two ways you can think about Aboriginal people. One is to say: "they were here first, and we stole their land, therefore we have to do something about it." This is a pretty naive view about the basis for recognition, because current Aboriginal peoples either killed or fully assimilated the people who were there before they arrived. Unless we get someone to figure out who were the very first persons and then give those persons everything just because they were first, that is not much of an argument. Curiously, however, if I were to say that in a public forum, I'd be vilified. But in fact, being "first" – even if you were demonstrably first – is not a good enough reason to claim territory. That is not a popular discourse when you move to discussions of Aboriginal rights today, because the current governments in the territory of North America are so obviously colonial reconstructions. But the problem is colonialism, not the fact that the occupation of the antecedents to these governments originated at some later time than First Nations peoples.

I reject the view that simply because they were here first we have to negotiate with them. However, there is also a different perspective, which is to say: the political community we know of as Canada cannot exist if it treats a significant part of its population, who is a rooted population, as disempowered and dependent. So, yes, we need to redesign political institutions, and we have to get to a very hard point, the point where Aboriginal peoples decide to call themselves Canadians, which is what they do not do now. Mohawks are Mohawks, they do not call themselves Canadians; if you want Aboriginal people to get angry, call them Aboriginal Canadians: they will deny they are Canadians. That is why, short of apartheid and short of building ghettos, we have to build a political community in which they are included, if we don't want to excommunicate them. So I think we have to build a political community in which they are in and find the terms under which they will come in: this is the challenge.

On the basis of your experience at the UNCITRAL, *how do you see the role of Canada as an actor on the international scene today? In particular, how do you see its role vis-à-vis North America, on the one hand, and Europe, on the other hand?*
In UNCITRAL, it constantly amazes me how much the rest of the world listens when the Canadian delegation speaks. It is the one delegation that everybody listens to, no matter what the topic is and no matter how the sides are drawn. And I think it's because the Americans are so self-righteous about their legal ideas! In large measure, these meetings are the rest of the world against the US. The Americans have an agenda, and they are trying to push it forward. The Canadian delegation actually agrees with most of those directions. But because people find the Americans just insufferable, they need to hear the message said by someone who is not insufferable, with a degree of nuance. Say, if we are playing poker, the US wants to win every last penny off the table. They just don't know how to play a game in such a way that the game keeps playing. They are much more interested in winning than in keeping the game playable.

You have been president of the Law Commission of Canada, and you have been involved in many sorts of law reform projects. Is there a tension between the idea that the informal is permeating the law and the attempt at conscious and formal law reform? If law is decentred in many social places and, tendentially, in every human being, how is it possible to carry on a centralized project about law itself?
That's the topic of "Recommissioning Law Reform." There I asked myself: how can I be a legal pluralist and sit in an institution that claims to be the centre? There are some pragmatic answers: you learn lessons of everyday law, and you consider them important in following a statute; you are more interested in opening up public debates about issues rather than coming to any particular conclusion; you are more focused on finding ways of characterizing social life using terms of everyday experience rather than terms of legislation. But let's face it: you are still an institution, you are still in the centre, you still have the authority to govern, absolutely.

Do you mean that you feel at the centre and that you have to act as if you were at the centre or that you actually are at the centre? Doesn't a legal pluralist consciousness lead to relativize the sense of centredness of law?
Others out there will ascribe to you, as an institution, a centredness, and make you the centre. You know that you are not. On the other hand, you also know that you *are*, because as a pluralist you believe that everybody

is the centre. So what you have to do is to use your own perception of being in the centre as a way of decentring others' perception of what makes the centre so that they may see the sense of centredness that you have. You have to show people that the reason why they are looking at you, as an institution – i.e., the necessity of finding a centre – is the very reason why they should not be looking at you.

Is the gap between a centred and a decentred, an explicit and an implicit perspective on law, bound to stay?
What presumably happens is the recognition that the first order of normativity is always implicit, is always tacit. Explicit law provides institutions, processes, and practices through which human beings can mediate between the immediate and the ineffable, between the practice of conversation in a room and a commitment to justice, rule of law, and fulfillment. Explicit law provides structure and guidance to make it possible for human beings to develop patterns of shared understanding and interaction. When you say to somebody whom you feel deeply about "I love you," you do not want to say, "and here are fifteen reasons why," you don't want to drive up from the implicit into the explicit. On the other hand, when you say "I love you," you also don't want to say, "and let me tell you what love means" in some transcendent sense. The expression "I love you" provides a linkage and a reflection towards what it really means to love somebody as an ideal and the practices and manifestations of that ideal in everyday life. That's how law works: explicit law works between the absolute, ineffable idea and the tacit practices of everyday interaction.

You have also been active in making explicit law, e.g., drafting secured transactions regimes in Ukraine – but let's not forget the regulation of the Faculty of Law of McGill University. Besides the professional commitment and study, is there a particular gratification, a particular feeling, in drafting a piece of legislation?
Sure, it's terrific. I have always found that there is more gratification in writing legislation than there is in writing a judgment or writing an article. Because when writing legislation, you can't explain what you are doing: the explanation of what you are doing has to be derived from what it is that you actually did; whereas when you're writing a judgment, that is all about explaining what you are doing. And that is easy, infinitely easier than doing it in such a way that those who read what you did can figure out what it is that you are trying to do without asking you. To be able to craft legislative instruments effectively is extremely powerful.

I would be tempted to call this conversation "The Many Activities of a Legal Pluralist around the World." You travel quite a lot around the world, to give talks at conferences and to join UN *meetings. Did travels contribute to your understanding of the particular situation of your Canada?*
If you travel in the right frame of mind, you will have a sense, wherever you are, of being at the margins, of being the *other*. I think there is something quite liberating about consciously understanding that you are other, because it means you do not have a direct responsibility for what is going on in front of you; therefore, you have the capacity to engage with it differently: you get a deep feel of where you are if you approach reality in that way.

The payback in your own society, if you have any sense of things, is that you can appreciate the perspective of those who are themselves *others*. That is, there are people within your own society who are positioned as others. As a result, you want constantly to be thinking about the experiences of the others in your own society. What do they think about what your society has to say to and about them? How can you take your experience of being other as a way to recognize and work to overcome the disempowerment, hostility, disenfranchisement, and disengagement that is often experienced by those who are the other in your own society?

41

Interview between Paul Kennedy and Rod Macdonald*

PK: Let me say before we start that your circumstances require special care here, so if at any point you want to stop, or feel you need to stop, let me know. Because the time is limited, I may sometimes interrupt you. Please don't assume I am being rude or anything if I do that. We're very sensitive to your time and to your energies right now.
RM: Well, I'm a professor. So it's important that people are rude with me. Otherwise I will give you a fifty-minute answer to every question. We're programmed that way.
PK: The good thing about broadcasters is that they can take fifty-minute answers and turn them into fifteen-second answers. We have that prerogative at the end. What can go on the cutting room floor can save us, but in this case I don't want to expend your energies excessively. So please at any point tell me when you are tired or would like a little break.
RM: OK, thank you.
PK: I've heard that you sometimes take out a guitar and you sing at workshops and conferences. And once even in front of a room full of judges?
RM: Yes. That's right. There was a meeting of all of the superior and provincial court judges of Quebec in Quebec City about five years ago. And the topic was the independence of the judiciary. I thought there was a particularly moving song by Phil Ochs about how one lives one's life, true to one's values, without being influenced by inappropriate considerations.
PK: What song is that?
RM: It's called "When I'm Gone."

* CBC Radio One *Ideas*, Executive Producer Greg Kelly, Host Paul Kennedy, Producer Alison Cook.

PK: Beautiful song, I know it.
RM: And you can understand how it resonates, for a sense of living your own life according to your own lights. And at the end of the speech I pulled out my Gibson Hummingbird that I have had since 1966, [PK: great guitar] and I serenaded them.
PK: There's no place in the world where …
RM: I belong when I'm gone. And I won't know the right from the wrong when I'm gone, and you won't hear me singing out this song when I'm gone, so I guess I'll have to do it while I'm here.
PK: How did the judges respond to that?
RM: Standing ovation!
PK: Wow!
RM: But maybe it's just because they were bored with all the regular speakers. It was just something new and different. I don't know.
PK: I think they might have thought you were Phil Ochs reincarnated.
RM: [Laughter]
PK: Another thing you're known for, widely known for, is that you wear a bow tie, and in fact it's a hand-tied bow tie.
RM: That is correct.
PK: Why is that?
RM: Well, I began my career teaching at the University of Windsor, which had a very relaxed dress code for professors. When I came to McGill, it was a much more conservative institution, and it was made clear to me that one always wore a tie, if not a tie and a jacket, to teach. And I thought to myself, well OK, if I have to wear a tie, I just don't want to be perceived as conforming to the pattern. So I decided to wear a bow tie. And I wore a clip-on bow tie to one class, and one of my students said to me that it was a bit disrespectful to them to wear a prefabricated bow tie. What was I? Some kind of a waiter at a restaurant? If I was going to wear a bow tie, why not wear a real one? So I picked up some real ones and taught myself how to tie them, and that became, I guess, just my trademark, to wear a bow tie.
PK: I understand that it is also a little bit crooked most of the time.
RM: Always.
PK: Always crooked. Why is that?
RM: If you tie your own bow tie, you will never ever tie it perfectly. And that's the way you know whether someone is wearing a prefab or wearing a real one, because a real one will never be perfectly symmetrical. And even if you try to make it perfectly symmetrical, it never will be.

And by the way, I could teach you how to tie a bow tie in thirty seconds. It's simply the same knot as the knot that you tie your shoelace, and you just tie it around your neck.

PK: I'd never thought of that. That a shoelace actually looks a little bit like a bow tie.

RM: That's right. There's a loop on each end, and a string on each end, and sometimes if a class is going a bit slow, I will surprise everybody by wearing a straight tie, maybe ten weeks into semester. And of course at some point the students will say, oh come on, Professor Macdonald, how come you didn't wear a bow tie, what's the problem? And I say to them, oh, you want a bow tie? Fine! Because you can make a bow tie out of straight tie. Mind you the loops go out as wide as your shoulders, on either side, but the knot can be tied with a regular tie, and so I use the bow tie as a teaching aid as well to try and break up the monotony of a course.

PK: Now, Professor Macdonald, I know that you are not only known for singing at conferences and wearing a bow tie, but you are known for a fondness for metaphors. And I am wondering if the bow tie could be seen as some kind of metaphor.

RM: Well, I think so. The point of a metaphor is that it enables somebody to learn something new about a familiar subject by thinking about it in an unfamiliar way. And so when one talks about structures, for example, in law, why do we have a particular way of formulating a statute, or why is a judgment written in a particular way, one can talk about a bow tie, a Texas string tie, a Windsor knot, a double Windsor knot, and various ways of wearing ties and framing ties, and ask what they tell us about the tie itself. When you tie a double Windsor, what are you giving up, and what are you gaining when you tie a bow tie? And the same with a Texas string tie? And so I don't often use the tie as a metaphor, but maybe once every course, there will be an occasion that I can use it to help students catch a particularly difficult point.

PK: I've never actually understood ties as deeply as I now do ... I was going to say the ties in some way signify that you are somewhat unconventional, you decided to wear a bow tie when everyone else was wearing a straight tie. And I know that in other parts of your life and career you have been somewhat unconventional. I want to ask you, have you ever said no to somebody in authority?

RM: [Long pause] Do you mean within the last fifteen minutes?

PK: [Laughter] No one has ever given me authority, so I will take it.

RM: Yes, of course. But there are a million different ways of saying no. And the most important thing to learn is how to say no to those in authority in a way that makes them think that you are agreeing with them.

PK: Now teach me about that, just as you taught me about bow ties.

RM: We'll take a simple example. Somebody in authority wishes you to do something that you don't think is the right thing to do in the circumstances. Very often, the person who is asking you to do that has conceived of the problem to be faced in a particular way, they've been examining it in their own lights. And what is required is to help them see that if you formulate the problem differently, then a range of alternative responses is open to you that wasn't open to you when you had formulated it in the initial way. So by changing the conversation with the person in authority, about the way the question has been framed, and why they have chosen to frame it one way and what are alternative ways of framing it, you can often lead them to frame the question differently, thinking that they have found the alternative framing themselves, and then it's a way of framing the question that allows you to say yes.

PK: Can you give me the most memorable example from your own life, of when you've said no to someone in authority?

RM: Well, I managed it the first time when I was about five years old, but let me give one from my time at McGill. I was asked by the dean who hired me to teach a course that I particularly did not want to teach because I thought it was a stupid course.

PK: [Laughter]

RM: It was a boring course and didn't give students much opportunity to learn. And so I started talking with him about why he wanted me to teach that course, what was there about the course that was so important to learn for students. And we began to talk about the purpose of pedagogy and how that course could be used to achieve certain curricular goals, and then we began to break down those goals and figure out what other things could be done to achieve that outcome, and at the end of the day, he said: "Can you suggest to me another course or another activity, that we could undertake that would do a better job of achieving those goals?" and I did. And he said, "Well, you're right. I had never even thought about it that way before. I will let you teach that course. But if it doesn't work, you're in deep trouble."

PK: Deep trouble meaning that he might have fired you?

RM: Well, he couldn't have fired me, but probably what he would have done was to give me four courses that I absolutely hate.

PK: Four courses instead of one.

RM: That's right.

PK: I guess this brings up a topic that you have dealt with in your academic work, namely the question of agency, and moral agency specifically. Is saying no a way of proving that you are acting independently as a moral agent and not just toeing the line, not just doing what the dean wanted you to do, and teach a boring course.

RM: Absolutely. Absolutely, and of course, that relates to my basic philosophy of law. Many, many people believe that law is a one-way projection of authority from law-makers or law-givers to citizens who are merely passive respondents to what the commands of the people in authority are. And I have always believed that law is created by the interaction of citizens among themselves and by the interaction of citizens with law-givers or those in authority. Very often, the best way to achieve a harmonious and peaceful society is to recognize that people have within themselves the capacity to do what is appropriate under the circumstances. The law should be designed to facilitate their agency and not to simply control them and set them on relatively constrained paths with predetermined outcomes that have been decided in the abstract and not by reference to the actual conundrums and problems that the people face on a daily basis.

PK: How does a person know when they are actually being an independent moral agent?

RM: Let me give an example. If I come across a red light and do not go through a red light, I could ask myself why am I doing that. And one reason might be: "it's a red light; if I go through it a policeman might stop me and I'll get a ticket." Another reason might be, "if I go through that red light, I run a risk that someone is going to smash into me, and that wouldn't be a good idea." Another reason might be, "I recognize that a well-ordered society depends on having ground rules that enable people, who have many different projects that point in different directions, to co-ordinate their activities in a most efficient and effective way." When you start thinking about your relationship with others in society and how your conduct will influence or not influence how they are able to live their lives with a maximum of freedom and independence, then you have moved your reflection from one of mere passive acquiescence in somebody else's decision to a conscious decision to act in a particular way because that's the most appropriate way of acting.

PK: When do you personally feel that you are acting independently and are a moral agent?

RM: Well, I suppose that is a two-pronged question, because one would hope that one is always acting like that. But the question is, when is one *aware* that one is acting like that? Are there particular circumstances when you become aware of your agency? And I think the most important circumstance is when your first instinct is to do something that goes against what you believe to be the appropriate way of acting because at that point you are engaged in a reflection about what is just, what is virtuous, what is appropriate that normally we don't face because our instincts tend to line up with social practice in a democratic society like Canada. Our personal instincts usually line up with a socially appropriate type of behaviour. It's when they don't that we realize that we actually have a choice and that it's up to us to choose the virtuous way.
PK: Did you grow up being sceptical of received authority?
RM: No, as a matter of fact I was very deferential towards my parents. And I think I began to become aware of authority when I was about twelve or thirteen, say, in Grade 9 or Grade 10, and did a lot of reading about and became interested in the civil rights movement in the US. I remember being impressed by Stokely Carmichael when he visited our high school in 1963, that was probably the origin of it.
PK: So that was the civil rights movement, basically the sort of New Left in the US. You also took it out in a characteristically cultural form. You were in a rock band, weren't you?
RM: I was, yes. Actually it didn't last very long as a rock band. It mutated into a folk band. And of course, Tom Paxton, Phil Ochs, Bob Dylan, Pete Seeger, and the Weavers were our standard repertoire. We were not a Peter, Paul and Mary folk group but a protest-song folk group.
PK: Do you remember the name of the group?
RM: Yes, it was called Les Chansonniers.
PK: Chansonniers?
RM: Why did we pick a French name? Because we wanted to tweak our noses at all the unilingual anglophones. We had a couple of songs in French as part of our repertoire. The famous patriot song celebrating the '37 patriots – "Un canadien errant."
PK: Beautiful song.
RM: It was one of our more popular songs.
PK: And you wrote songs yourself as well, didn't you?
RM: Yes, I did.
PK: Do you remember any of those?
RM: Oh yes. One title of that era was called "Born with a Silver Spoon," which was a critique of economic inequality. Another called "Nickels and

Dimes," which was about the banking system, so yes, I in my own little way I suppose I joined the protest.

PK: Now, what I'm interested in is that given that type of a temperament, which is slightly anti-authoritarian and on the edges, I suppose, what possibly could have attracted you to law school?

RM: Well, when I was completing my BA, I wanted to go to graduate school, and I was all set up to do a graduate degree with a Marxist scholar in Sussex, when my undergraduate advisor said to me, "you know there are no jobs left for Canadians in Canadian universities because they have all been taken by American draft dodgers. So if you really want to be a university professor," which I had decided upon as a career, "you better find a faculty where they are still hiring Canadians." And I did some scouting around, and the faculty that was still hiring Canadians was the faculty of law. So I applied to law school. That was where my best chance of becoming a professor was.

PK: Now, you wanted to go into the university, but did you at that age, as a young man, want to change society?

RM: Well, in the most simplistic terms, which now obviously I have thought beyond, I always thought of the priority of equality over liberty, whereas for most people in the sixties, liberty was a prime value and equality was a secondary value. In my view, the reverse was true then. The biggest problems were problems of inequality of opportunity, inequality of resources, discrimination based on social status, and so on. I thought that in political theory, or ultimately, as it turned out, law, there would be ways to work towards building institutions to promote equality. And that was what I was going to do.

I imagined that in my teaching and my scholarship, I would attempt to show where the possibilities of creating these types of institutions lay. For me, for example, the creation of medicare was one of the greatest triumphs of the equality agenda.

PK: That kind of equality is something that is not easy to achieve. Those are fairly lofty ambitions. What were things like in law school? Did you think you could do that by starting as a young lawyer?

RM: No, I had no illusions. Three and a half weeks of my classmates convinced me that this was going to be a lonely struggle.

PK: Three and a half weeks?

RM: Yeah, it wasn't long.

PK: And what convinced you?

RM: Well, I think I perceived really early on, through the questions my classmates were asking and the way most professors organized their classes, that the boundaries of permissible questions and policy issues to investigate were much narrower than I thought they ought to have been. And so we had very lively questions in class, of which I was not a part, about how to make the current system work more efficiently. But the question as to whether or not the design of the system itself was right was not really on the agenda.

PK: What did your professors think of those kinds of political or social ambitions you had?

RM: Well, to tell the truth, I was a pretty lousy student. Instead of resisting or challenging authority in the classroom, in the faculty, I withdrew and spent most of my time working for student groups or NGOs or other organizations outside the faculty. And it really wasn't until my third year that I really spent much time in the faculty of law at all.

PK: When did you decide that you didn't want to be a lawyer but might want to be a law professor?

RM: That was decided before I even applied.

PK: Oh really, you never had ambitions to be a lawyer?

RM: Never, no. And as I said when I was recruiting young professors when I was a dean, "Are you going to be a lawyer who practises law by teaching it, or are you going to be a professor whose field happens to be law? And if it's the first, this is not the faculty for you." I was trying to build a faculty at McGill of people whose primary commitment was to education and law happened to be the field but it was not their raison d'être. And I feel that was strongly the case for myself.

PK: I was just wondering, was there a time when you were a student that any professor told you to pack your bags and your books and go away?

RM: [Laughter] Well, yes, there was. The word got out early that I was interested in being a professor, and in my first assignment in evidence in first year, first term, I didn't do particularly well. And it was the habit of professors at that point to hand out the papers to the class in order of achievement. So all the students with As got noted together, and then the students with Bs, and I was in the last group. And the professor said to me, "Well, Professor Macdonald, I guess you will have to do a little better on your next assignment, won't you?"

PK: [Laughter]

RM: Dripping with cynicism, as you can imagine.

PK: Did you ever meet that man in later years?

RM: No. I never did, I never did.

PK: Probably a good thing.

RM: Well, I don't bear a grudge. Probably he was right.

PK: When you did enter the profession of being a law professor, what were legal teaching and legal writing like at that time?
RM: I started in 1975, and that was about the time, under the leadership of people like Harry Arthurs, where legal scholarship became focused more on learning and exploring law and the phenomena of law and less on providing research services to the profession. Up until that time, most of the writing would be textbooks or articles solving a particular problem that had been raised by the courts or something of that nature. Beginning in the '70s and significantly in the '80s, legal research began to look more like the kind of research that was being done in faculties of arts, where you look at underlying causes, you look at functional approaches, and interdisciplinarity. Sociology of law, philosophy of law, and legal history became important parts of the curriculum, which had not been the case, certainly during my studies.
PK: And you started originally teaching at the University of Windsor?
RM: I did.
PK: And then you went to McGill?
RM: That's right. I had a very hard time getting my first job.
PK: Why was that?
RM: Well, my marks at Osgoode were not stellar, for the reasons you can guess. And there was also a real scepticism at that point in law faculties about hiring Canadians who had done graduate work in Canada. I did my LLM at U of T. Law faculties were still hiring Canadians, but really you should have a graduate degree from Yale or Harvard or Oxford or Cambridge. The fact of having a graduate degree from a Canadian school was read as "you're just not good enough to get into a foreign school." I had an excellent, excellent supervisor at University of Toronto and really learned a lot there. But no faculty other than Windsor was willing to take a risk on me. So I wound up at the University of Windsor. And fortunately, under the leadership of Ron Ianni who was the dean, Windsor had a really creative and innovative public legal education program, the community law program. And I became involved in that, and as a result, access to justice has been one of the primary research elements of my career ever since. So it was fortuitous that I wound up at Windsor. And it has profoundly shaped my career.
PK: So when you went from Windsor to McGill, that was quite a big change. There eventually you published a text called "Office Politics," which is basically a set of memos written between a dean and the other members of a law faculty and the staff and the students about the allocation of office space. That doesn't sound like a typical law paper to me.

RM: No, it does not. It was written when the Law Reform Commission of Canada sponsored a conference on current issues in administrative law. One of the directions my career took early on was to be very interested in the way institutions work. I was less concerned about the control that courts exercised over institutions. That's called judicial review. And that's what most people do now studying administrative law. And most people did then. Administrative law was about what courts do to make sure that administrative agencies act appropriately. I was more interested in how administrative agencies work and the internal mechanics by which they fulfilled their legislative mandate. And so when it came time to produce a paper for this conference, I said, "I don't want to write anything about judicial review. I want to write about agencies." I had a huge disagreement with the conference organizers about my paper. And I said, OK, if you don't want me to write about the internal mechanics of the CRTC or the Ontario Labour Relations Board or whatever else, I will do it all allegorically. So I wrote this paper using the law faculty as an administrative agency and one particular decision within the law faculty, the allocation of offices, to make two points. The first is the complexity of authority and, of course, of the legitimacy of authority within institutions and second, that the quality of the way an institution treats its clients, the way the labour board treats its workers, or whatever else, is largely governed by how healthy the institution is on the inside. If you have a dysfunctional institution, it will do a lousy job vis-à-vis its clients; if you have a good institution where fairness and decency pervade the way authority is exercised, that institution will perform its statutory mandate better. So those were the two ambitions of the paper. And I used the allocation of offices within the law faculty as an allegory to make those points.

PK: How did your colleagues respond to your paper "Office Politics"?

RM: Well, at the conference they were equally divided, to my surprise. I thought they would almost all be sceptical. But there were about half the people in the audience who said, what the hell is this? is this a fraud? how much are we paying this clown? what's he got to do with law? And the other half followed up by writing additional memos that they [PK: Laughter] thought could have been part of the paper. And a couple of those ideas actually wound up in the published version of the paper. Again, it was 1989, and as I say, this was a period of great transformation and transition in law faculties. I think if somebody produced a paper like that today, not everybody would agree with it, but everybody in the room would say it's a legitimate scholarly exercise that is perfectly appropriate for a faculty of law.

PK: But were you in a sense putting on a revolutionary hat? You're issuing a challenge there. Writing just in an allegorical format in legal papers had not been a common practice. And you were in some ways pulling the beards of the establishment, tweaking the people in power.
RM: Yes. It's funny, a lot of people have characterized me as a bit of an enfant terrible or maybe a bit of a Don Quixote, an iconoclast, or whatever. I never feel when I am writing that there is somebody out there whom I want to get. I write what I believe. And I try to write passionately about what I believe and what I think important, and it turns out that these essays make people in power angry, but that isn't why I wrote them. I wrote them because that is what I believe. And I thought I had something worthwhile to say, and I wanted to say it. We talked about Phil Ochs: "When I got something to say, sir, I'm going to say it now." And I just did it.
PK: Was there a part of you that was gratified that you made some people angry?
RM: No, actually I'm actually a very shy person. You know, in social work language they talk about the world dividing into fighters and fleers. I flee conflict, I hate conflict, I feel terrible when somebody reacts negatively to what I say, and I try to patch over the differences. But somehow when I'm writing what I really believe, it makes some other people angry, and so I spend an awful lot of my life apologizing.
PK: Hoi Kong said at the symposium that your temperament of opposition is actually tied to something much more serious as a scholarly project. That is to shine light upon the dark corners of the law. And I'm wondering which dark corners you are most proud about. You're very interested in access and universal access, is that something that is central to your world view?
RM: Yes, it has been since my first days at the University of Windsor. I've been interested in how effectively people can understand how law works, how you can take advantage of law's resources, and how they can lobby in order to make the law more effective than it is. So access to justice, knowledge of law, has been a fundamental preoccupation of mine since the get-go.
PK: And why is that?
RM: I guess it was something that came from my upbringing and concern about social groups being excluded, concern that women systematically were squeezed out of opportunities that were available to men. A concern for the underdog has always been a part of my interest.
PK: And what was it about your upbringing that made that the case?
RM: I think, I think my parents were always involved in things like United Way. They were involved in activities around their church, looking after

the least well-off members of the community. They encouraged me whenever I expressed any kind of concern about segregation in the US instead of saying that's their problem, not ours. They would engage in that conversation. Situations like that around the home made a difference.

PK: You've published in a wide area. Many facets of the law have interested you, civil law, constitutional law, administrative law. You've also had a fairly big impact in the area of same-sex marriage. Why is that?

RM: Well, when we set up the Law Commission, we were given the opportunity to pick our own agenda, the topics that we would examine. And at that point, already there had been a significant lobby by the gay and lesbian community to change marriage laws in Canada. And in 1997 and following, the Law Commission thought that was a good topic to look at but expanded it. And what it wanted to do was look at all of the situations where adults form close personal relationships of interdependence and dependence with each other and ask ourselves whether the law was inhibiting the forming of these relationships or supporting them the way it does with a regular marriage.

And so we set up a project called "close personal adult relationships," and here we looked not only at issues with same-sex relationships but, for example, the situation of two sisters who may have lived together their entire adult lives or an elderly parent and an adult child living together in a relationship of interdependence, a whole series of relationships like this, some conjugal, some not conjugal, where there's a domestic unit. And we found incredibly discriminatory laws as between what happened to your benefit if you were married and things you couldn't do even if you were in a long-term relationship. So, for example, as between husband and wife, there's a question about pension entitlements. There's a question about who gets notified in respect to medical care and matters like that. Imagine two sisters who've lived together for thirty years, supporting each other. None of those rules apply to them. And yet they're in exactly the same kind of social situation. So we produced a report that tried to show how 837 federal statutes could be amended to treat close personal relationships more fairly than they currently do. And of course one of the most important types of close personal adult relationship was same-sex marriage. So one of the chapters of the report was specifically on same-sex marriage, but the other chapters were on non-conjugal close personal relationships. Some provinces have actually picked up these other chapters as well, and bits and pieces are going through tax legislation, survivorship legislation, home ownership, evidence protection, and so on to treat these relationships more fairly.

PK: Professor Macdonald, I noticed when you were giving that answer, your tone changed, and it seemed to animate you more than other things. Why would that be?

RM: Gee whiz, well it's another one of these equality issues and helping society, because we are publishing reports for Canadians, not just for governments, helping people in society see where the law that they are comfortable with may in fact create discriminatory consequences for their neighbours and others around them, and I'm animated by the educational aspect of producing reports like that. Now, of course, the benefit of being a government commission is you have a direct pipeline to the Ministry of Justice, and during the debate about same-sex marriage, our report figured prominently in discussions in parliamentary committees and figured prominently in discussions in the Ministry of Justice about how you can design such a regime. So there was the added benefit not only of public education but of actually moving the law forward.

PK: It must be very gratifying to see something that could be just a dusty report aging on a library shelf somewhere become a practical, tangible thing, with results in legislation.

RM: It is, but I have to tell you as an experienced law reformer, when it happens you jump up and down and spit wooden nickels!

PK: [Laughter]

RM: But it doesn't happen that often.

PK: Well, another that happened in an area that I think you are very much interested in is the residential schools question. You published a report that again had very tangible results.

RM: Yes, it did. And surprisingly, it was a report that was much like the same-sex marriage issue. Our report was actually designed to look at the sexual and physical abuse of children in institutions. And that included institutions for the deaf, institutions for children who had mental difficulties, for the blind, training schools for kids in trouble with the law, and residential schools. So we were able to take a very significant terrible chapter in Canadian history, residential schools, and show at the same time how the same types of abuses were taking place in other institutions that had passed under the radar screen. And so our report was written generally.

Now, by the time it was published, many provincial governments had already taken steps to set up mechanisms of redress for abuse that happened in provincial institutions. And so our report was not the thing to get the ball rolling but a push to keep it moving and keep alternative ways of moving ahead going.

But for residential schools, it was the first significant report which detailed, with empirical evidence and with survivor testimony, the extent to which there was not just deprivation of culture, but there was actual physical and sexual abuse that was widespread in residential schools. Many hundreds if not thousands of children were physically beaten up in these schools or were raped by those who were meant to be looking after them. And this report was a real shocker, because people knew that there's always one bad apple or two bad apples, but the extent of what was going on was not as well known as it should have been. The Royal Commission on Aboriginal Peoples started down this road, and we followed up. And in our report we attempted to show all of the various types of redress mechanisms that could be put in place to help deal with this problem.

We showed that civil suits for example, often re-victimized the survivor. But we showed that alternative dispute resolution processes, especially those that were run through the community, could be very effective in helping those who had survived abuse deal with it and compensate them for the harm they suffered. And you will notice that the current commission frequently makes mention of our report as providing models and alternatives and ways ahead that are particularly sensitive to what Aboriginal survivors really want. In other words, starting from their perception of their needs and what needs to be done for them, rather than having a top-down solution proposed by the government of Canada. And so we feel very, very proud about the impact of that report as well.

PK: We've been talking about the report, which is called *Restoring Dignity: Responding to Child Abuse in Canadian Institutions*, and you were talking about the impact. I think that everybody knows that in 2008, the Canadian government apologized to former students of Native residential schools. Tell me about the moment when you heard that apology was going to happen. How did that feel?

RM: Well, I felt very humbled by that. Something that we might have done to address a problem, to help get a recognition of a problem, had worked its way through the policy process and produced an outcome.

Now, there's a deep irony here, because that apology happened by a government which the previous year shut down the Law Commission. So the very institution which produced the report, which led to the apology and to Judge Sinclair's inquiry, the very institution which produced that impetus, was closed by the government as not useful, not doing anything that can't be done more cheaply by the private sector, and so on. You know the rhetoric. And so here at a moment of success, we're also lamenting the demise of the Law Commission of Canada.

PK: You said it was ironic. Some would say it was almost suicidal to do that.

RM: Well, that's not for me to say, I guess. But it was very disappointing.

PK: Now, at the symposium recently held in your honour, Phil Fontaine, who was the former chief of the Assembly of First Nations, made a point of going to that tribute session. As you know, in his own youth he was at a residential school. He was sent to one in Manitoba. What did the fact that he made a point of coming to your symposium say to you?

RM: Well, if I were an egotist, I would say he came to the symposium because I was there, and he was wanting to say thank you to me. But I'm not, and I think he came to the symposium because it was dealing with a matter that was of great interest to him. He's a very thoughtful guy, and he would have met people who are currently actively involved in pursuing these agenda items forward.

So I felt honoured that something that relates to me would be sufficiently well done and well attended by the right people that a person as important as Mr Fontaine would come, and I made a point of telling him so afterwards when I met him. But I don't think it had very much to do with me personally.

PK: I think you are being modest there.

RM: I guess you and I will differ on that one. [Laughter]

PK: Richard Janda was at the symposium as well, and he says you have built an entire body of work through an appeal to our better selves even though we have to confront, and you doing the line of work that you do, the worst abuses that people are capable of. And I'm wondering why confronting that dilemma hasn't turned you into a pessimist?

RM: I think there are two reasons. The first is the incredible resilience of the human spirit. When we, just to take an example, when we meet people doing access to justice work who have suffered terribly, and for whom the legal system has done nothing, and they are still optimistic about their lives and forging forward and moving ahead, that's really empowering to somebody who's working in this field. When we met and interviewed survivors of residential schools, many of them had been broken down terribly by their experience but were optimistic about their lives and optimistic about their children and the development of their communities and forward-looking. And so how can I as a researcher, as a scholar, looking at these terrible events become a pessimist? If anything, I would be betraying them if I could not translate the same optimism and the same desire, belief in the possible, into the reports we write and into the work that I do.

PK: Is there any one encounter, with any one individual person, that stands out particularly for you?

RM: Well, it would be inappropriate of me to mention her name in public, but during the institutional abuse hearings we met a woman who had been put away in the Grandview school, which was a training school for girls, and had been terribly abused: raped by several guards, physically abused, treated horrendously. And yet, here she was, at age sixty, full of humanity, full of optimism, working in a volunteer sector to improve the situation of training schools for youth in other situations, with just a sparkle in her eye and no sense of anger and no sense of bitterness at her past. She had completely transcended the anger and bitterness of her first reaction and had become an absolute model of somebody who was working for the common good.

PK: That sort of encounter is very inspiring, isn't it?

RM: It's unbelievable, and you walk away, when you are working on a report, and it just rededicates you to writing and doing the absolute best you can, because in some sense, you are doing it for people like that.

PK: Can you take me to the moment when you were diagnosed?

RM: Yes, I got the news on my birthday; 2010, in August.

PK: Ouch. Wow.

RM: And I was on holiday, and the oncologist said, well, we've had a look at the scan of the bump in your neck and the needle biopsy shows that it's cancerous. And so could you come in as soon as your holiday is over, and we'll set up a treatment program. And so I did.

PK: Did you have any premonition that that was what they were going to say, and what did you think about it?

RM: Well, I had this bump in my neck from about May. And it took my GP two months before he decided I should have it looked at by an oncologist. Perhaps because I'm a bit of a fatalist, I don't know, I wasn't surprised when the oncologist called me and told me the biopsy showed it was cancerous. No, I wasn't surprised at all.

PK: Now, he recommended a course of treatment. What was the prognosis? Did he give you either good or bad possibilities?

RM: Ah, at that point he'd seen many of these in his career, and the prognosis was very good. He's a surgical oncologist, and he wasn't going to cut me open to start. What they wanted to do was a combination of chemotherapy and radiation. I had thirty-seven doses of daily radiation in the neck and throat area. And he wanted to do that because, he said, "what we have here in your lymph is the secondary cancer, it's not the primary. We don't know where the primary is. So if we just try to do massive radiation across your throat, we hope we can get the primary, even though we don't know exactly where it is." And so that's what they did during the fall of 2010.

PK: So you were diagnosed on your birthday in 2010, and there has been treatment since then. What is the prognosis now?

RM: Well, I have just started another round of chemo. Can I give you a bit of history?

PK: Absolutely

RM: So everything went well, and I was back in the classroom in May of 2011. But by April 2012 some of my blood tests weren't looking right, so they did a biopsy on my tonsils and discovered in my left tonsil, there was cancer, and they did some more tests and discovered that in fact the whole soft palate tissue in the back of my throat on the left side was affected. So at the beginning of May 2012, I went for an eleven-and-a-half-hour operation in which they took a large part of my tonsil out, and they took a large part of the soft palate, which is why I can't talk clearly now, because I am missing too much tissue back there. And immediately after, while I was just coming out of recovery, he said, we couldn't get it all. So we're going to do a radiotherapy treatment called brachytherapy where they have a very intensive insertion of radioactive sources right next to the tumour up tubes into your throat. I did that for a week and was out of the hospital in four weeks. The problem that I have suffered since then is that I can't swallow, which means I can't eat or drink, and I suffer trismus, which means I have lockjaw. I can barely open my mouth, and I have to do very painful exercises just to be able to open my mouth wide enough to put a toothbrush in. And I went along with that, not getting any better, not getting any worse, but obviously unable to perform any kind of academic function.

Until, again on the day before my birthday, last year, the 13th, of 2013, I'm on holiday again, and he calls me and says: "I have bad news for you. The cancer has come back. It's come back pretty aggressively, and the only thing we can do for you now is put you on an intense chemotherapy program," which they did. I did that for eighteen weeks last fall. Unfortunately, it didn't do much, and the cancer spread into my lungs, and now it's showing up at the base of my skull as well. And so it's clearly fatal, but they're trying one more chemo drug, a different drug, which started this week, and it's running on a twelve-week cycle. And if it works at all, there's about a 40 per cent chance it will be successful, and if it's successful it will extend my prognosis. My prognosis without this treatment is three to six months, and if this treatment works, I may get another three to six months on top of that.

So at the outside I have about a year, but it could be as soon as three months from now.

PK: Given what you've told us about how it's affected your speech, and that is very important to somebody who is a law professor, how has it affected other aspects of your life? Is your hearing affected? Can you walk?

RM: Yes. The first round of chemo in 2010 took away all of my high-range hearing. So much of the pleasure that I had from listening to music has dissipated. Although one of the things that is interesting is that when you can't hear parts of a mix anymore, you actually hear other parts of the mix that had been sort of hidden by the parts you do hear. So on all our CDS and other recordings, I'm hearing things in them that I've never heard before. Which is quite fascinating. And I'm enjoying that new discovery.

Obviously, I can't drink, I can't swallow, so meals have become very boring. There's a product made by Nestlé that I just take three times a day through a tube directly into my stomach. So much of the social encounter of eating, which is part of an academic life, has gone as well.

Talking is hard, so that's a bit of a drawback, as well as hearing on the telephone is more difficult. So I have discovered how to make email serve almost all of the functions that these other academic encounters used to serve. And all I can say is thank heaven for email! [Laughter]

PK: I think it's fascinating that when you say that your hearing was impaired, and you lost the upper registers, that it opened new possibilities in the lower realm, something's lost and something's gained all the time.

RM: That's exactly right! You know, throughout this whole thing I've never felt any kind of anger, or bitterness, or whatever. It just is what it is. I've had a great life. And I'm going to have a great life for as long as I have it to live. And that's just the way it is, you get on with it, and try to derive the most you can from what you are still able to do.

PK: Not long ago, a fairly large group of your colleagues and friends and former students got together in a two-day symposium to, in many ways, celebrate your life. It was definitely something completely in your honour. How did it feel to go to that symposium?

RM: Well, the best thing about the symposium, when it was being organized, I said, this is embarrassing, I really don't want to do this, do it when I'm dead. And they insisted. So I said, OK, but it can't be maudlin. You've got to have people speak critically to where the flaws and defects and incompleteness in my scholarship and career have been.

And fortunately, the organizers picked wisely, and they got some really good people who, not in an aggressive way but in an honest and collegial way, were able to bring a critical perspective so that the symposium was a wonderful intellectual experience, because it amounted to a debate around some of the key themes that have animated my scholarly career. And that was fun for me.

PK: It was a bit of, if I can say, an academic roast, in which everything was done in complete respect but also unbelievable affection. I mean there was a lot of love in that room.

RM: Yes, surprisingly there was. I mean I was, I was really humbled by that, by how kind and decent people were.

PK: I'm really amazed, as I said, the people that spoke in that room, there was a lot of love. And yes, there was a lot of sincere and legitimate criticism. It really did put your career into a focus for me, which I never had before, because I didn't really know much about you. I'm wondering though, did having that kind of a celebration, did that make you look back on yourself and think about what you've done, about your career, about your accomplishments, your achievements, and your commitment and contribution as a teacher to two generations of lawyers in this country?

RM: Yes, I think coming out of the celebration, the thing I thought of most was all of the people along the way, along my life trajectory, who've made it possible for me to achieve what I've been able to accomplish. Often, often, we tend to forget that we wind up where we are in life largely because of the influence of others. And going right back to high school teachers, I can think of probably fifteen or twenty people who at key moments in my life helped orient me, or helped support me, or chastise me when that was necessary. Helped me overcome laziness or a failure to be as rigorous as I should be. And so that was a primary sentiment I had coming out of it – a sense of deep gratitude to all of the people who have helped my career. And of course, most notably, my wife Shelley and our two children have been a source of inspiration. Many of the ideas I have about law are derived from extrapolating from events and activities of everyday life. And of course, the family has been the crucible for that. And as a result, all through my teaching career, I have been fascinated by what I can contribute beyond the specific knowledge of a subject matter to my students, because in recognizing the importance of the influence of others on me, my own teachers on me, you see you have a trust, and it's up to you to be able to convey to your students not only knowledge but a sense of vocation, a sense of commitment, a sense of integrity, a sense of virtue about what they're learning and about their role in life.

PK: I can't help, though, but point out much of your life has been in a classroom and much of the kinds of interactions you are talking about involve you talking, and it's got to be one of the most painful possible ironies here when somebody like you in a sense loses their voice. You lose your instrument.

RM: It is. When I discovered after the operation that I would no longer be able to talk clearly, my academic life changed. However, even though I was on leave, medical leave, I maintained supervision of my graduate students, because with graduate students your availability is not set by a timetable. So if I just can't talk at a particular moment, I can postpone a meeting with a graduate student. You can do an awful lot more by writing. Graduate students are more interactive all the time. I also found that I was able to engage with my students much more in the process of writing letters of reference. They would ask me for a letter of reference, and I always show my students my letters of reference, because there are things in letters of reference that you say that are your understanding of the student you are writing about. And sometimes there are some negative things that nobody has ever bothered to tell the student. And so I show them a draft, and the student will come, and we'll talk about it. And when I produce the final letter, I can always write very positively about the student being aware of this particular problem and working on it to overcome it. And so I found that although there is much teaching that I can no longer do in the classroom, there are other aspects, like commenting on student papers by writing detailed comments, that are still available. So I sought other ways of interacting with students that don't require a voice, or require as much voice, in order to maintain that relationship.

PK: That's what the Internet's about. I read a long transcript of a conversation you had some years back with Andrea Brighenti.

RM: Yes.

PK: And in that you were talking about your "critics." You put that in quotation marks, saying that the people who reject what you say just reject it out of hand without really taking it on. The reaction you actually quoted was that of a fellow dean, who said, "Rod, this is crap." And then you were very candid, I thought, in what you said. Your more friendly critics, the people who accept your work, just accept it out of hand and don't really go into it and examine it and critically take it apart and take it on in some sense. Can you talk to that issue? What is it like not to have been really been taken seriously, either by your foes or your friends?

RM: Well, I think the hardest one is when you have people who uncritically accept what you say. And the reason why is that there are no ideas in law, there are probably no ideas in life, which are perfect, which fully capture the phenomenon or the idea at issue. And when people just say, this is a terrific piece of work, I have nothing to add, everything is perfectly set out, that means they haven't really engaged with it, because when you engage with an idea, you will always see weaknesses and gaps and inconsistencies. And I think as a professor, as a teacher, the one thing you hope more than anything is to be taken seriously. And whether somebody is lauding you or critiquing you doesn't matter as long as they are doing it seriously and being engaged with the ideas. So what I was trying to point out to Andrea was, the worst thing ever for a professor is to have is disciples, because disciples, typically, are uncritical.

PK: Those are the friends. How about the foes? You give a very specific example in the reaction to "Office Politics" the first time it was delivered. Tell me about that.

RM: Well, the "Office Politics" issue was very interesting, because the people who took that negative view never actually engaged with the argument in the article. What they said as a purely formal matter was "whatever else this is, it isn't law" or "whatever else it is or however useful it may be, it doesn't belong in this symposium because it doesn't speak to the issues we are discussing." Now, of course, that's about the most deadly type of dismissal you can have, to be told that you are irrelevant. One hopes to be told one is wrong from time to time. There can be some debate around that. But to be told that you are so irrelevant that you are not even worth discussing hits hard. And I think that that's happened more than a few times in my career, where something I have written has produced that kind of reaction. Just "whatever it is, it doesn't belong here." And you know, you scratch your head, and you think about it some more, and you try to reformulate the idea or the thought in a different context in another article or another speech or whatever else. But I don't think I have ever reacted to being told I was irrelevant by giving up. It's not in my nature.

PK: Quite specifically, what did the dean say to you when you first presented "Office Politics"?

RM: Well, the response was, "I just don't get it. What is the point you are making? Where is the argument? What's the logic? It doesn't start anywhere, and it doesn't end anywhere. It's just a story. Part of our job as scholars is to formulate consistent arguments and draw conclusions from our arguments, and your paper doesn't do that." That was essentially what the complaint was.

PK: You're quoted as saying somewhere that teaching is a way of being in the world, and I want to know what you mean by that.

RM: Well, I think that very often we are brought up to believe that a job or employment has no intrinsic value. You have a job to earn money in order to do the things in life you want to do. But a job is a job is a job. It's a means to an end. And I firmly believe that teaching is a calling, it's a vocation, it's something you do because it's a statement about truly what you believe and what you are committed to. It's not something you are doing simply to earn money. You believe profoundly that there is an ethic which attaches to being a teacher, an ethic of commitment to your students, an ethic of commitment to discovery, and that shapes your life. It's a part of your life, in the classroom, in the hallway, at home, on the street corner, and that's what I meant by teaching being a way of being alive. It's not just what you do to be alive.

PK: Well, plainly the life you've lived has had a great effect. Many of your students, former students, colleagues, who spoke at the symposium, said that they still sort of hear you in their heads, that you are still very much with them. When do you know that you have actually touched a student, that you have actually succeeded, that you have taught them something?

RM: You know, that's a very interesting question. Sometimes you can actually see the light in the eye. The lightbulb goes on, it's there to be observed, and it comes with an immediate follow-up question, which is rich and profound. Sometimes it comes in a casual conversation a week later, a month later, sometimes you never know. In the last three or four years, I've had dozens and dozens of letters from students whom I remember, students who were wonderful people, whom I would not have thought, gee whiz, I had a particularly profound effect upon, writing me, very personal and very, what should I say, touching letters about how my class or some experience I had with them was a turning point in their life or the most important thing that happened to them during their education. And I never would have guessed that. So the short answer to your question is, sometimes it's obvious, and sometimes you never know. And you discover it after the fact, many years after the fact.

PK: Is there any one student or any one story that stands out in your mind that you remember?

RM: Well, it would be invidious to compare, but I can say there are probably forty or fifty where I have at the tip of my fingers a specific thing a student said about a comment that I made to them. And sometimes it comes out as, "I remember when I was having a particularly rough time with something, and you said to me, if it's not impossible, it's not worth doing. And that has stuck with me my entire life, and it's the way I've been living my life ever since." There will be comments like that that come back, or there will be moments when a student is having a particularly rough time at a personal or emotional level, where they will say, "I remember the time I came up to your office, and you spent an hour just listening to me talk, and nobody had ever taken me seriously before then. And you are the first person I thought really wanted to hear what I had to say." So sometimes you get a story like that as well. But I think it would be invidious for me to pick one out.

PK: It must be tremendously self-affirming or gratifying to hear somebody say something like that to you, "You are doing something right."

RM: Well, that's a very tough question, because I really believe that you do what you do because it's the right thing to do. And there are many people whose view of teaching is you do a particular thing in a classroom because of the reward it will give you as a teacher, and I think that's absolutely the wrong way to think about it. Your relationship with your students and your relationship with your colleagues, from whom you are learning as much as they are learning from you, is not something you do for some gratification it will give you. It's something you do because that is what it means to be a teacher. When I hire research assistants, often I go through an interview process, talking with them, and the last question I will ask them is, "After this conversation now, what do you think it is you will be able to teach me this summer when we are working together?" Because it is very important for a student to realize that in a relationship like this, it's bilateral. If it's not bilateral, it's not a relationship – it's an imposition of power. Or an imposition of control. And students have to feel that I want to learn from their experiences and their insights, which will help me do the research I'm doing even better.

PK: When the general public thinks about or looks at a law faculty, a department of law at a university, the general perception is that they are there to produce lawyers, that you are churning out lawyers at the law faculty. What's your sense of what a law faculty should be doing?

RM: Well, I think, I think it is true that a law faculty will provide an education that will enable a person to become a lawyer, if they choose to become a lawyer. In other words, it's not a faculty of arts or a department of history. There is a responsibility in what we do which can't be ignored. But I think that if the purpose of a legal education is perceived to be to train lawyers, we're missing the point. If that's what we were about, why would you go through such an expensive process, time-consuming, labour-intensive, as a university education to learn a trade, a skill, which you can learn as an apprentice, by working for five years, four years, as an apprentice in a law firm? Surely there has to be something more about learning and understanding law than just acquiring the very important capacities which are necessary to practise law. And, you know, a very high percentage of our students become involved in international agencies, NGOs, public interest work, some are involved in business, some are involved in politics, many are involved in government. And one hopes that they learn important interpersonal abilities, they learn modes of reasoning, they learn how institutions work and how they can go off the rails. They learn how to formulate ideas, they learn how to marshal a consensus, they learn how to make an argument which is coherent and not inconsistent. And all of these are abilities which one hopes that a citizen has. They are essentially the fundamental tools of citizenship. And so, to capture the mission of a faculty of law is probably to say it's about engaging students in a profound reflection about what it means to be an active, involved citizen in a modern liberal democratic state.

PK: Is one of the underlying purposes, then, to make the world a better place, to enact social change?

RM: One hopes that students that graduate from your faculty will be committed to fundamental issues of social justice, fairness, equality, non-discrimination and that being committed to those values, they will work in their everyday lives, whatever they do, to advance them, and that as a consequence of that, the world will become a better place. But one thing that one should not try to do in the law faculty is pretend to have a recipe. Here folks, do the following fifteen things in this order, and you will make the world a better place. That completely misunderstands what it means to be educated. Because education is an ongoing quest for knowledge and understanding. And to assume that there is a formula that will always produce the right answer at any given moment is the opposite of what an education is.

PK: When you see where you students have gone, and they have gone in many of the places you have described, they've gone into government, they are working in business, working for NGOs, they're working around the world.

RM: One of them was on the Supreme Court. Marie Deschamps.
PK: You've had a great influence, right across the board almost. When you see what these people have achieved that you have taught, who have taught you as well, what does it make you feel? What do you feel when you see the results of your work?
RM: Ha! I often think to myself, it sounds ridiculous, but I think to myself, if I only knew, when I was teaching those students, what I do now, how much more I would have been able to help them along their career paths. That's a very common reaction, because I look back at my early years as a teacher and I think, oh my heavens, I really, I really didn't know what the heck I was doing in front of the classroom for much of my early life.

That's one reaction. Another reaction is, I feel very personally gratified when students whom I have had a close interaction with, whatever their careers are, are themselves devoted into an educational enterprise. Not just as a law teacher or university teacher but as a corporate leader. They are corporate leaders who are outstanding role models and teachers of those working within their institutions. The same with the trade union movement, the same with NGOs. And the deepest gratification is to see that your students are committed to passing on important life lessons in helping those with whom they interact to learn themselves.
PK: You've been teaching for decades now, and I'm intrigued that earlier in the conversation you mentioned that when you are interviewing people to be research assistants, you always ask the last question, "What will you be able to teach me?" And I'm wondering, what have you learned from your students?
RM: Well, I think the one of the most important things is that the world doesn't stand still and what I bring to the table is very much a product of the time and the period in which I grew up. Even if I am constantly trying to renew myself, I am always renewing myself against that background. Students whom I interact with year after year bring a different set of foundational premises to the table.

So the conversations, reactions, reflections, the way you formulate a life ambition, how you relate to technology, how you relate to different social institutions, changes from generation to generation. And like learning from your children, constantly being aware of how these background foundations are changing through time enables you to communicate more effectively with other people, not just of your own age but of every generation. It enables you to hear their voice more richly than if you are always filtering it through your own set of understandings, which were fixed twenty, thirty, forty years earlier.

PK: You knew from the beginning, when you decided to go to law school, that you didn't want to be a lawyer. You wanted to be a law professor, and it sounds like, having listened to you talk for so long now, you made the right decision.
RM: Well, I do not regret my choice of career. I've been extremely fortunate. I've been surrounded by colleagues who are thoughtful and understanding and intellectually curious. I've had extraordinary students. I've had academic leaders, my deans, university presidents, who've supported me. You know, it's been a fabulous life. It sounds silly to say, "I wouldn't have it any other way," but I genuinely believe that. I regret sometimes that I didn't take advantage of opportunities that came up or that I may not have invested as much in a certain thing as I should have done. But on balance, it's been a great life.
PK: Professor Macdonald. It's been an honour to talk with you. Thank you very, very much.
RM: My pleasure. Thank you so much.
PK: And if you are willing, I will come by to see you. In fact, I don't know whether you've seen it, but I saw on my bookshelf last night, and I was thinking about you, a biography of Phil Ochs.
RM: Ah ha.
PK: Have you read it?
RM: No, I have not. I have not.
PK: I will bring it along.
RM: I have two guitars.
PK: [Laughter]
RM: So when you come, I'll get out my Hummingbird, and you can get the other, and we'll play a couple of Phil Ochs songs.
PK: No, you're trying to keep me away from you now.
RM: [Laughter]

Appendix: Symposium Texts by Rod Macdonald

THEME 1: Producing Fairness | La production de l'équité

Restoring Dignity: Responding to Child Abuse in Canadian Institutions, Executive Summary (Ottawa: Law Commission of Canada, 2000) (with S. Zimmerman et al.)

"Parametres of Politics in Judicial Appointments" (Prepared for the Bastarache Commission on Judicial Appointments, 2010)

Lessons of Everyday Law (Montreal: McGill-Queen's University Press for the School of Policy Studies, Queen's University, and the Law Commission of Canada, 2002)

"Perspectives on Personal Relationships" (Opening address to the Conference on Domestic Partnerships, Queen's University, Kingston, 22 October 1999)

"A Theory of Procedural Fairness," *Windsor Year Book of Access to Justice* 1 (1981): 3–34

THEME 2: Pluralizing the Subject | La pluralisation du sujet

"Custom Made – For a Non-chirographic Critical Legal Pluralism," *Canadian Journal of Law and Society* 26 (2011): 301–27

"Here, There ... and Everywhere," in *Étudier et enseigner le droit: hier, aujourd'hui et demain – études offertes à Jacques Vanderlinden*, edited by N. Kasirer (Montreal: Blais, 2006), 381–413

"Legal Republicanism and Legal Pluralism," in *Human Diversity and the Law*, edited by M. Bussani and M. Graziadei (Brussels: Bruylant, 2005), 43–70

"What Is a *Critical* Legal Pluralism?" *Canadian Journal of Law and Society* 12 (1997): 25–46 (with Martha-Marie Kleinhans)

"Unitary Law Re-form, Pluralistic Law Re-Substance: Illuminating Legal Change," *Louisiana Law Review* 67 (2007): 1,114–60

THEME 3: Kaleidoscopic Federalism | Le fédéralisme kaléidoscopique

"Canada's Third National Policy: The Epiphenomenal or the Real Constitution?" *University of Toronto Law Journal* 59 (2009): 469–523 (with Robert Wolfe)

"The Political Economy of the Federal Spending Power," *Queen's Law Journal* 34 (2008): 249–304

"Kaleidoscopic Federalism," in *The States and Moods of Federalism: Governance, Identity and Methodology*, edited by J.-F. Gaudreault-DesBiens and F. Gélinas (Montreal: Blais, 2005), 261–83

"Three Centuries of Constitutional Making in Canada: Will There Be a Fourth?" *University of British Columbia Law Review* 30 (1996): 211–34

"The Design of Constitutions to Accommodate Linguistic, Cultural and Ethnic Diversity: The Canadian Experiment," in *Dual Images: Multiculturalism on Two Sides of the Atlantic*, edited by K. Kulcsar and D. Szabo (Budapest: Royal Society of Canada and Hungarian Academy of the Sciences, 1996), 52–84

THEME 4: The Priority of Distributive Justice | La priorité de la justice distributive

"A Model Law on Secured Transactions: A Representation of Structure? An Object of Idealized Imitation? A Type, Template or Design?" *Revue du droit uniforme* 15 (2) (2010): 419–46

"Transnational Secured Transactions Reform: Book IX of the Draft Common Frame of Reference in Perspective," *Zeitschrift fur Europaisches Privatrecht* (2009): 745–82

"Three Metaphors of Norm Migration in International Context," *Brooklyn Journal of International Law* 34 (2009): 603–53

"Core Principles for a Regime of Security on Property," UNCITRAL Working Group VI – Security Interests (2002)

"Article 9 Norm Entrepreneurship," *Canadian Business Law Journal* 43 (2006): 240–91

THEME 5: Contextualizing Governance | La contextualisation de la gouvernance

"Call-Centre Government: For the Rule of Law, Press #," *University of Toronto Law Journal* 55 (2005): 449–95

"Rabbits, Ravens, Snakes, Turtles: Analyzing the Political Economy of Aboriginal Communities," in *Gouvernance autochtone: reconfiguration d'un avenir collectif*, edited by Pierre Noreau (Montreal: Thémis 2010), 211–35 (with Thomas McMorrow)

"The Swiss Army Knife of Governance," In *Designing Government: From Instruments to Governance*, edited by Pearl Eliadis et al. (Montreal: McGill-Queen's University Press, 2005), 203–41 (with Eric Reiter)

"The Acoustics of Accountability: Towards Well-Tempered Tribunals" (Speech to the 14th Annual Conference of the Council of Canadian Administrative Tribunals, Ottawa, 31 May 1998)

"Understanding Regulation by Regulations," in *Regulations, Crown Corporations and Administrative Tribunals*, edited by I. Bernier and A. Lajoie (Toronto: University of Toronto Press, 1985), 81–154

THEME 6: Pursuing Virtue | La poursuite de la vertu

"Decolonizing Law School," *Alberta Law Review* 51 (2014): 717–38 (with Thomas McMorrow)

"Office Politics," *University of Toronto Law Journal* 40 (1990): 419–76

"Transdisciplinarity and Trust," in *Transdisciplinarity: Recreating Integrated Knowledge*, edited by M. Somerville and D. Rapport (Oxford: EOLSS Publishers, 2000), 61–76

"Curricular Development in the 1980s: A Perspective," *Journal of Legal Education* 32 (1982): 569–90 (1982)

"Legal Bilingualism," *McGill Law Journal* 42 (1997): 119–67

Contributors

ROSALIE SILBERMAN ABELLA, Justice, Supreme Court of Canada
ANNALISE ACORN, Professor, Faculty of Law, University of Alberta
KIRSTEN ANKER, Assistant Professor, Faculty of Law, McGill University
HARRY ARTHURS, University Professor Emeritus, Osgoode Hall Law School, York University
BLAINE BAKER, Professor Emeritus, Faculty of Law, McGill University
SUZANNE BOUCLIN, Assistant Professor, Faculty of Common Law, University of Ottawa
MICHAEL BRIDGE, Cassel Professor of Commercial Law, Department of Law, London School of Economics
KIM BROOKS, Dean, Schulich School of Law, Dalhousie University
NATHALIE DES ROSIERS, Dean, Faculty of Law, Common Law Section, University of Ottawa
THE LATE H. PATRICK GLENN, Professor, Faculty of Law, McGill University
KATE GLOVER, DCL Candidate, Faculty of Law, McGill University
HOI KONG, Associate Professor, Faculty of Law, McGill University
RICHARD JANDA, Associate Professor, Faculty of Law, McGill University
ROSALIE JUKIER, Associate Professor, Faculty of Law, McGill University
DANIEL JUTRAS, Dean, Faculty of Law, McGill University
NICHOLAS KASIRER, Justice, Quebec Court of Appeal
NICOLAS LAMBERT, Professor, Faculty of Law, Université de Moncton
ROBERT LECKEY, Associate Professor, Faculty of Law, McGill University
JEAN LECLAIR, Professor, Faculty of Law, Université de Montréal
H. WADE MACLAUCHLAN, President Emeritus, University of Prince Edward Island
DESMOND MANDERSON, Professor, ANU College of Law and ANU College of Arts and Social Sciences

JOHN D. MCCAMUS, University Professor, Osgoode Hall Law School, York University
THOMAS MCMORROW, Assistant Professor, Faculty of Social Science and Humanities, University of Ontario Institute of Technology
SALLY ENGLE MERRY, Professor, Department of Anthropology, New York University
YVES-MARIE MORISSETTE, Justice, Quebec Court of Appeal
PIERRE NOREAU, Professor, Faculty of Law, Université de Montréal
ERIC REITER, Associate Professor, Department of History, Concordia University
JEAN-FRANÇOIS RIFFARD, Maître de Conférences de Droit Privé, École de Droit de Clermont-Ferrand, Université d'Auvergne
KRISTEN RUNDLE, Senior Lecturer, Faculty of Law, University of New South Wales
DAVID SANDOMIERSKI, SJD Candidate, Faculty of Law, University of Toronto
COLLEEN SHEPPARD, Professor, Faculty of Law, McGill University
ANGELA SWAN, Counsel, Aird & Berlis LLP
JACQUES VANDERLINDEN, Professor Emeritus, Faculty of Law, Université de Moncton
SHAUNA VAN PRAAGH, Associate Professor, Faculty of Law, McGill University
CATHERINE WALSH, Professor, Faculty of Law, McGill University
JEREMY WEBBER, Dean, Faculty of Law, University of Victoria
JOHN WHYTE, Senior Policy Fellow, Saskatchewan Institute of Public Policy, and Professor of Political Science, University of Regina
ROBERT WOLFE, Professor, School of Policy Studies, Queen's University
ALISON HARVISON YOUNG, Justice, Superior Court of Justice of Ontario
SUSAN ZIMMERMAN, Executive Director, Secretariat on Responsible Conduct of Research, Government of Canada

Printed and bound by CPI Group (UK) Ltd, Croydon, CR0 4YY
15/09/2026
14962458-0002